FIGHTING THROUGH THE HURDLES OF MY LIFE

A Memoir

One Man's Inspiring Story of Survival,
Heartbreak, Redemption, and Beating the Odds!

ROBERTO ALFARO

Halo
PUBLISHING
INTERNATIONAL

ISBN: 978-1-63765-263-3
LCCN: 2022912210

Halo Publishing International, LLC
www.halopublishing.com

Printed and bound in the United States of America

ACKNOWLEDGMENTS

Growing up poor and living in one of the worst drug-infested neighborhoods of the South Bronx wasn't easy, and it was complicated even more and made worse by the frequent bouts of domestic violence I witnessed at home. Before long, I found myself facing an enormous array of challenges that at times left me feeling drained and helpless. Having no one to turn to, one day I prayed for God's blessings and guidance in overcoming some of the darkest and lowest moments of my life. My prayers were slowly answered, and before long, I started noticing many positive changes taking place in my life. But I still knew I had a very long way to go.

Over the years, I failed miserably many times. But against all odds, deep down inside my heart and soul, I never lost hope or faith for a better life and future. Yet, and most importantly, I always knew that God would one day bless me with all the right people to lead me through my journey.

Therein is where my story begins. With the amazing people God put in my path, the ones who somehow miraculously came into my life when I needed them most, the ones who ultimately inspired me to "Never Stop Dreaming!" Some of them were just chance meetings that led me to a different path because of what they said or did. While others inspired me with their kind words of wisdom and life lessons that encouraged me to dream big and to never set limits on what I can or can't do in life! Thanks, to those truly caring people who never stopped believing in me, who knew that one day I would grow up to be a success story and inspire others with my journey.

Today I am so proud, honored, and extremely grateful to say that without those people in my life, I wouldn't be the person that I am today! Thank you, God, for this amazing blessing!

First and foremost, I want to take a moment to thank my beautiful family. To my amazing and loving wife, Anna, I want to thank you from the bottom of my heart and soul for always being there for me through so much of my journey. You have been my partner and soul mate through so many of my biggest victories and continue to be a true inspiration in everything I do. Including the writing of my memoir; your editing talents made a big difference in the final draft of my manuscript! Thank you so much for all your love and support, babe!

To my amazing kids, Brianna, Christian, Bobby, and Bianca, thank you for being my biggest fans and supporters in all my ventures and dreams! For I know that I wouldn't be the dad and the person I am today without all your love and support! I love you guys with all my heart!

Thank you to my late brother, Valentine "Flaco," and my late sister, Mercedes, for always being there for me during some of my toughest times growing up in the South Bronx. Your unlimited love, care, and life lessons made a huge difference in my life and helped to mold me into the person that I am today. I love you and miss you both!

Thank you to my beautiful sister, Esther, for all your love and support! I love you, sis!

To all my uncles, aunts, nieces, nephews, and cousins, thank you all for being a part of my life and for all your love and support over the years! Included among them, my beautiful niece, Maria Scott, who although we've only known you for the past six years, thanks to Ancestry, you are one amazing and talented niece whom we all love and adore! Thank you so much for being in our lives! You have certainly made up for all those lost years! A special thanks also goes out to my wonderful niece and her husband, Cindy and Nano Alejo, for always being there for me when I needed them most!

To my late grandfather, Ezequiel Alfaro, for being an inspiration in my life, and for being the reason why I decided to become a police officer just like you, Grandpa! Thank you so much for setting such a great example and giving me something to aspire to in life!

Thank you to my late cousin, Wilfredo Rivera, for being such a big mentor in my life and in my law enforcement career. It was truly an honor to serve with you and our cousin, Orlando Allende, as a trio right out of New York City. Together, we took that journey into the Hartford Connecticut Police Department Academy, and graduated as a family. I love you both! And to my beautiful cousin, Maureen, a

Hartford police dispatcher! I thank you for always looking out for me, and for being there with all your love and kindness throughout my career! I love you, cuz!

Thank you to all of my lifelong friends, brothers, and sisters in the Hartford Police Department that I had the honor and pleasure to serve with over the years. Special thanks goes out to some of my partners, like Al Jardin, Rick Gutska, Harry Satterfield, Sal Abbatiello, Sergeant Eddie Resto, Jose and Becky Lopez, Carlos Santiago, Jimmy Doyle, Wayne Anderson, Joe Sikora, Ernie Scott, Jerry Johnson, Jon Fox, and a host of other amazing police officers and great people who always had my back!

To my lifetime friends of over fifty years, who grew up with me on 140th Street in the South Bronx. Misael Rivera, Orlando Rosario, Angel Rosario, Eddie Moran, and the late John DeJesus, I thank you all for being such an important part of my youth, growing up in a really tough area of the South Bronx. It was truly an amazing honor to have you guys in my life! As a team, we all did very well, considering all that we had to go through to be where we are today. You guys are and will always be my brothers, and I love you all! And to my other friends from the block, Edwin, Mickey, Johnny, and Andre, who also influenced me during my younger, elementary-school days. Thank you all for your friendship and memories!

To the many mentors who walked into my life and provided me with guidance, wisdom, and words of encouragement along my journey! Starting with my Alexander Junior High School 139, eighth-grade teacher, Mr. Robert G. Shapiro. Mr. Shapiro, your kind words of wisdom and heartfelt advice came at a time when I was hanging out with the wrong crowd and was heading in the wrong direction. You quickly intervened and put me on the right track, and for that, there are not enough words to say how thankful and grateful I am that you played such a big role in my life!

To Thomas, whose last name I don't remember, who made a huge impact in my life with his inspiring words of wisdom and life lessons. At the age of fourteen, I was a high school dropout and was working in a part-time job at a community outreach program in a South Bronx neighborhood. On the day you found out that I had dropped out of school, you immediately encouraged me to go back to school and get an education, just as you were doing. Your caring words made a big difference in my life. On that day, I took your advice and decided to go back to school. Thanks to your thoughtful efforts, that inspired me to turn my whole life around!

And finally, I want to thank two very important mentors who entered my life during my police career at the Hartford Police Department. First, I want to give a big thanks to Deputy Chief Fredrick Lewis, for always believing that I would one day have a great career as a police officer and public servant. Your words in the academy, when I was homesick and missing my family in New York City, convinced me to stick it out. Thanks to you I became a model police officer, both in patrol and years later in the mounted unit. Since then, we have remained close friends, and you continue to support my numerous careers and journey!

And lastly, to one of my biggest mentors and loyal friends, the late Hartford Police Chief Bernie Sullivan. Thank you, sir, for always looking out for me and believing that this Bronx kid would someday go on to do great things that would make you and the department so proud of me. You gave me an opportunity of a lifetime when you selected me to be a part of the recruitment team in order to induce more diverse candidates to sign up for this amazing career. But most of all, I am super thankful for the day you selected me to be a member of the brand-new mounted unit. A unit that I am proud and honored to say I went on to serve as the longest tenured mounted police officer in the unit's fifteen-year history! A true blessing!

Other friends and people who played big roles in my life are as follows: To Shana Sureck, a former photographer for the *Hartford Courant*, who one day back in 1992 asked me if I would be interested in doing an underwear ad as a model for the "Style and Fashion" section of the newspaper. I decided to give it a shot, not knowing that this one underwear modeling shot would one day lead to a very long and amazing career in modeling! Thank you so much, Shana, for being the catalyst behind such an unexpected new career in my life. One that never in my wildest dreams would I ever have imagined possible! A big thank-you also goes out to Officer/Model Ian Thompson, who got me my very first modeling contract and representation with his agency. I also want to thank Steve Prezant, an amazing photographer, who captured some of my very best modeling shots ever!

To Luz Ramos, an actress, model, and business entrepreneur, whom I once met during a modeling shoot. During our shoot, we talked about my acting aspirations and how I would one day love to go into the business, but just didn't know where to start. When she heard about my interest, she didn't hesitate to tell me that she had some connections in New York City with a casting agent from the TV show *New York Undercover*. She quickly gave me his name and contact information, and told me to send him a headshot and a resume. I did so, and a couple of weeks later, I was booked on one of my favorite TV shows. And the rest, as they say, is history! Thank you so much, Luz, for your friendship and for helping me get my acting career started! One that I still enjoy to this day!

To Larry Hoffman, a retired NYPD detective, actor, director, screenwriter, and author, thank you so much for your loyal and longtime friendship. As a first-time author, you were the one who inspired me to follow my dream as a writer, and continued to get on my case by reminding me to get that book done! Well, I followed your advice, my friend, and now I am proud to say that I am a published author! Thanks once again, my brother!

To Lalenya Lopez de Rivera, for giving me my very first motivational speaking engagement as a guest speaker at the Hispanic Heritage Month celebration at the Connecticut State Police Headquarters, back in 2015. Thank you so much for that awesome opportunity of a lifetime that gave me a start on a brand-new chapter in my life!

To others, such as Yana Comrie, former owner of Visage Models, who signed me to my very first modeling contract. Omar Nicodemo, another great friend and fellow actor, who one day got me work on my very first soap opera, *All My Children*, with his connections in the industry. Sergeant Bob Vignola, from Quinnipiac University and a retired assistant chief from Cheshire Police Department, a great friend and boss during my five and a half years at Quinnipiac University, for taking the time to honor me with numerous awards and commendations over my years of service to the university. Ray Ramos, a lifesaver at my former gym and all around great friend, who quickly came to my aid when heavy weights on a barbell suddenly landed on my neck, nearly strangling me, during a workout routine on the decline bench press. Brian Smith and Michael Lyle, two great friends and radio personalities at the former WQUN radio station. Where, over the years, I became a regular guest on their popular on-air talk show, sharing my life stories and experiences as a police officer and public safety officer. I thank you all for your loyal friendship and inspiration during my career and journey!

And last, but certainly not least, I want to take a moment to thank my mother, Gloria, and my dad, Calept. You brought me into this world and cared for me in the best way you could, while at the same time dealing with your own personal and traumatic shortcomings that ultimately affected all of our lives. Although they weren't the best conditions in which to grow up as a young child, and were overwhelmingly scary at times, I know I wouldn't be the person I am today had it not been for all those tough challenges I faced along the way. In the end, despite the chaos and discord that took place at home, I forgive you and still love you both with all my heart! May God bless you always!

CONTENTS

INTRODUCTION

One day back in the early part of August 2004, I was channel surfing on my TV, just looking for something interesting to watch, when I came across *The Oprah Winfrey Show*. That day the show's topic revolved around the theory that "everyone has a story to tell." During the segment, she interviewed numerous guests who all had one major thing in common—none of them thought their stories were worth sharing. But as the interviews went on, Oprah soon began to dig in a little bit deeper and discovered they all had amazing tales to tell. From struggles to triumphs, they all had interesting narratives to share that made their respective journeys unique and special. For some, it was a newfound journey. And yet for others, it turned out to be a new phase of their lives that they hoped to explore further and possibly even write about in their own little life stories.

That day after watching the show, in self-reflection, I started to look back at my own life's journey. Suddenly, some of my most traumatic experiences while growing up started to resurface. All were vivid memories of troubled times that somehow, by the grace of God, I was able to overcome, and to go on to live a normal and successful life. After thinking back in time to all the challenges I faced along the way, I knew right then and there that I had an inspiring story to tell…and one that was definitely worth sharing!

A few weeks later, on the evening of Thursday, August 26, 2004, I sat down in front of my computer and started writing my very first chapter. Over the weeks, months, and years that followed, I continued to write my life story. I wrote on and off in fact—although more off than on—for nearly seventeen years. But writing this book became a labor of love and passion that I just knew I had to finish and not put to the side. More importantly, this was a chance to share an inspiring story about overcoming hard times, facing tough challenges, and most of all, never giving up when failure is looming and threatens to change your path in life forever.

Chapters on occasion went untouched for months at a time, without any new entries or even the addition of a sentence or two. I realized that a part of it had to do with the many hours and long days I spent on the road, traveling to New York City to work on my acting and modeling gigs. The other part had to do with my hesitation when faced with revisiting some of the darkest moments in my past, bringing them back to life with my writing. This was extremely stressful, but deep down, inside my heart and soul, I knew that I would only be doing a disservice to myself if I didn't get back to writing about my journey, sharing my story.

It wasn't until much later that I started to focus on devoting more time to finishing my memoirs, completing what I started. Many years went by, and on April 30, 2021, I finally finished writing the last chapter of my book. It was the biggest relief and accomplishment; I had never before devoted so much time, energy, and emotion to a single personal project. And to know now that I'll be able to share my stories, and hopefully inspire others who might be going through some of the same tough challenges that I endured is truly the greatest feeling in the world!

However, in order to move forward, I first have to look back at my journey and visit how and where it all began for me and my family, starting with my parents and, of course, my life in New York City.

My parents, Calept Alfaro and Gloria Mariani, were both born and raised in different towns in Puerto Rico. My father was from a town called Isabella, while my mother was from a small town called Arroyo. At the age of eighteen, my father joined the United States Army, where he served for two years before leaving the military as a decorated World War II veteran. Shortly after serving his time in the armed forces, he returned to his hometown in Puerto Rico, where he thought that the opportunities of finding a job would be a lot greater. But after being there for a few months and not being able to find a job, he decided to get on a plane and head to New York City in order to try his chances there.

As for my mother, she lived in my grandmother Oliva's house in Puerto Rico, where she raised my two older siblings as a single parent. Like my father, who was living in poverty and having a difficult time trying to find a job, my mother found herself in a very similar situation. One day, she decided to pack up her clothes and her children and leave Puerto Rico. She ultimately ended up in New York City, in search of a better way of life for her and her family and a greater opportunity to find a well-paying job.

By the mid- to late-1940s, they both found themselves working and living in Manhattan. My father, fresh out of serving his two-year stint in the army, found a job working as dishwasher at a Midtown Manhattan restaurant. My mother, on the other hand, found work in an old garment factory in the South Bronx. During this time period, she met another gentleman, and they had my sister Esther. The relationship didn't last long, and she soon found herself a single parent once again, but now with three children.

At the time, my father just knew enough English to get by, whereas my mother didn't speak a word of English. This made it extremely difficult for the two of them to find good jobs that would pay at least the minimum wage.

One day, while out with some friends during the late 1940s, my mother and father met while dancing at the Tropicana Club in the Bronx. They soon began dating. By the early 1950s, as common-law spouses, they had moved into a tight two-bedroom apartment in Manhattan for all five of them. They elected to live together as a couple for many years, but never got married. In 1956, they had me, which made it six people living in a tiny two-bedroom apartment.

It could be said that my challenges in life started less than a year after I was born, when I nearly died. I fell into a coma after coming down with an E. coli type of bacteria that nearly killed me. But miraculously, I was able survive this near-death experience and continue growing up, only to face an untold number of challenges that came my way.

Shortly after recovering from this close call, we moved to a lower-income neighborhood in the South Bronx, where we were finally able to live comfortably in a three-bedroom apartment. Overall, life was good! But not for long.

Sadly, as the years went by, my father soon turned to alcohol and made our lives miserable, at least during the weekends. For the rest of the week, he was dedicated to his job as an upholstery worker and somehow managed to maintain his alcohol consumption to a minimum. However, as soon as Friday came around and he got paid, that's when he hit the bottle hard, and our troubles quickly began.

Growing up poor in one of the worst drug- and gang-infested neighborhoods of the South Bronx only added to our problems. For soon my father's violent domestic outbursts had us running for safety in the middle of the night, forcing us to seek shelter at either a friend's or a family member's home... sometimes for days at a time because we feared for our lives.

All this running around eventually started affecting my ability to learn at school. While under the umbrella of this chaotic environment, I was forced to miss many school days due to both the conditions at home and my chronic battles with asthma, which was worsened by the stress.

In school, I was living in a shell. My extreme shyness kept me from making friends, and I soon became a target for the bullies' name calling in my classroom. One day in fourth grade, it just got completely out of hand, and I reached a boiling point that ultimately forced me to turn my life around completely on the day I learned how to box!

This ultimately became one of the biggest and most important accomplishments in my life. I am so proud of myself for the person I've become, thanks to the strong stand I took on the day I decided that "enough is enough!"

The cover photo and the title I chose for this book came about after finding this old picture of me as a young kid wearing my boxing gloves. It symbolizes everything that I've gone through during my journey. To me, the boxing gloves, the stance, the look on my face, and my demeanor are symbols of all the tough challenges I've endured in my life. I guess, more than anything, they represent the many times I have had to literally fight my way through every tough hurdle that stood in my way in order to be where I am today. But more importantly, what I have learned from each and every negative experience in my life is that, with each failure, one can also be blessed with an abundance of victories. That's why I love using the catchphrase Never Stop Dreaming! I have relied on those words, for so many years, to help push me through every tough challenge I've had to face in my life. I always remind myself about this simple equation: positive thoughts lead to positive energy, which leads to positive accomplishments in life. As long as you believe in yourself and in everything in life being possible, it will become a reality!

In fact, here's a poem that I wrote back in 2020 on that same subject. I lean on it as an inspiration for everything I aspire to do in life.

When No Dream Is Too Big to Dream!
When no dream, is too big to dream
There are no limits
There are no caps
Only a destination
That drives you…
That pushes you…
Until you reach the top
And while obstacles may try to slow your ascent
Face them without fear
Never quitting…
Never giving up…
Always staying focused on the task at hand
And once you've reached that finish line
Only then will you know
That no dream is too big to dream!
And you can rejoice in victory…for you have finally made it!!!

In the end, I hope that by sharing my story you will see that if I was able to succeed with all the challenges I've experienced throughout my life, so can you!

Writing this book has been a true labor of love for me for so many years. But more than anything, it is truly a dream come true for me, a realization of the dream that I've been carrying in my heart and soul forever. I just want to take a moment to thank everyone for joining me on this journey and for supporting my book! It means the world to me!

CHAPTER 1

WELFARE ISLAND, 1956

In the wee hours of a late summer night in 1956, the silence of the night was quickly broken by the flashing red lights and blaring sirens coming from an ambulance racing across a city bridge, en route to the nearest hospital on Roosevelt Island, formerly known as Welfare Island, located directly across the bridge from FDR Drive in Midtown Manhattan. While the noise was pretty overwhelming, inside the walls of this emergency vehicle the sound of a screaming female was ten times louder. Legs kicking, fists clenching, the desperate mother-to-be is yelling at the top of her lungs in Spanish that she "can't take this pain any longer…please hurry…hurry…hurry!!!" She was holding on to my father's hand and arm so tightly that it caused a bruise, according to my father. She begged my father in Spanish, over and over again, to please tell the ambulance crew to "get me there quick… my baby is about to come out!!!"

Translating those words was not an easy task for my father, who did not speak English very well, so in his best broken English, all he was able to yell to the driver was "¡¡¡Avanza, conyo!!!" Please hurry, and a few other Spanish curse words in between. Whether it was because of my father's venting of his frustration or my mother's hysteria, someway, somehow, they managed to get her there "just in the nick of time." As my father would later tell me, "A few minutes more, and you would have been born in the ambulance and not in the hospital." I took that as a big blessing, considering everything else that happened to me soon after my birth.

I was born at 2:45 a.m. that very same day. I was a pretty normal baby with an average weight of seven and a half ounces and a height of twenty-one inches. I had bright-green eyes, pale skin, and a "big, bald head," according to my parents. My father said becoming a father for the first time was the proudest moment of his life. At the age of thirty, he had already been a stepfather to my three older siblings for many years, but this was different. It meant an offspring who would proudly carry the Alfaro family name, a traditional but rare last name that dated back to when the Spaniards first inhabited the island of Puerto Rico in the 1800s.

To my mother, though, it meant becoming a mother for the fourth time in her life and starting all over again at the age of thirty-nine. A good eight years had passed since my mother last breastfed a baby or changed a diaper, so this was going to be a big adjustment in her life. Luckily, however, she had my three older siblings—ages eight, fifteen, and eighteen—to help out and hopefully make it a smooth transition for the new baby in town.

For the next couple of months, things were going well for all of us. I had grown a little bit; I was eating well and driving everyone crazy with my middle-of-the-night hunger cries, according to my family. In general, though, I was basically doing all the normal things a baby my age was supposed to do, and more.

One day, I began crying uncontrollably for hours on end. This was followed by constant bouts of extremely high fever, vomiting, and diarrhea. The persistent vomiting continued throughout the day, to the point where I could no longer hold anything in my stomach. Because of that, I soon became extremely dehydrated from the lack of fluids in my system and got very pale and ill. My parents, fearing the worst, quickly rushed me to the emergency room at Bellevue Hospital in Manhattan, which was located not too far from where we lived at the time. I was immediately admitted for what was determined to be an "unknown, serious, stomach, E. coli-type bacterial virus" that required immediate medical attention. Before long, a team of doctors proceeded to work on me. They tried just about everything within their grasp to get me well and to get me eating once again, but it wasn't working. After a while, doctors were able to control the fever a little bit, but the vomiting and diarrhea continued, causing my condition to take a turn for the worst.

The next thing my parents knew, I was downgraded from serious to critical condition, and my prognosis for improvement quickly started looking very grim. My condition continued to worsen by the hour, to the point where doctors were running out of options on how to treat me, according to my father. Throughout the night, they worked feverishly to stabilize my condition, but no matter what they tried, they weren't able to succeed. While my parents kept a vigil outside of my room, doctors were busy inside, trying to do everything within their power to cure me of this debilitating ailment.

By morning, doctors cautiously approached my parents to give them the devastating news that my parents had been dreading. They were told that the doctors had tried everything possible, but that unfortunately I was not responding to treatment and had slipped into a coma. The condition was so bad that they could not guarantee with certainty that I would emerge from the coma and survive this battle.

Shocked and overwhelmed by the news, my parents became hysterical, especially when they went into my room and saw all the tubes and intravenous drugs and lines going into me. "That scared the hell out of us," my father exclaimed. The way I looked and the fact that I was not responding to their voices made this an extremely tough situation for my parents to endure. A priest in the hospital was soon sent for by the doctors to keep my parents' spirits up and to help them pray for my recovery.

For three days, all my parents could do was pray by my bedside and hope that something, anything, would happen that would give them a sign that I had a chance at beating this. For three or four brutal days, life was at a standstill for my parents. Nothing else mattered in their lives but to see that I would survive this horrible ordeal and go on to live a normal and healthy life. But as the hours went by, they were soon starting to lose hope.

Out of the blue one afternoon, I responded to their voices by opening my eyes and moving my fingers. It was the sign that gave them hope. A definite sign that maybe, just maybe, I was coming out of this coma. Their prayers were answered; it was all they could think about. Their emotions began to run wild with hope. They cried; they laughed; they jumped up for joy, all in one shot. They were so overwhelmed with happiness that their screams could be heard all over the hospital ward, drawing the immediate attention of both doctors and nurses, who quickly rushed into the room to see what was going on.

That day, as doctors and nurses continued to work on me, my condition and prognosis became better and better by the hour. I was slowly but surely, it seemed, coming out of this coma and was soon upgraded from critical to stable condition. Doctors could not explain in medical terms what happened to me that day. "Your hopes and prayers made this miracle happen, and I'm glad to say that it looks, at this point in time, that there is a very good possibility that he is going to make it and be a healthy baby once again," one doctor told my parents. In time, my condition improved dramatically. So great was my improvement that, within a couple of weeks' time, I was released from the hospital and into the care of my parents. My parents were so overwhelmed with emotion that they thanked God and everyone on the hospital staff for saving my life. "It was truly a miracle," my father went on to say.

Although I continued to suffer from other medical issues over the years—like eczema, chronic childhood asthma, and tonsillitis—and later discovered I was a sickle-cell carrier, nothing could compare to all the pain and suffering my parents experienced when they thought they almost lost me. In the end, the totality of the circumstances surrounding all my health issues are but a small asterisk in my life when you compare it to all the emotional and mental instability that later scarred my family and me for a lifetime!

CHAPTER 2

THE BIG MOVE TO THE BRONX, 1957

Manhattan had everything my parents had ever wanted when they lived there in 1956. A great neighborhood, a steady job, lots of shopping centers in the area, and a community in which they were surrounded by lots of Puerto Ricans from the island. You might say we had it all…except maybe enough space around the apartment.

But as the months went by, with a growing family of six people living in the tiny two-bedroom apartment, it became quite difficult for all of us to move around and sleep in those tight quarters. About a year or so after I was born, they decided to pack up the family and move to a more promising area and a bigger three-bedroom apartment in the South Bronx.

As my parents later discovered, the place they left in Manhattan was a paradise compared to the new place. The place that at the time I called home was 603 East 140th Street, which is located right in the heart of the South Bronx. It was here where I spent most of my young adult life and experienced some of the most memorable, and at the same time most difficult, moments of my life. I can honestly say that the trials and tribulations that I experienced were many; yet, somehow, someway, I managed to learn a lot from them and to survive despite my mistakes and those of others. However, when I look back at everything that I experienced on my block, in the South Bronx, and in New York City in general, I strongly believe that in the grand scope of things, those occurrences helped to make me a better person and contributed to molding me into the person that I am today.

If someone were to ask me to sum up what my neighborhood was like in those days, three words would immediately come to mind. It was fun, wild, and dangerous, all at the same time. Add the low socioeconomic status, scarcity of jobs, lack of money, and rampant availability of drugs, and the situation gets even more complicated for the residents of the neighborhood. In the end, it wasn't just one factor that made this neighborhood jump the way it did, but a combination of many situations, all rolled up into one, that played a big part in everything that was going on in my block. I guess what made it all so unique yet volatile had to do with a combination of two things: the large number of people living in a one-block area, which sometimes brought both harmony and friction to the inhabitants, and the large number of buildings, which made it possible to house so many people all in one place.

My neighborhood was a place where rows upon rows of attached buildings adorned both sides of the street. These tall, five-story brick buildings all contained at least four apartments on each floor, an average of two to three bedrooms in each dwelling. This layout made it easy to accommodate a lot of families like ours... all under one roof. Each apartment was also equipped with an exterior emergency fire escape, which were accessed by two adjoining windows in each apartment, and connecting steps that attached to each floor of the building, all the way up to the rooftop. Although the approximately four-foot-by-fourteen-foot wrought-iron fire escapes were made to be used for emergency situations only, for the residents of these apartments, including my family, they became a poor man's porch.

In general, it served as a great place to shoot the breeze or enjoy the scenery around or below you on a warm, hot summer day. It was especially entertaining just to watch the people in my neighborhood interacting with each other and enjoying the day. The traditional conga and bongo playing, along with folkloric singing of island tunes, brought out the Puerto Rican in all of us. The local *piraguero* selling his shaved-ice cones soaked with our favorite tropical fruit juices, would cool just about anybody's thirst on a hot, sunny day. Our block was also a place to view a game of stickball, which was played right in the middle of the street. To play this street game, all you needed was a broomstick, a pink Spalding rubber ball, your bare hands, and manhole covers for bases. Other activities, which usually took place at night, revolved around seeing four to five men getting together in front of a building's stoop—with a makeshift fire in a metal trash can during the cold winter months—and singing their favorite doo-wop songs.

The buildings' rooftops also became a great place to escape, hang out, and get a nice view of the surrounding neighborhood or the people congregating on the street below. The rooftops also served as a great spot to fly a kite or get a suntan on a sunny summer day. In the winter, a snow-covered rooftop was a fun place to stage a friendly snowball fight or to throw snowballs at the unsuspecting pedestrians below without getting caught. Since all that separated the adjoining buildings was a three-foot-high wall, anyone could easily jump to the next building without even breaking a sweat. It became a shortcut for accessing any of the buildings by way of their vestibules or hatchways.

The block, which was predominantly made up of poor or low-income Hispanics and Blacks, was rich in culture and history. The diaspora brought many first- and second-generation Puerto Ricans from the island to *Nueva York*. Together with those born in New York City, like me, we became one community known as Nuyoricans.

The large number of young Hispanics that saturated our area created a sense of brotherhood, a bonding based on shared culture and language. This eventually led to some groups of young Puerto Rican men and women unifying and forming street gangs to protect the neighborhood, or the "territory" as it was known in those days, from outsiders or other gangs trying to cause problems in our neighborhood.

As the years went by, the lure of attracting new friends and the feeling of belonging to a common cause became too hard for my older brother, Valentine, also known as Flaco, and my sister Esther; they ultimately decided to join our two neighborhood gangs known as the Spanish Devils and the Lady Devils. As it turns out, the presence of these two gangs in the neighborhood eventually became a huge problem for my parents to handle in our new environment. Before long, drugs and alcohol would enter the picture and create an even bigger crisis for my family to deal with, a crisis that would ultimately turn our lives upside down.

Clinging to a little hope and having faith that things would soon change for the better, my parents decided not to move out of our neighborhood. Instead, they prayed that over time things would get back on track.

CHAPTER 3

A NEW PLACE, A NEW BEGINNING

It is now 1960, and four years have passed since we first moved into our neighborhood. No longer are we the new family on the block, trying to make adjustments to a whole new environment and a different way of life. But now, as a family, we are starting to know people in the neighborhood on a first-name basis and have made lots of new friends. Overall, our family's life has changed as well. My father gave up his old job as a dishwasher in a downtown restaurant in Manhattan and has a better-paying position in a furniture-upholstery business in the Bronx. On the other hand, my mother, who was a stay-at-home mom when we lived in Manhattan, decided to follow in my father's footsteps and took a job working in a clothing-manufacturing factory in the Bronx. With both parents working, it made it a lot easier to feed a family of six and pay the bills.

As for me and my siblings, I was being cared for by a family friend in the neighborhood while my parents were both at work. My oldest sister, Mercedes, age twenty-two, was still living at home and was working in a factory in the garment district in downtown Manhattan. Esther, my next-to-oldest sister, at age twelve, was attending Junior High School 139, which was located just a few blocks from where we lived, but she was not adjusting well to school and was giving my parents a really hard time. My older brother, Valentine, age nineteen, on the other hand, who had already dropped out of school a few years before for medical reasons and lack of interest in school, was looking for work in between hanging out with his friends on the streets and staying at home.

While all of this was going on, my parents also had to deal with the crises of my sister Esther, who contracted polio in her left leg when she was only about four or five years old, and my brother's pretty serious bouts with epileptic seizures, which were the result of a sudden fall from a playground swing when he was about seven or eight years of age. He nearly died from the head trauma, according to my parents. Though my brother and sister both suffered from serious, debilitating setbacks in their lives, with the assistance of medical intervention, they miraculously were both able to overcome, or at least control, the long-term effects of their medical conditions and to live somewhat-normal lives.

With all these sudden changes happening in their lives, my parents soon realized that their search for a better and more stable life had hidden consequences that could turn our world upside down in an instant.

CHAPTER 4

UNFATHERLY LOVE

My oldest half-sister, Mercedes, a striking twenty-two-year-old who was five feet four inches tall and had auburn-brown hair and a face that could grace the cover of any magazine, fell in love and became engaged to my uncle Radames. I know it sounds weird, but they were not related by blood. He just happened to be my father's younger brother, and my father is my sister's stepfather. It's a bit confusing, but I hope that clarifies it a little bit more now. Anyways, their budding romance began one day when they met for the very first time at a family gathering and hit it off immediately. In fact, they got along so well that they soon started dating and eventually became a couple. He was about my sister's age and had been in the air force for quite a few years; he was making a career out of it. As destiny would have it, they soon fell madly in love with each other and ultimately decided to get engaged.

Before long, he was shipped overseas on an extended tour of duty, and it soon became apparent that this would become a long-distance love affair between the two. The letters they wrote to each other were enough to keep any mailman busy for weeks and months at a time. And the long-distance phone calls kept the phone constantly unavailable for anyone else in the household, other than my sister and her fiancé.

Although most of the time it seemed he was away on tour for months and sometimes years at a time, when they were back together, they were inseparable, and you could clearly see how truly in love they were. With my sister's love life moving full steam ahead, behind the scenes something really strange was beginning to take place with the family dynamics. It was something so incomprehensible and so unexpected that it took the family completely off guard.

It turns out that my father, whose dual role of being my sister's stepfather and her brother-in-law at the same time, began to show a somewhat odd and consuming interest in my sister's love life. After a while, it became obvious to everyone that my father's interest in the relationship was more than just keeping a watchful eye on my sister in his brother's absence. He was the hawk hovering in the sky, watching his prey's every move, or so it seemed. My father's awkward behavior was especially evident when he was drunk on a Friday or a Saturday night; he became very inquisitive and upset if he got home and my sister wasn't there.

It turns out, that the heavy drinking provided an escape from my father's introverted and extremely shy personality. It quickly transformed him and made him into a daring, boisterous, and angry individual who had no boundaries or respect for the rights of others. That was my father on the weekends, in complete contrast to the quiet persona you would encounter during the week when he would say nothing while observing everything in silence.

For a while, my family questioned my father's feelings toward my sister. We each had our personal theories; we hoped that maybe, just maybe, we were overreacting. Maybe he was just being a little bit overprotective, merely acting as a concerned stepfather. It didn't take long, however, to figure out that wasn't the case at all.

He was persistent, always wanted to know my sister's whereabouts, the circle of friends she was keeping company with, and the hours she left home and came back. It soon became apparent to my sister, and to everyone else in our family, for that matter, that the man whom she had come to know as a caring and loving stepfather, throughout most of her young-adult life, had ulterior motives in mind besides parenting.

Annoyed, scared, and frustrated, my sister decided that the best way to confront the situation was to tackle it head-on. So, every time my father would question her about anything that had to do with her personal life, she would lash out at him and basically tell him off, saying, "I'm a grown woman," and adding, "It is none of your business what I do with my life!" It wasn't long before my sister began to feel resentment, distrust, and betrayal towards my father. This led to numerous heated arguments between the two and gave a new meaning to the catchphrase "family feud."

Even with my mother in the picture, serving as both the judge and jury in all of this, the problems continued. Since it seemed my father could not stay out of my sister's personal life, my mother had a very difficult time trying to sort things out, justify my father's actions, and determine his true motives.

In the months that followed, things appeared to be cooling down somewhat. The arguments seemed to be less and less. The tension eased, and my father's drinking slowed down a bit. My mother appeared to be less anxious, and so were we as a family. We thought that finally we would be able to live a normal life and breathe a sigh of relief without all the tension and fear caused by the constant infighting between my father and my sister. It was definitely something we had all been wishing for, for a very long time. It seemed that the months and months of torment and agony were behind us, and a more tranquil and serene future lay ahead of us.

It didn't take long, however, for our family's rebuilt facade to come crashing down on us like a ton of bricks, literally, overnight.

CHAPTER 5

A NIGHTMARE TO REMEMBER

I remember it being a weekend, sometime during the years of 1961 and 1962. That day, I was fast asleep in my bed, tired from a long day of playing with my toys. My mother, on the other hand, was relaxing on the living-room sofa, watching some of her favorite TV shows. Other than that, our home was relatively quiet for a weekend. That particular night, not even my older sister Esther and my brother, Flaco, were around. It was just my mother and I. My oldest sister, Mercedes, had still not arrived home after visiting some friends in another part of the South Bronx. As for my father... well, it was payday. So as usual, he did what he did on most weekends when he had money in his pockets and friends to hang out with—he spent a good portion of his earnings on having a good time with his friends and drinking up a storm until the wee hours of the mornings.

Although things had cooled down immensely between my father and sister, there was always that air of uncertainty or unpredictability, a fear that the problems might start up again... at any given time. At times, it felt as though everyone in our family were walking on eggshells in anticipation of yet another heated verbal confrontation between the two of them. This was especially true when you had the toxic mixture of my father going off on one of his drinking binges, and my sister not being home when he returned. At times, it felt as if we had a time bomb strapped right underneath our feet, not knowing when it was set to go off.

From the best of my recollection—for most of what I'm about to say is a blur to me—that night I was awakened abruptly from a deep sleep, as if I were being pulled by my feet from the middle of a pleasant dream and into a painful nightmare. There was this earth-shattering, loud, piercing scream that appeared to be coming from the living room, a troublesome commotion the likes of which I had never heard before. I remember the sound of a struggle and of things being tossed around. But most of all, I remember being petrified of lurking into the unknown and not wanting to see what was going on, on the other side of the door.

One thing I knew for sure, even at the young age of five or six, whatever was awaiting me on the other side of the bedroom door was not going to be pleasing. As I built up the courage to open the door, I remember my hand trembling as I slowly turned the doorknob and heard the click of the door. With my eyes wide-open, I cautiously peeked through the crack in the doorway. It was then that I remember seeing total chaos taking place right before my eyes. I immediately felt helpless as I opened the door and entered the living room area. My mother, father, and sister Mercedes were all entangled in what appeared to be a "fight for your life" struggle. I remember how the stench of booze was all over the place. With every exhaustive breath that my father exhaled while battling my mother and my sister, the smell of the alcohol in the air got stronger and stronger.

In the midst of this chaotic scene, I saw it! My sister Mercedes's face had been slashed. She was incapacitated and screaming at the top of her lungs as she tried desperately to stop the bleeding coming from the cut to her once-flawless face. She had been slashed with a razor that my father so cowardly used; he cut her face from her right ear, all the way down to the side of her mouth. I can only assume it happened in a matter of seconds.

I felt so helpless and paralyzed that my body and my brain quickly went into total shock. Everything seemed to be moving in slow motion. A big blur. A nightmare that I just couldn't awaken from. About all I could do at that moment was cry and scream for my mother, my sister, and my dad to put an end to this nightmare. I had absolutely no control whatsoever. In my own little way, I prayed with all my heart and soul that this nightmare would magically go away so that everything could go back to normal. But it wasn't working.

The ruckus continued for what seemed to be an eternity before my father somehow managed to break loose and run out the door and onto the street below, leaving everyone involved exhausted, shocked, and in total disbelief that this unimaginable tragedy had just taken place.

From what I could recall, the cops and the ambulance arrived at our home right after this all ended. And my sister was quickly rushed to the emergency room for treatment at the nearest hospital, where I later learned it took doctors over forty-five stitches just to close the deep facial laceration.

As for my father, I later learned that he left the country and went back to Puerto Rico in an attempt to avoid being arrested. My father, in his own absurd and selfish way, not only scarred my sister for the rest of her life, but deeply wounded all of us, both psychologically and emotionally. In the end, this became a family secret that was twisted to appear as though what happened on that horrible night was nothing more than an unintentional accident gone wrong. The lie was conjured up by my family in an attempt to protect me from the mental trauma I experienced on that fateful night.

CHAPTER 6

THE AFTERMATH OF A TRAGEDY

As the months went by, I tried desperately to block out of my mind everything that took place on that dreadful evening, classifying it as just a bad dream that never really happened. I wanted so badly at that point just to live a normal life similar to those of the rest of the kids I knew. My family wanted me to believe that it was merely an accident.

And for a long while, I too was convinced that it was just that… an accident. Perhaps, in the long run, I thought believing it to be an accident would help me cope with the all the pain and suffering in a less traumatic way. An accident was more acceptable to my well-being than the reality of this family tragedy.

I soon learned, however, that no matter which way I tried to come to grips with this, it was of little use. For it seemed that every single time I would look at my sister's face, I couldn't help but wonder why it even had to happen. These were questions that I really didn't have the answers to, but I was always wondering, *What next?*

What will be the long-term effects on the rest of Mercedes's life? I often wondered. At other times, I would ask myself if the consequences of this dreadful incident would lead her to a lifelong struggle with depression, heartbreak, and even ridicule in the public's eye. I even struggled with the fact that a few terrifying seconds of fighting for her life might later turn her world completely upside down. But more than anything, I just thought about how her life would never, ever be the same again after this traumatic experience. For it was on that frightful night that she lost her youth and her sense of safety and well-being.

Over the years that followed, I remember how my sister would try her best to cover the scar on her face by wearing heavy makeup and a colorful scarf that went from the top of her head, down to the bottom of her chin, where she would tie it in a knot. This soon became a ritual every time she left the house and had to face the public. A simple trip to the store to go clothes shopping, to visit her friends, or even to go to work became a time-consuming effort.

In her own private moments, I suspect that she must have struggled with the pain and anguish, must have asked, "Why me?" Must have suffered the humiliation of living life with a visible scar, a modern-day scarlet letter that constantly reminded her of a dark family secret that one day destroyed her innocent and promising life.

Fear and anxiety also consumed much of my sister's thoughts. With my father still on the loose, leaving the home was not an easy task. Constantly looking over her shoulder became the norm for her. She feared for her life and her safety. It's creepy to think that the man who once protected the household as her stepfather was now the same man whom she feared the most.

Luckily, however, approximately six months after the incident happened, she was able to breathe a sigh of relief when my father was arrested. FBI agents working on the case, along with local authorities, were able to track him down and pick him up as he arrived on a flight from Puerto Rico to Newark, New Jersey. It was there that, according to my family, he was placed under arrest and charged with being a fugitive from justice for the assault charges brought by my sister.

It would be months before my family would be called upon to appear in court for my father's criminal court case. I remember it all happening like one big flash in my mind. One moment he was out of my life completely, and the next day he was in my presence in a courtroom. Because I was so young at the time, about all I recall was being in this big, dimly lit room with very dark, cold wooden benches that felt very uncomfortable. I also remember gazing at the enormity of the courtroom we were in, its high ceilings and faded-white walls with a few picture frames. I also noticed a huge stagelike area right in front of me, which I later learned was where the judge sat to listen to my father's court case. I also learned that this judge would be the one to determine my father's fate, either sending him to jail for a very long time or setting him free!

I waited patiently for something exciting to happen to break the silence in the courtroom. It was extremely boring, but exciting at the same time because you didn't know—or at least I didn't—what to expect next. The seconds ticking in my head only added to the anticipation, waiting for what was going to happen. Suddenly and without warning, the next thing I remember hearing was this loud, resounding voice that echoed throughout this quiet room, addressing everyone in the courtroom, and at the same time bringing the room to complete silence. About the only sound I could hear came from my own inhaling and exhaling with each moment of silence. With nothing else to do, I felt my eyes start to wander around the courtroom; I was in limbo, just waiting for something big to happen to break the silence. It was certainly a tough and uncomfortable situation for me to be in.

I must have fallen asleep, from all the boring legal jargon that took place that day, because the next thing I recall is hearing the judge pounding the gavel on the podium; then my mother, a few family members, and I quickly exited the building. About all I remember about my father that day was seeing a glimpse of him as he was being led away in handcuffs by the court officers as court adjourned for the day. It was the end of a tension-filled day for all of us, and now it was time for all of us to slowly heal as a family and to reflect on what would happen next in our lives.

CHAPTER 7

EXPECT THE UNEXPECTED

In the year or so that followed, quite a few changes took place. I was enrolled in kindergarten at Public School 65, located about two blocks from where I lived. Still reeling from the nightmarish experience in my household, I had a very difficult time adjusting to the school environment. I found myself afraid of being away from my home and in the presence of a lot of people. I became reclusive and introverted, even at the young age of five or six, petrified to say a word to anyone, including my fellow classmates.

I remember one day being in class and desperately having to go to the bathroom. I kept squirming in my seat in hopes that by moving around, the urge would go away, class would end, and I could eventually go home. That was wishful thinking on my part because it was too early in the morning; I still had a long way to go before dismissal. However, that morning, when I finally built up enough courage to raise my hand and ask my teacher if I could go to the bathroom, it happened! Just as I stood up, I couldn't hold it any longer and literally peed on myself right in front of my teacher and the whole classroom.

I remember standing there motionless for what seemed like hours, although it was just seconds, with my pants drenched in urine while I stood on my feet in a big puddle of urine. It was one of the most humiliating moments in my life, standing there in a puddle of my own urine while all the kids in my classroom laughed at me. I will never, ever forget it!

Looking back now, I could clearly see that everything that was happening to me was the result of my basically suffering in silence after having my whole world turned upside down because of the violence I witnessed at home. It was a personal betrayal that destroyed my heart and soul in a matter of seconds, leaving me confused about how fast love can turn into pain on the spur of a moment.

To make matters worse, I had the most difficult task of trying to sort all this out by myself, without any help whatsoever. *To whom can I turn?* I constantly asked myself. I was not offered professional counseling or intervention. Instead, I turned to my family for answers, but they kept reminding me that what happened that horrible night was merely an accident. And since I had no concrete evidence to the contrary, I wanted so hard for it truly to have been an accident. But as hard as I tried, the horror of it all kept lingering in my thoughts. I even had nightmares on a regular basis. As matter of self-preservation, I knew that I had no other choice but to keep saying to myself that someday the truth would be known, and my mind and my heart would be vindicated.

While my mind dwelled on what the future might hold, other changes were quickly happening all around me. My father got out on bail from his arrest, gathered all his belongings, and moved out of our apartment and into a private furnished room in the South Bronx. While my mother, now the sole breadwinner of the household—my sister Mercedes helping out in whatever little way she could—was forced to quit her job at the garment factory and go on welfare, public assistance, in order to survive and make ends meet.

My sister Mercedes, on the other hand, was pregnant with her first child from her fiancé. And because of all the problems that were swirling around after "the accident," they decided together that it was best to postpone their wedding. My sister's fiancé was still having an extremely difficult time coming to grips with something so terrible, so unimaginable having been done by his own flesh and blood. This was the same person whom he once looked up to, loved, and trusted so dearly. It was just so mind-boggling that such an unspeakable crime took place at the hands of someone he admired so much. Ultimately, it led to the sad and heartbreaking end of the relationship between two brothers! With one hating the other for the rest of his life!

It was a drama that unfortunately we could all relate to as a family. For it was on that day that my father's violent actions destroyed many lives, shattered many dreams beyond repair, and hurt so many people. In the end, it left my family in a state of total disarray, with so many unanswered questions and very few solutions to the problems.

CHAPTER 8

A SURPRISE TURN OF EVENTS, 1962

In one year's time, things in my family took a turn towards the unexpected. In a bold move that shocked everyone, my sister Mercedes and my mother both decided to forgive my father for the unmerciful assault and dropped all the charges against him in court. That bombshell took everyone within the immediate family and close friends by total surprise.

But what's even more unbelievable is that within a few months, he had moved back into our apartment! From that moment on, the tension-filled atmosphere was forever present, especially when my sister and my father happened to be in the same room at the same time. Although neither my sister nor my father would utter a single word to each other and avoided each other's presence at every cost, the tension was always so high you literally could cut it with a knife. Everyone knew that this volatile situation could explode at any minute.

For a very long while, we, as a family, tried to make it as normal as possible for everyone. We tried to carry on with our lives as if the tragedy had never occurred. But as much as we attempted to mask the incident as a thing of the past, somehow the thoughts and the horrifying images still stayed in my private thoughts.

My sister, especially, tried desperately to put everything behind her so that she could concentrate on raising her now-one-year-old son, Radames Jr. She became pregnant with her second child and had a daughter, whom they named Sandra. Unfortunately, as it turns out, soon after giving birth to her daughter, the marriage plans faltered due to the constant strain of maintaining a long-distance relationship and the lingering aftereffects of that unforgettable incident.

While all this was going on, my brother, Valentine, also known as Flaco, had just been released from prison following a felony conviction involving an assault. And although talks of retaliation by my brother on behalf of my sister were overheard, they never materialized, and that gave my mother one less thing to worry about. What my mother didn't know then was that her problems were just about to start once again. My brother reunited with his fellow gang members from the Spanish Devils, and my sister Esther dropped out of school to hang out with her female gang members. My mother's headaches soon would be more than an aspirin could cure.

CHAPTER 9

PUBLIC SCHOOL 30, 1962

I was only at Public School 65 for one year before I was transferred to Public School 30, which was closer to my home and in my school district. Public School 30 was a newly built school that was added to the neighborhood to relieve some of the overcrowding that Public School 65 had been dealing with for many years. For me, it was a great opportunity to start over, meet new people, and try to forget my painful past.

Initially, everything was going great for me. I looked forward to getting up in the mornings and going to school every day. Being at this new school gave me a reprieve, even if it was only temporary, from all the stress and turmoil that existed at home. In the meantime, the freedom from having less anxiety in my young life felt great, and I was truly enjoying it! But unfortunately, it didn't last long.

Before I knew it, I was back in my lonesome shell once again. I became extremely introverted and shy, to the point that teachers quickly took notice as the years went by and documented it all in my report cards. From first grade all the way up to fourth grade, most teachers stated that my personality was "too quiet" and that I needed to "speak more often in class." "He is very shy in class; he does very good work," a teacher once wrote.

My extreme shyness soon caught up with me. Because I was so shy and afraid to talk in class, I also stayed away from the other children and did not socialize with anyone. It was so bad that I don't remember having any friends in school at all. As a result, I started skipping school and looking for any excuse not to attend classes. In my first two years alone, I was out a total of eighty-five days. Although some of the days I was out legitimately suffering from my asthma attacks, a lot of the time I would just fake it to avoid going to school. In all, I was out an insurmountable amount of time during the five years I was there, a dreadful trend that continued into my later years in school. To say that all these years of missing school, combined with all the problems I was having at home at the time, had a negative effect on my ability to learn is truly an understatement.

Through the years, it was apparent that I had a huge problem on my hands. Just trying to master some of the basic skills of reading, writing, and math in order to stay within my grade level of comprehension became a challenge. I soon pushed myself into a whirlwind of confusion and second-guessing myself, asking if I was as smart as the other kids in my class or worse, if I was even "fit" to be in school. Hence, after a while, I was so overwhelmed with feelings of negativity that I felt as if I was an underachiever who wouldn't amount to anything in life. It was a terrible feeling to have as a kid, and one that took me many years to overcome.

Today, when I think back to my young academic life, what I find most amazing is that even though my school attendance was extremely poor, my grades were suffering, and I was behind in all my classes, amazingly, I was still being passed and never had to repeat any of my grades or classes.

Looking back now, I can clearly see that all the warning signs of a troubled child were there, but no one in the school system picked up on it. As a result, nothing was ever done to help me. Internally, my inner voice was desperately crying for help to break out of this all-consuming, shy personality, but my inner voice was never heard… because no one ever asked.

CHAPTER 10

ENOUGH IS ENOUGH, 1965

By the time I got into fourth grade, I was still that shy, quiet, and reserved kid who entered the school nearly four years before. Being skinny and the tallest kid in the class only added to my already fragile, low self-esteem issues. It also didn't help that because of my height, my teacher would always place me in the back of the line during lunch and at dismissal, making me stand out like a big giant palm tree in a field of tiny shrubs. I was, by far, the tallest Puerto Rican kid you had ever seen by the age of nine.

Even though I was so tall and skinny, my height wasn't intimidating at all. Instead, kids would take turns poking fun at me and calling me all sorts of names like "the jolly green giant," "toothpick," and "slim Jim," just to name a few. After a while, I felt like an oddball that just couldn't fit in with the rest of the kids in the school, no matter what.

That year turned out to be particularly bad for me, not just because of all the name calling and self-esteem issues that confronted me every day, but also because of an unforgettable incident that eventually left an indelible mark on my spirit as a child and forced me to take a hard stance in making changes in my life for the better. That one humiliating incident took place during the fall of 1965.

One day, I was in the cafeteria, trying to find an available table to have my lunch. I was minding my own business and not bothering a soul. Just as I was finding my way to an open table, I encountered Alexander. Alexander was considered one of the most feared bullies in the whole school. He intimidated just about everyone with his big size and presence and not surprisingly, was always in trouble in school. That day, as I passively made my way towards my table with my food tray in hand, I had the misfortune of having to pass by Alexander's table before getting to mine. That's when he decided to do the unthinkable just for a good laugh in the presence of all his school buddies. He tripped me. Without skipping a beat, that's exactly what he did. I was just about to go past him, when he stuck his foot out in front of me, causing me to trip and fall on my face. I suddenly found myself on the floor, my lunch food scattered all over the place, while everyone, including Alexander, was laughing their ass off at my expense.

I felt like crap, embarrassed beyond reason. At that moment, I just wanted to run out of the school cafeteria, go home, and punch the hell out of the cement wall in my room, just to relieve some of the pain and frustration. Instead, I just sat there on the floor and took in the barrage of laughter, taunting, and abuse that came my way. But as the laughter continued to intensify with each second that ticked by, so did my anger! Without warning or thinking about the consequences of confronting this big bully, I immediately jumped to my feet and leaned right into his face, angrily clutching my fist. I wanted to kill the bastard. I had fire in my eyes and was about to explode at any minute. As I confronted him, I said not a word, but stared right into his eyes, face-to-face. I was just waiting for him to make the first move so that I could punch the hell out of him.

This surprise challenge shocked everyone, including big Alexander, who was now forced to defend his reputation as one of the most feared bullies in the school. However, before any punches could be thrown or the confrontation could escalate, a couple of teachers quickly intervened, and the big fight between Alexander and me in the cafeteria never happened. That angered Alexander more than anything else because he wanted to settle the score right then and there, in front of all his cronies. Instead, he left me with these last haunting words, "Don't worry, your ass is mine after school," and then he calmly walked away. At that moment, I wished the incident had been resolved while I still had the fire in my chest. Instead, I had to wait until later when the fire in my system would surely literally be burned out.

The thought of my fighting this bully in front of all his buddies and other students after school scared the hell out of me, to say the least. That afternoon, I kept looking at the clock in the classroom, hoping that 3:00 p.m. would never come. But the more I stared at the clock, I knew deep down in my heart and soul that the moment in question was inevitable... and I would have to face Alexander sooner or later.

Up to that point, I had never had a fistfight in my life, and the thought of fighting someone his size was incomprehensible. Luckily, or so I thought, he was in another class, and a fifth grader at that, and I was in the fourth grade. I figured that maybe, just maybe, my class would be dismissed before his class, and I could avoid him altogether and go home without having to deal with this bully.

But it wasn't to be. For just as I left the school and was halfway up the street towards my home, Alexander suddenly ran up from behind me and sucker punched me right in the back of head. The impact felt as if I had gotten hit with a bat. Instead, it was just his bare knuckles that slammed into the back of my head and knocked me right to the ground like a bowling pin. It all happened so fast. The next thing I knew, I was lying facedown on the pavement. I remember getting hit so hard that it left me all dazed and confused. He then turned me around and immediately proceeded to pound on my face with his fist while he pinned my body to the concrete pavement with his over-weight, massive body. He continued his attack, punching me in every part of my face until I went unconscious and was bleeding from the beating.

Before I knew what was happening, someone in the neighborhood decided to intervene and pulled Alexander right off me. By the time this happened, I was semiconscious. The Good Samaritan rushed me to the hospital in his own private car so that I could receive medical attention. That afternoon at the hospital, I was treated and released to my parents with a diagnosis of "concussion and numerous facial bruises." The attack by Alexander was reported to the school author-ities the next day by my parents, and Alexander was suspended from school.

School ended shortly thereafter that year, but the incident left me extremely bitter and angry. It was then that I made a promise to myself that enough was enough! I decided that from that day forward I was never, ever going to let something like that happen to me again! Once more, it was a promise I made to myself… that I vowed to keep!

It was during that summer of 1966 when I approached my brother, Flaco, about the incident and told him that I wanted him to teach me how to fight so I could defend myself! It was a challenge that my brother willingly took on; he told me, "Don't worry, my little bro. I promise you that before the summer is over, you're going to be really good with your hands. You'll see," and gave me big hug and a smile.

I knew right then and there that things in school were going to be a lot different for me come next school year.

CHAPTER 11

A ROCKY IN THE MAKING, 1966

Just as a prizefighter makes his purse for putting up a good fight against a boxing opponent, my brother's payment for a good fight came in the form of "getting respect." In street lingo, it basically means someone who's proven himself to be a tough guy, both on the streets, and in his own neighborhood. As my brother bluntly put it to me one day, it is "someone who doesn't take shit from anyone…and everyone knows not to fuck with!"

That was my brother in a nutshell. A streetwise, quick-witted, humorous, highly explosive-tempered, daring individual who would say or do just about anything on a dare, who could just as easily beat you with his fists or hurt you with a selection of weapons he was known to carry—knife, zip gun, bat, etc. It was a street credibility that followed him whenever or wherever he went, including the prison system, where he spent quite a few years behind bars for various crimes, including what he termed "having consensual sex" with a minor. She, months later, gave birth to his first child, but more on that in a later chapter. That being said, it was my brother's same type of crazy, charismatic personality that made him a magnet for friends who loved being around him. That's also how he made a lot of friends while in prison and got a chance to hang around with some of the toughest guys in the prison system at the time.

I recall my brother once telling me that if you can "kick some ass and you're quick with your hands, nobody will ever mess with you, brother!" Although he was already quick with the hands before he landed in prison for the first time, once in there, he managed to polish up his street skills even more by learning from "some of the best" hard-core street fighters in the prison system while serving time in the Bronx House of Detention and on Riker's Island. In the long run, this ultimately helped him become a better street fighter and to sharpen his fighting skills, something most proponents of anti-violence would wholeheartedly detest and would counsel walking away rather than standing your ground. But when you happen to live in such a tough neighborhood, like ours, knowing how to fight ultimately becomes a welcomed talent to have at your disposal; in the end, it becomes a vital part of surviving the streets of New York City. Not to mention, what my brother calls "the respect" you get from having such skills is something you must have for your own protection in our neighborhood. It was those same basic fighting skills that I was surely lacking, but I was more than willing to learn from a "street survivalist" like my brother.

On the day I approached my brother about my situation at school, he said, "No problem, brother! I'm going to teach you everything I know, so that no motherfucker will ever fuck with you, ever again, bro." That was my brother. Always to the point and telling it like it is!

Within weeks of having that talk with my brother, we started training. I first started out by learning some of the most basic techniques in boxing, from defensive hand positioning to protecting your face. He then taught me some of the different types of body punches—jabs, uppercuts, and knockout punches—that one would deliver to an adversary. He also taught me to never stay flat on my feet, to always keep dancing, moving around and swinging my fist, in order to throw off my opponent. As he always said, "A moving target is harder to hit!"

After weeks of going over the basic skills, it was time to put it all to work against him, of all people. To say I was a bit intimidated about boxing against my brother and mentor is an understatement, especially after he told me he was going to "hit me hard just to toughen me up"!

To prepare for the training, my brother brought a couple of pairs of those big, twenty-ounce boxing gloves; although they appeared to have a lot of cushion in them to soften the blows, they would still sting pretty hard when you got hit. My brother was a little bit taller than I was—he was five eight to my five six or so—but weightwise, I don't think he had me by much. Hence his nickname, Flaco or Skinny, was perfectly fitting for a guy with his build.

We began our boxing sessions, in the living room of our apartment, with a slow, almost shadowboxing-type speed. Trying to remember everything we had gone over the past couple of weeks, and finally attempting to put it all together to make it work, I knew it was going to be an extremely difficult task for me to put into action, but one that I was willing to give a hundred percent on our first day of physical training.

At first, my timing and coordination were completely off. I felt a bit clumsy and uncoordinated at the very beginning, which I guess was to be expected for a kid my age. But more concerning to me during our sparring sessions was feeling that my punches were going all over the place. At times, I was swinging wildly and completely out of control, while at others I was on target and swinging with precision.

As uncoordinated and unpolished as I was, my brother refused to give up on me. He kept encouraging me to "come on… hit me… you can do it" as he danced around me in circles as if he were a moving target that just could not be hit. The more he pushed me, the more frustrated I got… and the more determined I became. I guess that was exactly his plan.

One day, when his verbal teasing—calling me every name in the book to get me pissed off—was within inches from my face, I let him have it, right smack in the jaw. In my astonishment, I thought, *This is it; he's going to beat the hell out of me and will never want to work with me again.* But surprisingly, it didn't happen that way.

Instead, he said to me, "That's exactly what I'm talking about. That's the way I want you to hit every single time. You hear me, brother?"

That day, for whatever reason, I finally felt that I had reached the pinnacle of my own expectations and was ready to move on. With my brother's blessings, that's exactly what I did. After weeks and weeks of training, I finally got the confidence I needed. In fact, during some of our sparring sessions, my brother would punch and throw me off-balance, but I would bounce back and hit him even harder. I guess what he was trying to teach me is that sometimes you're going to get hit hard, but you can't back down; you must make every effort to stay in the fight.

After a few minor bumps and bruises during my training, I not only learned to take a punch, and give two or three punches back in return, but also the psychology of how to bounce back, stay in the fight, and never give up finally came into play.

From that point on, he helped me develop all the self-confidence and the physical tools I needed to confront the bullies of my world. When we finished with all our training by the end of that summer, I was all pumped up and couldn't wait to put my skills to the test. "Bullies of the world, I hope you're ready for me…because I'm coming after you," I kept repeating over and over to myself! I was excited because I knew that this was something that I'd been waiting to do for a very long, long time: a chance to finally confront a bully just to give him a taste of his own medicine!

In addition to all the boxing training I got from my brother, I also learned some truly valuable life lessons that I wasn't even expecting, but I felt really blessed that he took the time to talk to me about them. He started by saying something to the effect of, "Brother, I just want to give you a little advice on a few things that I've learned in life. Just like what you did in boxing, you should never be afraid to take on new challenges in your life. And I'll tell you why. Because with each challenge you take on, you're always going to learn a little something and hopefully do really well at it. It's the experience and the journey of it all that means the most. But just remember that it doesn't matter how hard or how difficult the challenge might be… as long as you can say that you gave it your all and never gave up. That's all that matters! So remember to stay positive, believe in yourself, and never set limits on what you can or can't do in life! And if you do that, I'm willing to bet you that you will be able to accomplish anything you ever wanted to do in your life! You got it, my little bro?"

I nodded my head in agreement and said, "Thank you so much, brother!" It is exactly those same words of encouragement that I took to heart then, and something that is with me to this day.

As it turns out, it didn't take long before my new skills were put to the test. I was about a month into my fifth-grade class in my last year at Public School 30 and was really looking forward to finally graduating and going on to Alexander Burger Junior High School. I was still that tall, shy kid who kept to himself a lot and didn't bother a soul. But for some reason, it's usually those quiet ones with very few friends who are on the bully's target list of people to pick on. Well, I guess it was my turn once again to make it to the top of that hit list.

Meet Cornelius. Cornelius was the class bully everyone avoided. He was as tall as I was, about five six or so, but approximately twenty pounds heavier. He was also known to have a very mean temper and a reputation for knocking people out on their asses with one quick punch if you so much as gave him a dirty look or brushed by him and accidentally bumped into him… as I soon found out firsthand.

One day, we were lining up in the back of the classroom to go to our gym class when Cornelius purposely bumped into my left shoulder as he made his way to the back of the line. He stopped momentarily and gave me a threatening stare from top to bottom as if to challenge me, and then he slowly walked away from me without excusing himself or saying, "I'm sorry."

Right away, this really pissed me off. Flashes of the old picked-on kid from the past ran through my head at lightning speeds, and I said to myself, *It's either now or never*, for I refused to be another hash mark on this bully's hit list, or any bully's, for that matter, ever again! So right before Cornelius made it to the end of the line, I bravely shouted out in a loud, "Yo, what the hell is your problem, man?"

This took everyone by total surprise, including Cornelius, who by now was slowly making his way back towards me to confront me. He definitely had that angry and pissed-off mood written all over his face as he approached me, as though he was saying, "How dare you talk to me that way?" In his mind, he had just been embarrassed in front of the whole class, and he was not about to let that go by without making an example of me… or so he thought!

Within seconds, the whole classroom became quiet. So quiet, in fact, that you could practically hear a pin drop. As far as I know, no one had the slightest idea as to how I was going to react to this sudden challenge that came barreling at me out of nowhere, or what was going to happen next. Little did they know that I had been waiting for a moment like this for a very, very long time. It was finally my turn to shine in the face of adversity, and I was prepared to show the world just exactly what I had in store for this moment.

By the time Cornelius got in front of me, I was ready, as ready as I could ever be, and I had all the confidence in the world that I could handle anything he would dish out. I was reborn as a street fighter and itching to put my newfound skills to the test!

I wasted no time and went to work on him right away. I stared him down just as my brother had taught me during those training days in my home. In doing so, I quickly reversed any fear I had in my heart and soul and projected it onto the enemy, whose protective wall of courage I had now whittled away. After that…it was all about me. All I can remember hearing from Cornelius was, "No, I don't have a problem. Do you?" It went back-and-forth, from that point on, as we stood chest to chest, challenging each other to see who was going to make the first move or take the first swing.

The next thing I remember, I was pushing Cornelius away from me really hard, just to get him off-balance. That gave me ample time to load up my cannons and prepare for battle. Before Cornelius could retaliate, I was ready and knocked him on his ass, backward onto one of the tables behind him, with one quick, powerful right-hand punch to his face. From that point on, it was all about me. Before he could regain his composure from the punch, I put him in a headlock and just started punching away with a vengeance. It was as if my frustrations from all those years of being picked on and tormented hinged on this one encounter with this one bully. To me, he represented all the bullies of the world, and I felt as if I were a hero, in my own little way, for having the courage to take him on, and in doing so, for fighting for the less fortunate.

The fight was eventually broken up by my teacher and a few of the students. That afternoon, we both ended up in the principal's office, where we got in trouble for fighting in class. In the end, it was a discipline that I accepted with pride. On that day, I fought hard to finally get the respect I so well deserved, not only from Cornelius, who ironically later on became one of my best fifth-grade buddies, but also from some of the other bullies of the school, like Tony, Victor, and Angel, who also tested my fighting skills and lost in a big way… with their pride!

CHAPTER 12

MY MOTHER THE DISCIPLINARIAN, 1966

My mother was an extremely strict parent with a quick temper; she ran a tight ship and always kept a short rein on me while I was growing up. Because we lived in such a tough neighborhood, she was constantly paranoid about my safety and well-being. My limited freedom was monitored at all times, it seemed. "Who are you with? What are you doing?" and "Where are you going?" became a regular part of her vocabulary whenever I wanted to get together with any of my short list of friends from the block. It didn't take long to figure out that out of all my friends, my friend Johnny and I had the least amount of freedom. One of my mother's famous threats would always be, that if I broke any of the house rules, I would pay dearly for it with a good beating. I tested this many times, and guess what? She wasn't kidding!

My mother was a tough disciplinarian who followed a stringent protocol for punishment or time-outs from the old school of discipline, unlike my father who very rarely punished me. It was a discipline that in the eyes of many would be considered cruel and unusual punishment. Way too harsh for today's standards of discipline.

For my mother, though, a first-generation Hispanic from the island of Puerto Rico, growing up under the umbrella of strict house rules was the norm, the natural way of life, and not the exception to raising kids the right way. Basically, if you broke the rules of the house, then you would pay for it in a big way. It was that simple!

In fact, when I think back to some of the most memorable painstaking time-outs I endured in those days, the pain and the anguish of the moment comes back to me so vividly that it feels as if it just happened yesterday. A typical time-out consisted of putting me in a corner, kneeling with bare knees on the floor, on a spread of uncooked rice... for about ten to fifteen minutes. Another form of punishment included forcing me to kneel, on my bare knees again, on a metal cheese grater, or *guajo* as they would say in Spanish, until my knees bled and I was in a lot of pain. Lastly, the use of a leather belt or an extension cord was also an option for a good, old-fashioned ass whipping. Ouch, it hurts just to think about it!

Perhaps one of the most painful and most embarrassing moments of my life didn't happen until I was the age of twelve. During the early part of the fall of 1968, three of my best junior high school friends—Freddy, Mexicano, and Oscar—and I decided to skip school so we could hang out at People's Park, a small, well-known park that was located directly across the street from my junior high school. It was known for being a notorious hangout spot for kids playing hooky, skipping classes, or spending time with street gangs.

That day, we met a few of the girls from the school, who had also skipped school, and we were having the time of our lives, conversing and flirting, when suddenly one of my buddies in the group came up with the bright idea of scaling down this large rock wall that was located in the northeastern section of the park, near the softball field, between the rear yard of a residential building and the park. This particular wall—a good twenty feet in height, about sixty yards in length, and stacked with protruding, sharp rock edges that were used to scale it—was pretty intimidating. The idea was to see which one of us could climb down the fastest. The challenge, although a bit risky, was all aimed at impressing the girls with our talents, at least that's what we thought. The end result, we hoped, would be a date with one of the girls.

Moments after staring down this wall and seeing how steep and dangerous the climb would be, we quickly began having second thoughts and wondered if it was all really worth it, just to win over the girls. After talking it over briefly, we all decided to go for it, even though we knew that the rewards certainly did not outweigh the risk of getting hurt. However, deep down inside, we all knew that one small slip on any of those sharp rocks could mean a broken leg, ankle, or worse yet, a bruised ego and no dates with the girls.

With the girls cheering us on, we got into our sitting positions at the top of the wall in preparation for this daring, stupid feat. As I looked down, my first instinct was *Whoa, if I beat these guys down the wall, these girls are going to love me… and I'll be their hero.* However, no sooner than that thought came to my mind, I realized I wasn't dressed for this occasion. While my buddies were all dressed in jeans, I, on the other hand, was wearing a brand-new pair of sharkskin dress pants that my mother had just bought me the day before. Those pants were very popular in the '60s and were made of this very fine, shiny fabric that made them really stand out among the other dress pants of that time period. My first thought was, *I better not get them dirty, or worse yet, mess them up…or that's my ass!* But I quickly reassured myself, *Everything is going to be just fine.*

By the time the girls were ready to say, "Get on your mark, get set, and…," I was so pumped up and raring to go that I feared nothing and no one. Absolutely no one, that is, except my mother. That last thought for some reason just continued to attack my brain and kept reminding me of what could or would happen to me if I got caught doing something I wasn't supposed to be doing… like playing hooky. But I brushed it off as just a crazy thought and continued to focus on my challenge, which was to win the girls over… and that, to me at the time, was more important than anything else in the world.

Seconds later when the girls yelled, "Go," I immediately began to drag my butt over the ragged edges of the rocks to get into position. I felt and heard what appeared to be a ripping of some kind; it seemed to be coming from the back of my pants. I ignored the sound, thinking it was just a snag in the material, and continued on my descent, never once stopping to think that maybe I ripped my pants.

By the time it was all over, not only did I come in last place, but I also discovered that I had accidentally ripped my pants in the process. Now, in addition to losing so terribly on this dare, I had to deal with the fact that my pants had ripped so badly that my white underwear was showing. Embarrassed, I instinctively took my sweater off and tied it around my waist to cover my rear end. So now, instead of making an good impression on the girls, I looked like a fool in distress!

From that point on, it didn't take long before all the laughter and the jokes started to kick in. It seemed as though the laughter and the roasting went on for what seemed like an eternity. After the laughter and the jokes died down a bit, we decided to walk over and sit on one of the park benches located right near the entrance to the park…just to kill some time. As we sat on the benches, we talked and laughed some more. A few in the group even lit up some cigarettes as we kept ourselves busy just watching the passersby. Bad idea, as it later turns out.

It was almost noontime when in the course of watching some of the people go by, I suddenly realized that this one lady approaching us lived in my building. Immediately, the first thing that came to my mind was, *Oops… I'm in big trouble now!* As if not to make it obvious that she knew me, she just give me a big smile, but didn't say a word as she slowly strolled by us. This led me to believe that maybe she really didn't recognize me and just smiled as a friendly gesture to say hi. After this quick interaction, I was feeling a bit nervous and uneasy, my biggest fear of course being that she was going to tell my mother about seeing me in the park. I shared my concerns with my friends.

But to ease my nerves, they laughed it off and collectively and said, "Don't worry about it. She's not going to tell on you. She probably doesn't even know who the hell you are, anyway!"

Although their intentions were good and it helped calm my nerves a little, deep down in my gut I knew the situation wasn't good. Not only was I worried about getting busted in the park for skipping school with a bunch of friends whom my mother didn't even know, much less would have approved of my hanging out with them, but also just knowing that I tore my brand-new pants was enough to scare the crap out of me. Especially when my mother had specifically warned me the day before, "These are brand new pants, so you better take care of them. Do you understand what I mean?" I had nodded my head in response to my mother and promised to take good care of them.

I soon became consumed with questions. *What do I do about my pants now that this has happened? How do I explain myself and get out of this once I get home?* With each question now becoming harder and harder to answer, the stress level just kept mounting by the minute, leaving me with plenty of excuses in my head, but not a lot of solutions to my overwhelming problems. *So what now?* I decided I would just keep my sweater on all day, and hopefully my mother wouldn't notice a thing once I got home.

It turns out I wasted so much time worrying about the status of my pants that instead of packing up and leaving the park, I decided to stay with my friends. That would turn out to be just another stupid mistake on my part.

As luck would have it, about a half hour or so after I saw my tattletale neighbor, my biggest fear was soon realized when my mother came storming into the park. Before I could even react, she was at the bottom of the park steps with hands on her waist, foot tapping on the pavement, and a look that would scare the crap out of anybody.

When this happened, all my friends, who had been laughing and having a good time, quickly got up from the park benches and nonchalantly walked away from me in different directions, acting as if they didn't know me. In essence, they were saying, "See you later, I'm so glad I'm not in your sorry-ass shoes." I felt so alone, as if everyone had abandoned ship and left me all by lonesome self to fight a no-win battle of survival with my mom.

The next thing I recall happening is my mother yelling at me, "Come down here right now," as she pointed to the ground where she was standing.

As I worked my way down the steps and looked at her now-steaming-red face, I felt my heart slowly work its way up into my throat, beating faster and faster by the second. By the time I made it to the bottom of the steps, I remember seeing my mother's left hand moving towards my face in what appeared to be slow motion, as if she were about to slap me, but instead she grabbed on to my right ear like a lobster claw, twisting and turning her fingers harder with every "ouch" that she got out of me… and then she quickly dragged me away.

"What the hell are you doing here, you son of a bitch, when you're supposed to be in school? Answer me… answer right now!!!" I clearly remember my mother yelling me in Spanish as she continued, "Who the hell are those people that were with you anyway?" But before I could get a single word in, she said what I had dreaded hearing all along. "Wait till we get home. I'm going to beat the living crap out of you!!!" Her menacing words echoed in my head like a nightmare. It was then that I knew I was in big, big trouble.

I remember how my mother's actions, towing me by my ear, got a lot of attention from neighborhood onlookers. I could clearly read the looks on their anguished faces; it was if they were saying, "Boy, is he in for a beating." And they weren't wrong. The drama in all of this did not phase my mother one bit; instead, her determination to punish me got even more intense the closer we got to our home.

By the time we made it to our fourth-floor apartment, I had already broken into a big sweat. I suspect it was a combination from our fast-paced walking and all the adrenaline that had built up inside of me, starting from the minute I got busted. Add to that the numbing pain in my ear from my mother's iron grip. It felt as if my ear were about to be ripped from my head. I was truly scared to death!

As soon as we walked into the apartment, she didn't waste any time and went right to work on her threats. I remember that the first few words that came out of her mouth. "Now take off your pants, and give me your belt," she screamed at me. Naturally, I refused, which infuriated her even more, prompting her to yell, "Don't you worry. If I can't get you with that one"—meaning my leather belt—"I'll get you with another one; that's the least of the problems." The next thing I knew, she pushed me onto the sofa and told me, "Sit there, and don't you dare move, you son of a bitch!" She soon left the living room, only to return a few seconds later armed with an even bigger and thicker leather belt than the one I was wearing. *How was she able to find a belt that fast?* I wondered. To this day, I don't really know, but somehow she managed!

Without warning, she started beating my ass as if there were no tomorrow. Each swing, it seemed, was so carefully calculated to hit its target; she never missed. And although I made every attempt possible in the world to dodge each of her swings, it just didn't work. Her strokes were quick, accurate, and to the point… and boy, did they hurt!

As I squirmed and maneuvered under the onslaught of more belt swings, I failed to realize that she had yet to discover the approximate four-inch-wide rip in my brand-new pants that I was supposed to take care of. It was during one of my feverish defensive moves to avoid getting hit that I inadvertently exposed the damage to my brand-new pair of sharkskin pants.

The angry and shocked look on her face said it all. The next thing I remember is this mountainous assault of Spanish curse words that came my way, followed by the following phrase I've translated into English: "You fucking ripped your pants, you son of a bitch. Now, you're really going to get it from me." As if the beating I was getting at the time wasn't enough!

In desperation, I made the courageous and crazy decision to try to make a run for it to prevent further punishment. To do that, I knew I had to be quick and agile, and I could not look back or stop in my tracks, no matter what, or it would be my ass. So before she could come down with another swat of the belt, I saw an opening in between her left leg and the edge of the sofa, and I decided to go for it. It took her by complete surprise.

The next thing I knew, I was hauling ass, running into the master bedroom like a running back going for a touchdown, my mother right behind me. I could literally feel her breathing down my neck. She swung the belt several times in her desperate attempts to stop me. I recall the scary swishing sound made by the leather belt as it whizzed right by me, just nicking my back. This only made me run faster as I dashed towards my escape route to safety. Without a moment of hesitation, I spotted my safe haven and went for it.

It was underneath my mother's bed, a spot that I had used on many occasions before to fend off a good ass whipping whenever I got in trouble, and it worked every single time. So before she could take another swing at me, I took a giant leap of faith and slid headfirst on the floor, just as a baseball player slides home to score a run, and in one swoop, I made it under the bed.

"Safe at last," I remember sighing to myself over and over and over again. *Now, if I can just stay clear of the broomstick that Mother will use to try to flush me out from underneath her bed, I'll be in good shape,* I thought.

That day, I stayed underneath that bed for what seemed like hours until my mother cooled down a bit, and I was able to plead my case for forgiveness. I promised it would never, ever happen again. At least, that was my hope, and it worked.

In time, all was forgiven. I had learned my lesson the hard way one more time. However, deep down inside, I knew that, no matter how much I tried, this would not be the last time I'd find myself in this predicament or worse yet, the last time I'd find myself diving for safety under my mother's bed!

CHAPTER 13

"TELL ME WITH WHOM YOU'RE WALKING, AND I'LL TELL YOU WHO YOU ARE," 1966

Dime con quién andas, y te diré quién eres is a common Spanish idiom that basically means tell me with whom you're walking, and I'll tell you the type of person that you are. It was a common principle that my mother used to always impress upon us: people will judge you by the company you keep. In other words, pick your friends wisely and make the right choices; in the end, you'll be a better person for it.

On that note, when it came to picking my friends, I knew right from the beginning what I was up against. I may have picked my friends wisely, as my mother used to say, but when it was time to determine who stayed and who didn't stay in my circle of friends, my mother had the final say. Basically, I had no other choice. It was either her way or the highway, as they say.

Looking back now, it seemed that my mother scrutinized every single one of my friends with a fine-toothed comb. From wanting to know about their family background, to wanting to know about any bad habits that could influence me in a negative way. It was that simple. I guess in retrospect it was her way of protecting me from the bad elements on the streets, and frankly, who could blame her. We literally lived in one of the worst neighborhoods in the South Bronx. It was better to think in terms of survival first and friendship later. Because of that, my choices were limited to the point that I could literally count the amount of neighborhood friends I had on one hand. There were the two brothers, Edwin and Mickey, Johnny, and last but not least, Andre.

Edwin, my best friend at the time, was a street-smart kid who was very inventive and always had an idea or a solution for anything we encountered. Being eleven, one of the oldest in the group, he was also very charismatic and assumed the leadership role on most occasions when it came to finding activities for playtime. Although he and his family were very poor, and they were always strapped for money, somehow it didn't affect his attitude or his happy demeanor. He and his brother, Mickey, were fun to be around, and they always made us laugh. As far as school was concerned, he was a good student when he attended. But he was out a lot, which negatively affected both his schoolwork and his grades.

Since Edwin lived in my building at 603 East 140th Street, on the first floor, we were always in each other's homes, and at times his mother, Maria, would watch over us, keeping an eye on me to make sure I was all right after school.

Mickey, on the other hand, was the complete opposite of his brother, Edwin. At age ten, he was on the quiet side, but very inquisitive about everything. He looked up to his brother, as if he were a hero, and was always with him wherever he went. Unlike his brother, however, who was very streetwise, Mickey was the complete opposite, treading more on the side of naive than anything else. He was also the type of person who had to be pushed into coming up with creative ideas to keep us busy. When it came to going to school, he was also absent a lot, just like his brother, and although he was a very bright kid, his grades were often not a reflection of how smart he really was.

Then we had Johnny, who lived in the apartment below ours. By the age of ten, he was considered by many to be one of the smartest kids in the school. He was known mostly for being a straight-A student, and for having really strict parents who only allowed him to leave his home on occasion to play with his friends. However, during the times when he was allowed to go outside to play with us, it was always under the watchful eye of his mother. She, just like my mother, would often monitor his every move through their third-floor apartment window that overlooked the front of the building. Johnny was considered to be on the quiet side. However, when he was around us, it was quite the opposite. He knew how to have fun, and we always managed to laugh a lot at some of the stupidest things we did while playing with our toys and games.

And last, but certainly not least, you had Andre. At age eleven, he was also one of the oldest in the group. He lived somewhere in the adjacent neighborhood, on 139th Street. I met Andre through Edwin and Mickey one day, and we quickly became good friends. He was the radical one in the group and had a bit of an attitude. His nonconformism set him apart from the rest of us; he got bad grades in school, had what seemed to be unlimited freedom from home, and was feisty and combative at times with the guys when things weren't going his way. Andre was different all right, but he was also a good friend who wasn't afraid to speak his mind. Although we saw that as a good trait, in the eyes of our parents, he was somewhat of a "wild kid" who always needed to be watched whenever he was around us.

Together, in time, we formed a tight-knit bond as friends because we had so many things in common, and they brought us together as friends. Everything from living in the same neighborhood, attending the same schools, to having a very similar family background, as well as the same lower socioeconomic status. Last, but certainly not least, sharing the same cultural ideas, language, and even ethnic background, being Puerto Rican, created a solid base for friendships that lasted for years to come.

Since we had so much in common, it was never a problem for our parents to approve of our friendship. Coincidentally, after a while, even our very own parents became good friends.

I guess, like most kids in our age group, we did pretty much all the regular things that we were expected to do. Playing cops and robbers, battling with our G.I. Joes, playing hide-and-go-seek and board games, and finally, playing with toys in general. With a little imagination and a competitive drive, we also spent a lot of our time building things to keep ourselves busy and avoid boredom.

One of our favorite things to do was to build our very own makeshift wooden go-carts, without a motor of course. It was every kid's dream in those days to build the fastest and most unique go-cart on the block. Our biggest problem at the time, it turns out, was just trying to find the right equipment with which to build it. We scrounged around backyards, alleyways, garbage cans, local *bodegas*, grocery stores, and yes, even our own closets, just to put this contraption together. To build it, we used wooden milk crates with one side cut out to serve as the driver's seat. We then got a couple of two-by-four pieces of wood for the framework, a saw, some nails, a hammer, and finally, to put our dream cars in motion, a pair of old grocery-shopping-cart wheels that had been tossed in the garbage when they became a bit wobbly and unusable.

When our wooden go-cart was completed, we loved showing off and boasting about our finished product to our competitors on the block. Teasing and bragging rights were all part of the game, especially when it was time to finally launch your speed machine down the sidewalk on a nice summer day; it became the excitement of the day. The speed of your go-cart depended upon how hard a push you got from your teammates. The main goal, of course, was making it to the finish line first.

You might ask, so how did we make it stop once the go-cart was going at full speed? Let's just say that it all depended upon how much rubber tread you had on your old, beat-up Converse sneakers. In the end, the reward for participating in the neighborhood go-cart race was an old-fashioned pat on the back and the fun and excitement of being recognized by your peers for having the best go-cart in the block!

Building go-carts wasn't the only thing in which we took pride and enjoyment. We also spent many hours in our homes, building and painting hard-plastic model airplanes, cars, boats, and monsters based on popular horror movies, like *The Creature from the Black Lagoon*, *Frankenstein*, *Dracula*, and *The Mummy*, just to name a few. These things, for the most part, kept us busy throughout the day and provided a sense of security for our parents, who knew where we were at all times.

However, somehow, somewhere along the way, we began drifting away from some of those innocent things that kept us busy for hours and instead, started searching for new, riskier ideas, adventures, and activities that captured our attention. As stupid as this may sound, my guess is that, at the time, we were probably trying to shed some of our good-boy image. The new things we tried brought sudden changes in our characters, and we began to act in ways contrary to how we were raised by our parents. Sometime near the end of 1966, that's when most of these crazy changes started taking place and having adverse effects on our lives. Some of the negative outside influences of living in a tough neighborhood like ours slowly began to creep into our previously somewhat-innocent lives.

It was during this time period when we became disloyal to our once-good family values and upbringing by betraying our families' trust in all of us. For some of us, it was a change that we welcomed with open arms. For others, like me, traveling down that road of uncertainty and wrongdoing required a lot of second-guessing on my part. I quickly thought, *Am I doing the right thing?* Nevertheless, when the time came for me to take part in acts of petty larceny and reckless behavior, I decided to go along with the program.

While some in the group were experimenting with various things, such as drugs, glue sniffing, cigarette smoking, and even breaking and entering, I made a conscious effort not to venture down that road. In part, I think I was afraid of getting caught and having to face my parents. Yet at other times, I just listened to that gut feeling deep down in my stomach that told me something was just not right. Although, as you will soon learn, it didn't always work out that way. Nevertheless, whatever were the facts and circumstances that caused me to change my mind at the last minute, I have to admit, in the long run, it saved my ass quite a few times down the line and prevented me from getting involved in some crazy stuff that could have been disastrous during that early part of my life.

One day in early spring of 1967, Mickey and I decided to go with my sister Mercedes to the local five-and-dime to buy a few things that she needed. I remember it was during the Easter season, so once we were at the store, I asked my sister if Mickey and I could go check out some Easter eggs they had on a display table near the entrance to the store.

"Okay, but just be careful," she said in a stern, forceful voice!

It didn't take long before we were off and running to check out the large display of beautiful, colorful Easter eggs. Once there, we couldn't believe our eyes. Right in front of us stood this massive display table containing hundreds upon hundreds of the most colorful, eye-catching collection of prize-filled Easter eggs that we had ever seen in our lives. After rummaging through this very large selection of Easter eggs for what seemed like hours, we finally narrowed it down to ten or so of the best Easter eggs of the bunch. After we made the final cut, there was only one big problem on our hands. How were we going to buy them if we had no money?

That's when we decided to do the unthinkable—steal them! We knew right away, for it to work, we had to devise a slick plan in order to avoid getting caught. This was our first time going down that road; we were both extremely nervous, and it clearly showed by the way our hands were shaking every time we picked up an egg to carry out our desperate scheme. Our elaborate plan worked like this: while leaning over the table to grab an egg with one hand, the other hand kept busy stuffing eggs into our oversized pants pockets.

After filling one pocket with eggs and not getting caught, we thought, *Boy, this is pretty easy.* Emboldened and undeterred, we continued to fill our other pockets. As beginner's luck would have it, I think we got a little bit too greedy and completely forget that maybe, just maybe, we were being watched. When that came to mind, I decided to take a quick peek over my shoulder just to see if anyone was watching us. And sure enough, someone was; he was looking right at us. When I told Mickey that an undercover store detective was on to us, we both froze. *What now?* we both wondered. The store detective was taking dead aim at us as he slowly made his way towards the egg display; we knew right away we were in big trouble.

Our first thought was to look for the nearest exit and just run for it. Luckily, the two nearest exits were about fifty feet or so away from where we were standing at the time. Within a flash, I was blessed with a sprinter's ability to haul ass, and I made a mad dash towards the right-front exit. I was able to make it out the door and avoid getting busted. Mickey, on the other hand, wasn't as lucky. He chose to run towards the left-side exit and was immediately apprehended by the store detective… just as he had one foot out the door and was a mere couple of inches away from freedom.

I had made it outside without getting caught and was in the storefront of the business located next to the five-and-dime, peeking through a corner while struggling to catch my breath after running. That's when I noticed Mickey putting up a fierce struggle to break loose, while at the same time crying and pleading with the store detective, "Let me go; please let me go!!!" It wasn't long before he was let go by security and sent on his way, but not before all the Easter eggs were recovered from his pants pockets.

Unfortunately for us, that incident—which, by the way, my sister miraculously never found out about—didn't suppress our hunger to do it again. Although this was Mickey's and my very first experimentation with stealing something, others like Edwin and Andre, on the other hand, had long passed that stage and had become old pros at it.

For whatever reason, this deviant behavior never caught the interest of our friend Johnny, who, over time, slowly began to distance himself from the group after finding out all the crazy stuff we were doing; he knew it would eventually lead to big trouble. Instead, he decided to focus on schooling, not stealing. Eventually, the rise in crime in the neighborhood, along with all the other negative influences, became too much of a burden for Johnny and his family to bear; they moved to another part of the Bronx.

After Mickey and I stole those Easter eggs, it became a rite of passage into a different world, a questionable world of wrongdoing. At the time, we had no idea where it was going to lead us. However, in the eyes of Edwin and Andre, the two oldest in the group, we had done something to which they could both relate. And in a weird kind of way, we had broken the mold of that good-boy image we had been trying to change over the years. It didn't take long before Edwin and Andre took us under their wings to teach us, as they said, some of the tricks of the trade.

In the months to come, I started to steal little odds and ends just to go along with the program. Although I felt extremely guilty afterwards and knew that what I was doing was wrong, I continued to do it until the day Edwin got busted. That's when things really changed for me.

CHAPTER 14

THIEF-IN-TRAINING

As time went by, Edwin and Andre became pretty proficient at stealing from Alexander's, one of the biggest department stores in the South Bronx. It was there that they were able to perfect their craft and score on a regular basis. The idea to steal from Alexander's happened by accident one day when Edwin discovered a big hole in the lining of his full-length winter coat. He put his right hand in his pocket, and it went through the hole and resurfaced outside his coat. In other words, he could literally lean over any display table, put his hand through the hole in his pocket, grab an item, pull his hand back into the coat pocket, making the item disappear. Soon, the idea of "holy pockets" had a totally different meaning.

It must have been a pretty clever idea because as soon as Edwin and Andre put it to the test, it worked every single time. Before long, Edwin and Andre were bringing in more pairs of leather gloves and other items than they could count. The new lean-and-grab method became their ideal way of stealing things. Soon, the hole in the coat pocket became a new standard for all of us. For Edwin and Andre, it also became an easy way to make some pocket change from the street sale of their leather gloves.

One day during the early weeks of the winter of 1967, Edwin approached me and asked if I would be willing to skip school the next day so that we could go "get some gloves from Alexander's." I hesitated for a minute, but agreed to go along with the plan. That night, however, a mixed bag of emotions ran through my head. On the one hand, by taking part in this scheme, I would be able to prove to Edwin and Andre not only that I was "one of the boys," but more importantly, that I "belonged" because I was willing to take the risk, no matter the cost, and was willing to take it to the next level. On the other hand, I worried about the consequences at home if I got caught. However, all that paled in comparison to what would happen if I made a stupid rookie mistake, got busted, and exposed the group. Their unblemished record of successfully beating the system would undoubtedly come to a halt, *all because of me*, I kept telling myself.

The next day, I was all pumped up and raring to go on this new adventure. I had done this before—the egg incident with Mickey—so in a sense, I wasn't completely green, but at the same time, this was a completely different ball game. I was moving into the big league of the petty-theft world, where the odds of getting caught were much higher and the penalties much more severe.

Although I was extremely nervous and excited at the same time, I tried to go about my business as usual, so as not to tip off my parents that I was up to no good. In keeping with my routine, I had my usual morning breakfast, gathered my books, and then got dressed. Everything was basically a carbon copy of the day before, with only one exception. When it was time to leave my home, I had to make sure that I was wearing the right coat. In my excitement to go on this risky journey, I had to make sure that I picked up the old, raggedy-looking coat with the hole in the right pocket, and not the other somewhat-better, everyday school coat. I waited until my parents were completely distracted in the house, grabbed my old beat-up coat, and said, "Bye… I'm leaving now," and ran out of the apartment without my parents even taking notice.

I met up with Edwin downstairs at his first-floor apartment, where we managed to hide our books in his bedroom closet and shortly thereafter, to sneak out of his home without his parents ever noticing that we had left our books behind. Soon, we were on our way to our destination, which was a good forty-minute walk from our block. I expressed my fears to Edwin about getting caught and what would happen to us if we got arrested. Edwin, not one to show any fear, quickly calmed my doubts by basically saying, "Just watch me, and do what I do, and you'll be all right!"

As we neared the store, I could literally feel the palms of my hands sweating out of control from the anxiety of it all. My heart was pounding so hard that I could've sworn it was visible on the outside of my coat. I was such a nervous wreck that the closer and closer we got to the store, the more I just wanted to turn back and go home. Then there was that other part of me that said, *You're here now, so you might as well just do it and get it over with!* In the end, it was that now-or-never mentality that really turned out to be the deciding factor in my going with the plan.

While my mind was going through all these changes, Edwin's attitude and demeanor did not change. He was steadfast on what he was going to do from the very beginning, so it seemed there was no stopping him, even if I suddenly decided to back out at the last minute.

Standing right outside the store and watching the heavy traffic of customers coming and going, we concluded that it was the perfect day to carry out our masterful plan. The more people who saturated the store in one tight area, the more cover we had and the better our chances of taking the gloves without getting caught. We took a moment to give each other a quick good-luck slap of the hands, a low five in those days. Without giving it any more thought, we said, "Let's go for it," and entered the store.

Edwin walked in first; I trailed closely behind like a three-dimensional shadow. We moved swiftly in a serpentine motion through the crowded store, as if we were following a road map to a temple full of riches that only we knew where to find. Edwin, having been down this road before on numerous occasions, knew exactly where to go to find this treasure in disguise. Within a matter of seconds, we were there. All the planning and talking boiled down to this one moment. The moment of truth. The moment to either sink or swim. To think that it was all up to me at this point was a really scary thought at my age, but I knew I had made a commitment to follow through on our joint plan, and I wasn't about to back out of it now, especially not at this stage of the game.

Like a kid in a candy store, I marveled at the sight before me: hundreds upon hundreds of beautiful, multicolored black, gray, brown, and rabbit-fur-lined leather gloves all stacked up on a display table as if it were a mountain of gold just waiting to be discovered.

Looking back, if there was any viable justification in my mind, it was that we were just a couple of poor kids from the South Bronx, with no money, a poor sense of direction, and trying desperately to seek attention from all those around us in the wrong way.

With all the trepidation leading up to this moment finally out of the way, we were ready to make our move. We cased the area for any suspicious characters who fit the prototype of an undercover security guard: standing in a general area for long periods of time, faking interest in buying an item, but whose hawklike eyes are more fixated on what's around him than on the item itself. Once we determined the coast was clear, we cautiously approached the table, making sure that we stayed close to each other in order for our plan to work. With everything in place, we were ready to implement our lean-and-grab strategy.

After grabbing and sweeping into my coat pocket the first pair of gloves, a big chill came over my body. It was as though I could feel the presence of the authorities standing right over my shoulder, grabbing me by my arm, and saying, "Okay now, son, come with us; you're in big trouble now!" However, that terrifying moment of stress soon disappeared when, to my surprise, nothing happened. It was then that I let out the biggest sigh of relief.

In the meantime, while I was all stressed out about the whole situation, Edwin, on the other hand, was as cool and collected as you could be, considering the circumstances. He even had a big grin on his face, as though he'd just enjoyed a big meal and was intent on leaving without paying his tab.

After a few grueling minutes at the table and each of us grabbing two pairs of leather gloves, Edwin signaled with his head towards the exit. It was time to get out of there. Following almost the same path that we took when we first entered the store, we managed to squirm our way through the crowded store as fast as we could and headed out the doors undetected.

Once outside, a temporary feeling of both relief and guilt soon took over my body. I was extremely relieved that it was finally over and that we were able to accomplish what we set out to do without getting caught. But on the other hand, I was trying to deal with the guilt of taking something that I knew deep down inside did not belong to me. I was a bit uneasy about the whole situation. It was as if I had just taken from the fire a burning piece of hot coal and stuffed it into my coat, knowing darn well that it didn't belong there in the first place and that it was going to burn me eventually. As insignificant as this incident might appear, it was surely an early sign that I might be heading in the wrong direction.

That day, after all was said and done, Edwin and I returned home and celebrated our victory with the rest of the group. We laughed at how nervous I was about the whole thing and after all that worrying I did, how easily and swiftly our lean-and-grab method really worked. As a matter of fact, it worked so well that when I was asked if I would do it again, I didn't hesitate to say, "Let's go!" It turns out that I kept true to my word once again, and about a month later, I went back with Edwin for another round at the same store.

As to what I told my parents about the sudden presence of a brand-new pair of leather gloves in the home, "I found them on the way to school" was my response. As for the other pairs of gloves that I took, I managed to get rid of them by giving them away at school to some of my friends.

Ironically, as luck would have it, a few weeks after my last trip to Alexander's, Edwin bravely decided to take a chance on his own when none of us wanted to go; he was busted by security just as he was about to leave the store. That really took us all by surprise for some reason. I guess it was a rude awakening of sorts; it hit us like a ton of bricks and made us all realize that we were not invincible, that the odds of dipping into the same pot one too many times were against us. It was time for us to make changes in our system... or it would soon be over.

Within the next couple of months, many changes did take place, but not in the way we had planned. Edwin getting busted spun off a downward domino effect that affected all of us in different ways. While Mickey and I had second thoughts about doing anything like that again, Andre saw it as the perfect opportunity to move on to bigger and greater things that he thought would be less risky, but more rewarding in the long run. It seems Andre, who was the only one in the group who didn't live in the same block, had met some new friends in his neighborhood who were breaking into freight trains at a local freight yard nearby. They asked him one day if he wanted to join them, and he said yes. After he committed himself to the new group of friends, Andre was never the same from that point on; we saw less and less of him as the days and the weeks went by.

Within a matter of months, not only was Andre breaking into freight trains and stealing all sorts of valuable goods, but also he had picked up other dangerous habits. He was sniffing glue from time to time, which was the ghetto's version of a cheap high. Cheap because glue was the least expensive "legal high" you could buy at any five-and-dime in the area. Instead of using the glue to build model airplanes or cars, as we used to do, you poured the glue into a brown paper bag, sealed it tightly around your mouth and nose, and inhaled it into your lungs. It was that simple. Once inhaled, the drowsy effects of the drug were quick and very dangerous, sometimes rendering the individual out for the count within minutes. Inhale too much of it, and it could kill you. Unfortunately, those were the scary facts that presented themselves on every street corner in our neighborhood. Neither Edwin, Mickey, nor I wanted any part of sniffing glue when Andre first approached us about trying it.

Smoking cigarettes, on the other hand, was something that we all experimented with at one time or another. Mickey and I tried it once and didn't do it again; Andre and Edwin became occasional smokers. Since a pack of cigarettes was so expensive, and thus not affordable for the average kid on the street, neighborhood *bodegas*, grocery stores, were willing to break open a pack of cigarettes and sell them individually for a nickel a piece. I knew this firsthand from all the trips I made to the store on my sister Esther's behalf to support her smoking habit.

While there were certain things that Andre couldn't convince us to do, other things, such as breaking into freight trains, proved to be too tempting for someone like Edwin, but not for Mickey and me, who saw it as too risky a gamble. Although it worked well for them for a while, at the beginning of the summer of 1968, the party basically came to a screeching halt when, to everyone's surprise, Edwin and Micky's mother decided that she had had enough of the decaying neighborhood and was ready to move her family to a more peaceful and better, more stable environment before things got any worse. According to what she voiced openly to friends and family members, a number of incidents over a period of time culminated in her having to make one of the toughest decisions of her life. She cited incidents such as Edwin's and Mickey's lack of interest and bad grades in school, the decline in the neighborhood that they once loved, Edwin's increased involvement with Andre, whom she did not particularly care for, and last but not least, Edwin's problems with the law, which most certainly proved to be the most overwhelming problem of all and the hardest to handle.

When the day finally came and they had loaded their last belongings on the truck, it hit me really hard. To know that my best buddies in the world were moving out of the neighborhood was an extremely tough situation to handle, especially since they were the only true friends I had left since I was banned from even associating with Andre. The only other friends I had at the time were a few I had met at my new school in the sixth grade at Burger Junior High School 138, but they didn't even live in the same neighborhood, so they could not hang out with me after school.

As the truck finally pulled away, and I waved my last goodbyes, I stood there motionless for a minute, trying to take it all in. It was a moment that I had dreaded because I knew that from that day forward, things would never be the same. I was suddenly overcome with a feeling of sadness and emptiness that quickly took over and reminded me that there were going to be a lot more of those tough changes coming my way. No longer would I be looking forward to the end of a school day to go hang out with my friends or to be able to do some of the stupid things we did as kids that got us in trouble. The weekends in particular were going to be especially hard for me since I no longer was allowed to go outside and hang out, not even in front of the building, because of how dangerous and bad the neighborhood had gotten, according to my mother.

Now that my best friends were gone, I couldn't even look forward to skipping a day from school to steal from Alexander's, as I used to do with Edwin. I guess, for my well-being and mental stability, it probably worked out well for me and my family that it happened the way it did, or so I thought. Little did I know then that my little escapades to Alexander's to steal weren't going to end once Edwin and Mickey moved out of the block. For a short time after they moved out, I started taking trips to Alexander's with, of all people, my older sister Esther, serving as her lookout while she helped herself to some of the goods from the store!

That only lasted for a little while, however. Esther's inexperience finally caught up with her one day when she became a little greedy and stuffed one too many bras and panties down her pants. I remember clearly how proud and happy she was as we made our way towards the exit doors; she thought we had beaten the system. It was a joyous moment that lasted less than the amount of time it took her to steal the items. She, like Edwin, found herself in handcuffs and was led off to the security office, with me in tow. My sister, who was a young, tough, feisty, streetwise twenty-year-old at the time, had the most amazing vocabulary when it came to using four-letter words. That day, she cursed everyone and their mothers, yelled to be let go, and put up a vicious fight all the way down to the security office. It took more than a handful of security personnel to bring her under control before the cops were called in to arrest her for theft.

Although I didn't get into any kind of trouble with the law that day, the incident scared the hell out of me so much that I never stole from there again. From that day forward, the only time I entered Alexander's was to make a legal purchase or just to browse. I managed to keep both my hands in my pockets and to stay out of trouble!

CHAPTER 15

LIFE WITHOUT MY BUDDIES

As the months and the weeks went by, I became very lonely and bored with my life. Although my sister Mercedes's kids, Junior and Cindy, lived with us at the time, they were younger than I was by five and seven years, respectively; thus, we did not share the same interests when it came to playing. My whole world revolved around keeping busy with the toys I had at home and watching black-and-white television, the five or six channels available to us. Not fun!

Although color television sets were available for purchase during that time period, unfortunately my family was so poor we could not afford to buy one. Instead, we did as every other poor family living in our neighborhood did: bought a colorful plastic sheet for our TV screen. The tricolor, transparent plastic sheet made the image of our black-and-white TV appear as though it were in color. Well, not really. But with a good imagination, anything is possible. Anyway, the plastic sheet was orange on top for the faces on the screen, blue in the middle for the bodies, and green at the bottom for the feet. You taped it on your TV screen to get a color-like experience on your black-and-white TV. It's a laughable situation now when you look back, but one that served its purpose and gave everyone in the family hope that one day we'd have the real thing.

When you have no friends and live in the ghetto, the only other thing to do is spend your day drawing cartoon characters on a piece of paper, color in your favorite coloring book, or do every kid's least favorite thing…homework. All things considered, I guess what I really enjoyed doing the most during those dark and lonely days was, believe it or not, looking out of my fourth-floor bedroom window, just observing all the sights and activities taking place on the action-filled streets below. Watching the way people lived, interacted with each other, and resolved conflicts on the streets was enough to keep me busy all day. It was news as it happened, right before my very own eyes. I saw activities such as violent gang fights, drug deals and busts, stolen cars being stripped, and the occasional stabbing or shooting incident. Our block filled with colorful flashing red lights and the blaring sirens from responding police cars and ambulances became a regular occurrence.

It was lawlessness at the best of times, yet those incidences doubled as both a form of live entertainment for the residents and something to talk about. After a while, you got to know what happened to whom on a first-name or nickname basis. Whether it was Seven Fingers, Negro (black), Flaco Pescuezo (long neck), or Skinny—coincidentally, all members of my brother's gang, the Spanish Devils—who got busted or got into some type of confrontation or incident, or it was Shorty, Leon (lion), Gypsy, or Flaco—my brother, of course, who was otherwise known as the Other Flaco—who got in trouble the next week, the news spread quickly and became the talk of the block. These were just some of the many characters from the block—or the badasses, as some called them—who received notoriety not for all the good that they contributed to the neighborhood or society in general, but for always defying the laws of the land and being different. These were our neighborhood heroes or as some might see them, our role models of the time; they defended our block and ruled with authority in the most intimidating and most fearful way possible, which was through violence.

A young kid like me, growing up under extreme conditions, formed impressions at a very young age and grew up, quicker than one was expected to in those days, in a world of uncertainty, always questioning what the future had in store for him and his family. In fact, there were times when I would often ask myself if I would I grow up to be like Negro, the leader of the gang, or like the hero cops who worked our neighborhoods so bravely while attempting to control the violence and drugs so that my family and I could have a better life and future.

Those were some of the challenges that I faced from a very young age, and would continue to struggle with during some of the most critical moments in my life. While not everything I saw on a daily basis was newsworthy or shocking, it provided me with an insight into which roads to take and which to avoid as I was growing up.

The way I saw it, although my neighborhood was filled with so much potential and with so many amazing people, it was also a place with a lot of broken dreams, sadness, helplessness, poverty, and dismay, which painted a bleak picture for those with very little hope and faith for a better life and future outside our troubled neighborhood. Witnessing so much of this firsthand taught me how to survive the rigors of a tough life in order to make a better life for myself down the road. In the end, although I saw so many lives literally turned upside down, right from that fourth-floor apartment window in my bedroom, I had no idea that someday those same problems and obstacles would ultimately become challenges that I would have to confront and overcome in order to stay alive and succeed in the ghetto.

CHAPTER 16

MY LITTLE SANCTUARY, 1967

In the silence of my bedroom, I used to love to just lie in my bed without any distractions from the TV, radio, or people around me. I was alone with thoughts… and that was it!

Sometimes, I would prop my head on the slightly deflated, feathered pillow on my bed and just stare at the decrepit, cracked ceilings or the white, peeling paint that once belonged to a solid-cement structure that was clearly falling apart. The condition of the cracked and peeling white ceiling paint went hand in hand with the visibly run-down walls. The entire room looked old and in distress due to many years of neglect by an uncaring landlord and the building's old age. Because of the building's decaying condition, it soon became a haven for mice and roaches to run amok. Despite my parents' greatest efforts to get rid of the annoying little critters with pesticides, mousetraps, and even a cat to fight the rodent problem, it seemed that it was simply a never-ending battle. These tough conditions, along with all the distractions that surrounded my life, only added to my overall negative view of the world.

Drifting in and out of a fantasy life became my favorite way of coping with some of the stresses in life. My bedroom, therefore, became my own little sanctuary that protected me from everything that was going on around me. I saw it as the ideal place to get a reprieve from all the turmoil. Life was tough on the streets, but at home it wasn't any easier. My home was a little war zone at times. Heated domestic battles between my parents became a regular part of my life. I was trapped in a war that I didn't declare, much less want to be a part of that early in life. Unfortunately, I had no choice but to get caught up in the middle of every major dispute my parents had.

But this was my biological father, so I kind of felt I, not my half siblings, should be the one to intervene and try to bring peace between my parents every time they raged a war against each other. It was a duty that I didn't take pride in, and one that I felt left me with no other choice but to deal with it. As detrimental as it was to my health and well-being to see them both entrenched in highly emotional and at times very physical altercations, it truly tore at my heart and soul. Thinking about it now, I should've just let them fight their own battles. Eventually, my mother would've had enough courage to finally put an end to the volatile relationship for good by walking away from it before somebody got hurt, but that never happened. My mother once said to me, "Your father only gets like that when he's drinking; he's really a good man when he's sober." Which was so far from the truth.

Looking back at the whole picture, I guess what she was really telling me was, that as long as he was sober and a "good man" the next day, after drinking and wreaking havoc the night before, she was willing to forgive and forget in hopes that it wouldn't happen again. But as long as she was willing to forgive and forget, my father saw it as an open invitation to break all the rules and continue with his drinking. The fact that he was a working alcoholic whose drinking didn't affect his job only supported his unsavory drinking addiction. In the end, it soon became a vicious cycle that ruled and tormented our whole family.

It took me a while to finally realize that as long as my father had an undaunted desire to keep on drinking, and money in his pocket to spend on booze, the battles were going to continue for a long time to come. And that, to me, was such a scary thought. As the months and the years went by ever so slowly, it became eminently clear that the more he drank, the more reckless and destructive his behavior became. One incident in particular, which to this day still sends a chill up my spine when I think of it, happened when I was about twelve years old.

It was about 4:00 a.m. on a Saturday morning. My mother and I had been waiting patiently for my father to arrive home from a night out drinking with his buddies. As was customary in my household, and a common practice with a lot of the Hispanic families I knew at the time, when the head of the household was out of the house, no matter what time he arrived at home, he was always expected to have a hot plate of food waiting for him at the dinner table. At a time when most mothers and their children were sleeping, I stayed awake with my mother and waited for my father to get home. The reason for that was simple. I had to stay up just in case there was a problem or fight when my father got home; I might have to intervene. It seemed I had a way of calming my father down whenever he went into his rages; I cried and talked to him until he fell asleep. Sometimes he was so incapacitated that he fell asleep at the dinner table, on the sofa, or yes, even on the toilet seat in our bathroom.

Eventually as time went by, we came up with a system that worked for all of us. Wherever he fell asleep, we left him and let him sleep it off until he sobered up enough to crawl into bed, with our assistance of course. Sometimes, we just let him labor through the pain or embarrassment of waking up half sober to discover he'd fallen asleep on the toilet seat and still in his work clothes.

After years of dealing with my father's drinking problems, my mother and I would perch ourselves on the ledge of the window, waiting to see the extent of his inebriation as he walked towards our building. There were two main reasons for this mad ritual. First, we wanted to make sure that he got home safely and in one piece after a night of drinking; second, we would monitor, believe it or not, the degree to which he wobbled when he walked. If he was staggering, we knew right then and there that it was going to be a very long night for all of us. If his walk was pretty controlled and deliberate, then we knew he wasn't very drunk, and he would be manageable, as compared to other times when he was a handful.

This one particular night, when he got home reeking of booze, he sat down, as usual, at the dinner table. After a little bit of small talk with my mother and me in his slurred, sometimes-hard-to-understand, alcohol-induced speech, he grabbed his fork and took one quick bite of his awaiting meal, which many times consisted of white rice, red beans, and fried pork chops, before losing it. He immediately went into a ranting rage because he claimed the food was not hot enough to eat. The next thing we knew, my father jumped out of his chair and in one sweeping arm motion, cleared the table, everything crashing into the kitchen wall. I remember the sight of all that food, which my mother so tirelessly took the time to cook and serve my father in the wee hours of the morning, sliding down the kitchen wall ever so slowly, just like the molten lava after a volcano eruption. Only this volcano eruption came from my father's alcohol-induced temper, which was always erratic and at times unpredictable.

I was heartbroken to say the least. When I looked into my mother's eyes, I could see the hurt and the immense fear of my father's raging outburst. Her eyes soon welled with tears. That sudden outburst was soon followed by more erratic behavior: chair tossing, bottles crashing, and a slew of curse words. That was just the beginning. What happened next took us both by complete surprise and scared the hell out of my mother and me.

Unbeknownst to either of us, my father was armed. He had a handgun concealed under the waistband of his pants; it was covered by his button-down shirt. Without warning, he walked to the kitchen window, lifted his shirt, reached into his waistband, pulled out a small black handgun, and slowly lowered it to the right side of his body, shocking the hell out of both of us. At this point, we were so scared that we were frozen stiff and afraid to say anything or make any sudden movement that would startle my father and force the unthinkable: one of us getting shot and killed. Before my mother and I could even react to what we just witnessed, my father stuck the gun out of the open kitchen window and began firing into the rear alleyway below.

I must have counted at least three or four shots before my mother, fearing that my father's anger might turn towards us, bravely jumped on top of my drunken father's back in an attempted to disarm him. When I saw my mother basically put her life on the line, fighting with my father over control of the gun, which could have accidentally gone off and seriously wounded or killed anyone of us in the process, I instinctively jumped in. Together as a team, we fought a fierce battle to disarm my father.

The momentum of the intense struggle forced us to the kitchen floor, where the fighting continued. From that point on, we battled for what seemed like hours, trying desperately to gain control over the gun and avoid a tragedy. Finally, after a few tension-filled moments of fighting and screaming at my drunken father to surrender the gun, somehow we were able to pry it out of his hands and take control of the situation. It was then that my mother, operating on pure guts, adrenaline, and fear, instinctively decided to make a quick dash into one of the bedrooms, where she hid the gun from my father.

After the intense struggle, my father literally had nothing left in him. He was so drunk that he couldn't even get up. Before we knew it, he was doing what he usually did after drinking that much; he crashed on the kitchen floor. The kitchen was in shambles, and it took us forever to clean it up. My father, on the other hand, slept through the whole thing and didn't wake up until later on that morning.

That day, no cops were called to our home by my mother. Believe it or not, even after all we went through, my father wasn't even thrown out of the house by my mother the next day. In fact, when it was all said and done, my father took the easy way out by saying the usual, "I don't remember doing that." As far as the gun was concerned, he claimed to have borrowed it from his best friend, Pablo, who gave it to him so he could protect himself going home. Although he asked for my mother to give him back the gun, my mother refused and told him she had already gotten rid of it. In reality, the gun was still in the house, but it was so well hidden that my father never found it. Later that day, she gave it to my brother, who ended up disposing of it somewhere on the streets.

As far as my mother's status with my father after that horrific incident that could've ended in a tragedy, they resolved the issue by not talking for a good couple of weeks, but then things were mended once again. As he had done on previous occasions, my father apologized profusely for his actions and promised not to let it happen again. That, as we will later see, turned out to be just another big lie coming from someone who had serious a drinking problem.

CHAPTER 17

THE WINDOW ON THE FOURTH FLOOR, 1967

While hiding in the seclusion of my bedroom, I allowed myself the freedom and peace of mind that I needed to elude, at least temporarily, everything that was troubling me. I saw it as my "therapeutic medicine," a way to live a normal life beyond the problems that surrounded me. Having the freedom to think clearly and resolve a lot of the issues in my life made everything in my world a lot easier to handle. I found that for whatever reason, I was drawn back more and more each day to the world I could see from my bedroom window. It became addictive, something I had to do to entertain my mind.

In general, after a while, my bedroom window became the entertainment capital of my world, where anything and everything was possible, if only you took the time to look, watch, and listen. I began to make little mental observations of some of the crazy things that were happening in the neighborhood, things that I didn't quite understand. For example, what would cause so many people, teens and adults alike, to tie the shoelaces of their old, worn-out, beat-up sneakers together, then send them soaring away boomerang style, to end up hanging around the neck of a streetlamp or wooden street pole, or over telephone and electrical wires? Well, believe it or not, this little-known tradition was as popular as a bottle of Coca-Cola back then and made the average posts and wires look more like a decorated Christmas tree with an array of colorful sneakers, instead of ornaments. In a weird kind of way, it served more as a burial ground for old beat-up sneakers than anything else.

Over the years, I actually had the privilege of seeing this rare ritual take place numerous times. It turns out that just a mere fifteen or twenty feet below my window stood one of those same light poles that I just mentioned. Being that I was so close to the action, I got a chance to see it happen at least half a dozen times while we lived in that apartment. Just watching how the lace of those old sneakers wrapped the posts or intertwined the wires was a sight. Moreover, having the opportunity to see firsthand the elated looks on the faces of the people involved in tossing the sneakers was worth a thousand words. In all, I saw it as their own personal way of saying their last goodbyes to a piece of their history, one that they would remember for a lifetime. As I later discovered, that tradition was conceived in the ghetto. It was a way of saying goodbye to your beat-up "old kicks" and welcoming the new ones that will most certainly have their own little story to tell someday.

I actually admired this tradition so much that I couldn't wait to one day take part in it. But sadly, for whatever reason, the opportunity never arose. My sneakers ultimately ended up in a more popular place: my own garbage can.

Another tradition that I learned about from my window was the opening of a fire hydrant full blast on a hot summer day. To celebrate, a couple of people, usually members of my brother's or sister's gang, stood in the strong, splashing current of the hydrant's water and got soaking wet. The first people to get wet grabbed someone else and shoved them into the cold water. After that, it was like a tag-team match; if you were anywhere near to the open hydrant, you were almost guaranteed to be forced into the water by the ever-growing mob of people. This went on forever, it seemed, until the cops or the fire department came around and shut down the fire hydrant. It was like a big joke, for as soon as the authorities left the neighborhood, someone pulled out a wrench and popped open the hydrant. And then it was party time once again. Sometimes it happened so often that the loss of all that water caused low water pressure in the area's apartments for extended periods of time.

In the end, it was a bittersweet trade-off that many in the neighborhood didn't mind. As long as there was peace and harmony in the neighborhood, and no one was getting hurt, to the residents of the neighborhood it was a great trade-off. One less day of violence in our neighborhood in exchange for one day of fun, peace, and tranquility… and everyone is happy and content.

While not all of what I observed through my window had to do with traditions or rituals of the neighborhood; other things worth mentioning were just as interesting or mind-boggling to watch. For example, two particular individuals from the block were interesting to watch because of the type of offbeat entrepreneurial lifestyle they lived as expert car thieves. Their wild and crazy story centered around taking risks, lawlessness, and reinterpreting the notion of good deeds; they stood out like modern-day Robin Hoods of our neighborhood.

Although I really never got to see the pair actually stealing a car, I'd heard enough about them from my brother, who was close friends with the dynamic duo, to know a little bit about them and their risky lives. Seeing all the different cars these guys drove and stripped on an almost-daily basis just confirmed everything that my brother had told me about them. He said they were the best car thieves in the Bronx. At first I had a hard time believing that fact, but as time went by, the legend of these two bad boys from the neighborhood grew; they surely were the best at their trade.

The leader of this two-man car-theft ring was Cheo, as he was best known to many on the block. Cheo, who was born and raised in Puerto Rico, had light skin, blue eyes, and curly, Afro-like, shoulder-length blond hair that made him look more Caucasian than Hispanic. Cheo was always known to sport brightly colored, casual dress shirts, which you could spot a mile away, multicolored, patched denim overall jeans, and platform shoes or Converse sneakers to go along with his fashionable outfits. Another trademark or Cheo characteristic was his almost ever-present cigarette or joint. It dangled off the corner of his mouth when he talked, but somehow never fell out. It was a talent that went well with his sometimes-offbeat humor and wired-up personality. His uncanny and somewhat charismatic personality made him a very popular guy to have around the neighborhood; as a result, he was never short on friends.

Like a rock star whose concert is conducted on a big stage in front of a large audience, Cheo's performance was based on his illegal activities. He had a reputation as a badass car thief. The "best in the business," some called him, and he loved it. It was a reputation that was solely based on how many cars he could steal in one day. At other times, it wasn't how many cars he could take in one day, but the type of car, the price of the car, or the challenging situation that truly characterized the type of person that he was known to be. In the end, it was all about making a big splash; the more cars he stole in one week or a day, the more attention he got and the more it fed his ego and his addiction.

After a while, it seemed he was living just for the adulation and attention he got from the people on the block, which made it an even more personal task and fueled his internal drive to make an impression or a name for himself, as silly as that may sound. Comments such as "How the hell did you pull that one off?" or "That's a really nice car," or "Where did you find that one?" only served to fuel his hunger to continue to do what he did best: earn a living and attention by stealing cars!

Most intriguing for all who knew him was his matter-of-fact, and brazen "I don't care" attitude. He wasn't shy about sharing his stories and adventures with people in the neighborhood. In fact, he actually bragged about them. It seemed there was always that cynical smile that accompanied all his storytelling. "This is how it all went down" was always the start of his stories. He would actually brag about some of the close calls he had, the type of cars he took the most pride in stealing, and some of his most challenging feats in locating special-request orders he got from some of his customers on the streets. In all, he had many stories to tell, and that's what made him such "goof" to be around, according to my brother.

As the saying goes, it takes two to tango, and this duo wasn't any different. Cheo wouldn't have been able to pull half the stunts he did were it not for all the help he got from his old buddy, his best partner in crime, Hector-Juan. As a pair, they worked perfectly together in establishing themselves as the best car thieves around. While each specialized in different things, it was their great chemistry that made them so good at what they did.

While Cheo was the brains in this operation and clearly the expert in stealing cars, Hector-Juan, a young, goofy, likable guy with a very similar background, was the all-important lookout during the car thefts. Besides being the lookout, he was also the one responsible for spotting the locations they would hit next and for driving them there. But more than anything, it was his job to hustle up customers, or buyers, from the neighborhood in order to pull off the thefts for profit, according to my brother.

Since both were in their early- to late- twenties, they appeared to be in pretty decent shape, considering they weren't even athletes. Having a slim body, with long, skinny legs to match, came in pretty handy in their line of work, especially when they had to take off running at a moment's notice. For it was those same long legs and overall street smarts that they had to rely on when they were being chased by the cops or the owner of the car they were attempting to steal.

According to my brother, the pair initially started stealing cars for two reasons: one, joyriding, and, two, just for the thrill of doing something that was both illegal and risky. As the months went by, they soon discovered that stealing cars for the purpose of joyriding was one thing, but once they realized they could make a profit from stealing cars, it gave them a whole new perspective and opened their eyes to the huge profit potential of this illegal and risky activity.

They started by setting up a parts-by-request operation. For example, let's just say the transmission in your 1966 Oldsmobile suddenly went kaput. If you went to the dealership or your local junkyard to buy it, it would probably cost you an arm and a leg. But when you placed your request for that part with Cheo and Hector-Juan, that same purchase would cost you a mere third of the actual price. Soon, what once started out as just a hobby, for two aspiring car thieves on the streets, turned into a very profitable but risky business.

Before long, word about their business started spreading like wildfire, and they were getting customers from not only our neighborhood, but different parts of the Bronx as well. Almost immediately, my brother said, they were bringing in all sorts of cars and stripping them for parts right there on our block. It was a sight that after a while I got accustomed to watching from my bedroom window. To keep from getting caught, they even paid the local junkies on the street to look out for the cops while they stripped the cars. It was a process that could take anywhere from only a matter of minutes to as long as an hour or so. In any case, they were impressively quick at what they were doing and wasted no time whatsoever.

Once the ordered parts were removed from the stolen car, the rest of the car was left for the sharks, as they called them, to do with it as they pleased. At times it was a shark feeding frenzy, every man looking out for himself and taking off the car what he wanted. That continued until the car was considered worthless, or the cops intervened to save whatever was left of the stolen car.

While not all cars ended their life span so sadly or in a state of ruin, others especially the convertibles, stuck around a lot longer. It seemed convertibles were the "it" cars of those days. Chicks were attracted to them like refrigerator magnets, and Cheo and Hector-Juan knew that. It wasn't uncommon for Cheo and Hector-Juan to be seen driving a convertible, especially on weekends when going out to the dance clubs or to a party became their fun activity of the week.

One car in particular, as best I can remember, was their car of choice. It was a blue-and-white 1963 or '64 Chevy Impala Classic convertible that got everybody's attention whenever they made their way slowly up the street. At times, it seemed that they were their own Macy's Day Parade, cruising the block with the salsa music blaring, a couple of cute girls in their ride, and wearing fancy, bright-colored disco clothes. They were the talk of the block.

In the end, they made quite a few bucks, but the law finally caught up with this dynamic duo one day. They were both arrested, but ended up serving very little jail time, if any, for their car thefts. Soon, they moving to a more challenging, yet more lucrative, way of making money on the city streets: selling drugs.

CHAPTER 18

THE BAD BOY IN ME

L ooking back now, I don't know if some of the things I'm about to say happened as a result of my frustration or just out of pure boredom, but they weren't nice, to say the least. It seems that whenever I would lock myself in my bedroom, some stupid, outrageous, mischievous ideas would always come to mind. I soon discovered that isolating myself up in my bedroom didn't always have to be about getting away from all the frustrations in my life; it could be a way to get creative and have tons of fun at the expense others without getting caught.

Out of the blue one day, I picked up this World War II-vintage toy rifle that I had gotten for Christmas a few years back. It was a rifle with which in my playtime I used to fantasize and mimic being in one of the war scenes similar to those I'd seen on TV. I always played the hero of my block, protecting my home from an invasion by enemy troops. As the idea evolved, suddenly my window and bedroom were converted into my own personal war bunker from which I fired shots at the enemy hiding in the buildings directly across the street from me; it became a fierce battle.

One day, during one of my imaginary battles, my rifle accidentally slipped out of my hands and fell to the floor; the wood handle that encased the front barrel of the rifle cracked upon impact, and the barrel of the rifle came loose. The sight of my damaged rifle really broke my heart. I became desperate and didn't know what to do to repair one of my favorite toys. With no glue to seal the crack in the wood frame, I decided to use a bunch of rubber bands, which I kept in a storage box in my bedroom, as a way of holding the rifle's stock and barrel in place. Using one rubber band after another, I wrapped them tightly around the wood frame of the rifle until the crack was mended shut and the barrel of the rifle was secured. And guess what? It worked!

While going through my collection of rubber bands, what looked like a twelve-inch rubber band caught my attention. It was then that this crazy thought came to my mind. Maybe I could use that rubber band to make some type of homemade slingshot. Holding the rifle in one hand and the rubber band in the other, the idea of converting my rifle into a slingshot soon became a reality. Before I knew it, I had taken this twelve-inch rubber band and somehow secured it around the barrel of my toy rifle with a bunch of other rubber bands. After creating that makeshift slingshot, I stretched the rubber band until I was able to hook it to the lip of the rifle's fake loading chamber. In no time, I had what I finally thought to be a powerful working slingshot at my disposal. But there was only one problem; I really had no workable ammunition available to put it to the test.

I decided I would look in every single room in my apartment. I was not looking for anything in particular; I was just searching for any ideas that would work with my slingshot contraption. I walked into my sister Mercedes's bedroom not expecting any miracles, but feeling hopeful. I happened to look down on the floor by her dresser, and there it was, staring right at me. It was a flat, two-inch metal clip that I later discovered was used on women's garter belts to fasten their stockings. It was just the perfect object that I needed to make my makeshift slingshot work.

It turns out, that once I found that garter clip, it was like striking gold! Since my sister worked for a garment factory in Manhattan, she would on occasion steal garter belts by the dozen and sell them to her friends or members of our family. And because she sold garter belts as a little side job, she always had numerous garter-belt parts, such as that metal clip I used for my slingshot, and other accessories in boxes that she stored in her dresser drawer.

Armed with my ammunition and a desire to make the slingshot work, I took my position in between the curtains of my bedroom window, loaded my slingshot, and randomly fired my first shot towards the adjacent six-story building across from me. It took off like a rocket, rotating and spinning in the air with such velocity that it made a whizzing sound similar to that of a spinning top as it left the tip of my slingshot rifle. The pinging noise of the projectile making contact with the brick building could be heard from my window. I knew right away this wasn't your typical toy slingshot you'd find in any store.

That day, I shot a few more times in the air just to see if I could tell how far it would travel and to measure by sight the distance, but it was impossible. Let's just say it traveled way beyond the six-story roof of the building and then some before it finally came crashing down on the street below or on the rooftop above that building. In time, I became really good at using my makeshift slingshot and started experimenting with real targets to perfect my aim. Before long, I found myself shooting at and breaking windows, hitting passing cars, and yes, at times even people just walking along on the street below me.

One of my most memorable moments happened one day that summer when during one of my shooting sprees, I ended up striking a kid about my age on one of his right-hand fingers as he stood on the front stoop of his building and talked with his stepfather, who sold *piraguas*, snow cones, during the summer. I immediately saw him grimacing in pain as soon as the metal clip hit his finger. It was by far the weirdest feeling ever. For even though I had fired my slingshot at numerous people in the past, this was the very first time I had actually witnessed it making contact firsthand. I felt really bad about the whole incident and vowed from that day forward that I was never going to shoot at anyone ever again. Ironically, as luck would have it, the kid, whose name was Orlando, would months later turn out to be one of my best lifetime friends from the neighborhood.

Although I learned a lot that day, and the guilt really bothered me for a while, my shenanigans and bouts of misbehaving unfortunately didn't end there. Soon after, I was up to my old tricks again and started coming up with new, innovative ideas to have fun in my neighborhood from my window.

One day as I was tossing paper airplanes out of my window, again out of pure and reckless boredom, I came up with this other crazy idea to put pinhead needles on the tips of my paper airplanes in order to sting the pedestrians below. This awful idea worked to perfection as it turns out. I can't tell you how many people I stung just to get a few laughs and to see their angry reactions. However, luckily, no one was seriously hurt, at least not to my knowledge. Eventually, I decided to put an end to my airplane-assault madness, before someone got seriously hurt, and grounded all of them.

It was only a little while before I got bored again and moved on to my next pastime: green-pea shooting. This one was one of my favorite ideas because, unlike the others which required a lot of work to put together, this one only required an oversized straw with a big opening and a bag of hard, uncooked green peas. Green peas are something that Latino families always have at their disposal for cooking *arroz con gandules*, rice and green peas, one of our favorite Puerto Rican dishes.

This game was less dangerous, or so I thought. And unlike my other projects that exposed more of my body through the window, this one only required a slight opening in between the window curtains in order to shoot out the window. So I was less likely to get busted. Also, with this particular idea, all that was needed to operate it was a strong set of lungs to blow the peas out of the straw and good aim. The only hazard with this particular stunt, as it turns out, was that you had to make sure not to inhale the green peas down your throat as you prepared yourself to fire them through the straw. Again, just like my previous pranks, this one got a lot of people pissed off, and the risk of injury to others, although less to a certain extent, was always there.

Wanting to find a less severe way of entertaining myself, I decided to move on to water balloons. Though harmless, water balloons were messy and a lot of fun. Just as with my other forms of entertainment, my main objective was to have a good time and hopefully have a great laugh or two.

One particular incident that really stands out in the back of my mind happened during one of those hot summer days in July. It was a daring act that presented itself merely because I was in the right place at the right time. Unfortunately, for the unsuspecting victim, the complete opposite was true. That afternoon, I gathered a bunch of water balloons in a box, just as I'd done on previous occasions, and lined them up by my window. This was all in preparation for picking my first victim to shower with some refreshing cold water.

When my victim appeared, he was a Hispanic gentleman wearing these dark sunglasses that perfectly matched his cool and inspiring trendy style in clothes. His flashy and distinctive demeanor easily complemented his chariot on wheels, which can best be described as a relatively new and shiny red Chevy convertible. It appeared that this was definitely his pride and joy, and he was here just to show off his most precious investment. The salsa music in his car was blaring so load that it could be heard as soon as he turned into the block. He was cruising and kicking back with his right arm stretched all the way from the top of the driver's seat to the front passenger's seat. He drove really slowly and deliberately as he maneuvered his car with his left hand, and he appeared to be enjoying the sight of all the young ladies standing in front of their respective stoops. It was a perfect day. Good weather. Nice music. Good sights. A beautiful, relaxing summer day. What could possibly go wrong? Unfortunately for him, his gorgeous, sunny day was about to change very quickly.

Wanting to make a big splash, I decided to select the mother of all water balloons to toss out of my window. It was a large, bright-red balloon that coincidentally matched his car perfectly. While the car inched ever so slowly in front of my building, it gave me plenty of time to set myself up for an accurate toss. Once the car was within the right target range, I grabbed the water balloon with both hands, took one deep breath, and using all my might, just let it fly out the window in one motion.

As the balloon made its way, everything around it appeared to be but a blur, with the exception of this red car. I guess I couldn't have timed it any better because, the next thing I knew, this oversized water balloon exploded on the driver's head, showering both the operator and his car with a torrent of cold water that left him completely drenched. This unexpected surprise shocked the hell out of him, prompting him to bring his car to a screeching halt right smack-dab in the middle of the street, where he immediately exited his car and went off on a cursing rant.

Streams of fresh water could be seen running down the driver's enraged face. It was as though he had just been caught in the middle of a powerful thunderstorm that somehow only managed to affect him. This once-happy-go-lucky guy, who only minutes earlier was having the time of his life while riding around in his red Chevy convertible, was beyond upset and just didn't know what to do or say to let out some of his frustration.

From a small opening in between the curtains of my window, I saw all this drama unfold right before my very eyes. I was stunned to know that something as simple and as harmless as a stupid water balloon could cause so much ruckus within a matter of minutes. Once again, I felt really bad for my stupid actions. But in my young age, I guess I still had a lot to learn about respecting other people's rights, boundaries, and rules, and about crossing the line or going a bit overboard just for a quick laugh. Unfortunately, hitting this guy on the head with a water balloon that day was one of the dumbest things I could've ever done, and I definitely should've known better. But I didn't, and for that I'm really sorry, man!

In the end, while dozens of people attracted by all the commotion on the street just stared in disbelief at this stranger's water bashing, surprisingly no one offered to help. The stranger was certainly in desperate need of some type of consolation or assistance, and was shocked to learn that no one was coming to his aid or seemed to care about what had just happened. It didn't take long before he realized that he was basically on his own. One man, in an unfamiliar neighborhood, in the wrong place at the wrong time. He finally decided it was time to call it a day, and he left the block in a flash of fury.

Within a matter of seconds, all that was left was a white cloud of smoke from the screeching tires and whispers of a revving engine slowly dying in the distance. *¡Adios, amigo!*

CHAPTER 19

MY ROLE MODELS

As I have mentioned before, although at times I felt isolated and lonely from being stuck by choice in my room on a regular basis for extended periods of time, it was also a time for me to reflect on how I viewed the world and what I wanted to do with my life as I got older. Growing up in those days, I envisioned myself as just a marginal kid, stuck in a world of confusion about what I wanted to do with my life and which road I had to follow to get there.

On the one hand, I saw my brother, Flaco, and my sister Esther and the type of free-spirited lifestyle that they were living, and often I wondered what it would be like to live like them. They both had lots of friends, were very popular on the streets, hung out late at night, and had very little, if any, real responsibilities in their lives. Both had dropped out of school at a very early age, and neither was concerned with working. They had it all.

Seeing and absorbing all these negative influences as a kid often made me wonder if I should aspire to do the same once I grew up? In fact, there were times that I envied my brother's and sister's lifestyle and wanted to be just like them to enjoy the same types of freedoms: hanging out with their fellow gang members and getting love, respect, and admiration from the people in our block just because of their affiliation with the gang. Thriving in a really tough neighborhood, like ours, meant a great deal and held a lot of weight!

On the other end of the spectrum, my thoughts were influenced by some of the positive role models I saw or came in contact with on the streets. For example, the beat cop working the streets, his mere presence made a difference in people's lives. There were also the dedicated teachers at my school; they could easily influence a student's life with their kind mentorship and caring. Other role models, such as the local firemen working at the firehouse just two blocks from me, they changed lives just by saving people while fighting building fires. Finally, the doctors I came in contact with during office visits with my parents, they kept us well so that we could have a healthy life and future. These were all people who were known for the good they contributed to society and for the way they changed lives with just with their mere presence.

However, of all these amazing careers, my favorite of all and my wish was to someday become a police officer. In fact, there were times when I envisioned myself being a cop similar to those on TV and fighting crime in some of the coolest ways imaginable. Using these futuristic gadgets that always badgered the criminals into surrendering and culminated in the good guy always winning in the end. Some of those shows influenced me so much that at times I mimicked some of the roles I saw on TV. Some of the big hit shows from the '60s were *The Man from U.N.C.L.E.*, *Batman*, *Superman*, *Car 54...Where Are You?*, and perhaps my favorite TV show of all time, *The Lone Ranger*. These all played a role in my upbringing and planted that early seed in me of someday being a real-life hero and changing lives.

As the years and the months went by, a little bit of everything that I saw or experienced as a young child stuck with me and helped mold me into the person I am today: a dreamer with a positive attitude in life, a dreamer who believes that everything you aspire to be in life is possible!

CHAPTER 20

MOVING ON UP

As the years went by, my brother's involvement with the Spanish Devils started to intensify. No longer was Flaco just one of the boys in this violent gang of about fifty members; he had moved up in the ranks and was now the president's right-hand man. Because of his strong loyalty and backbone as a warrior in the battlefield of gang turf wars, he was appointed the war counselor by Negro, the gang's president.

A war counselor—or warlord, a common term used by most gangs in those days—is the person responsible for starting or settling a turf war. It was his responsibility to throw the first punch, inflict the first knife wound, or worse yet, fire the first shot before all hell broke loose. It was also his responsibility to make peace and settle disputes with rival gang members before things got out of hand. All in all, it was probably the most dangerous position in a gang because he was on the front line, the first to do whatever it took to jump-start combat, a situation that put him in the most vulnerable spot for sustaining an injury or risking his life. I can't tell you how many close calls he had while in that role; however, what I can say is that on many occasions the cuts and bruises on his body far outweighed those sustained by many of his comrades in the gang.

Luckily, many of his wounds were not life-threatening, but he made quite a few trips to the emergency room to get treated. And as with most gang members at the time, his refusal to cooperate with the investigating police officers made it extremely difficult to make an arrest, let alone get a conviction. Gang members preferred to deal with the situation on their own terms instead of involving the police.

The gangs' choice of weapons consisted mostly of bats, knives, brass knuckles, ice picks, and zip guns, the makeshift weapon of preference, according to my brother. The zip gun, I learned, was the poor man's .22 caliber handgun and was known to be used by gang members everywhere because, as my brother used to brag, it was so easy to make. However, it was also an extremely dangerous and deadly weapon for both the individuals getting shot by one and those firing them. Making one involved using a hollow car antenna for the barrel, rubber bands to hold it in place, a piece of wood in the form of a gun, a nail for the firing pin, and of course a .22 caliber bullet for firepower. It seems that on many occasions these zip guns would misfire and explode on contact, right in your hand. And no matter how well they were put together, once the bullet was fired there was no telling where that bullet would strike because of the gun's lack of accuracy.

Identifying who was in a gang and who wasn't in those days was pretty easy. That's because they all wore jean jackets bearing the name of the gang and gang symbol—the face of a devil was my brother's gang's logo—displayed on the back of the jacket. Another gang identifier was the use of specific color of sweater with a particular letter of the alphabet affixed to it to declare gang affiliation. In my brother's gang, for example, they wore bright-red sweaters with the capital letters *SD*, for Spanish Devils, on the front.

In those days, gang members had to take a pledge of brotherhood and draw blood to show solidarity and commitment to each other and the gang. This was done by pricking their own fingers using a needle or a knife; then they clasped each other's bloody fingers to create what they called a brotherly bond for life. This ritual, unfortunately, was not just limited to the guys, but also required of the female gang affiliates. The Lady Devils, a female gang led by my sister Esther, performed the same rituals, including, having a dress code. In keeping with gang standards, the women wore red sweaters, blouses, or T-shirts in order to conform with the symbolic tradition of the red devil.

Unlike my brother's gang, whose membership numbered somewhere near fifty, the ladies were a lot fewer in number and were a lot less violent than the guys. While the guys were known to carry all sorts of weapons in order to protect themselves, the girls would settle their disputes or fights by using their fists, a stick, or an occasional knife.

One such fight I recall witnessing; it happened in a backyard one summer day approximately two buildings away from where we lived. According to what I was told by my sister Esther, a rival gang member who lived in the neighborhood attempted to flirt with my sister's boyfriend at the time. When my sister heard of the incident through a rumor going around on the streets, she decided to confront her rival and challenged her to a fight right in the backyard of her rival's building. Rumors of the big fight spread like wildfire on our block that day. To see two young ladies fight over a man was one of the biggest highlights of the day, especially when it involved members of two opposing gangs going at each other in an all-out fistfight.

My sister, who had a permanent limp from having polio at a very young age, did not shy away from anyone and was as tough as nails, with the heart of a female lioness who feared no one. She was known on the streets for having a bad temper and for having a natural ability to pack a good solid punch.

When the time came for the fight, herds of people from the block, including fellow gang members, gathered in the concrete backyard and waited for the big brawl to begin. Within a matter of minutes, both opponents were in each other's faces, laying out their dirty laundry about what led to this confrontation. Since it was to be a fair fight, no one was allowed to jump in or intervene until it was all over.

As tempers flared and the intensity of the surrounding crowd grew, it was only a matter of time before all the taunting and chanting from the people pushed the embattled opponents to an all-out fistfight. Not surprisingly, it was my sister who threw the first punch to her opponent's face. That was soon followed by a barrage of fist throwing, hair pulling, clothes ripping, and pushing on both sides. The ultimate goal was to be the first one to knock her opponent to the ground and hopefully beat them into submission.

As the battle intensified, it was my sister who still had the power and strength, even after an exhausting fight, to somehow flip her nemesis onto the ground and get the upper hand. Once down, my sister proceeded to pummel her opponent's face with her fists before the fight was mercifully stopped. My sister was able to walk away with the victory, and she won back her man. In the end, it was all about keeping intact her reputation as both a leader and a warrior and putting on a big show for everyone in the neighborhood.

That day after witnessing my sister put up a hell of a fight in front of me and all those people, I truly believed she was all that they made her out to be: a tough street fighter with a lot of guts who didn't back down from anyone or anybody, despite her disability.

As insignificant as that moment might have been to many who saw the fight that day, for me it had more to do with watching my sister overcome a handicap, the post-polio limp, than anything else. I witnessed her using all the brutal strength, fighting ability, and courage within herself to step up to the challenge and come out victorious, despite her physical disabilities. And for that, there are not enough words to say how truly proud I am to have her for my sister!

CHAPTER 21

WHEN THE CAT'S AWAY, THE MICE WILL PLAY

Even though being in a gang might seem as if it is all about being tough and defending one's turf, for my brother and sister it was also about having a little fun. The phrase "When the cat's away, the mice will play" couldn't have been more fitting for the two of them; they literally took it to heart.

When my mother left the house to go to work, my brother and sister took full advantage of the great opportunity to have their gang parties. It was during those parties that both sides of the gang, males and females, got together and had a huge party instead of going to school or work. Anything and everything was possible at these home parties, most of which I either witnessed as a young child, while staying home from school because I was not feeling well, or heard about from my two siblings, Flaco and Esther.

Our apartment was literally a wild party house. There were everything from orgies that sometimes took place right in Esther's locked bedroom, to all-out dirty dancing to slow jams in every corner of the apartment, including our kitchen.

Besides all the dancing, there were also games that encouraged physical interaction between the partygoers. One game in particular was called spin the bottle. An empty glass bottle of beer was placed in the middle of the living-room floor, and members of both sexes would gather around it in a circle. Whoever spun the bottle had to make out with the member of the opposite sex to whom the bottle was pointing at the end of the spin. Let's just say that by the end of the game, there was plenty of spit swapping and heated matchmaking going on.

Aside from all the liquor consumption and the pot smoking that I witnessed, there were also your usual blood-brother or blood-sister initiation rituals at most of these gang parties.

One day, I decided to spill the beans and tell my mother everything that was going on behind her back while she was busy at work. It all unraveled when my sister failed to give me some of the hush money, which consisted of a dollar or some candy, that she had promised me to keep me quiet. So when it was time to collect and she didn't pay me… that's when I decided to tell my mom.

Since both my sister and brother had dropped out of school by that time, it was not unusual for both of them, and sometimes me, to be at home when my mother left for work. However, after I told my mom about this big party my brother and sister were planning, she decided to pull off a little surprise of her own.

The next day, my mother left the house, as usual, to go to work at about eight in the morning. As soon as my mother was out the door, my brother and sister immediately went to work calling people on the phone and telling them to spread the word, "We're having a party at our place, so bring your own drinks and weed! It's going to be a great time!"

Within a couple of hours, the apartment was packed with party-goers. Drinking, smoking, dancing—you name it, and they were doing it. Although I wasn't showing it at the time, deep inside I was smiling because I knew that at any moment my mother was going to raid her own home and catch everybody, including my brother and sister, by total surprise.

As the morning went by, and the partying intensified, no one, not even I, could have predicted what was about to happen. Suddenly and without warning, my mother busted into the house and shocked the shit out of everyone. What was once an all-out party scene for my brother, sister, and all their friends soon turned into chaos. My mother was so pissed off that she quickly went into a frenzy and immediately started yelling and screaming at everyone, "Get the hell out of my house, you motherfuckers!!!" along with a barrage of other Spanish curse words, some of which I had never even heard her say before. She even took a few swings at people as they scrambled to get past her and out the front door. While this was going on, others ran out the fire-escape window located in my bedroom in order to avoid being hit or yelled at by mother.

During this insane time, I remember seeing how scared my brother and sister were in anticipation of what was going to happen to them once the air cleared and all my mother's anger turned on them. More than anything, they were in total disbelief, and I could tell they were wondering how my mother was able to find out about the party.

Within minutes, all this frustration really got the best of my mother, and she was all over my brother and sister. She began by screaming and yelling at them like never before, and even slapping them about the face and body a few times to relieve some of her anger.

When this happened, they were both left speechless. They knew they had a lot of explaining to do about what they had been doing behind our mother's back. But down inside, they also knew that there was just no justification for that type of party and the total mess it created because of their actions. Our home was left in a complete mess!

In the end, besides the good Spanish tongue lashing and slaps they got from my mother, they also got some good old-fashioned housecleaning punishment that they weren't used to doing. That day, I was highly commended by my mother for turning in my siblings. But on the other hand, I got chastised by both my brother and sister for being a little rat and telling on them.

In the days and weeks that followed, I felt really bad and was full of a lot of guilt for what I had done that day. I know that although it was the right thing to do, deep down inside I knew it was for all the wrong reasons. I turned them in because they failed to come up with the hush money or candy they owed me. That really bothered me for quite a while. I felt that I had betrayed their trust and the special bond that we had as siblings and that they would never, ever trust me again. But, thank God, that never happened.

They were pissed off at me for a very long time, but we finally made up, and I was able to apologize and promise I would never do it again! Luckily, they accepted my apology, and I was soon back on their good side once again.

Although the parties continued after they got busted, in the end they were few and far between. As far as the payoff part of it, I got a little bit of change and candy here and there, but it wasn't the same. Hey, but who's complaining? I still got their love, and that's more important than any money or candy!

CHAPTER 22

WE GOT YOUR BACK

Having both of my siblings involved in gangs placed me in what I like to call a comfort zone of protection. I felt untouchable and feared no one because I was indirectly a member of the "family." I knew that all I had to do is tell my brother if I ran into any type of trouble or if someone was picking on me, and the problem would be taken care of in an instant.

Instead, I decided to only call upon my brother's services and those of his gang if I felt I was being outnumbered. Luckily, however, that only happened once or twice in my life when two overbearing fifth-grade thugs from my classroom threatened to beat me up after school for no apparent reason. I probably looked like an easy target because of my physical appearance. I was still that tall, skinny, lanky, and believe it or not, extremely shy kid from years past.

I remember leaving early from school "not feeling well" and running home to get my brother to help me with the situation. Within a couple of hours my brother, a fellow gang member of his, and I were outside the school grounds, waiting for the students to be dismissed. As soon as school let out, we looked into the crowd until I was able to point out the thugs who had threatened me that day.

Before long, we approached the duo and cornered them by a chain-link fence located along the north side of Public School 30 on 141st Street. The surprised reactions and the fear in the faces of these so-called tough guys said it all. They were afraid and didn't know what to expect from the adults that accompanied me. They quickly denied ever threatening me.

This prompted my visibly upset brother to say, "Brother, I want you"—pointing at me—"to fight these guys"—pointing at the bullies—"one by one… and we'll see how tough they are." The next thing I remember was my brother handing me this big-ass bulky ring to use as a "stinger." He took it off one of his fingers and told me, "Put this on, brother!" No sooner had I put the ring on my right index finger than my brother looked at me straight in the eyes and said, "Now go fuck these motherfuckers up with everything I taught you. And if you don't, I'm going to fuck you up, so you better take care of business, bro!"

I nervously nodded yes. The flame inside of me had been ignited. I was now on the spot, and the focus was all on me. My adrenaline was on full throttle, and I was all pumped up. I had fire in my eyes. And similar to a lion that is about to attack his prey, my eyes were trained right on those two targets. I was more than ready, and I knew there was no turning back. In my mind, this was the boxing ring, and I was the main event. The bell was just seconds away from ringing, and it was payback time! The stage was set for the battle of my life, and I was not about to back out!

Not surprisingly, my brother was like my corner man, or manager, prepping me for the big fight. That day, there was no title or belt at stake, no prize money on the table. It was just a battle of guts and determination. Without skipping a beat, my brother patted me on the shoulder, indicating his confidence in me, and quietly whispered into my ear, "Now go kick some ass!"

And off I went! With my brother and his buddy loudly cheering me on, the fight was finally on. One by one, I fought those two punks, using all the bravado, frustration, and energy that had been boiling inside of me all day. Soon punches were flying all over the place on both sides until all of us nearly collapsed from exhaustion. The fight, which drew a small crowd of onlookers from the school, was finally stopped my brother and his buddy after what appeared to be five or so grueling minutes. It was eminently clear that the tough guys had had enough of me for the day and were ready to go home to heal their wounded egos.

Although I too sustained a few bumps and bruises, it paled in comparison to the two bullies I dealt with that day. They got the worst of it, their faces visibly swelling and bruising, including their eyes, which took the brunt of the punishment. In the end, although the physical bumps and bruises eventually healed with time, the damage and permanent stain on their egos was not so quickly forgotten. They had just been just beaten by a shy, skinny kid whom they thought would be an easy target. I'm sure that stayed with them for a lifetime.

Thinking back now to that time and place in my life, it's refreshing to know that in a very small way I reached a personal milestone in my early life. I had decided to take a stand and beat the odds by fighting each bully one on one. That day, not only had I proven to myself that I was a worthy opponent, but I was also proud of how I handled the situation when I refused to give into their threats and intimidation, and instead confronted them head-on.

I can honestly say that although I was extremely pleased with the way I handled myself in that street fight that day, no one was happier for me than my very own brother. The big smile on his face said it all that day. He was super proud of me, not only for the way I handled myself, but also for the brave way in which I took a stand on bullying and never backed down. This was the very first time he actually got a chance to see me in action, using all the mentoring tools and boxing skills he had taught me during our training sessions. In all, it was a truly memorable bonding moment for the two of us, one for which I will always be extremely grateful.

While some of the things I learned from my brother were somewhat controversial, they were, nevertheless, useful tools that worked for me and will be with me forever. Some of the most valuable life lessons he taught me are to never back down from my adversaries, no matter what the situation might be, to never show fear, to always believe in myself and my abilities, and to believe that I can do anything I want in life. It was through him that I also learned the tough street-survival skills needed to succeed in a really rough neighborhood of the South Bronx like ours. And last, but certainly not least, he taught me that no matter where you go in life, you never forget where you came from and what you did to get to where you are.

In all, they were lessons learned from someone whose troubled environment from an early age had taught him a lesson or two about life and the tactics needed to survive in a tough world. That's my brother in a nutshell; he's a true warrior of life with a great big heart!

CHAPTER 23

THE NEEDLES, THE JUNKIES, AND ME

Jumping from the battles of the streets to tackling and dealing with everyday fears for survival in my neighborhood could sometimes be an overwhelmingly scary situation, especially when it involved the mind of a young, impressionable child in his preadolescent years.

One sunny summer afternoon, while trying to keep myself busy, I decided that it was a great day to fly a kite on the roof of our building. With no one at home, I gathered up my favorite kite, locked up the house, and headed up two flights from my fourth-floor apartment to the rooftop of my building. Other than leaning too close to the edge of the rooftop while I flew my kite, I really wasn't all that worried that something would happen to me.

After about an hour or so of flying my kite, I decided it was time to call it a day, and I started heading towards the vestibule doorway that would lead me back to my apartment. However, just as I was about to open the door, I heard the faint voices of two people talking. Not having the slightest idea what to expect on the other side of the door, I cautiously opened it and peered in. What I saw on the other side of the door gives me chills when I think about it to this day.

As I peeked around the door, I saw what appeared to be two really disheveled and dirty junkies sitting on the landing. I couldn't tell who was more surprised of the three of us when I first opened the door, but I think it is safe to say I was, because I was frozen stiff.

They were in the process of what I later learned was shooting up heroin. Both had one of their sleeves rolled up above the elbow, that arm strapped with an elastic band around the bicep to engorge the veins. One junkie held a syringe in his hand and appeared to be in the process of injecting his friend, just as a nurse would do at the doctor's office. When I opened the door, they both stopped what they were doing and stared right at me.

The silence and pure tension of the moment only added to the horrific scene I was witnessing. My heart was beating out of control, while my mind was swirling in my head with a thousand different scenarios that all spelled trouble for me. I was immobilized with fear. I was afraid to make any type of movement or say anything that could jeopardize my life.

Soon, ugly visions of stories I had heard from people on the block about what junkies had done to people started playing in my head like a horror movie. *They're going to shoot me up with drugs then throw me off the roof,* I quickly thought. *Or maybe they're just going to shoot me up with so much heroin that I'll get hooked and be a junkie just like them for the rest of my life.* I wanted to scream for help, but I was too afraid. I wanted to run away from the scene, but my legs just weren't responding to my commands. Finally running out of options, I just stood there and prayed with all my heart that nothing would happen to me.

Out of the blue, one of the junkies must have noticed my fear and broke the silence by muttering, "Hey, bro, you live here?"

I was shaking to death and really didn't know if answering yes was a good thing or a bad thing. I nervously calculated the answer in my mind many times over before I finally got the nerve to say yes. I dreaded to hear what their responses were going to be.

"All right, kid, go on home," one of them said as they moved out of the way to open up a pathway for me to go down the stairs.

I said thanks and hurriedly found my way past them. As I was making my way down the stairs, I could still feel their stares. Before I made it to the last step and could finally put this drama behind me, one of the junkies called out to me. *Oh no,* I thought, *they must have had a change of heart. I'm really in trouble now!* My heart dropped; I didn't know what to expect next from those hard-core junkies.

"Hey, by any chance, are you Flaco's little brother?" one of them asked.

Again, I was petrified because I didn't know where this was going. I knew that my brother had made a few enemies along the way, and giving the wrong answer could backfire on me. I hesitantly answered yes. It turns out that was just the right answer they were looking for. It seems those two junkies knew my brother very well from the streets and had recognized me from seeing me around the block with my brother.

It was a welcoming thing to hear all the good things they had to say about my brother, the gang, and the block in general. In the end, it made me feel a little bit more relaxed and not as scared. I remember the conversation being quick, but in it they mentioned how they knew my brother from the gang and how they thought he was "a really cool dude" who "put up a good fight" and was somebody you "didn't want to mess with."

While they talked, I noticed that the effects of the heroin were slowly starting to take place. Their voices were shallow and lacked energy; their eyes made them seem sleepy and tired, but in this case they were reflecting the high from the drugs. Their eyelids appeared heavy, almost as though they were squinting to see what was in front of them. I was really uncomfortable, and I couldn't wait to get the heck out of there and run home.

Finally, when it was time to say goodbye, they ended the conversation by telling me to tell my brother they said hi.

I walked down the stairs, ran into my home, and reflected on everything that happened that day. It felt great being home, but more importantly, it felt great being safe and sound, especially when I thought back to what could've happened had things gone in a different direction. Thank God, they didn't; that's all I can say!

As for going to the roof, let's just say I learned a big lesson. After that day, every time I went to the roof, I made sure to take precautions by telling someone in the household where I was going. I also made a pledge to myself to be more aware of my surroundings and to use a little bit more common sense before going into potential drug-shooting galleries. And last, but not least, I decided to never, ever go on such a journey by myself again, for who knows if being "Flaco's bro" would always be synonymous with "This kid is all right!" Boy, that was a close one!

CHAPTER 24

PUERTO RICO, JULY 1967

"*Levántate, muchacho, levántate,*" my mother called out to me! "Get up, boy, get up."

"But, Mom," I said in a half-sluggish sleep mode, "it's only three o'clock in the morning!"

"You know what the rules are, son," she quickly responded. "So get your ass up right now!"

It's the Fourth of July weekend, and that morning we were flying to Puerto Rico, out of John F Kennedy Airport, on what seemed like an annual visit. At the age of ten, I just wanted to stay on the block with my friends and have a fun time in the good ole Bronx. Unfortunately, I had no other choice. It was either get up and start getting ready for our trip, or risk getting an "ear pull" from my mom as she ordered, "Now! Let's go!"

Thinking back to that earlier time in my life, I guess it was kind of nice to get away on a little summer vacation to visit some of my relatives on the island… especially my grandparents from my father's side, whom I hadn't seen for many years. Deep down inside my heart, I knew that escaping to the island would also serve as a big relief for me and would give me an opportunity to get away from all the troubling issues affecting my family because of my father's addiction to alcohol.

That day, I was up and ready to go in a flash. However, before leaving our home that morning, there was a set of rituals that we had to perform every single time we went away or left our home for an extended period of time. These rituals were put in place by my parents from as far back as I could remember. These basic house rules were made to protect our home from intruders. In short, it was just another way of trying to implement as many safeguards as possible in order to prevent our home from being burglarized by our neighborhood junkies.

As I previously said, we lived in one of the worst drug- and gang-infested neighborhoods of the South Bronx during the heroin epidemic of the '60s and '70s. It was a place that was well known not only for its high level of poverty, but also because of the boarded-up, abandoned buildings that were visible everywhere! Many were as a result of intentional or accidental fires that left poor tenants homeless in the poverty-stricken neighborhood. Eventually, the rash of abandoned buildings all over the Bronx, due to those fires, sadly gave rise to that 1970s term "the Bronx is burning," which became synonymous with the Bronx of that era.

Performing this type of ritual every time we went on a trip was not something out of the ordinary for our family, for we knew that it was either take these precautions to keep our home safe, or risk the chance of being victimized by the neighborhood bad guys. In other words, sneaking out of our building or neighborhood in the wee hours of the morning had its purpose. It was all done to prevent ourselves from being seen by the neighborhood junkies, who for the most part, thank God, were sleeping during those hours of the morning. Ultimately, we figured out that by taking these proactive measures, it made it less stressful for us when leaving our home with our hands full of luggage. In our minds, it decreased our chances of becoming an easy target for a break-in. But as weird as this system may sound, it was the truth! The bad element in the neighborhood would always look for golden opportunities—for example, signs of a family going on vacation—to take advantage of empty homes.

Yet as bad as it might sound to live under crazy conditions like these, to me this was my home. It was the only place I'd known since I was a little kid. Taking extreme precautions every time we stepped out of our home was a way of life for us. One thing that's ingrained within you when you live in the ghetto is to never let your guard down. Always try to outthink the bad guys. It's imperative that you beat them to the punch. In other words, implement whatever survival tactics you have at your disposal in order to come out on top and avoid becoming a victim. As you will see later, that wasn't always possible.

We managed to gather up all our belongings for our trip and quietly tiptoed out of our third-floor apartment undetected. However, there's one thing that clearly stands out about that morning that I will never forget. That day, my father, in the rush to leave the building and head to the airport, literally stopped our taxi so that he could run back upstairs to our apartment. "We forgot to turn on the radio and disconnect the phone!" he said. These actions, although they might have seemed a little over the top when you think about it now, became two more safeguards that my family used in those days to outsmart the neighborhood thieves into thinking that someone was still at home. And it worked!

At the time, I really didn't understand the whole logic behind such a routine, but the way it was explained to me later made a lot sense to me for two reasons. First, keeping the radio on gave the uninvited listening ear the impression that someone was at home. Second, pre-answering-machine days, if no one was at home to answer the phone, it could ring off the hook for hours, signaling to the bad guys that no one was home and that it was safe to break in. They could easily kick open the front door or climb up the front or rear fire escape to gain entry through a window.

The fire escapes were made of wrought iron and were attached to the rear or front of every building in my neighborhood. The purpose of a fire escape was to provide tenants with an escape route in the event of a fire. Each floor was equipped with a zigzag ladder that ran from the first floor, all the way to the top of the building. While the fire escapes were initially built for safety reasons, the druggies in the neighborhood considered them a gold mine that made it so much easier to burglarize your home.

Over the years, it became common knowledge to the bad guys that if they entered through the rear fire-escape window, their chances of getting seen, or even caught in the act, were certainly less than trying to force their way through the front door of an apartment. All they had to do was smash your rear window, enter, and leave the same way they came in, all without being detected. A row of abandoned buildings in the rear alleyway only served to encourage this type of criminal activity.

For this reason, we could never travel together as one big family. It would usually be either my mom and I, or my mom and my nephews and nieces. My brother and sisters were doing their own thing and very rarely traveled with us. My father, on the other hand, worked a full-time job and would take alternate trips to the island once we got back. By doing it this way, there was always someone at home to keep an eye on the place.

Since we lived only thirty minutes away from John F. Kennedy Airport, we made it to the airport with plenty of time to spare. Once there, we said our goodbyes to my father, and off we went on our approximately three-and-one-half-hour flight to the island.

It was about 12:30 p.m. when we finally taxied into the San Juan, Puerto Rico, airport the next morning. Looking out the airplane window, I recall seeing the tall palm trees swaying back and forth with each gust of the wind. It was surely a strange sight from what I was used to seeing in the Bronx, which is very little trees, a ton of brick buildings, and instead of palm trees, towering lampposts that adorned the front of every building in my neighborhood. Once we landed, I also remember all the excitement on the plane, with passengers clapping and some even yelling out loud, "¡¡¡Que viva Puerto Rico!!!" Their emotions showed just how happy they were to visit the island again.

I gathered all my belongings from the plane, making sure that the wings pin, which I got from one of the Pan Am pilots when we first boarded the plane that morning, was clearly visible on my shirt. To me, wearing that special pin was like displaying a medal of valor for flying such a long distance.

As I waited for the cabin door to open, my heart raced in anticipation of what awaited me outside the plane. I thought about my uncle, Tio Cruz, and his son, Pedrito, who were usually the ones to pick us up at the airport. I also thought about all the fun my cousin and I were going to have once we got to our hometown. The fact that we were the same age and got along great was definitely a bonus. However, the one thing I dreaded the most was taking that long and exhausting four-hour car drive from the airport to my mother's hometown of Arroyo. It was a very difficult drive that would take us through *las Curvas de Cayey*, the curves of Cayey. The drive would involve taking us through a mountainous, curvy, and winding road that almost always got me dizzy and would force me to throw up on the side of the road.

However I decided, I wasn't about to let that "little inconvenience" stop me from enjoying our beautiful island and all that it had to offer. Instead, I preferred to marvel at what made the island so special and inviting, at what made us come back to visit almost every single year. I thought about all the tasty tropical fruits that adorned the island—for example, the oversized, ripe, juicy mangos, which would melt in your mouth with every bite, and the addicting, juice-filled coconuts, which would conquer any thirst, yet leave you thirsting for more of this fantastic, natural fruit drink. I was also excited about the unlimited sunshine, the warm tropical breezes, the warm, crystal-clear waters, and the white, sandy beaches that added to this majestic and alluring paradise. Topping it all off are the island's wonderful mountainous views, its cultivating plantations, and last, but certainly not least, the historical pride of its amazing monuments, culture, and traditional folklore. Together, this all amounts to what is commonly known to all Puerto Ricans as living in *la isla del encanto*, the island of enchantment. In short, Puerto Rico was vastly known to all of us as a total paradise. It was a place for having fun, enjoying amazing adventures in its tropical forest, and relaxing in some of the most beautiful and wonderful beaches in the world!

Finally, the long-awaited moment had arrived. I was soon making my way to the front of the plane with my mother, where the pilots and stewardesses waited by the cabin door to greet the departing passengers. As we approached the crew, I remember them sporting the biggest smiles as they told each and every single passenger exiting the plane, "Welcome to Puerto Rico. We hope you enjoy your stay."

We said, "Thank you," as we exited the doorway!

As I stood in front of the doorway, before I descended to the ground via these long stairs that were rolled up to the plane for passengers' use upon exiting the plane, I felt like a United States president standing at the top of his very own private jet, Air Force One. I enjoyed the magnificent view of all the palm trees, the warm tropical air, the sunshine, and the large crowd that was gathered in a fenced-in area of the terminal, waiting for their relatives to arrive. *Wow, what a view!* I thought to myself.

After finally meeting up with my uncle and cousin, we soon left the airport and headed towards Arroyo. We made our usual stop to get a bite to eat before continuing on to our destination. Near the airport, we stopped at this very popular restaurant called *Aquí Me Quedo*, I'm Staying Right Here. At first, I had reservations about eating, knowing my history with going up that unforgiving, whirly ride up the mountain, but the lure of the food and the temptation to not pass up a good meal was just too much to handle. So I gave in, hoping that maybe this time around I wouldn't get sick. Within minutes, I was sitting down with my family and having the most delicious plate of *arroz con pollo*, rice and chicken, that I've ever tasted in my life.

After spending about an hour there and downing my delicious meal, we headed back on the road again. Approximately two hours into our travel, I started feeling nauseous. I guess going up that winding, mountainous road really got the best of me, and I felt myself wanting to throw up. My mother quickly picked up on it and told my uncle's taxi driver to pull over to the side of the road. The driver quickly pulled over, and I immediately began puking my brains out. After I vomited, I felt weak and tired. I fell asleep for the rest of the ride to my mother's *pueblo*, town.

Once we arrived, it was the greatest feeling in the world—a chance to finally see my family in Arroyo, a small town of about thirty thousand or so residents, located in the Southern Coastal Valley of Puerto Rico. It was a place where everyone seemed to know each other, and greetings abounded from the crack of dawn when roosters crowed to sundown. The amazing and unique sound of a rooster crowing at the crack of dawn served as an alarm clock that reminded everyone to wake up, enjoy the rich sunshine, and start your day!

Many of the homes were made of wood frames with aluminum siding sheets as rooftops. The combination of the two gave these beautiful homes a very nice look to them and coincided with the way traditional houses were built back in the day in Puerto Rico. I especially loved when it rained at night. The sound of the bouncing raindrops off the aluminum roof shingles provided a white-noise effect that gave me the most calming and relaxing feeling in the world. I knew I was in for the best sleep ever!

My cousin Pedrito was born and raised in Arroyo and knew all the ins and outs of the town. Somehow, he always managed to stay busy by coming up with some adventure or idea for us to explore every day. Whether it was climbing up our next-door neighbor's giant mango tree, to fetch some delicious mangos without her permission, or swimming in the aggressive ocean waters without our parents knowing, he always had something up his sleeve. I used to say that he was the Puerto Rican Dennis the Menace of Arroyo, for he was constantly getting into some type of trouble. He gave my poor elderly grandmother, Oliva, more premature gray hairs then she could count. She was always worrying. "I wonder where he's at" and "What is he doing?" were constant thoughts that never left her mind when he wasn't home.

All in all, I think Pedrito was just your average kid looking to have a good time in all his natural surroundings. Although he gave our grandmother a headache on a regular basis, he also loved her dearly and would always attend to her every need.

Approximately three weeks into our vacation, I got a chance to visit other parts of the island and was finally able to spend some time with my grandparents and a host of other relatives from my father's side of the family in the town of Isabela, which is located in the northwestern region of Puerto Rico. I also did a little sightseeing in Old San Juan, the place where the famous fortress El Morro became a symbol of where the Spanish-American War took place way back in 1896.

I was having the most amazing time back in Arroyo, until one day when something happened that got us both in big trouble. My cousin and I were watching a nest of ants attacking a caterpillar they had just captured. We were literally right across the street from my grandmother's house at the time. One of the neighborhood kids, Miguelito, approached us with some exciting news. He told us that today was the big motorcycle race we'd been waiting for at the plaza, otherwise known as the town green. It was taking place in the center of town, about a half a mile or so from where my grandmother lived, and he asked us if we wanted to join him.

This was awesome news because I had never seen a motorcycle race in my whole life! When my cousin asked me if I wanted to go, I said, "Of course, I want to go!" In an instant, we all took off running without asking permission or even worrying about the trouble we would be in if my mother and grandmother found out.

We were about a long block away from the site when my cousin decided we should "race to the plaza to see who gets there first." Not one to turn down a challenge, I quickly accepted. Since I was tallest in the group and had the longest legs, I figured I stood the better chance of beating them all.

Before we knew it, the race was on! Miguelito started in front of the pack, my cousin a close second, while I was desperately in last place but gaining on my cousin. I remember being less than one hundred yards away from the end of the street, with all three of us laughing out loud as we pushed ourselves to the limit to beat each other. I also remember running blindly as I tried desperately to catch up to my cousin and Miguelito.

Suddenly, out of the blue, my feet left the ground. I was being tossed up in the air like a rag doll. My mind was spinning out of control. My vision was a big blur, and I heard a loud thumping sound as my body hit the ground; I was knocked unconscious.

The next thing I remember is opening my eyes, my cousin, Miguelito, and an unknown gentleman standing around me. They were all worried and asking me if I was okay. I soon realized that I had just been struck by a car.

I was dazed, confused, and had a lot of pain radiating from the back of my head to my lower extremities. My back landed on the cement pavement, and the excruciating pain from the impact was traveling from the left side of my pelvis, all the way down to my legs. The smell of burnt rubber was still in the air from the tires grinding against cement as the driver of the car came to an abrupt stop. The front bumper of the car was within inches from my face, the motor still generating heat from the car that was still running.

I was so scared for my life. I didn't know if I had broken my legs, damaged my pelvis, or worse yet, suffered internal injuries that needed immediate medical attention. An ambulance and a police officer soon responded to the scene, and before I knew it, I was en route to the nearest local hospital to get treated for my injuries. My cousin, who was shitting in his pants from the trouble he suddenly found himself in, had to take the long, unceremonious ride with the police officer to my grandmother's home to give them the bad news.

Luckily, I didn't sustain any serious injuries, other than a slight fracture in my left leg, extensive bruising and swelling to the left side of my pelvis and lower back, and a concussion from hitting my head on the ground. An accident investigation by the responding officer determined that the driver of the vehicle was speeding out of his driveway when he struck me. Because I had temporarily lost consciousness after I got hit, I didn't remember a thing and had to rely on others to tell me what happened. From what I was told by my cousin and Miguelito, the accident happened just as we ran past this one particular long driveway that stretched from the street curb all the way to the back of the house, approximately thirty or forty yards. The operator of the vehicle, who was barreling out of the driveway, apparently never saw me cutting in front of his vehicle. As he hit me, according to my cousin, he came within inches of running me over when I landed in the driveway, in front of his car.

The driver, who was eventually found at fault in the accident, was ticketed by the investigating officers at the scene and ordered to appear in court a few months after the accident. Nearly a year later, my parents reached an out-of-court settlement with the insurance company that netted me and my family a few thousand dollars.

I later learned in life that all the money in the world couldn't lessen the pain and embarrassment of a good beating with a leather belt, a tongue lashing, and being grounded for a week. All and all, I think my mother took a little pity on me because of my injuries; otherwise, I know she would've given me the beating of my life for breaking the rules and going somewhere without her permission. My cousin, on the other hand, wasn't as lucky! That day my mother and my grandmother both agreed that since it was my cousin who dragged me into this, it was only fair that he should get the harsher punishment. Let's just say that the whipping that I was supposed to get that day...he got it two times more!

Looking back now, I can see why my mother was so upset at me. As it turns out, that incident was the third time in the previous six years that I had gotten hit by a car. The other two happened in the Bronx, with the last one taking place just about two years prior to this one. Thank God, they weren't as serious as the last one; otherwise, who knows how different my life would've turned out to be.

After all was said and done, two quick lessons came to mind. One, always look both ways before crossing a street, no matter what the situation is. Second, never—I mean, never—be in a hurry to get somewhere. Sometimes, it's just not worth it!

CHAPTER 25

MY REBELLIOUS STAGE

By the time I reached the seventh grade in Alexander Burger Junior High School 139, the shell that I once used as a shield to protect my extremely shy and introverted persona was beginning to crack, and a new me was slowly emerging. I was getting a little older, and my character and way of being was gradually starting to change. I guess you might say that I was entering what I can only define as my rebellious stage, a time in my life when I felt that change was needed in order to survive in the outside world and be a better person, not a bitter person after all that had happened in my life and with my family. And while my intentions might have been good, somehow, somewhere, I ended up taking the wrong turn and wound up on the wrong road with the wrong crowd.

In just a short period of time, I became a very disrespectful, irresponsible, and at times, lawless kid who wanted to break all the rules just for the sake of breaking them. I went from being a quiet kid who barely said a word to anyone, to an untamed monster who was at times totally out of control. I was disrespectful to my parents, teachers, family, and even the law. I joined a gang, did minor street rips, and even stole from the school. About the only thing I didn't do was use drugs; they didn't come into play until my early teens.

Along with this bad behavior, my schoolwork and education suffered as well. From the time I entered my freshman year of junior high school in September of 1967, until the time I barely graduated three years later in June of 1970, I amassed a total of 101 days absent, and that doesn't even include the days I showed up to school in the morning, only to skip out of school in the afternoon. Though at times I missed school because of my chronic asthma attacks and the fallout from my dad's alcoholism, most of my absences were choices I made of my own free will. Just as I was promoted in elementary school to the next level even though my grades and my attendance were not up to par, the same thing happened in junior high school. How the school and the administration continued to pass me to the next grade level is beyond me, but it happened!

Because of my absenteeism from school, my grades took a big hit. It was so bad that when I finally did graduate from school three years later, my grade point average was a mere 69 percent. My disruptive classroom behavior also landed me in the principal's office quite a few times. In the end, these were all factors that contributed to my downfall as a student and basically crushed my chances of making something positive out of the education I received.

Where did I go wrong? I've often wondered. And the answer can always be traced to my tragic life as a child. I was basically crying for help on the inside, and nobody was there to help pull me through my own inner battles and the violent domestic environment. So in the interim, I sought help in the best way I knew how—through my friends, most of whom were having similar problems. In a sense, that was what forged our bond as friends. Most of us lived under the umbrella of a dysfunctional family, broken homes, drug use in the household, or unaware, uncaring parents.

CHAPTER 26

HOW IT ALL BEGAN

Thinking back now, I can vividly recall when everything changed for me and where all my troubles began. One day, I was walking to school, using the same old path down 141st Street that I took every single day. That morning, something really strange happened that unexpectedly changed my life.

I remember being entrenched deep in my thoughts about what kind of a day I was going to have at school. Out of the blue, a kid whom I'd just passed yelled, "*¡Oye, amigo!*" I slowed down a bit, not thinking he was referring to me, and continued to walk, but then I heard him say, this time in English, "Yeah, you, with the funny walk!"

Those last words certainly caught my attention. *Me with the funny walk?* I wondered to myself. *Is he really referring to me?* So out of curiosity, I quickly turned around to see what was his problem. He was quite a few steps behind me, so I waited patiently without responding; I wanted to see what he was going to say next. As he approached me, he had this great big smile on his face, which had me wondering, *What the hell is so funny?*

He was a skinny kid, just as I was, and had tan skin and dark, wavy, medium-length hair; he appeared to be in about my age range, twelve or thirteen. He introduced himself as Mexicano, and we shook hands. He said, "I don't mean to offend you, but are you walking with a funny hop?"

A bit bewildered and confused at this point, I asked him to show me what was wrong with my walk. He took a moment and imitated my so-called funny walk. As soon as I saw what he was referring to, I was dumbfounded. *If this is true,* I told myself, *then I must be walking like a total goofball in the eyes of everyone around me.*

I don't know if odd was the best way to describe it; however, let's just say it was weird and made me look like a total geek. But then again, I shouldn't be totally surprised. It kind of fell into place with my little shy and introverted personality that I'd been carrying around with me for all those years. I became self-conscious of my walk and thanked him for making me aware of something I was totally oblivious to doing. We ended our conversation with a big laugh about the whole thing and an agreement to talk some more at lunchtime as we continued on to school.

The thought of walking weirdly kind of bothered me all day, so I knew, if I ever made changes in my life, that would be one of them. By the time lunch came around, I was already consciously working on my walk. I was pleased that I was making a big effort to remove that hop from my walk so that I could blend in with the rest of the kids in my school and not stick out as much.

I picked up my lunch in the cafeteria and was in the process of looking for a place to sit down to eat when I heard that now-familiar voice from that morning saying, "Hey, Roberto, come here, and have a seat with us!" I looked in the direction of the voice to discover that, sure enough, it was Mexicano.

This time, however, he was sitting smack-dab in the middle of a bunch of guys that I didn't know. They were all dressed in the Wrangler jean jackets typically associated with gangs throughout New York City, but without the colors or identifying gang insignias on the back... which were prohibited from being worn on the school grounds. He waved me over and started introducing his friends one by one. "This is Freddy, Oscar, Jose, Luis, Mousey, Herman, Johnny 'Rubber Band', Luis, and last but not least, *Cebolla*, Onion Head."

Since I had so few friends at school, meeting people and having an opportunity to make some new friends was just what I was looking for. I shook hands with all of them and received a nice warm welcome in return. They made me feel really comfortable, as if I were already the newest member of the group. We talked for a little while during the limited amount of time we had for lunch, and I was able to tell them a little bit about myself before we parted ways and went to our respective classrooms.

As the weeks and months went by, meeting in the lunchroom became a regular thing. In time, I started feeling less of an outcast and more like one of the guys. I became a lot more outgoing and sociable as I fought hard to overcome the shy, introverted personality that had plagued me. Over time, I became really good friends with everybody in the group, to the point that I found myself hanging out with them more than I had ever anticipated, both within the school and outside.

It didn't take long for me to figure out that this daily meeting among friends in the lunchroom and at recess every day was more than just friends hanging out. This was a school gang. A school gang that, I later learned, had over twenty members on its roster and was still growing. The gang was called the Seven Diamonds.

One day, the leader of the gang—Freddy, a tough, streetwise, charismatic individual who always seemed to be surrounded by lots of people—approached me privately in the schoolyard and asked me if I would like to become a member of the Seven Diamonds.

Me, I thought to myself, *in a gang like Esther and Flaco? Well, why not?* Right away, I thought about the popularity and the many friends I would have. I thought about the positive effect on my introverted personality, my self-confidence, and my low self-esteem. I mulled it over before finally coming to the conclusion that, for me, it would be a really good change all the way around. After thinking about it for what seemed like an eternity, I finally said, "Yes, of course, I'll join your gang!"

Freddy smiled and extended his right hand towards me. We shook hands, and he said to me, "Tomorrow at recess, meet me in the schoolyard, and I'll let all the boys know that you want to join us."

From that moment on, I knew life was going to change for me in a big way. Although I realized that joining the gang came with lots of risk and uncertainty, in the long run, it would also provide me with all the confidence and assertiveness I needed to become the new me.

That early afternoon at recess, I met Freddy and the rest of the gang in the schoolyard, just as he'd asked me to do. As I approached the group, I could tell right away that they all appeared to be pretty excited and all pumped up. I couldn't help but wonder if my joining this gang was creating all that excitement, or if maybe there was something more sinister about to take place. I was still a bit nervous and apprehensive about the whole thing.

Freddy proceeded to gather the group—which, as I said, numbered in the twenties—in a huddle, as if he were preparing for the next big play on the football field. At his request, I patiently waited in anticipation of what the hell the group was talking about and what was going to happen next.

After a few seconds, the meeting was over, and Freddy approached me to tell me what it was all about. He said, "Are you sure you still want to do this?" Without hesitation, I said yes once again! "Okay then, you see that line over there?" He pointed to the members of the gang who had divided into two equal lines facing each other. I said yes. "Well," he continued, "to make it into this gang, you have to able to make it from the beginning of that line, all the way to the end, without falling. Everybody, including me, is going to punch the hell out of you to see if you've got what it takes to be a member of the gang."

This gang initiation thing isn't what I had in mind, I thought. *But if that's what it takes to be in the gang, then I'm willing to take the chance, even if it means getting the shit kicked out of me.* I kept saying to myself, *Hopefully, in the end, it will all be worth it, and I will officially be one of the guys.*

In no time, I was ready to take that dark plunge into getting the beating of my life, something I was hoping I wouldn't regret later on. Without further ado, I stood in the front of the line, took one quick, deep breath, and said to myself, *Well, ready or not... here I go!* I dove in headfirst!

As I nervously started up the line, I tried desperately to shield all the vital parts of my face, like my mouth, eyes, and nose, using both my hands and arms as protection. But that, it turns out, was extremely difficult to do. The first hit caught me right in my lower lip, and that was followed by a barrage of hard-fisted knuckles that hit me everywhere on my body. By midway through, I had taken a serious ass whipping, but I didn't want to raise the white flag and quit. *I have never been a quitter, and I'm not about to start being one now*, I kept assuring myself as I staggered my way up the line.

I was hurting everywhere, but my will to continue kept pushing me closer and closer to the end of the line. After experiencing the beating for what felt like an eternity, I was finally able to see the light at the end of the tunnel, literally. Luckily, I somehow managed to make it all the way through the line without falling. That day, although I received numerous bumps and bruises, the relief of making it and finally becoming the newest member of the gang numbed the pain a little and made getting the beating of my life a lot easier to take.

No sooner had I completed the grueling task of getting my ass whipped at the hands of my *compadres*, than I was being flanked by all the members who proceeded to congratulate me on making the gang. It was especially nice when Freddy, as the gang's president, approached me with a handshake and personally told me, "Congratulations, brother, you're now one of us!"

It wasn't until Freddy actually said those words that it really hit me as to what I had just done. *I'm in a gang now... I'm really in a gang... Wow, what a feeling*, I kept repeating to myself as if I had just reached the biggest milestone or aspiration of my entire life.

After all the fanfare and excitement of it all had quieted down, I went home and thought about it some more. Above all, I wondered, *What kind of an impact will being in this gang now have on my life? How will it change me as a person? But more importantly, what happens from this point on, now that I'm one of them?*

As it turns out, it wouldn't take long for those hard questions in my mind to be answered. The changes would come fast and in bundles!

CHAPTER 27

THE NEW ME!

Within three or four weeks of joining the gang, I completely lost any interest in school. I was skipping school at an alarming rate, way more than the usual. My quiet and shy personality soon became raw and abrasive. I was disrespectful to others, from my teachers to my parents and everyone in between. I became a distraction in class and spent many a days in the principal's office for my disruptive behavior. I also engaged in everything from fighting in class to annoying and distracting other students and teachers from their work. *I'm cool now*, I thought. On the outside, I was a changed person with a big ego and a tough-guy persona, just the way I always wanted to be.

Deep down inside, however, it was a different story. I was still that insecure kid who was dealing with a lot of emotional and traumatic family issues at home. Nothing outside of school had changed. So for me, going to school and cavorting with my fellow gang members, who were constantly engaged in troublesome activities, subconsciously turned out to be my way of relieving stress and feeling better about myself.

My first true test of what it meant to be in a gang happened about a month after officially joining it. Freddy gathered a bunch of us in front of the school one day and told us, "Tomorrow, we're going to skip school, and we're going to hit Public School 49"—located at 388 Willis Avenue, about three blocks from our school—"to take some hats." The hats he was referring to were called beavers, a very expensive, popular hat that kids wore in those days; they were made of a mohair-type fabric and had a Green Beret-type shape. They were very popular because they came in a variety of colors and could be combed with a brush and a little hair gel, or grease, to give them a very appealing look.

The plan on that day was to case the elementary school during recess, pick out our victims within the crowd, walk right up to them, grab the hats off their heads, and run away as fast as possible.

It was early afternoon by the time we made it to the school and cased the area. Only a few teachers could be seen within the school grounds, so from what we could tell, it had the appearance of an easy hit. There were kids everywhere wearing beavers, so we basically had a variety of choices. After waiting around and picking our targets, we decided it was time to make our move.

I had never done anything that even came close to this in my life, so I was extremely nervous about the whole thing, and my adrenaline was at an all-time high. I thought about what would happen if we got caught or if someone got hurt. The seconds were ticking by faster than my heart could keep up.

When Freddy finally yelled out, "You guys ready? Let's go," the reality of it all set in. The last thought I remember having was, *I can't believe this is really happening*, and in a moment's time, we were off.

We went running after the students as though we were in a western movie featuring cowboys and Indians in a battlefield, except we had only our legs, not horses, to rely on to get us in and out of there in a moment's time. Before long, our plan had succeeded without any one of us or them getting hurt. We went in there like a storm, grabbed our hats, and left just as fast as we went in. It was such a weird feeling because taking somebody else's personal property was something that was totally foreign to me, other than stealing from the department store. Nevertheless, I knew that if I wanted to stay in the gang and be respected and accepted as one of them, I had to do what was expected of me, and that was to partake in everything and anything that the gang was doing, without asking questions or going on a guilt trip.

As it turns out, that day each of us left the school grounds with at least one hat. Because it turned out to be so easy and went off without incident, a bunch of us returned to that school a few more times, executed the same plan, and succeeded each time. After a while, it became like a dare—since most of us already had hats and didn't need any more—to see how far we could push the envelope without getting caught.

Everything was going great. We even decided to expand our little scheme by hitting some of the other schools in the area, using the same methods. Our reckless and lawless behavior was riding in high gear. I guess we felt that we were the untouchables and that absolutely nothing could go wrong. Well, we were dead wrong! As it turns out, our arrogant, careless, and somewhat-lackluster way in which we carried out our little operations eventually caught up with us.

Everything started as usual one morning. A bunch of us had skipped school, and we were hanging out in People's Park, a favorite gang hangout located across the street from the school. That morning, Freddy, Oscar, Luis, Mexicano, and I were just hanging out with nothing to do. Oscar mentioned that maybe we should go back to Public School 49 to see what we could find. Freddy declined to go for some reason, but suggested we four should take a trip over there and see what we could come up with.

Without giving it much thought, we collectively decided to go for it and headed for the school, which was roughly about three or four long blocks away from our school. It took very little time to get there, and we quickly established our positions and our plan of attack. However, something in the air that day just didn't feel right. Unlike on our previous hits, this time it appeared as though there were more kids than usual outside during recess for some odd reason. This kind of took us by surprise a little bit. But after giving it some thought, we decided to stay the course and go for it anyway. And that's exactly what we did.

After picking out our targets and trying to go in for a scoop, we were shocked to learn that the extra group of kids that were mingling about the school grounds that day were members of a rival street gang that happened to be hanging around the school at the same time we were there. So as soon as we made our presence known and grabbed our first set of hats, all hell broke loose. We had unintentionally walked into an ambush, and we didn't know it. Suddenly, a swarm of about ten to fifteen gang members—some armed with sticks, bottles, and knives—were upon us. We started to run in all directions as we were being pelted with rocks and bottles and threatened with bodily harm. We were totally unprepared for this, so none of us had any weapons of our own with which to fight back.

Oscar was about thirty feet ahead of me, running down Willis Avenue and trying to get back to our school, when one of the gang members appeared from in between two parked cars and grabbed Oscar just as he was about to turn the corner of 141st and Willis Avenue. As he grabbed Oscar from behind and stopped him in his tracks, I ran to his aid and pushed the guy off Oscar's back, forcing him to break free of the hold. However, what I didn't know then was that the guy was armed with a knife.

So as the guy let go of Oscar to go after me, he turned around wielding a knife and said to me, "Oh, so you want some of this..." He took a wild swing at me that just missed me by inches. I jumped back instinctively as he took another crazy swing, only to miss me again. This time, however, the momentum of his swing was so powerful and wild that it literally forced him off-balance and allowed me to dodge right past him to freedom.

I remember running so fast that day that I made it back to my school in no time. I proceeded to head to People's Park because, in all likelihood, that is where I would probably find the rest of my friends, hopefully in one piece. One by one, we all gathered in the park, and I was happy to see that no one got hurt in the close call.

It's safe to say we were all pissed off and a bit embarrassed that we had to run with our tails between our legs because we were outnumbered. About all we could think about was getting revenge. It got so heated that Oscar was even willing to go home to get his zip gun so we could wage a war on this gang. That idea was immediately shot down by our leader, Freddy, who decided it wasn't worth the payback, especially since we started the whole thing by going into their territory. His was a valid point that had a lot of merit to it, so before we knew it, the thought of revenge was quickly squashed.

After that ordeal, you would think that we learned our lesson... but we didn't. About a month or so after our shaky ordeal, we were back at it again. This time we decided that our target would be Elijah Clark Junior High School 149, which was located on Willis Avenue, about five or six blocks from where our previous school, Public School 49, was located.

Clark Junior High School was very similar to our school, Alexander Burger Junior High School, in size and all, but their grade levels went all the way up to ninth grade, not eighth grade like ours. So, of course, they had bigger and older kids, which made our task a lot riskier to carry out there, instead of at the other grade schools in our area. We did not let that deter us from what we wanted to do, which was go after some more of those beaver hats!

One particular day, there were about five or six of us, minus the president of the gang, who was hitting another school with a bunch of the other gang members, who decided to pull off our plan. Anytime you go into a new territory, there is always a risk that anything could happen or go wrong at any time. So we proceeded to the site with a bit more apprehension and caution than usual, being mindful not to let what happened to us at that other school take place again.

After casing the school for a little bit, we only found a few potential victims who were wearing beaver hats right outside the front of the school. After waiting around for a couple of minutes and not seeing any more hat-wearing students, we decided it was time to make a move. As we approached our targets, we found that no one really put up a good fight, which I guess only encouraged us to continue ripping people off. Although we were only able to make off with two hats, it was just enough to complete our task, and we left the school with a mission-accomplished mindset!

Because it turned out to be so easy, we took our time leaving the area, not one bit worried that we were going to be caught by the cops or attacked by some of the rival gang members from the school. But, man, were we wrong! Within minutes of pulling off what we thought was a perfect hit, one of the guys in the group happened to look over his shoulder and noticed a throng of about fifteen to twenty Black males, all wearing the gang colors of the Black Spades, running our way. Instinctively, we knew they were gunning for us!

Within a matter of seconds, we took off running like bats out of hell in all different directions on Willis Avenue, trying desperately to find our way back to our school. But this time, unlike the previous occasions, we were farther from our school and quite a few blocks off course, making it extremely more difficulty for us to make it back to our safe territory!

In the meantime, Mexicano and I stuck together, and we decided to cut through one of the side streets somewhere in the vicinity of 144th Street, desperately trying to elude the gang members... but it was a little bit too late. By the time we made it midway down 144th Street, a group of about eight to ten gang members soon caught up to us. That day, I remember getting thrown up against a car by about four or five Black teens who then proceeded to beat the living crap out of me.

Another group of about four or five Black teens managed to grab on to Mexicano and did the same thing to him. I got punched, kneed, and kicked in just about every part of my body. It seemed that the more I struggled to fight back or tried to get away, the harder I got hit. After a while, I felt as if I were drowning in a whirlpool of flying fists and ass-whipping kicks that just kept on coming nonstop.

I was just about to go down for the count when the assault suddenly stopped. I heard the muffled voice of one of the attackers say to the others, "I think he's had enough of this shit. Let's get the hell out here right now!" And they all calmly walked away laughing and giggling all the way up the street, satisfied to the max, knowing that they had just beat the crap out of us and taught us a lesson or two about entering somebody else's turf to start trouble.

By the time they left, I was a complete mess. I was hurting all over and bleeding from a bloody nose and cuts on my lower lip. I staggered to one knee as I attempted desperately to regain my composure and catch my breath before getting up. I was tired, shocked, and in a daze, all at once, and felt as though I had just run a marathon, only to be rewarded with a good ass whipping, instead of a trophy, at the finish line!

Looking over to my right I could see that Mexicano, who was about six yards away, was unconscious and not moving. I immediately called out his name, but got no response. Fearing something seriously wrong had happened to him, I quickly approached him and started shaking him as much as I could, until I finally got some response out of him. It was eminently clear from what I saw that he got the worst beating of the two of us. He was hurting from cuts and bruises to his face, head, and ribs, and obviously needed a lot of help in getting up onto his feet and walking again.

We were both mad as hell. We wanted revenge in the worst kind of way, and we wanted it now, not later, but we knew that it would have to wait. For one, we knew right away we were dealing with a well-known notorious gang, the Black Spades from the South Bronx, whose membership numbered probably in the hundreds. And two, they were a lot older than we were, so we knew from the very beginning that taking revenge wasn't going to be an easy task.

After a little while, we managed to make it back to our own stomping grounds in People's Park, where we immediately started looking for Freddy. Freddy was hanging out with a few of the other guys when we found him. They were completely shocked at what happened to us. A few of the other guys involved in this fiasco, who were also beaten up, started trickling in one by one with their individual stories of what happened to them.

For the first time since I'd been in the gang, I could see it in our president's face that he was a bit worried and uptight about the whole situation. His silence as each one of us shared our stories wasn't a good sign. We were outnumbered both in age and pure numbers, and we knew it. It was a David-versus-Goliath situation, and deep down we knew we didn't stand a chance. We knew we would need outside help from another gang or gangs, and we knew exactly where to go for assistance.

My brother, who was the warlord of the Spanish Devils, and Freddy's brother, who was the president of the Social Seven, a chapter of the Spanish Devils, were just who we were looking for. We knew this would be a huge bloody battle if these gangs went at each other, especially since we later found out they were at peace after a previous encounter.

The more we thought about it, the more we realized that the reason this whole thing even took place was due to our stupidity for going into someone else's territory. As soon as we thought about that, we became less inclined to push the issue of payback. Freddy, after discussing the issue with all the members of our gang, came to the same conclusion; it wasn't worth the headache of telling our godfathers, the Spanish Devils and the Social Seven, about this incident. After all, the whole thing would not have happened had we used a little bit of common sense and not entered someone else's territory. Overall, it was pure stupidity on our part, and we paid for it with a big beating.

In all, it was just another lesson in life that leaves you wondering, "What the hell were we thinking?" Oh, and by the way, when I got home that afternoon, I had to tell my parents a big lie in order to explain all the bumps and bruises on my face. I told them I got into a little fight with a kid from another school after he bumped into me outside the school. Case closed!

CHAPTER 28

A BRAND-NEW START

It was the summer of 1969, and boxes were piled up approximately six feet high on the living-room floor . The walls were empty of the decorative mirrors and pictures that once adorned the white, cracked walls around the apartment. The dimly lit kitchen where we once sat as a family to have our dinners was now empty of all the food in the cabinets. About all that remained were a few remnants of uncooked rice, red kidney beans, and dry breadcrumbs on the beat-up linoleum floor. It was a sad day in the life of the tiny little critters and roaming mice that used to feast on any speck of food they could find whenever the lights went out.

And then there was my bedroom—my sanctuary, as I preferred to call it—where dreaming and hoping for a better life became my daily ritual in order to maintain my sanity and peace of mind. The age-old room with decrepit walls and ceilings kind of reflected what my inner fragile soul had endured during my younger years growing up in this apartment, which was now empty and full of cracks.

This was my home, a place that secretly harbored a mixed bag of some of my most painful childhood memories, combined with some of best times of my life. Ironically, it was those same good old times that in the long run had helped me cope with all the adversity I faced as a young child. Moving out of this apartment that held so much personal history wasn't going to be easy. I could only wish that this time a new apartment meant a new start in life and a more tranquil, stable environment for all of us. At least, that's what I hoped!

Our big move was just down the street to 586 East 140th Street, but it was a far cry from the decaying conditions of our present building. The new building, as it turns out, was part of the rebirth of the South Bronx; old run-down and boarded-up buildings were being gutted and refurbished to look like new. It was a slow transition that would eventually spread to other run-down buildings, including my former building in the neighborhood.

Our new building was one of three or four refurbished structures that were finished at about the same time. There was a lot of buzz and excitement about who was going to be picked to move into the finished building; there was a long waiting list. We were one of the lucky ones to get chosen to occupy this new dwelling, so you can just imagine all the joy and enthusiasm we were feeling at the time.

Ironically, my sister Esther, who had gotten married by then and had a daughter, also ended up getting selected from the list. She moved into the building right next door, 584 East 140th Street, about a year or so later.

One of the major changes that would take a little getting used to—besides the new security system equipped with an intercom and a buzzer to monitor who was allowed access into the building—was our apartment's location within the building. Besides the obvious that we were now on the third floor as opposed to the fourth, our view of the street was no more. Now our view of the outside world was limited to the rear of the building, where several big, unflattering, boarded-up vacant buildings only served as a sad reminder that the line that separates hardship from prosperity is sometimes a very thin one. Nevertheless, it's a change we were all looking forward to and one that we hoped in the long run would be worth the transition. Despite the fact that some of the buildings on the block experienced incredible transformations, the ever-present evidence of gangs, drugs, poverty, and signs of a troublesome neighborhood would remain until years later.

By the time the early 1970s rolled in, membership in the neighborhood gangs had started to lose its luster. With its members growing older and finding interests in other venues, the overall makeup of the gangs began to change over time. While some members just quit outright and walked away from it to become better people, others weren't as lucky and ended up serving time in prison for a variety of crimes or getting killed. In fact, many got hooked on drugs and ended up becoming hard-core junkies, while still others took the other route and sold drugs on the street corners in order to make a quick, but risky buck.

One particular person who comes to mind from those distressing days of the late '60s and early '70s was a Puerto Rican guy nicknamed Skinny. This five-eleven to six-foot-tall individual was nicknamed Skinny by members of the Spanish Devils because of his slender, somewhat-lanky build that made him stand out from the rest of the guys in the gang. However, what Skinny lacked in stature, he more than made up for in his ability to put up a good fight or use violence to intimidate others.

In time, Skinny who was also a first cousin of Negro, the leader of the gang, would turn to drugs and become one of the most notorious and menacing criminals to ever roam the city streets of our neighborhood. His brazen and sometimes-risky ways he committed heinous street robberies in order to support his drug habits became his trademark. He was probably the only guy we all knew who could rip off a local drug dealer's drugs and cash, be shot a total of six times, and live to talk about it next day. The guy had nine lives, everyone said; he had one close encounter after another and still managed to get away with it, over and over again.

One particular day, I had the scary misfortune of actually witnessing Skinny in action. It was a bright, sunny summer day; I was about twelve or thirteen years old at the time and living in our new complex when I decided to step outside onto the stoop to get some fresh air. It was one of those late-summer, hot afternoons, and the streets were full of people enjoying the day. I happened to look up the street and saw Skinny walking down towards my building; he was about thirty yards away. He appeared to be all strung out. His clothes were all disheveled, and he truly looked a total mess.

In the meantime, a young Black male, about eighteen to twenty years of age, had just passed my building and was slowly walking in the opposite direction, right into Skinny's path. That scene gave me a deep, gut-wrenching feeling that something terrible was about to happen. That's when I noticed that as soon as the young Black male was about to pass shoulder to shoulder with Skinny, the unthinkable happened.

Skinny, who gave no outward signs of what he was about to do, quickly turned around and without warning put a claw-type grip around the young man's neck with his left hand, while at the same time violently threatening him with a carpenters-hook knife held to the victim's neck with his right hand. He forcefully demanded that the young man hand over his money, yelling, "Give me all your fucking money, or you're fucking dead, motherfucker!!!"

The shocked young man, who had put up a brief struggle while screaming for help, finally decided that his life was worth more than his money; he handed over all the money he had in his pants pocket. A strung-out Skinny immediately grabbed the victim's money and told him, "Now, get the fuck out of here!!!" Once freed from this ruthless thug, the young man hauled ass up the street, not even hesitating for a second to look back over his shoulder to see if the menacing junkie was pursuing him.

Skinny, on the other hand, with a wad of visible cash clutched in one hand and the knife in the other, calmly put the knife back into his pants pocket and continued to walk off down the street towards my building as if nothing had happened. Without skipping a beat and wearing a deadly smirk on his evil face, without a worry in the world, he slowly proceeded to count the money from his latest robbery.

As he walked past my building that day, no words were exchanged between us. Although he knew that I saw the whole thing go down, he also knew I was Flaco's brother and would not rat him out to the cops, out of fear of being the next victim. So at that moment, the only communication that transpired between us was a quick nod hello and a menacing stare that emanated from Skinny's small, drugged-hazed beady eyes.

Looking back now, I clearly remember how the silent threat from his scary-looking eyes spoke volumes to me that day. Although he said not a single word in that dreadful moment, somehow deep down inside I knew exactly what he was telling me. With that one look, he was reminding me of the street creed or mantra that comes from living life in the ghetto: "You see nothing, you say nothing…you understand, or else!" Those harrowing words can sometimes bear down on you like a ton of bricks and scare the hell out of you, especially when you find yourself in a situation as I did that day, feeling helpless, scared, and confused all at the same time. I wanted to do something to help, but something much more powerful kept pounding in my head and reminding me not to get involved. So I did what most people in that situation would do; I looked the other way and just hoped for the best. One thing that was drilled into my head, even as a young child in my neighborhood, was that a dead hero tells no tales!

In the end, this see-no-evil, say-no-evil mentality plays out like a vicious cycle that has no ending or beginning. As a friend once told me when we were discussing a situation in which someone tried to stop a fight between two people and had gotten shot and killed for his efforts, "If you mind your own business, you'll live a lot longer!"

CHAPTER 29

WHAT GOES AROUND,
COMES AROUND

There's only so much you can get away with as a criminal. So was the case of the notorious Skinny, who over time went on to rob and steal from many innocent victims after that last encounter I had with him. From that day forward, I knew, and so did everyone else in the neighborhood, that it would only be a matter of time before the torrent of violence that governed his life would strike back at him and bite him in the ass.

As luck would have it, it didn't take long before his brazen hunger for the bigger fish took him from robbing people on the street to the more lucrative sticking up of *bodegas* and illegal after-hours joints, or social clubs, in the neighborhood. After a while, the word on the street was that he was on a roll, preying on and ripping off one business establishment after another and getting away with it every single time. Everything was going extremely well for him. He was striking on sevens and elevens on each drop of the dice and winning each time. He was winning big, all right, until one day when he made the mistake of dipping into the same cookie jar one too many times.

It turns out, that this one particular place, a record shop that was a front for an illegal numbers and gambling outlet for a popular neighborhood game called *bolita*. This one particular place had been robbed by Skinny at gunpoint several times within the past couple of months, each hit netting him quite a few hundred dollars. According to the word on the street, Skinny liked this particular store the most because he felt it was an easy hit and he would get away with it every time. During each robbery, he daringly went in without wearing a face mask or any type of disguise to shield his identity because he just didn't give a fuck what happened to him, it was commonly said. Additionally, it was believed he liked working by himself so he wouldn't have to split the money with anyone.

This front, which was located at 276 Saint Ann's Avenue, right around the corner from my home, was familiar to and popular with my family, who liked to gamble on the numbers as well. Coincidentally, one of the biggest *boliteros*, or numbers dealers, at that location happened to be Skinny's very own first cousin Negro, the same well-known and respected tough guy who was the former president of the Spanish Devils street gang. According to neighborhood gossip, when Skinny first hit the illegal numbers joint, the owner approached Negro and pleaded with him to have a talk with his cousin and warn him not to do it again or he would pay for it, in one way or another.

Negro relayed the message to his strung-out cousin, who took it as a challenge instead of a threat. When Skinny robbed the numbers joint again, he was given a final warning. Skinny apparently took it as a joke since there were no repercussions after the second theft, so he decided he'd rob the gambling joint a third time. It was after the second hit, according to rumors, that Negro told the owner to do what he had to do. Negro had warned Skinny many times about this shit, but he didn't want to listen.

When word got out to the owner of the record store that Skinny would make yet another daring attempt at hitting his business on a specific day, the owner prepared himself and hired two hit men. According to the talk on the streets, these two men were ordered to be on the lookout for Skinny and to take him out the minute they saw him anywhere close to his business. It didn't take long before that confrontation would become a reality, and Skinny's days of pulling off robberies would finally come to an abrupt halt.

Approximately two weeks after that warning, Skinny walked in and announced a robbery just as he was accustomed to doing. Little did he know that, this time around, he had a big surprise waiting for him right outside the store. Once inside, Skinny pulled out his gun and proceeded to rob the store for the third and last time. As soon as he opened the record store's door and exited the business, he was immediately confronted by the two hit men who quickly shot him in the head and took off running. Skinny instantly dropped to the ground and was left there to die.

At the time of the shooting, I was hanging out in front of my stoop when one of my friends in the neighborhood came running up to me and yelled, "Skinny was just shot at the record store!!!" I immediately stopped what I was doing and ran down the street.

By the time I got there, a small crowd had already gathered around the scene near the entrance to the record store. Neither the cops nor the ambulance had arrived at the scene yet. It was a fresh scene. As word got out that Skinny had gotten shot, more and more people could be seen running to the scene to take a quick glimpse. It was like a scene straight out of *The Wizard of Oz*, the one in which Dorothy's swirling house comes crashing down on the body of the Wicked Witch of the East, killing her instantly; then all of Munchkinland gathers around to confirm that at last "the wicked witch is dead!"

Although Skinny appeared to be dead, his feet were still twitching slightly as a stream of blood slowly found its way down towards his feet, to right where I was standing. Seeing his feet twitching gave rise to the thought that maybe, just maybe, he still had one more ounce of life in him. However, based on the massive amount of blood loss and the pretty messy scene, we all knew that Skinny's chances of surviving this one were going to be pretty slim.

Skinny was transported in very grave condition to the hospital by ambulance; he later died in the emergency room. Looking back now… it was a scene that I will never, ever forget!

CHAPTER 30

AND THE BEAT GOES ON...

S adly, similar cases to Skinny's became a way of life for so many in my neighborhood… and would continue to do so in the months and years to come! After a while, you kind of get used to it and are not surprised. In fact, before the age of sixteen, I had witnessed, or been personally affected by, tragic incidents of this caliber on numerous occasions.

For example, there was the time when I stepped outside my building one evening and saw a big commotion. Two men were engaged in a heated domestic dispute, right in the middle of the street. Before long, one of the men, who was about six feet tall and weighed a good 250 pounds, punched the other shorter and slimmer guy in the face, knocking him off his feet. As the shorter of the two attempted to get up from the ground to defend himself, he was brought down once again and pinned under the aggressor's 250-pound frame. Having no way to escape, the victim lay there helplessly as the aggressor proceeded to pull out a knife and repeatedly plunge it into the victim's chest, eventually killing him. It was a horrifying scene for anyone to watch, let alone a young child. It stayed with me for a very long time.

Over the years, I noticed that carrying a knife or a gun for self-protection in my neighborhood had become a way of life. In fact, because there were so many guns and weapons on the streets, it wasn't uncommon to hear gunshots and altercations on a pretty regular basis. Sometimes, shots were fired into the air for the pure fun of it; at others, it was done as a way of getting back at someone who either did you wrong or owed you a debt, usually drug related. It got to the point that all you had to do to determine if gunshots were a prank or an assault was wait a few seconds to see if you heard someone screaming for help. That's when you knew someone just got shot.

That was exactly the case one day when Richie, a local drug dealer, got shot in broad daylight. That day, I was at home when I heard a couple of loud bangs that appeared to be gunshots. For a moment after, there was dead silence, and then suddenly I could hear the wailing screams of a female yelling that someone had gotten shot. As the seconds went by, the screaming intensified, and so did my curiosity.

As soon as I left my building to investigate, I found out it was Richie. His body was sprawled out in the middle of the sidewalk, right next door to my building. He was lying facedown on the pavement, his motionless body surrounded by a pool of blood. As I got up close, I could see that he appeared to be bleeding heavily from a gunshot to the head. He was not moving and appeared to have stopped breathing. An unknown female was crouched over his body and crying hysterically while yelling, "Please don't die, Richie; please don't die!" Only a handful of people were with the victim and the female at the time I arrived.

Standing there in this chaotic situation I felt helpless. I just stared and internalized everything I saw, lost in the silence of my thoughts. Once again, I was a bit surprised, but not shocked, that another person I recognized from the block had fallen victim to yet another act of violence. This body just part of the rhetoric in the story of life in my neighborhood, another sad tragedy, another voice silenced forever in the good old South Bronx.

Soon droves of people started arriving at the scene to get a glimpse of the body. Although I noticed that a few people did jump in to try to revive the motionless body in the best way they could, to no avail for he appeared to be a goner, according to a bystander at the scene. Even though this guy was no doctor, he had probably seen this scene repeated many times in his lifetime, certainly enough to know that this gunshot victim was more than likely not going to survive.

Minutes later, the familiar sound of blaring sirens could be heard, the echoing sound no stranger to me or to the residents of the block. Before long, a string of cops and an ambulance had arrived at the scene. Richie was whisked away to the nearest hospital; we later found out he was pronounced dead on arrival.

As is usually the case in situations in which the victim dies as a result of a drug deal gone wrong, nobody claimed to have seen anything or to have known the identity of the culprit when the cops asked. The response was always the same—no! And yet, who could blame them? As horrible as it may seem, nobody wants to be caught in the middle of a drug feud gone wrong by serving as a witness to a crime and thus putting their very own life on the line. Sometimes, it's just not worth it.

The sight of yet another life lost for a senseless reason really tugs at your heart after a while. You instinctively start wondering what his life could've been had he not elected to get involved in the world of drugs. What his family must have gone through to see his life just wasted over a stupid cause. It's unfortunate, but scenes like these are repeated over and over again in a lot of the poverty-stricken neighborhoods throughout the US, where drugs, weapons, and casualties go hand in hand. In the end, it leads to just one thing—another tragic ending!

Over the years that followed, others whom I knew and who decided to go down that same dark path, tragically paying for it with their lives, were Joey, Cano, and Tito, just to name a few.

CHAPTER 31

ONE CLOSE CALL

There were other incidents that affected me personally, but did not have tragic endings, even though the potential was always there. For example, there was the time that I heard the sound of glass breakage coming from somewhere below my apartment, in the rear fire escape of the building. This quickly drew my attention, and when I looked out the window, I saw a former gang member by the name of Ralphie, a junkie from the Spanish Devils, breaking into our downstairs neighbor's home by way of the fire escape. This could have easily been my apartment that he randomly chose to break into that day. And because this guy was a nutcase who was known to carry a weapon, who knows what the consequences would've been had he been confronted or startled by me.

Immediately, creepy thoughts about what could've happened filled my head, especially since I was all alone. The visions of having to confront this guy to defend myself and my own home were just overwhelming. Anyway, I kept as quiet as I could, watching his every move as he slowly made his way into the apartment. He stayed there for only about five minutes or so, before exiting out of the apartment with a pillowcase full of items he had taken from the home. He looked as if he were a deranged, drugged-out Santa Claus carrying a bag of toys. Only this Santa was not there to deliver goods, but to take them away from the less fortunate. To my relief, he left quietly down the fire escape and through the rear yards below, where he soon disappeared in between two abandoned buildings that led on to 139th Street.

Hours later, as soon as she got home from work, the victim's screams and rants could be heard from inside my home. She cursed at the culprit who had the nerve to break into her home. But who could blame her? In essence, this junkie violated her space, he violated her sense of freedom, and finally, he violated her sense of feeling safe and secure in her very own home. All of which were taken away within the blink of an eye.

Ironically, a couple of months later, I saw Ralphie engaged in a fierce knife fight with another junkie, right in the same backyard where he'd last made his escape. Though, that day, no one was seriously hurt in the battle, the potential for someone getting killed was there. The fight was ultimately stopped by a few of their mutual friends before it ended in a tragedy.

A few years later, unsurprisingly, it was also Ralphie who made breaking-news headlines one day when cops and arson investigators moved in to serve him with an arrest warrant for an arson he was accused of committing. Ralphie opened fire on them with a handgun just as they were about to enter into his apartment, which was located in another part of the South Bronx. That incident left several of the investigators dead. Ralphie was wounded and taken into custody by authorities, according to what I read in the *Daily News*. It was a sad story—which didn't surprise anyone, including me—about a man who was literally on the road to self-destruction because of his addiction to drugs. While his case was not an isolated one, it was typical of how the use of and addiction to drugs can destroy a person's life.

My brother, Flaco, was another example of how drugs can literally turn your world upside down in a very short time. As the years went by, my brother's use of casual drugs, like alcohol and marijuana, which is also called pot, started increasing. Soon, his attention started shifting to other drugs, like cocaine, also known as coke, and LSD and sometimes even heroin, in order to get a better high.

And when the lure of making money from the sale of drugs, instead of using it, became a better draw, he decided to get into the business himself and began selling it. Before long, he was hobnobbing with Pepe, one of the biggest local drug dealers in the neighborhood; they became a team to be reckoned with in the drug business, selling drugs out of Pepe's apartment. Thankfully, during my brother's drug-selling years, not once did he sell drugs from our apartment, out of fear that my mother would find out and beat the crap out of him.

In time, my brother was bringing home wads of cash from his drug profits and buying everything he ever wanted—clothes, jewelry, booze, and women. You name it, and he had it. He even carried around two fully loaded guns that I clearly remember. One was a snub-nosed .38 caliber handgun, and the other was a small six-shot .22 caliber handgun. One day, while hanging around in our room, he even pointed one of the guns at me and said, "You see this here, brother; this is power. With this, nobody will ever fuck with you!" To say I almost shit in my pants when he did that to me is an understatement, but he quickly put it away as fast as he'd pulled it out. "I bet I scared the shit out of you, didn't it?" he said before breaking into a big laugh.

His reckless and senseless behavior really pissed me off that day, and I didn't hesitate to let him have it. I told him angrily, "Don't you ever do that again, you fucking idiot!!!" Steaming mad, I immediately walked out of the bedroom! It wasn't until moments later that my brother's pretentious, stupid prank really hit me. *He could've killed me had he accidentally pulled the trigger and let a round go,* I kept saying to myself. And all for what for what reason? So that he could have a big laugh at first, only to cry his ass off later?

I had a tough time sleeping that night because I wasn't sure if I should tell my mom or not. But I decided that, instead, I would let it go for the time being. My hope was that my brother would learn a big lesson from my yelling at him and not talking to him for the rest of the day. The very next day, he apologized to me for the whole incident and promised to never do it again. We made amends, and I'm happy to say he kept his word.

Weeks later, my brother's happy days in the drug business would come to an abrupt end when a bunch of narcotics detectives from NYPD busted his partner, Pepe, and him during a big drug raid at Pepe's apartment. They were both tried and convicted. My brother got the better end of the deal; it called for him to serve two years behind bars, followed by probation. Pepe, on the other hand, ended up getting three to five years behind bars.

After his short stint in prison, my brother came out and, for a good while, stayed out of trouble. Then he was back at it, this time teaming up with a different drug dealer by the name of Joe. It was during this time that he almost lost his life because of another incident involving drugs.

A rival drug dealer, Flaco Pescuezo, who happened to be a former Spanish Devil, got busted by the cops for possession and sale of narcotics. After bonding out of jail a few days later, he decided to come after my brother when he was told by an unreliable snitch on the streets that he had been busted because my brother had ratted him out to eliminate his competition. Enraged over the rumor, he decided to get even with my brother.

On this one particular day, my brother was hanging out on the stoop when Flaco Pescuezo approached and told him, "Hey, Flaco, I want to talk to you about something that happened the other day."

My brother, not suspecting any malice, agreed to talk to him and calmly made his way down the cement steps. My brother told me later that, just as he got to the bottom of the steps, he began to get this eerie feeling that something just wasn't right. He quickly noticed that Flaco Pescuezo was a bit jittery and had this almost-cold-blooded look about his eyes that instantly made my brother feel very uncomfortable. My brother suspected that the conversation they were about to have wasn't going to be about the good old days.

As my brother made small talk with his old buddy, he noticed that Flaco Pescuezo kept one hand in his coat pocket; he was also constantly moving and appeared agitated, as if something was bothering him. The next thing my brother knew, he was being viciously attacked with a big knife by his longtime friend and former fellow gang member. My brother was in the fight for his life, trying to dodge this maniac of a friend who had just lost it and wanted desperately to end my brother's life. Flaco Pescuezo, intending to kill him, violently stabbed him in the neck, stomach, and left arm, while my brother tried desperately to shield himself.

My brother would later tell me that as Flaco Pescuezo was taking stabs at him, he kept repeating, "This is for snitching on me. I'm going to kill your ass!!!" My brother, who had made the mistake of not picking up his guns when he left the apartment, pleaded that he had nothing to do with the bust. Flaco Pescuezo didn't want to hear it.

My brother somehow was able to escape from his attacker and run upstairs to our apartment before collapsing. For a few of days, my brother was in really serious condition at the hospital; he was released after a couple of weeks. Soon after this close call, my brother armed himself with his two guns and began hunting for Flaco Pescuezo around the neighborhood to, as he said, "do him in!"

My brother, not wanting to tell the cops the true story of what happened to him that day, felt that the best way to settle the score with his old friend was to get even on his own terms, to get street justice without involving the police. As a result, he was very uncooperative with the authorities and never told them the truth about what actually happened to him or who tried to kill him that day.

Surprisingly, a few months after the incident, the real truth came out about who really ratted on Flaco Pescuezo. That prompted my brother's old buddy to come looking for him. However, this time, it was to beg him for forgiveness, not to hurt him.

In the end, although the incident nearly ended my brother's life, my brother and his old friend decided to talk it out and put the incident behind them, once and for all, for the sake of friendship. They shook hands, embraced, and continued to remain friends from that day forward.

CHAPTER 32

THE EIGHTH ROUND

By the fall of 1969, I couldn't wait to get back to school. Not only for the educational purposes, mind you, but because I knew that this was going to be my last year of hanging out with most of my junior high school buddies and fellow gang members before we bid farewell and went our separate ways. With that in mind, I wanted to make this last year in school my most memorable and exciting year yet!

It was the first day of school, and just as we had done the previous years, we all met in front of the school prior to the start of classes. However, unlike the years before when everyone was happy and excited to see each other after summer vacation, this year the mood was quite somber and disturbing. No one was talking about the excitement of the summer. Nor were they talking about the fights, the criminal activities, or the girls, for that matter; in short, most of the things that got us in trouble or that we enjoyed throughout the summer were not even mentioned. Instead, there we stood, some with our heads bowed down, some near tears. I had no clue at all what the hell was going on.

Confused and out of the loop, I was afraid to ask any of the guys what the problem was, for fear that maybe, deep down inside, I really didn't want to know. Finally, I decided to take Freddy, the leader of the gang, to the side and ask him what was going on and why everybody was so down.

Without skipping a beat, he put his arm over my shoulders and slowly walked me away from the group. I instinctively knew, right then and there, that what he was about to tell me wasn't good news. He said, "You obviously don't know what happened, right?"

"About what?" I quickly responded.

"Luis"—he paused—"Luis...Luis is dead."

"Luis is dead?" I quickly repeated. "No way. There's no way he's dead!" *Why, he was just with us the other day... on the last day of school,*

I thought to myself, *and having the time of his life with all of us. How could it be?* The questions we all had in our young minds had no real answers or solutions; we'd never know why this had to happen to our dear old friend. It was truly heartbreaking.

I was without words. I was confused, shocked, and in a state of disbelief, all in one shot. I waited for a few minutes to see if maybe Freddy would say he was just kidding, or if Luis would suddenly appear among my friends, and the joke would be on me. But it never happened. Out of disbelief, I instinctively put my head down and began to cry, shaking my head from side to side, not wanting to accept the fact that Luis was dead and gone at such a young age. But he was. And we immediately began to hug and cry on each other's shoulders to console one another over this horrible loss.

That day, out of all the things that I was expecting to hear from Freddy, this was definitely not one of them. The last thing that you expect to hear after a break from school is that of one your dear friends is gone forever. This devastating news hit me like a pile of bricks, for this was the first time in my life and the lives of most of my friends that we had lost somebody that close to our hearts and that young. What a tragedy.

Freddy went on to explain to me, in the best possible way he could, just how Luis so tragically lost his life during the summer. He said, "From what I've been told, Luis and a couple of his friends went swimming at Randall's Island"—a river that runs through a neighboring little island located about five or six miles from where we lived—"one day to cool down, and something went wrong… He ended up drowning."

The dreadful news pretty much ruined my whole day. Physically, my body was in school, but my mind wasn't there. I couldn't even think straight in class. I just wanted to go home. Throughout my whole body, I had this numb feeling that I just couldn't shake. Luckily, I wasn't alone; it affected most of us in the same way, so we kind of had our own little way of supporting each other.

In the end, it was this strong, bonding friendship and brotherhood of the gang that ultimately became the support system we needed, that ultimately helped us deal with this unforeseen crisis so early in our young lives.

CHAPTER 33

LIGHTNING STRIKES AGAIN

A few months had passed since the death of my friend Luis. Most of us, although still mourning his death, were slowly recovering from that tragic incident and were ready to move on with our lives. We were back to doing the normal things we were accustomed to, such as skipping school, getting into fights, and doing the same old little, stupid things that got us in trouble on a regular basis.

Anyway, as I mentioned before, for me and the rest of the gang, slowly but surely, things were improving and getting back to as normal as they could be, considering the circumstances. Pretty normal, that is, until one day my sister Esther called me to her home to tell me, "I have some bad news to tell you."

Bad news, I quickly wondered, *what the hell could it be?* Within a matter of minutes I was at her home.

The worried look on her face told me that what she had to tell me was really bad. She sat me down and slowly broke the devastating news that another one of my best friends had died over the summer. According to my sister Esther, she'd bumped into Maria, the mother of two of my closest friends who once lived in our neighborhood, and she told Esther that Edwin had died from a terrible accident at home. He had just finished taking a shower and was playing around with the air conditioner while still soaking wet, trying to get it working right. He somehow touched a live wire, got electrocuted, and died instantly.

Edwin and his brother Mickey were two of my closest friends growing up in the neighborhood; they used to live in my building at 603 East 140th Street. To hear that I had lost another close friend within a matter of months from each other was devastating, to say the least, and extremely tough to handle, especially at my age. He was only about fourteen at the time of his death, just a kid.

Again, I took this heart-wrenching news extremely hard. I cried for days because, as I said, this was one of my best friends growing up; never in my wildest dreams could I have ever imagined something this tragic happening to him. Who knew that on the day he and his family moved out of our block a few years ago it would be the very last time I would ever see him alive?

Looking back at that time and place in my life, it makes me wonder how I was able to deal with those two very tragic, back-to-back deaths. To lose one close friend at such an early time in your life is pretty traumatic, but to lose two friends within a time span of a couple of months is beyond words, beyond comprehension, and beyond understanding.

I was dumbfounded for many years after that, with little or no solace at their passing. However, what I didn't know then was that those two early incidents were just the beginning of a string of heartbreaking incidents that happened to my friends. It's hard to imagine that by the time I had reached the age of sixteen, I would lose still more friends who succumbed to tragedies and died before reaching the age of adulthood. Here are some of the others.

Cebolla, or Onion Head, as he was known to many because of the shape of his head, was a fellow gang member who died a few years after graduating from our junior high school; he was shot and killed in a drug-related incident that went bad.

Luisito died of an overdose at the tender age of fourteen.

Angelo was tragically shot and killed by a mutual friend of ours by the name of Hector; they were playing with a loaded gun they thought was empty. Hector pulled the trigger and shot Angelo point blank in the head, killing him instantly.

And, finally, John, or Mono for monkey, as he was known to us, was another one of my great friends; he was shot in the back, in a crowded club in Boston, when he was mistaken for someone else who was having an affair with the wife of an enraged and jealous husband.

In total, by the age of sixteen, I had lost more than twelve friends from the old neighborhood. Sadly, many years later, my family and I suffered another heartbreaking tragedy when both my nephew and cousin got ambushed and were murdered in separate incidents. And then, more than three decades after that last horrific tragedy, I lost a second nephew; he committed suicide.

In the first incident back in 1987, my nephew Carlos was at a party, having a great time with his two older sisters, when a male subject at the party got fresh with one of his sisters. Carlos intervened, and heated words were immediately exchanged. During the verbal altercation, the male suspect challenged my nephew to step outside so they could settle the issue man-to-man.

My nieces immediately pleaded with Carlos to just forget about it, but he ignored their pleas and ran out of the door to meet up with the suspect and fight it out. My two nieces ran behind him, still trying to stop him, but by the time he stepped outside to confront the suspect—who, we later found out, was a gang member—the suspect and one of his fellow gang members were waiting for him. Without warning, they pulled out guns and started firing shots at my nephew. With bullets flying all over the place, he jumped to shield his sisters, and in doing so, got shot once in the back, killing him instantly. He was only eighteen years of age at the time of his murder.

The two armed suspects were later arrested, but somehow were able to beat the charges in court. Witnesses, who had positively identified them both as the shooters, refused to testify out of fear of retaliation; instead, they said in court that the two suspects were not the individuals who shot my cousin. Both ended up getting away with murder and never served any time in prison.

This truly devastated everyone in our family. To this day, we are heartbroken over the loss of my nephew and this outlandish verdict!

The other heartbreaking incident took place in April of 1990. That is when my young cousin Nelson and three other young children were ambushed and shot numerous times. According to what we learned from the investigation, the accused had lured the four teens into the back of a schoolyard to talk to them about an incident that took place that week. Unbeknownst to them, the suspect was enraged because he said they had insulted his girlfriend. He told them the truth about why he had asked them to meet, and then he pulled out a 9mm semi-automatic pistol, according to the detectives. At gunpoint, he had all four of them kneel on the ground and shot them one by one. He shot a total of fifteen rounds at point-blank range, killing two and wounding the other two. Sadly, my cousin was one of the two kids who did not survive this horrific ambush. The dead were only fifteen years of age.

The next day after the murder, an arrest was made, and the seventeen-year-old suspect was charged with two counts of murder and two counts of attempted murder. At the trial, he was convicted of all charges and never saw the light of day ever again!

Then many years after these last two tragedies in our family, my nephew Jacob committed suicide by hanging himself in his grandmother's, my sister Esther's, house. His suicide really shocked the whole family, because he was always smiling and was a happy-go-lucky kid who would light up the world with his smile. Because of that, we never suspected that, behind that big, infectious smile, deep down inside he was suffering from depression. We were all so heartbroken because he was only twenty-two years of age at the time of his death; he had so, so much potential…and we thought a bright future ahead of him.

One thing that always stands out in my memory is his lovable attitude and personality. Every time someone in our family would say, "I love you Jacob," he would respond, "But I love you more"! And that's how we will always remember him.

Yes, the tears and the heartbreaks were many through the years, but the memories of the great times I shared with all my departed friends and family will last a lifetime. May they all rest in peace!

CHAPTER 34

BOUNCING BACK

As the school year rolled along, my interest, attitude, and behavior in school was plummeting faster than a skydiver jumping out of a plane without a parachute. My problems began when I started skipping school at an alarming rate, disregarding the what-if-I-get-caught mentality that would normally deter someone from engaging in irresponsible behavior. But my I-don't-care attitude went right along with the new person inside me who was using my bad behavior to mask everything that was troubling me.

In a nutshell, I guess what I was really seeking was a major overhaul in my life, one that would somehow release me from all the baggage that had stigmatized me all these years. At the time, the best way I knew how to channel my anger and hurt was to become a rebel, or what some might call a rule breaker, and just do whatever the hell I wanted to do, instead of what others expected me to do.

As a result, skipping school became part of my daily routine. It was so easy and something I just loved doing. Why, there were times that I would just report to my homeroom class for attendance and slip out the back door while everyone was changing classrooms. I'd then meet up with my friends in People's Park. It was really that easy.

At People's Park, we would plan our day and come up with some of the wildest, craziest things to do with our time. It was during one of those days when I decided to go on my first date. Freddy asked me if I wanted to skip school the rest of the day and go on a double date with him and the girl he was seeing. I took a bold step forward and said, "Sure," knowing darn well that what I really wanted to say was "Let me think about it." I remember being a nervous wreck because while most of my fellow gang members had girlfriends, or at least were seeing someone, this was going to be my first time going on any type of date. I knew this was a big step for me, due mostly to my shyness and inexperience.

Immediately after I said yes, my heart started pounding a mile a minute, and the second-guessing soon began to consume my body and my brain. About all I remember repeating to myself was that phrase made famous by the dynamic crime-fighting duo from the hit TV show *Batman and Robin*—*What now, Batman?*

After skipping school that morning, we proceeded to go to Blanca's apartment; she was the girl to whom Freddy was going to introduce me. Blanca lived about a block away from the school, on East 142nd Street, in a five-story brick building like mine; hence, we didn't have to travel far in case something went wrong, and we needed to run back to the school right away.

As we walked to her building, the tension and the nerves started building at a rapid pace. I was nervous about meeting my date, but I was also just as nervous about going into the unknown and getting busted by her parents, who had no idea that their daughter had skipped school and was bringing some boys home for a good time while they were at work.

After going up the stairs, we finally made it to her doorstep, and I was introduced to Blanca by my buddy's date. Blanca was a stunning, tan-skinned Puerto Rican girl with dark, shoulder-length hair, and a slim build; she was pretty tall and physically developed for her age, which I assume was about thirteen or fourteen at the time.

She invited us into her apartment, and we proceeded to walk right into her living room. One thing I noticed very quickly as I sized her up was that, unlike me, she did not appear to be the shy type. Her personality was bubbly and outgoing. I knew right away that she would be the one to carry most, if not all, of the conversation on this so-called blind date. First impressions told me she had some experience in dating. Right from the jump, her conversations appeared to be very direct and flirtatious; they went right along with the way she carried herself.

"Why don't you sit right here"—pointing to the large sofa in her living room—"and make yourself at home," she told me, "while I get some sodas." She gave me one big, sensuous smile before disappearing into the kitchen.

I said to myself, *Oh boy*, for I knew right away this was going to be one hell of a learning experience for me. And believe me, it was!

Within about a half hour or so, my buddy Freddy took off into one of the bedrooms with his date, leaving me all alone with Blanca in the living room. My nerves were at an all-time high, so I said very little and just smiled a lot, nodded my head in agreement while Blanca just kept talking and talking nonstop.

I was about three feet away from her on the big sofa when Blanca said to me, "Why don't you move closer to me and sit right here," indicating with her hand on the sofa where exactly she wanted me to sit. It was right next to her.

After a bit of small talk… well, about basically nothing, Blanca casually got up and sat right smack down on my lap—a move I wasn't expecting, but accepted with open arms. I was shocked, but pretended not be, and instinctively reacted by wrapping my arms around her like an octopus. Although I was a rookie at this, my intention was not to come across that way and embarrass myself, so I just kind of tried to relax a little bit and let her take the lead, instead of the other way around.

Well, she wasted no time. For as soon as she plopped onto my lap, it was less about talk and more about action. She stared right into my eyes, as the snake charmer that she was, and began to play with my hair in a very seductive and innocent kind of way. I was captivated, spellbound, and hooked, all in one shot, for I didn't know what else to expect. About all I knew is that it felt really good. Whatever she set in her mind to do to me, it was working, and no one knew that better than I did. I was really enjoying the moment, frame by frame, and then it happened. I got physically excited, if you know what I mean. And that's when things got really interesting.

That excitement, which was boiling on both ends by now, started leading to other things, like kissing. *I'm in heaven*, I thought. The feel of her soft lips tenderly kissing mine was out of this world, something that I just could not put into words. Then she shocked me even more when she unexpectedly stuck her silky, wet tongue right into my mouth and started twirling it around my tongue as if there were no tomorrow. Whether it was naïveté on my part or just pure lack of experience, I honestly never knew that when people kissed, they used their tongues to make that ultimate romantic connection. In fact, to be honest with you, about the only thing I knew about kissing at the time was from the images I saw in the movies or on TV. Not even my parents kissed that way at home, as far as I could remember. So, boy was I green!

Although I was shocked and a bit nervous during my very first kiss, I was starting to really enjoy it and didn't want it to end. With my eyes now peeking through my half-closed eyelids, I made sure to take in every impressive moment that Blanca initiated. That helped me relax more and more by the second, leading me to really get into this exhilarating moment of romance, or at least that is how I saw it.

After a few more kissing sessions, I was starting to feel like a pro. I immediately felt as though I was finally taking control of the situation, instead of the other way around. It was great, *perfecto*, magical— And then suddenly, out of the blue, we heard what appeared to be a knock and a tugging of the front entrance door's handle. We immediately thought the worst, that it was one of her parents at the door.

I jumped up in one shot and ran into one of the bedrooms, hiding inside the closet, scared shitless. While Freddy, on the other hand, found a great hiding spot underneath one of the beds. The girls hid as well. But after waiting a few minutes and not hearing anyone enter, we figured it must have been a false alarm. It was; it turns out it was someone knocking on the wrong apartment. Close call though!

The scare was enough, however, to put an end to our little romantic hooky get-together, and we ended up calling it a day. I left the house content, still marveling at the wonderful experience I just had on my first date.

The little romance Blanca and I started that day continued for about a week or so before it was all over. We remained friends in school, and although we parted ways for no apparent reason, deep down inside I knew that a lot of it had to do with the fact that I was so shy. I literally had nothing much to say during our brief relationship to keep it going strong, or at least to make it interesting and fun. So what else can I say, but it was good while it lasted.

In the end, although our little interlude was short-lived, the thrill and excitement of that very first kiss left me thirsting for more!

CHAPTER 35

A CHASE TO REMEMBER

While some of the crazy things we did with our time away from school stand out more than others, like the aforementioned, perhaps none more than the time we almost got busted by the cops for sneaking into a neighboring Catholic school with the intent to steal.

That day, Freddy, Herman, Oscar, and I had skipped school and were hanging out in People's Park when one of the guys suggested that go to St. Luke's School—a school located at 604 East 139th Street, about three blocks from our own school—to try to sneak into the school and see what we could take. It was a great but risky idea, considering school was still in session, and that would mean trying to sneak inside the school while all the teachers and students were still around.

Regardless, we decided to give it a try anyway. When we showed up at the school, we staked it out for a little while before we made our move. We tried several doors around the school, looking for one that was left unlocked or one that we could possibly pry open with one of the folding knives we had in our possession. After trying several doors and not having any luck, we were ready to call it a day, but then Herman yelled that he'd found an open door.

The door, which was located near the 139th Street entrance into the building, it turns out, led right into the boys' locker room. It was a large open area with lockers on all four sides of the wall and wooden benches and chairs that covered a big portion of the locker room. Just inside the door was a long single set of stairs that went from the street level to the locker-room floor below. The wide-open floor plan was perfect for what we wanted to do, which was to hit-and-run with whatever we could find.

We got all excited because this was like a gold mine for us. We knew that wherever there were lockers, there would also be pants with money and other valuables, which was just what we wanted. We decided that only two of us would enter the building, while the other two would serve as lookouts. Freddy assigned me and Herman to serve as lookouts, while he and Oscar would go into the locker room and do the actual stealing.

As soon as they entered the locker room, they began to feverishly search through every unlocked locker they could get their hands on. As they rifled through at least a dozen or so unlocked lockers, they found a few bucks here and there and began stuffing them into their pockets as fast as they could.

Without warning, it happened. Somehow, one of the nuns in the building must have spotted us entering, and she surprised us in the locker room, wasting no time in screaming and chastising us for being in the locker room. She yelled, "What are you boys doing in here? Get out of here right now!!!" But what made us jump into action right away and vacate the premises was when she said, "The police are on the way, and you boys are going to be in big trouble."

That was all we needed to hear. Immediately, Freddy and Oscar grabbed whatever they could get their hands on and ran up the stairs in lightning-bolt fashion, meeting up with us on the street. The school was located near Cypress Street, way at the top of 139th Street; before we were clear of the area, we would have a pretty long walk in the opposite direction towards St. Ann's Avenue. With that in mind, we proceeded to walk as fast as possible down the street.

Although we were a little bit jittery from being busted by the nun, we nevertheless made a good joke of it all as we made our way down the street. And while our little heist didn't get us a lot of money, just chump change, in the end I think it was more about providing us with the subconscious rush of doing something illegal and getting away with it, than about the actual money we sought to make from sneaking into the school.

As it turns out, just when we thought we were pretty much in the clear because we were about one hundred yards from turning the corner onto St. Ann's Avenue, out of curiosity, I decided to take a peek at the school behind us to see if anything was brewing. And sure enough, it was. A cop car was already at the scene, and the police were talking to a few of the nuns who were pointing in our direction, indicating to the cops that we were the culprits who broke into the school. Before I could yell, "Cops," the police were on our asses.

This shit all happened so fast. The next thing I remember is hearing the police siren blaring full blast and the loud sound of screeching tires as the police car slammed to a halt in their attempts to apprehend us. They had pulled up ahead of us, in order to block our path, and were just about to bail out of their police car to grab us. We decided to make a run for it and took off in the opposite direction, towards Cypress Avenue. The screaming and the yelling that went on as the cops told us to "Stop right there" fell on deaf ears as we boldly and completely ignored their orders to stop in our tracks and surrender.

By not stopping, we really pissed them off, and they wanted nothing better than to get their hands on one of us and teach us a lesson or two about disobeying an officer. The cops knew that the only way they were going to get us was if we got tired of running and gave up, but we weren't having it. With the cops hot on our trail, we ran back and forth on the street, forcing the police car to come to a screeching halt every time they thought they had us cornered. This played on like a cat-and-mouse game for what seemed like hours.

I was exhausted and tired, and my legs wanted to give up on me, but I was not about to let it happen and give into the cops. Deep down inside, I knew that the penalty that was waiting for me if I got busted meant big trouble for me from all angles—the law, my school, and most importantly, my parents. In the frenzy of it all, I lost sight of all my friends. As far as I was concerned, at that moment, it was down to just the cops and me, no one else.

In the desperation of it all, winded and out of breath, I decided to make one last-ditch effort to escape by running into an alleyway that was located in between two brick buildings that led to a rear yard. Luckily, it just so happened that the alleyway in between the buildings led to a fenced-in area that divided 139th and 140th Streets, my block. So basically, I ended up in my own backyard after all of that.

Scared straight and not wanting to look back to see if the cops were chasing me on foot, I climbed the six-foot fence and made it to the other side. When I hit the ground, I took a hard fall, but soon recovered and continued to run until I made it all the way to 140th Street. Once there, I hid in the hallway of one the buildings until the coast was clear. After stalling a bit, I later made my way back to People's Park, where this mess first started, and waited there for the rest of the crew to show up.

Nearly an hour after our little ordeal, we were all back together again in the park, counting our blessings and acknowledging how close we came to getting busted over some stupid pocket change that, it turns out, wasn't even enough to buy us a sandwich at the corner deli. After a good laugh and a few what-ifs, we decided it was best to chalk it up as a lesson learned. We vowed that if we ever found ourselves tempted to do something as stupid and as risky again, it better be worth our while and net us more than a little pocket change, a deli sandwich, and a soda.

CHAPTER 36

A CHASE OF A DIFFERENT KIND...
IS STILL A CHASE INDEED

You would think that after that close call, I'd be scared straight, but I wasn't. Shortly after that brush with the law, I was chased again on the streets. This time, however, it wasn't a cop who was hot on our trail, but the school's truant officer who spotted us hanging out on a building's stoop on Brook Avenue, which was about two blocks away from the school.

That day, when the truant officer approached us and identified himself, he told us we had to return with him to school after we told him that we were students at Alexander Burger Junior High School 139. He proceeded to point in the direction he wanted us to start walking and said in his slightly raspy but authoritative voice, "Let's go, fellers. Right now!"

As we got off the building stoop, we started walking slowly towards the school, the truant officer slowly tagging behind us. It didn't take a genius to figure this one out; we were not planning to go easily. After all, this was not our first time dealing with the authorities of the school system or the law, for that matter. So right from the jump, we were already planning to take off on the truant officer, even if it meant one or all of us would get in trouble later on at the school. We just didn't care.

When the truant officer got a little bit complacent and thought he had everything under control because we appeared to be so cooperative, we decided it was the time to make a run for it. And that's exactly what we did. Midway up the block, we took one quick look at each other's faces, and that's when Freddy yelled, "Let's go!" We all took off running. In fact, we were running so fast that we looked like a bunch of horses racing in the Kentucky Derby.

It happened so fast that it caught the truant officer completely off guard. By the time he reacted to the sudden turn of events, we were so far out of his reach that he never really had a chance to catch us, prompting him to quit halfway through the chase. And just like that, he was done for the day!

Luckily, however, since the truant officer didn't really know who we were by name, none of us ever got caught or ended up in the principal's office over this incident.

CHAPTER 37

THE REVOLVING DOOR AT THE PRINCIPAL'S OFFICE

After those last few close calls, you would think I would just, as they say, hang up my sneakers and start working on turning my life around, but it didn't work out that way. Instead, it just added more fuel to the fire and gave me the false sense of security that everything I was doing was the right thing to do. In the long run, it seemed that the more I treaded on thin ice, getting in trouble with the authorities at school, the law, and my parents, the more exciting it became to do the complete opposite of what was expected of me.

Before long, I had made more trips to the principal's office than you can count on both hands. Fighting in class, being disrespectful to teachers, and being disruptive in class landed me in more trouble than I care to remember. However, of all the incidents that classified me as a troublemaker, the one that really stands out the most is the day I was labeled as a thief and someone you couldn't trust. At first, I couldn't think of why they would think of me in that way, but the more and more I thought about it, I could easily see why.

One day when one of the doorknobs from a storage closet in art class went missing, I was the first person whom they accused of taking it, because of both my proximity to the door and my reputation. And although no one really saw me take it that day, my reputation for being a troublemaker and untrustworthy caused everyone to suspect me as being the culprit.

The day I was accused, I wholeheartedly denied it with a straight face. All along, because of my attitude, I guess the art teacher suspected that I had been lying to her from the very beginning, and she was absolutely right. I did take the doorknob! I took it for no good reason other than to do something disruptive or malicious that would get me out of class and in trouble again.

Well, that day when I landed in the principal's office for the suspected theft and I denied it again, the principal said to me, "Since you are not willing to come up with the doorknob, as a punishment, you and the whole class will have to stay after school for a full week of detention until the doorknob shows up."

In those days, a whole week of detention meant an extra two hours of schoolwork after school—which I definitely did not want any part of—and not only for me, but for the whole classroom. *Oops*, I quickly thought to myself, *I really screwed this one up!*

That afternoon, when I got back to the classroom, and the announcement was made about the after-school detention for the whole class, the students all looked at me and gave me the nastiest look ever, as if they were ready to kick my ass after school. Again, I denied taking the stupid doorknob, but they weren't buying it; they immediately started putting pressure on me to either come up with the doorknob or else...

After two days of detention and with the pressure mounting from all those around me, I decided to come forward and admit to taking the damn thing! That day, I remember apologizing to everyone in the class and feeling really bad about putting them through this whole detention and wasting of their free time. Luckily, they accepted my apology, but only after threatening me with some consequences if I let anything like that happen again! I wholeheartedly agreed!

The very next day, I brought in the doorknob, handed it back to the art teacher, and took the punishment handed down to me with pride. But as far as the punishment was concerned, not only did I have to finish up the remaining three days of detention that I had left, but to make things worse, as a bonus I was given an additional two weeks of homeroom detention by the principal. As if that wasn't enough, I also got a big-ass whipping from my mother when the school notified her about my latest episode at school.

All in a day's work! All in the life of a troublemaker in school!

CHAPTER 38

A LESSON LEARNED ...
IS A LESSON EARNED

I was in my final year in junior high school, and I was failing miserably in many of my classes. School was hard. But honestly, I really wasn't putting in the effort I required to get the good grades I desperately needed to graduate that year, and my negative attitude and behavior only made matters worse.

One day, I was in art class, the place where I got in trouble the last time for stealing a doorknob, when I had the misfortune of being in the wrong place at the wrong time. Once again, I ended up getting into trouble. This time, by the same art teacher, I was accused of stealing the wallet from her pocketbook. What happened next will turn out to be one of the biggest life-changing experiences of my life.

That day, the teacher stepped out of the classroom to get some art supplies from another room and left her open pocketbook sitting on her desk. Instead of in the back of the classroom, where I usually sat, I happened to be sitting in the front, right near her desk, so that she could keep an eye on me. A few minutes later when she returned and happened to look into her pocketbook for something, she immediately realized that her wallet was gone. She was infuriated and started coming down on the whole class about her missing wallet.

Since the class had gone crazy—people out of their seats, stuff being thrown around, and a lot of noise being made—as soon as she left the class to pick up her supplies, it could have been any one of us who took her wallet while she was gone. As for me, I was playing around in class, just like everyone else, so whoever took it did it while I wasn't at my desk. I didn't see who swiped her wallet.

The next thing I know, the teacher storms out of the classroom all pissed off and returns less than a minute later with the vice principal, whose office was right next door to our classroom. By now, the classroom is so quiet that you could literally hear a pin drop. As they stood by the doorway, I could see that the teacher was whispering something into the vice principal's ear as they looked my way.

The vice principal nodded his head as though he was in agreement. And then he slowly started walking towards me with a look on his face that could only mean someone was about to get in trouble. Yeah, and that somebody, unfortunately, was me again!

He stopped in front of my desk, called me by my name, and said, "Come with me, young man. We're going to my office."

Feeling embarrassed and humiliated that I got fingered for doing something that I honestly had nothing to do with got me really pissed off. I angrily spoke out in my own defense and said, "What did I do wrong this time?"

To which, he responded, "I don't want to hear it, young man. Just follow me to my office right now!"

Once in his office, the vice principal told me to take a seat in a chair right next to his desk. As soon as I did, I felt the pressure and stress of being in an interrogation room similar to those you see in the movies. The bright lights, the solitude of being around two stone-faced adults staring me down, and the overly tense mood that surrounded the whole environment. To top it off, no one was saying a word. The silence in the whole room only added to the tension and frustration I was starting to feel. It was a horrible position to be in. I started feeling very uncomfortable. As my teacher stood by with her hands crossed over her chest, the vice principal began pacing back and forth within arm's reach of me, as if to employ some type of prosecutorial tactic that would force me to confess to something that I swear I didn't do.

This is some serious stuff, I remember thinking to myself over and over again as I watched the seconds of the clock in front of me tick away. My mind quickly became clouded with what-ifs. I started thinking, *How in the world am I going to prove my innocence when they have already made up their minds that I am guilty beyond a reasonable doubt, even before hearing what I have to say?* I bowed my head in disgust and told myself, *I'm done; these guys really think I did this.* And before I knew it, the questioning began.

"Where is the wallet, young man?" was his first question. That was immediately followed by "You better come up with that wallet right now, or you are going to be in some serious trouble, son."

My throat started to dry up as I struggled to respond to all the questions. It took a little while, but I finally got the courage to speak up and say, "I have no idea what the hell you're talking about. I swear… I didn't take the damn wallet!"

Immediately after I said that, the vice principal got really angry at me and started violently, physically trying to shake the truth out of me by grabbing me tightly around both of my arms. He started yelling right in my face at the top of his lungs, over and over again, "Tell me what you did with it!"

I began to get so nervous that I started crying and professing my innocence. Each time I denied having anything to do with taking the wallet, the vice principal got insistently angrier and angrier by the minute and said he wasn't buying it. He added that I better come up with the wallet, or else he was going to call the police, and I would be arrested.

The nervousness in me soon started morphing into anger, and I began to lash out at the vice principal. "Leave me alone. I already told you I had nothing to do with this!" I told him repeatedly.

Since he knew he wasn't getting anywhere with me, and he saw how upset I was, he let me go and started to back off. But he wasn't done yet, and he wasn't about to raise the white flag and say it was over. Instead, since he'd tried every tactic in the book and come up empty, he decided that a better idea would be to bring in the police. Not wanting to waste a minute longer, he got to his phone and called the police.

Minutes later, a cop, Officer Burr, who walked the beat around the school, showed up. He began to interrogate me as well, but got nowhere. After what seemed like a twenty-minute interrogation, including threatening me with the possibility of facing criminal charges, they gave up. Ultimately, the vice principal, the teacher, and Office Burr came to the unfavorable conclusion that maybe, just maybe, I was really telling them the truth this time; perhaps someone else did, in fact, take the wallet.

Well, wouldn't you know it, after all those tense moments accompanied by malicious accusations and scare tactics, not to mention all the humiliation and embarrassment that I was put through during that time, they finally discovered that someone else in the classroom had taken the wallet and had hidden it in one of the closets just to give the teacher a big scare. Unfortunately, I was the one who paid the price on this one, and in the end, I didn't get the last laugh.

That day, no one apologized to me, no one excused themselves for pointing a finger at me, and no one even thought to think I was innocent because, after all, I was a known troublemaker.

In the end, no one really cared. In their eyes, I was, and would always be, that troubled kid with a cloudy future, traveling down the wrong side of life. It was up to me to prove them wrong!

CHAPTER 39

SOMEONE WHO TRULY BELIEVED IN ME

Throughout my tumultuous behavior in and out of class, I unfairly offended many people who were just trying to help me turn my life around while I still had a chance. Of all those who tried to lend a helping hand, perhaps none was more inspirational or played a bigger role in my life than my homeroom teacher, Mr. Shapiro, class 8-432.

Mr. Shapiro was one of the nicest, most caring people you could ever meet. More than anything, he cared deeply about all his students. He always preached the value of getting a good education, being respectful to each other, and most importantly, striving to better yourself for the future in order to be successful.

When I acted up in class and gave him a hard time, he didn't take it personally. Instead, he would pull me to the side after class and take the time to give me a pep talk about what I did wrong and about the consequences of my offending character. He was truly an amazing and caring mentor whom I greatly admired and respected.

While I never really opened up to him about all that was troubling me throughout the school year—including all the problems I was having at home, because I was just too embarrassed to even talk about it—somehow he just knew. He could read through the facade of that tough-guy image I so proudly tried to portray. But more than anything, he knew that under that tough shell I was constantly trying to hide behind stood a kid who had the potential of one day becoming somebody in life… if only he was given the chance and the right guidance.

What I will never forget about him is that of all the teachers I encountered while in school, he was the only one who really stood by me during those tough times in my life and never gave up on me. Never was the value of that more evident than on the day I was wrongly accused of stealing the teacher's wallet. They eventually discovered I had absolutely nothing to do with it, but because of my bad reputation and my history, it was only natural that I would get blamed. Let me tell you, that wasn't a good feeling at all. It really made me feel like crap.

That day, just as class was about to be dismissed for the day, Mr. Shapiro called out my name and said that he wanted to talk to me after class. I guess he must have seen that I was still a bit upset about what happened that day, and he wanted to have a chat with me just to make me feel better. Well, as soon as class was dismissed and I approached him, I could tell by the look on his face that he wasn't too happy with me. But more than anything, I could easily tell that he had quite a few things on his mind that he wanted to talk to me about.

He began by telling me to take a seat, and then he sternly lectured me about all the troublesome things I was doing that were really bothering him. He chastised me on just about everything that I was doing wrong in school, from missing classes, fighting in class, and not paying attention, to being disrespectful to him and to some of the other teachers. Lastly, he also reproached me about getting in trouble, both in and out of school, over a barrage of stupid and meaningless activities while hanging around with the wrong crowd.

However, I guess what really hit home was when he touched on the fact that behind this tough persona of mine was a good kid. Someone who, in his eyes, wanted to do the right thing, but just needed some direction. He started with "I see so much more potential in you than being this tough guy," and added, "I see a kid with a lot of dreams, a big heart, and the ability to move ahead to bigger and greater things in life, rather than just wasting your time on the streets with no future. But in order to make that happen, you have to start by making those changes now, and not later. Because if you don't, I can promise you one thing right now; you will never, ever amount to anything positive in life. Other than being that typical guy hanging out on the street corner, trying to hustle up a buck or two. And going nowhere! So, if this is what you want out of life, then by all means just keep doing what you're doing. But if you want a better life for yourself…and you're willing to do all the right things to turn it around… then now is the time to step up to the plate and start making those changes... before it's too, too late!"

Finally, he finished our talk with these words, "Just remember that you, and only you, have the power to make those changes in your life. You just have to believe in yourself. Believe that you can do it, and I can guarantee you will make it happen! And that's it! For in my heart and mind, I honestly believe that one day you will grow up to do great things and be very successful! So here's what I want you to do. I want you to go home and think about everything we just talked about today... and hopefully, just hopefully, it will make some type of sense to you... by the time you come back to school tomorrow, okay?"

After that inspirational speech he gave me, I really didn't have much to say other than "Thank you very much for this wonderful advice, Mr. Shapiro!" before I packed up my books and went home.

By the time I got home that afternoon, my mind was going in a million directions all at once. So much so, that as soon as I got home, I went directly into my room and lay on the bed for what seemed like hours, just to really think this through. To say I was overwhelmed with everything Mr. Shapiro had said to me that day would be an understatement.

But what are my choices, I thought? I could stay the course and continue doing what I was doing, which was really nothing productive, and hope for the best way down the road. Or I could actually do something about it right then and work on taking the proper steps to turn my life around before, as he said, it's too late!

Over the days, weeks, and months that followed that conversation, my attitude towards school and my behavior changed dramatically. Starting with my grades and school attendance, which showed a commendable "big improvement," as compared to my first two years at the school. Even though that meant hanging out less with my school buddies in order to focus more on my schoolwork, I was okay with that.

Going into high school was not something I was considering until Mr. Shapiro sat me down once again and motivated me to start thinking about my future and what I wanted to be when I grew up. I started contemplating possible careers. One in particular kept tugging at my heart more than anything else. And that was to become a professional basketball player, believe it or not. That had been one of my biggest dreams ever since I first got my hands on a basketball, especially knowing that at my age, I was one of the tallest kids in the school and was still growing with every year that went by.

So I started thinking, *Why not? Why not make playing basketball my career? Hey, you never know; maybe someday I'll become the first Puerto Rican basketball player to ever play in the NBA. Wouldn't that be something nice?*

Not wanting to limit my options, just in case that didn't work out for me, I started thinking about a more realistic career, one in which I could possibly help others, doing for them what Mr. Shapiro did for me. I decided that my next-favorite choice would be to become a police officer, a career not only that is known for changing and inspiring the lives of others, but also one where you make a difference just by your mere presence. It was a wonderful field that wasn't foreign to me because my grandfather served honorably as a state police officer in Puerto Rico for quite a few years. Besides my grandfather, I had a handful of cousins who were police officers. So I just knew that being a police officer was something that was already in my blood; all I needed to do was to stay focused and hopefully make it happen one day.

By the time the end of the school year approached, I had narrowed down my choices of schools to just one—DeWitt Clinton High School. DeWitt Clinton High School was an all-boys high school located in the heart of the Bronx, and it was known for having one of the best sports programs in all of New York City. It was there where some of the best basketball players the city, some of whom ultimately made it to the pros, had come from. My hope was that by going to this school and eventually making the team and doing well, it would hopefully be my ticket into the NBA someday. Although, realistically speaking, I knew that my chances of making it into the pros were probably going to be a million to one. Nevertheless, I knew that as long as I kept the dream alive in my head, regardless of the outcome, it would hopefully be enough to keep me motivated to stay in school and out of trouble.

By the time graduation came around, it was sad to leave a school where I had so many good, and quite a few bad, memorable moments with some of the best teachers, friends, and fellow gang members. I'd entered school as a shy kid carrying a ton of baggage from a troubled life at home. But thankfully, I was leaving with a more confident and positive attitude, thanks to all the help, encouragement, and words of support I received from so many of my friends and caring teachers during this really tough journey, especially Mr. Shapiro!

Although I was still a bit shy in my own little way, I was now able to do the things that I wouldn't have even dared to do before I entered this school. I was well on my way down the right path, but I knew that before I could fully commit myself to achieving my goals, I had to do something that I knew deep down inside was going to be very tough for me.

And that was severing the ties with my faithful gang buddies who had a lot to do with helping me through my crises when I needed them most. This somewhat-painful and gut-wrenching move, I knew right away, wasn't going to be an easy one. But it was one that I knew I had to make if I was ever going to turn my life around for a better future. And that's exactly what I did.

As graduation came around—unfortunately some of them didn't even make it to that point because of their grades—we bid our fare-wells. I sadly said my last goodbyes with some reservations, just knowing that this would probably be the last time I would ever see some of my junior high school friends. That day, as I walked down the school steps with the tune of our alma mater still ringing fresh in my ear, I left with no regrets and only smiles. I knew that deep down inside of me I would always have the memories of the good times, the friendships I made through the years, and the life lessons I learned with my friends and from the teachers; they were all stored safely in my heart.

It didn't take long before I was off to the next challenge in my life: high school.

CHAPTER 40

FALLING OFF THE WAGON

While I was excited to be moving on to a brighter chapter in my life after graduation, back home flashes from the past were starting to come back again. My father had taken a bit of a break from his heavy drinking after slashing my sister Mercedes's face with a razor and basically destroying her life. But by this time, he had fallen off the wagon and was back to what he loved doing the most—drinking.

The prospect of alcohol creeping once again into my father's life was definitely the last thing me or my family wanted to deal with after all the horror and turmoil it had previously brought into all of our lives. As in the past, work, money, and hanging out with his friends after work were the key catalysts to this vicious, nightmarish cycle that just never quite seemed to end.

At first, it started out slowly. Hanging out with his drinking buddies once a month on Fridays soon turned into twice a month, and so forth, until it became a part of his weekly routine. Before long, just hanging out on Friday nights was not enough to satisfy his craving for drinking himself into a stupor. Soon Saturdays and even Sundays were added to the equation, once again creating that monster we all dreaded.

Within no time came the sleepless nights once again. My mother and I waited for my father to stumble through the door in the wee hours of the morning, not knowing what to expect next. Just as in the past, the food had to be served hot and steaming by the time he sat down at the dinner table to have his dinner. But it's what happened after he sat down that had us all walking on eggshells.

Conversations would automatically shift from talking about the casual events of the day, to inquiring about my sister. He would make little comments about my sister's love life and dating status, always wanting to know about her every move and whereabouts.

It was for that reason that, come Fridays or weekends, for that matter, my sister, fearing for her safety, would pack her bags, sometimes with her two kids in tow, and stay at a friend's house for a couple of days until it was safe to return home after my father sobered up for the week.

But as the months went by and my father's alcoholic binges and increasingly stalky behavior continued, we all started fearing for our own lives. This was especially true one day when my father took his large 007 folding pocketknife out of his pocket, opened it up, and began making verbal and menacing threats as he spoke about my sister's life. The dining room's wooden table served as a scorecard. Each visible knife serration represented a deviant thought that consumed his troubled mind. Every stab, a moment of anger. Knowing his past history of violence, the sight of my father in possession of that knife was enough to scare the hell out of all of us. The mental abuse and anguish we were enduring at the time would drive any one single person crazy, let alone an entire family.

After each drunken outburst, my mom and I would always follow up with our regular routine the next day—namely, bashing him about all his threatening and out-of-control behavior that made our lives miserable in those wee hours of the morning. But even in his sober state of mind, he couldn't grasp just how much hurt and upheaval he was bringing to his family. He always blamed his booze-induced amnesia for not remembering what took place the night before. His favorite morning-after speech started off with "What did I do...?" or "I don't remember doing that," or "What did I say?" etc., etc., etc. After a while, it was as if it were a broken record that just played the same old tune, over and over again, until you were ready to throw up.

To my mother's credit, she was a fighter. She literally fought tooth and nail to try to keep our family together in the best way she could, as a caring mother and wife. Her tireless efforts to try to discourage my father from drinking always landed on deaf ears. When that didn't work, she even tried threatening to leave him or kick his butt to the curb if he didn't stop drinking, but even that never worked. He knew that she never really followed through on her threats, and so he continued with his drinking binges, always pushing the boundaries more and more with each passing week.

The line started to draw thin after a while. It soon became evident to my mother that he was not going to change, and that his behavior would become more radical, dangerous, and aggressive the more and longer he drank. The threats at home hit the boiling point one day when he threatened my mother with physical harm, thus putting us all in danger.

My mother, in her efforts to protect herself and her family, especially after what he did to my sister Mercedes, came up with an escape plan: leave home at the first sign of danger. Although she knew this wasn't the best plan available—the ultimate plan would have been to walk away from the relationship altogether—but at least it was a temporary plan that would keep us all safe.

As soon as she put her plan into effect, we were literally running around like gypsies, going from house to house whenever my father threatened that there would be trouble when he got home after a night of heavy drinking. After a while, it became a simple equation. (Heavy drinking) times (threats of violence) equals (packing up our bags and leaving the household).

In time, this routine of packing up and running for our safety soon started taking its toll on all of us. On weekends, it was especially hard because sometimes I was sleeping when my mother would wake me up in the middle of the night, saying, "Wake up; wake up. We have to get out of here!!!" And in pajamas, out the door we went. It got to the point that on average, we were literally vacating our home two to three times a month, and sometimes even more, seeking refuge, mental sanity, and safety.

At times, a friend of my sister Mercedes, Carmen, offered us shelter in her apartment, which was located on the opposite side of the street in the same block. From her window, we were able to monitor when my father got home, as well as when he left the building in the wee hours of the morning to look for us. There were times when we saw him exit our building, after not finding us home, and sit on the stoop to drink some more. Angry and blabbering to himself about everything in the world that was pissing him off. Once seated, he would stay outside until he'd finished his beers, and then he would go back into our apartment and conk out.

Hours later, when we gambled that it was safe for my mom and me to go home, my sister Mercedes would stay behind for fear that my father would start up again and do her harm. When my mother and I reentered our apartment, we never knew where we would find my father sleeping. It was always a surprise and a wild guessing game. As before, there were times when he would fall asleep on the sofa, dining-room table, floor, bed, and sometimes even on the toilet. In fact, coming home drunk, he once fell asleep on the train and was robbed of all his money, but that's a whole other story.

Instead of moving my father or trying to wake him up so he could climb into bed, my mother just let him sleep it off until he sobered up. And depending upon how much he'd drunk that night, it could take a very long time. In the meantime, we never disturbed him; we let him wake up on his own and slowly find his to bed. In those days, for whatever reason, my dad and my mother did not sleep in the same bed. Instead, my dad slept on this little sofa bed that was in the bedroom I shared with my brother. My mother, on the other hand, always slept on the living-room sofa.

Once my father was up and about the next day, the stress immediately started up once again. It usually began with my father saying something to the effect of "Where the hell were you when I got home last night?" And that automatically led to a verbal altercation between my parents, which, in turn, then eventually led to another drinking binge. It became a cycle of mental control with no end in sight.

Amazingly, however, through it all, even under all the mental duress and stress that my father inflicted, my mother never gave up the names of the people that protected and shielded us, even when my father insisted on wanting to know who they were. Some of the people involved, like my sister Esther and Carmen, lived right in the neighborhood, so we didn't have to run far at the spur of the moment. Yet others, like Edna and Dalila, both longtime family friends of my sister Mercedes, lived on the other side of town; taking a taxi or a train became our escape form of transportation that took us to their respective homes.

On many occasions, my father suspected that perhaps we were at my sister Esther's home, but he could never prove it. At times, he did knock on my sister's door looking for us, but she always refused to open the door and yelled through it, "Go home; we're all sleeping!" Feeling completely ignored, my father would get pissed off, but he eventually left and went home to sleep it off.

While most of what I've mentioned so far took place on weekends, during the rest of the week there was always a sense of uneasiness and tension that filled the whole apartment. That's because, deep down inside of all of us, we always had this gut feeling that at any time, something terrible could happen.

One particular day, I got home and found my mother crying hysterically. When I asked her what happened, she told me that she had gotten into a big argument with my father, and he had threatened to hit her. As I've mentioned before, my mother was one tough cookie, and I just knew that she was not going to allow any man to hit her or push her around. And that was the scary part!

While venting her anger and frustration, I could tell that she'd just about had enough of the abuse and was willing to do whatever it took to protect herself and her family. Her eyes had this shallow look about them that I'd never seen in her face before. Her body began to tremble uncontrollably, followed by a river of tears that suddenly began rolling down her cheeks. Whatever she was thinking or experiencing at the time was both troubling and alarming.

What happened next really took me by total surprise. She looked me right in the eyes, got on her knees, and said, "*Hijo*"—son—"I promise you that from this day forward, if your father so much as lays one hand on me, I'm going to kill that bastard, so help me God!" She continued, "I love your father with all my heart, but this has got to stop. I am just so sick and tired of all of this abuse, and I refuse to take it anymore!"

The look of hurt and frustration was written all over her face, so I just knew she wasn't going to hesitate to follow through on her threat. I knew she meant business. After hearing this, about all I could do at that point was hope and pray that that day would never, ever become a reality.

Ironically, as bad as my father was and as much turmoil, disruption, and heartache he brought into our family, I could never bring myself to hate him. For whatever reason, I always saw the good side of him. The side of him that was well liked and admired by all his friends, and even family members who didn't know his dark side.

To me, he was a man who gave me everything I ever wanted or asked for. He bought me toys, candy, and would take me out on local trips to the museum, aquarium, theater, playgrounds, and even amusement parks. The shy and gentle man I knew when he was sober was the complete opposite of the monster that surfaced when he was drunk. It was like living with a person with two different personalities, one who went through a wolf-like transformation as soon as the sun went down. As a young child, and later on as a young teenager, I actually got a chance to see this gradual change firsthand.

On quite a few Saturdays and Sundays, he would take me with him to the place where it all happened. It was a small grocery store—or *bodega*, as it is commonly referred to in Spanish—where I could actually see my father's physical appearance morph into that ugly side of him that we all hated and detested. This *bodega*, which happened to be owned by his first cousin Juja and her husband, Felix, became my father's hangout of choice right after work on Fridays and on weekends.

The store, which was located right on the corner of Forest and 160th Streets in a mostly all-Hispanic neighborhood, became the social gathering place for my father's friends and family. It was there that he spent time not only with family members, but also with some of his drinking friends from the neighborhood. The *bodega* became his perfect place to discuss the problems of the world, politics, sports, and even women. There was no topic that was out of the question or not worth talking about. For one, it gave them an opportunity to kill some leisure time, and, two, it was a place where they were able to hang out as friends, share some bonding experiences, laugh, play cards, and sip on cold beer or other alcohol.

On many occasions, the gatherings took place right in front of the store, especially during the summer; they sat on top of empty wooden milk crates that adorned both sides of the store. At other times, they hung out inside the store in an isolated back room that was built especially for that purpose. It was there, in the makeshift room, that you found a game room equipped with a table, chairs, dominos, and playing cards for a perfect night out. It was also there where the combination of alcoholic drinks and food went hand in hand like one happy marriage.

While hanging out at the *bodega* garnered most of my father's attention, a social club that was located on Forest Street was just as popular for a good time with the guys. Although the social club had a dark underground feel to it, it was nonetheless a legal establishment that had a license to serve beer and alcohol up until the wee hours of the morning.

This social club, which was located underneath a six-story, occupied dwelling, was just off the sidewalk. To get to it from the street, you had to go down a set of about six steps to this dark, kind-of-gloomy entrance. Above it was a makeshift sign that carried the name of the club in bold, hand-painted letters. Once inside, there were a bunch of tables and chairs that were used for games of cards or dominos. The social club was also furnished with a regulation-size, coin-operated pool table, a jukebox, and finally a little bar with high barstools for people to gather around the bar to have some drinks. In all, the bar was just like any other bar you would find on any busy street. In this social club, they had all the drinks, food, and amenities that you needed to have a good time. And although it wasn't a big place to hang out in, socializing and having a good time with all your friends is what made it so special.

It was during some of these trips that I took with my father on weekends that I got a chance to see firsthand some of the things that went on during these so-called social gatherings. It was a party of sorts, from what I recalled, where boozing it up was all that mattered. I witnessed how people went from being sober to being inebriated within a matter of hours. At times, it was fun to watch how people's behavior changed over time, as they became silly and said or did the stupidest things. The slurred speech, the dazed look in their eyes, and even their stumbling walk when they went from the card table to the bar to fetch a drink, were just simply amusing. Yet, at other times, it was also scary because I knew firsthand the other side of what alcohol can do to you and all the damage it can inflict on the lives of family members.

After a while, I got used to the overwhelming stench of booze all around me and watched in amazement as the bottles of empty beer cans and cups would pile up on top of the tables as the night went by. I also observed how people became happy, boisterous, or belligerent from the effects of alcohol. I noticed how some individuals' personalities changed right in front of my eyes, and they became aggressive and at times violent, exactly like my father.

I remember, on more than one occasion, witnessing a few arguments and fistfights over trivial nonsense. I guess when you're drinking, any word or statement can easily be misconstrued and lead to trouble. Sometimes a simple game of cards, dominos, or craps, a dice game, led to a big fight, especially if there was money involved. At other times, a mere mix-up of words said over a couple of drinks during a competitive game of pool resulted in a fistfight, even among the closest of friends. Ironically, as bad as that may sound, the heated arguments and fistfights meant absolutely nothing the next day, once everyone involved was sober. A simple handshake and a "Come on... I'll buy you a drink" is all it took to settle the score.

While I witnessed a lot of this negative behavior, I never once got tempted to take a sip of beer or alcohol out of curiosity. The thought of behaving as some of the people I saw just didn't do it for me at the time. Instead, I would spend my time doing other things, such as playing a game of pool, cards, or even a hand or two of dominos with some of the other kids, without the slightest temptation of drinking alcohol. Looking back now, I had a great time just learning and playing some of the same adult games that kept my father busy. In fact, I even went as far as to emulate some of the adults at the club by playing a game of pool for quarters against some of the kids my age who stopped by the social club or went there with their fathers.

But perhaps the main reason I used to love going with my father on those weekend day trips was because it gave me an opportunity to hang out with my cousins, whose parents owned the *bodega*. Although David and Nelson were a few years older than I was, and their two sisters, Irma and Helen, were a little younger, we all got along just great. They were my favorite cousins growing up, and they took me everywhere. It was through David and Nelson that I made a bunch of friends in that neighborhood and learned how to play pool, stickball, and even bowled. I also went to a few parties that included older kids, young teens, and had a blast.

Because of them, I got my first glimpse of what the future had in store for me when I got older. The partying, the socializing, and the flirting with girls were all things I wanted to do, but couldn't because of my age. But I just knew that someday it was going to happen.

One thing that I remember about hanging out with my cousins was the way I was introduced to everyone. "This is my little cousin Robert," they would always say. And although in reality we were really distant cousins, third cousins at that, they always treated me as if I were their own little brother, rather than their cousin. Because we got along so well, there were times that I didn't want to go home and have to deal with the garbage that was taking place there, especially when my father was drinking. Their home was like my second home, and everyone treated me great; I truly loved them for that.

In fact, I discovered that whenever I slept over at my cousins' home, the stress in my life would temporarily disappear. It was a big reprieve from all the worries, frustrations, and sleepless nights I was accustomed to, not knowing what to expect with my father from one moment to the next. The trade-off of not being home was having peace of mind and fun. In the end, getting away from my home turned out to be my own form personal therapy that provided me with an outlet to be a normal kid. It also allowed me to venture into a world of normalcy, even if that sense of normalcy only existed for just a little while. But whatever the amount of time I could get away from home, it was certainly well worth it!

When I look back at what life was like then, the one thing that I remember most of all was how peaceful their homelife was, in comparison to ours. In their home, there was no fighting or arguing—at least not when I was there—between their parents that kept them up all night. No one had to stay up all night because they feared for their safety when their father went out drinking and came back home stone drunk. Instead, everything that I saw and experienced told me they were just one big, happy family in which everyone got along great and treated each other with kindness and respect, the way it should always be!

This is what I wanted in my life. This is what I dreamed about every day, to have peace and tranquility, not only in my home, but in my life in general. Instead, I had to depend on others to calm my inner turmoil and bring peace into my life, even if it was just for one day.

During one of my sleepovers, the world once again came crashing down on me. I remember it being a Saturday when I had one of those busy days at my cousins' house. Towards the latter part of the day, we decided to go bowling at one of the local bowling alleys not far from the neighborhood. After packing a bunch of people into two cars, we headed out to the bowling alley. My father did the usual and stayed with his friends, drinking up a storm at the *bodega*. By the time we got back late that evening, I was too tired to go home, so I went directly to my cousins' house and fell asleep.

When my father got there to pick me up that evening after the *bodega* closed up, I was already out for the count. So instead of waking me up and dragging me out of bed to take me home, they convinced him to let me sleep over, and he agreed. Because my father was pretty intoxicated that night, and they didn't want him walking alone to the bus stop at that time in the evening—making him an easy target for muggers—my father's cousin's husband, Felix, decided to put him in a cab and instructed the cabdriver to take him home. So home he went.

It was about eight the next morning when I was suddenly awakened by my cousins with the frightening news that my father had been critically wounded during what they called a robbery attempt in front of my building. I immediately gathered up all my stuff and headed with them to Lincoln Hospital in the Bronx, where we later learned my father was being treated for a stabbing to his chest.

That morning, I remember breaking down and crying all the way to the hospital as my family rushed me to the emergency room. As soon as we got there, I ran into the intensive care unit where I saw my father lying on a bed. He had tubes everywhere on his body, it seemed. I ran over to him, crying hysterically. He was heavily sedated and in a lot of pain, suffering from a single stab wound to his chest. He could hardly talk and just squeezed my hand as he looked me straight in the eyes to comfort me. His skin was pale, and he looked really bad. As I took a close look at him, I could see that he had tears in his eyes.

A stream of tears quickly started rolling down my father's face as he struggled to speak. He was able to muster a few shallow words, and I was able to pick up a little of what he was trying to tell me. He said something to the effect of "Don't worry, pop"—as he would sometimes call me—"I'm going to be okay." And then suddenly, he fell into a deep sleep, a side effect of being heavily medicated.

The fact that he was able to talk to me brought a big sigh of relief. That day, my cousins and I stayed by his bedside for a long while as he slept.

Soon a doctor walked into the room and called us over to the side to talk to us. He said, "Your father is one lucky man." He proceeded to lift up his fingers to show us just how close my father came to losing his life. He continued, "Another couple of centimeters this way, and it would've pierced his heart…and it would've killed him instantly."

The fear of losing my father this early in my life was an unbearable thought. I fought hard to believe he would be okay and prayed with all my heart he would make it through. Although he was in extremely grave condition when I got to the hospital, the strong hope and faith I had within me somehow assured me that he was going to pull through and make a full recovery from his injuries.

As I prayed by my father's bedside, I was on a roller-coaster ride of emotions and hurt. I noticed that no one from my immediate family was at the hospital. I mean no one! My mother could not be reached at home, and my sisters and brother were nowhere to be found. *Where are they?* I wondered all day. *They should be here with me and Dad.* About all I could think of was my father's grave condition and the whereabouts of my mother and siblings. After waiting many long hours at the hospital, it was clear to me that they would not be showing up. I was totally confused.

It wasn't until I got home later that day that the puzzle pieces started falling into place. As soon as I opened the door to my apartment, I could tell right away that something terrible had happened in my home. The apartment was a complete disaster. It was as though a tornado had swept through the apartment and destroyed everything in its path. Lamps, picture frames, clothes, and glass figurines were broken and strewed all over the place. In all, the place looked like a mini junkyard.

Finally there, among the ruins of the war zone, was my mother. She was sitting at the kitchen table, crying hysterically. The petrified look on her face told a sad story that she just couldn't find the strength to tell me. As I took it all in, I noticed that not far from where my mother was sitting were splatters of blood going from the kitchen entrance all the way to the end of the hallway. Although my mother had not spoken a word to me while in her state of shock, my instincts told me what I really did not want to hear from her. The injuries that my father sustained in the wee hours of the morning did not happen as result of a robbery. Instead, something went terribly wrong between my parents, and it led to my mother stabbing my father in the chest.

But before my mother could utter a single word to me, I gave her a great big hug, and we held on to each other tightly as we both cried. Although it was only minutes, it seemed like hours; we embraced until my mother was able to compose herself enough to tell me exactly what transpired. She started out slowly and proceeded to tell me step-by-step exactly how it all happened.

On Sunday when my father arrived in the wee hours of the morning, he was drunk out of his mind as usual. She said he did what he normally does when he gets home drunk. He had his dinner, engaged in some small talk, and then got onto the subject of my sister Mercedes's not being at home when he got there. Before she knew it, they got involved in a heated argument about my sister's personal life. The argument soon spewed into more sensitive issues about my sister's love life, and my mother just about had enough of the whole ordeal. When the argument got out of control, and my father's threats of physical harm became more and more imminent, she began to fear for her life and started to prepare for the worst.

According to my mother, things started getting really ugly, and my father became enraged, like a mad man, and began to break everything in the house. He was totally out of control and then started focusing his attention on my mother. She says he began to "push and shove" her around the apartment like a rag doll. She didn't know how it was going to end or where it was all leading, and immediately began to fear for her safety.

When the shoving continued and the threat of violence began escalating, she knew she had to do something right away in order to protect herself. She decided that the best thing she could do was to try to make a run for it. She immediately ran into the kitchen and grabbed the first thing she could find to defend herself, a steak knife that she hid in her pants pocket before my father had any chance to see what she was doing.

As she tried to exit the kitchen, my father was "right there." He forcefully grabbed her by the right arm, and in an unprovoked rage, he punched her once in the face. It was at that point when she says she "had to put a stop to this once and for all!" And when my father reached back to hit her with his fist again, that's when she says she "had to do the unthinkable." Without hesitation, she took one quick step back, pulled the knife from her pocket, and "let him have it," stabbing him once in the chest "before he knew what hit him."

According to my mother, as soon as she stabbed him in the chest, the look of hurt and disbelief was written all over his face. He immediately froze in his tracks. He remained motionless and speechless for what, to her, felt like an eternity, before clutching his bleeding chest and staggering out the door, presumably looking for help, while leaving a trail of blood behind him.

"I felt like I was slowly dying and needed help quick," my father later told me, "and if it wasn't for my friend"—a neighbor—"who rushed me to the hospital in his car, I think I would've died right there and then."

I continued to press my mother for answers, and although she felt terrible about what happened, she confessed, "Protecting my life, and the life and safety of my children, was more important to me than anything else. And just as I promised you the other day, even though I love your father with all my heart, I will never, ever let any man put a hand on me. I will kill him first before that happens."

Looking back now, it's amazing how close she really came to putting an end to my father's life; that would have been just one more tragedy for our family. In the end, it was a deep, heartfelt sentiment coming from a woman who had gone through so much trauma and had endured so much misery in her life, all in an effort to keep her family together. It was an ideology that I had a tough time understanding, especially when caught right in the middle of a vicious storm that never seemed to end.

After my lengthy conversation with my mom, I felt drained, helpless, and overwhelmed. I was hurting emotionally, and my mother could see that. She assured me that everything was going to be all right. Yet I had a hard time believing that. About all I could think of at the time was the daunting and painful task of having to go through yet another tragedy in my life because of my father's drunken stupidity.

While I was going through all these emotions, I began to look in the direction of the kitchen and hallway, where all this had taken place. I guess it was my way of trying to put it all together in my desperate search for answers. I shook my head in disgust when I started to think that the reason for all this turmoil in our lives had to do with an emotionally enraged person who had a serious drinking problem. I got extremely upset at that moment and just wanted to punch the hell out of the wall to let out some frustration, but I didn't. Instead, I used all that energy and pent-up anger to pray that things would eventually get better…if not today, then hopefully in the days, weeks, or months ahead.

In the aftermath of this incident, while cleaning the mess left behind in the apartment, I accidentally came across the bloody steak knife that was used by my mother to stab my father. The dried-up blood, which had caked around the blade of the knife, all but assured me that this wasn't just a dream. That it actually did happen.

I started feeling guilty for not being there to stop this horrible tragedy from taking place. But then again, was it really my fault? I wasn't the one who was drinking, I wasn't the one who decided to hit my mother, and I certainly wasn't the one who brought all these problems to our family. It was my father, and only my father, who brought this on himself. I was ready to move on, to leave all the blame and finger-pointing where it should be—on my dad.

That day, the horror of holding in my hand the knife that had caused so much pain and anguish in all of our lives brought back a lot of bad memories from the day my sister Mercedes's face was savagely slashed by my father. As if to wash away all those dreadful memories, I instinctively took the knife and tossed it in the garbage can as soon as possible. I made it a point not to look back as I exited the kitchen, satisfied in knowing that the knife that was used in the stabbing of my father would never, ever be used to hurt anyone else in my family!

Over the months and years that followed after this last ugly incident, the incredible love-hate relationship that my parents carried on between them went on for a very long time. Even though the stabbing would have ended most marriages, common law in my parents' case, it seemed that the longer they stayed together, the more they were willing to forgive and forget, acting as if nothing of that magnitude had ever taken place. For as far back as I can remember, my siblings and I always had a big problem with that unorthodox love-hate relationship. Although we all voiced our strong opinions against their wacky union at one time or another, somehow, someway, they always convinced us that they loved each other and that they were better off together than not.

Looking back now, the one thing that really bothers me is how quickly this whole tragic event was swept under the rug and how nothing was ever done about it. After it was all said and done, there was no judicial intervention because my father blamed the stabbing incident on a robbery gone wrong. There were no counseling or therapy sessions. Each one of us internalized our feelings and dealt with it in our own little way. I prayed for a better life and a better tomorrow!

CHAPTER 41

THE DAY MY PARENTS MADE AMENDS

It took a little while before my parents decided to work things out once again for what felt like the fiftieth time in their lives. Even though they were back together again, it didn't mean my dad had stopped drinking. Instead, it meant that as a condition of his reconciliation with my mother, he was not going to drink as much, and he promised to stay out of my sister's love life for good. He also promised to be a better husband and father and not to put my mother and the family through so much grief and agony ever again!

It had been months since the last tragic event, and so far, so good. He was still functioning at work, but had cut down on his drinking and partying on weekends pretty dramatically. To our joy, his stabbing must have been a wake-up call that really struck home. We were hoping that maybe, just maybe, he had finally realized all the damage his out-of-control drinking had done to all of us over the years, that he was finally starting to feel remorse, and that he was on a mission to change.

But who knew for sure? We had been down this road before many times, and those changes never really stuck. And since we heard these terms from my mother, never directly from my father, we were a bit leery about the whole situation. Our only hope was that this time his actions would speak louder than his words, as they say, and that he would emerge from this whole ordeal a different person.

It had taken some time, but it appeared that he had been making progress and was sticking to his plan as promised. However, although he had made many changes in his life, and we are all breathing a sigh of relief, internally my father was fighting a different battle of sorts that was affecting his health and well-being in ways he could never have imagined.

It seems that after all the years of partying, drinking, and smoking, he had neglected his health to the point that it had started affecting his heart. He had put his heart and body through so much stress and neglect that one day it finally caught up to him. Within a matter of a couple of years, my father suffered two mild heart attacks that basically shut him down for good.

It was while my father was receiving treatment for his second heart attack that his doctor finally told him, "You either give up your drinking and smoking, or you're going to die. It's that simple!"

As sad as that may sound, it took that last statement from his doctor for my father to realize that he had hit rock bottom. It was totally up to him to determine his future. Was he going to live or die? He chose to live.

CHAPTER 42

A ROAD TO RECOVERY

Trying to live a normal life after nearly drinking himself to death wasn't going to be an easy task, and my father knew it. But in the overall scope of things, he also knew that he had no other choice. Although he had cheated death before, having survived a stabbing and two heart attacks, he knew it would only be a matter of time before the tide turned against him and killed him. Having no other alternative, he did what he never foresaw: he decided to live a sober life. That being said, what lay ahead for my father was the difficult task of trying to live a life without the booze, which was easier said than done.

After all, it was the booze that made my dad feel like a different person. It was the booze that transformed him from that quiet, introverted personality we all knew, to that wild, no-holds-barred, daring, out-of-control individual who lived life on his own terms, and who in the end chose to rule his household in the only way he knew how: through the force of intimidation and threats. Losing the power and control that was such a big part of his alter ego became a daily monumental task to handle. Drinking was an addiction that worked as a demonic force that took over his body and soul and made him into a totally different person. Now the moment had come to break free.

It was time to make changes for the betterment of not only his life, but also that of his loving family, whom he single-handedly destroyed and traumatized for so many years. It was time to move forward, to build a new life for himself. It was also a time to start the healing process for those whom he'd hurt; there were so many of us. Finally, it was time to work on gaining back the love and trust we once shared so that we could live happily together once again as a family.

Those were our hopes. Those were our prayers. And those were our dreams. Only time would tell…

CHAPTER 43

THE FOLLOW-UP SAGA

It took a little while for my father to adjust to his new sober lifestyle. In fact, it took quite a few years before we all felt comfortable enough to be around him and his newly transformed self, but he adjusted very well over the months and years that followed. Luckily, he never gave into the temptation of going back to the bottle that once ruled his life.

For in the end, after all was said and done, I think he finally realized that staying clean and sober not only saved his life, but it also brought the entire family all the freedom and happiness we had been missing in our lives while we were under his reign of terror and misery.

May we pray that from this day forward, our family will be able to live a normal, healthy, and happy life... once again! Amen!

CHAPTER 44

MY HIGH SCHOOL DAYS

With my life slowly but surely going back to normal without the evil that alcoholism brought into my life, I was now looking forward to a new beginning of sorts. Starting at a new school, DeWitt Clinton High School, was going to be my key to a better future. Also, by going to a school outside of my community, I would have an opportunity to explore new neighborhoods, make new friends, and finally, meet and mingle with people who shared the same goals and aspirations that I had of being a better person.

In all, I guess what I was really looking forward to was a second chance at a new life. A chance at being able to redeem myself, a chance at being able to live a life without drama, a chance, just a chance, to live in a better world outside of all the gangs, drugs, and alcohol that I was accustomed to living around. All, so that one day I could prove to myself and others that I finally made it! Again, those were my heartfelt hopes… those were the dreams that I planned to make a reality one day.

Over the months that followed, I found myself on a personal crusade, around my old neighborhood and in my new school, to find friends who were not affiliated in any way with the gang culture with which I was so familiar. By weeding out as many negative people in my life as I could, I ultimately found myself surrounded with a good selection of trustworthy friends with whom I shared the same common goals, and who surprisingly liked going to school for a change. However, none of that happened right away.

At my new high school, it was a couple of months before I started making friends; some, it so happens, lived in my block. Soon, not only did I have a whole new set of friends at the school that I could depend on and trust, but also I found myself making new friends in my old block. By mere coincidence, these friends also shared the same big dreams and aspirations of making it in life as I did. Over time, this whole new set of friends from the old block turned out to be life-long friends.

Back at school, life for me could not have been any better. Although I was having a difficult time with the amount of schoolwork, and my grades were not very good, I made a promise to myself that I was going to try to stick it out and give it 110 percent, no matter the circumstances. And let me tell you, it was tough. Because as it turns out, all those days that I either skipped school or did not pay attention in class were finally starting to catch up with me. My reading, writing, and math skills were not even close to the rest of the kids in my classroom; they seemed to be breezing through the work with no problems. I felt like crap, to be honest. And although my confidence was really low, I knew I wasn't about to give up.

As the days and the months went by, some of the work was starting to sink in. I made every possible effort to not allow some of the distractions surrounding me to get the best of me. Over time, even my test scores started improving. So much so, that I went from getting failing or just barely passing grades, or what I call sympathy grades, in my first marking period, to passing most of my classes—with the exception of two classes, English and health education, which I failed miserably—on my final report card.

By the way, it also didn't help that I still had some of the old bad habits that got me in this predicament in the first place. I was absent from school a total of seventeen days in my very first semester alone. Much of that I attribute to health issues, but some was due to just being too lazy to take the long thirty-minute subway ride to school.

This isn't good at all for a kid who wants to be the first Puerto Rican basketball player in the NBA, I thought to myself. *I have to focus more in school if I'm ever going to make my dream come true.* And while I was aware that the odds of making the school team were against me, I knew I had to improve not only my game skills, but also my schoolwork.

DeWitt Clinton High School had one of the best basketball programs in New York City; over the years, they had competed in numerous city and state championships. In fact, quite a few players who graduated from my school actually went on to play professional basketball in the NBA. So I just knew that the caliber of players had to be high; they must've been some of the best all-around students, in both academics and sports. That only motivated me even more; I wanted to be a part of that special group of students who excelled in both.

From this day forward, I tried to convince myself, *I am going to try to work harder and improve my grades in order to become a better student.* But that was easier said than done.

By the end of the first semester, although I had brought my grades up a little, I was still struggling mightily. And as I mentioned before, I failed two out of six of my classes; the others, I just barely passed, which didn't say much for all the effort I thought I was putting in. I guess I was spending too much time trying to perfect my basketball skills, outside of school, and not enough time hitting the books. I was really disappointed in myself. In my mind, I had failed once more on my quest to better myself and ensure a bright future. With that dreadful semester finally over and the Christmas vacation coming up, I knew I would have plenty of time to reflect on my failures and to try to reignite that fire in my belly that got me to this wonderful school in the first place.

The second semester started, and I was doing fantastic! Better than I expected. Not only was I passing all my classes, but also I was passing with flying colors. So much so, that a couple of the teachers even wrote positive comments on my evaluations: "good student, works hard" and "good work and attitude." Seeing those comments only served to motivate me even more and to keep me on track. Everything was going great for me, and I was really enjoying going to school every single day. Things could not have been any better. That is, until my whole world was turned upside down once again…in an instant!

It was about three in the afternoon when school was dismissed. I was on my way home, walking along my usual path towards the train station. I heard footsteps running behind me, as if someone was hurrying to catch up with me to tell me something. I stopped momentarily to look behind me and see if it was someone I knew, but it turns out it wasn't. It was three Hispanic males whom I didn't recognize; they were fast approaching. Since I didn't know them and didn't think they wanted to talk to me, I turned around and continued to walk towards the train station. Out of the blue, I felt this hand tapping me on my right shoulder. I turned around right away and realized it was the same three guys I had just seen running towards me. I soon found myself surrounded, and since I had been in several situations very similar to this one in the past, I knew right away this was not a good thing.

Not much of a conversation took place. They were on a mission to rip me off, plain and simple. I was the target they randomly chose to rob. Not having on me my folding 007 knife—a very popular knife with a five-inch blade and carried by many people in those days—with which to defend myself, I clutched my right fist as tight as I could, while holding my loose-leaf notebook in my left hand, and waited for the inevitable to happen: a mugging.

Surprisingly, it didn't happen. Instead, the tallest of the three got right in my face and tried his hardest to pressure and intimidate me into giving them some money. My refusal to cooperate with them only served to piss them off. Frustrated from not getting any money out of me, the tallest male forcefully grabbed me by my right arm and said to me, "Since you're not giving us any money…we better not see you get on the next train…because if you do…we are going to kick your fucking ass!"

As they marched away ever so slowly towards the train station, they took one quick moment to look back at me to see if I was still standing there or walking away. I could tell they thought this was a big joke, and they were having a big laugh over the whole thing as they made their way into the train station.

By the time they disappeared into the train station, I was still standing there in total disbelief at what had just happened to me. My first instincts were to just walk away and take a bus, or wait until the train left with those punks on it and then hop on the next one. But the more and more I thought about the whole situation, the angrier and angrier I got. *Am I going to let these assholes do this to me and get away with this? No fucking way!* I said to myself.

Soon, visions of my old self started creeping into my mind. So much so, that before I knew it, the ghetto in me had been released, and I was on the warpath once again. Armed with nothing more than a good pair of hard-fisted knuckles and a reinvigorated old South Bronx mentality from my past, I was ready to do battle!

At this point, I was so pissed off that I didn't care if they beat the crap out of me. I was running on pure adrenaline, blinded by the memories that kept pushing me in the back of my mind: being bullied and disrespected in my elementary-school days. Armed with all these hurtful thoughts going through my mind, I was off on a mission.

I quickly entered the train station and rushed up to the platform upstairs before the next train arrived. Knowing that most of the students liked to congregate towards the end of the platform to get into the last car, I decided to head in that direction in the hopes of running into the thugs. As it turns out, my instincts were correct. For right there, at the end of the platform, stood the three thugs I just dealt with; they were surrounded now by a bunch of their friends.

They took notice of me right away as I purposely came to within thirty feet from where they were all standing. They seemed shocked to see me there; the looks on their faces clearly said, "How dare this asshole come up here after we told him not to!" It didn't take long for me to find myself surrounded by the three thugs and the rest of their stupid cronies.

Surprisingly, even though I knew the odds were against me when it came to getting out of this situation without an ass whipping, I wasn't afraid! For in my heart and soul I wanted to fight, believe it or not, just to show these guys that I wasn't going to let them push me around and get away with it. I was ready!

Just as I expected, the leader of the group who had threatened me earlier came right up to me and started pointing his finger right in my face. He said, "What the hell are you doing here? Didn't I just tell you not to come up here? Didn't I tell you that you're not getting on this train? Huh?"

I reached deep down inside my heart and just blurted out the first thing that came to my mind. "I'm getting on that train, and I don't care what you say!" Immediately there was complete silence, as though they could not believe what had just transpired.

I knew that what I just said could get me an ass whipping right then and there, but at that point in time I didn't give a damn. When I got to this level of anger, it was the voice within my heart that took over.

Tired from all the years of being bullied in elementary school, I found myself pulling from all that built-up rage from the past. Regardless of what happened to me, there was just no way I was about to back down from these assholes. *There's no way!* I kept repeating to myself.

As we went back-and-forth for a little while, I could see the train fast approaching, and I knew I had to make a decision right away. It was either skip this train and have them have the last say, or hop on the train and stand my ground! I bravely chose the latter!

The train pulled up, and the thugs all started moving towards the doors. I lagged behind them just a little bit. However, as soon as I saw that all the thugs and their cronies had entered the last cab, I made my move! As I got on the train, the doors quickly closed behind me. I found myself in no-man's-land, with not one friend in that car to help me out if I got jumped.

It didn't take long before I found myself being the center of attention. No one was sitting down, and I felt their eyes glued to me as if they were just waiting for something to happen, as if they were a bunch of hyenas just waiting to attack their prey. At this point, it didn't take a genius to figure out that as soon as the train pulled away from the station, I was in big trouble.

The instigator in this whole thing was in the middle of the crowd and wasted no time in approaching me. Once again, he was right in my face and started yelling, "I see you don't fucking listen! What the fuck is your problem, man?" His voice and tone immediately showed signs of shock and anger, as if he was thinking, *How dare this fucking guy not listen to me? He's making me look bad in front of all my people.*

I began to slowly back off as he inched his way closer and closer to me. The whole time, I was watching his hands, in preparation for any flying fist coming my way. My whole body tightened and got into defensive mode; I was just waiting for the inevitable to happen. I held on to the loose-leaf notebook with my left hand and curled my right hand into such a tight fist that it almost felt as though I was cutting off the circulation. The closer and closer he got to me, so did the crowd who followed right behind his every step.

Soon I felt as though I was being backed into a corner with nowhere to go. It was at that point that I decided I had to do something right away to protect myself, or my ass was in big trouble. I quickly put down my loose-leaf notebook in preparation for a fight. Like a wrecking ball on a crane getting ready to strike a brick building at full force, I pulled my right fist as far back as I could and was ready to let him have it. In one swooping motion, I struck this idiot so hard on the left side of his face that it sent him barreling backwards into the crowd.

Once that happened, I knew I had him. He lost his balance and looked dazed and confused. From that point on, I wasted no time and went right after him again with everything I had in my power. Before long, I was able to put him in a headlock with my right arm around his neck as I pounded his face with my left fist like there was no tomorrow.

In his desperation to break free of my ironclad hold around his neck, he tried everything in his power, including grabbing me and hitting me where he knew it would hurt the most—my balls! When that didn't work, and he found himself in a no-win situation, he started yelling to his boys, "Get this motherfucker off of me right now!!!"

Within seconds, one of his cronies came to his aid and wasted no time in helping out his buddy. I quickly found myself under siege with what appeared to be a five-inch blade with its point right up against my chest. He threatened, "I'll kill you if you don't fucking let him go right now!!!"

Scared for my life at this point, I had no other choice but to let him go. I then braced myself for whatever was going to happen next. The tables had turned. Now I was the one who was put in a choke hold by my nemesis, while two of his buddies, including the one holding the knife, held my arms so I couldn't move or try to get away. I was all by myself on that part of the train. No friends, no Good Samaritans, not even a conductor who could come to my aid. It was just me versus the thugs. That's it!

I was nervous and scared, all at the same time, for I had no idea what was going to happen to me, or how or when this was going to end. About the only thing I knew for sure at this point was that whatever they had planned for me next, it wasn't going to be a good thing.

Somebody in the group began to chant softly, "Throw him off the train...throw him off the train...throw him off the train!" Soon the others joined in, and the chant got louder and louder by the second.

I knew for sure that I was in big, big trouble! Although my nemesis was out of breath from all the fighting, I knew he wasn't going to let me have the last word on the outcome of this intense fiasco.

Instead, he told his boys, "You know what, that's a good fucking idea! When we get to the next fucking stop, let's throw this mother-fucker right off the train!!!" And the chant continued.

I knew it was just a matter of time before they followed through with their threats, and I was kicked off the train just as they said. As the seconds ticked by, the only thing that kept racing through my mind was whether or not I would be set free at the next train stop without getting hurt. *Who knows what these assholes have planned?* I thought to myself. Before I could ponder my fate any longer, the train arrived at what would turn out to be my final destination.

As the doors on the train opened up ever so slowly, about the only thought that ran through my mind was, *Freedom!* The train platform in front of me was my safety zone, and if I could manage to land on it, then I knew at least I had a chance of getting some help. But the bas-tards weren't going to be nice to me and just let me walk off, especially after the hurting I put on my nemesis's pride and ego. So I knew I was in for a rough landing.

It didn't take long for my biggest fears to become a reality. As soon as those doors were wide-open, the bastards followed up on their threats and threw me off the train headfirst. Luckily, however, the only injury I sustained was scraped knees and hands from the impact with the cement platform. I turned to look at them; they were all standing there by the doorway, pointing and laughing at me as though I was the biggest joke in town. This only served to infuriate me even more. I wanted to get even with them in the worst way, but I was easily out-numbered and had no weapons at my disposal.

Instead, I just sat there on the platform, shaking my head in total disbelief and wondering what the hell I did to deserve this. In an instant, everything I had fought so hard to achieve was disintegrating right before my eyes. And for the first time in a very long while, I felt so helpless. More than anything in the world, I guess what really hurt me the most was my pride. I could've just let this one go and not done anything about it, or I could've fought back. I chose the latter, and I paid the price for it in more than one way.

To add insult to injury, the bastards decided to go after something they suspected would really hit me hard in the gut: my loose-leaf notebook. My notebook meant everything to me. It represented all the hard work I had put in during the semester to get back on track. To me, having better grades meant better opportunities in life. And looking at the bigger picture, it also meant big changes in my life. A big change in the way I handled my future. In short, my loose-leaf notebook was a symbol of my commitment to the pledge I made to myself to live a more productive and meaningful life. And now, all the hard work and investment that I put into myself was basically looming in the hands of these idiots who were now in possession of my notebook. About the only thing I could do was pray that somehow I could get the notebook back in one piece so that I could go on with my life, but it wasn't to be.

Soon after these thoughts started piling into my head, there in the center of the train's doorway stood my nemesis holding on to my book and laughing. While two of his cronies held the doors open, my nemesis opened up my loose-leaf notebook and began tearing out pages and throwing them up in the air as if he were throwing confetti down onto a parade route. Only, I was the lone recipient of this sad and painful debacle. And it really hurt!

I recall that the wind was blowing so hard that day that the pages were literally flying all over the place. They were on the platform, the tracks, and the stairs nearby. In short, everywhere! I tried my best to grab as many of the flying pages as I could, but it was a lost battle. The majority ended up on the tracks, especially after the train took off and swept many of the pages from the platform to the train tracks below.

As the train took off, I remember vividly the faces of those punks still laughing from the rear glass window in that last cab of the train. But most importantly, I remember the last words they said to me right before they let the pages go flying: "I'd like to see you do your homework now, asshole!" In a flash after that, the train doors closed, and so did my desire to continue to pursue my education. I was done and deflated.

After this heartbreaking incident in my life, I went home that day looking a mess. And when I told my mother what happened to me, she didn't waste any time calling my brother and telling him everything. Bright and early the next day, my brother and I, along with a couple of his friends from his old gang, all armed with knives, soon found ourselves on the school grounds, searching for all the individuals who'd messed with me. After searching long and wide for more than an hour and not finding them, we came to the conclusion that maybe they were not students that went to my school, but were outside gang members from a different school or neighborhood that hung around with some of the kids in my school. For several more days, we went back to the school at different times during the day, but never got to see them again or found out who they were. So we gave up!

Overwhelmed with everything that had happened in my life, I decided to do the worst thing anybody my age could do: drop out of high school. In doing so, I became just another statistic on the charts of minority high school dropouts, joining my sisters and brother, who all had also dropped out of school at a very young age.

When I told my parents what I intended to do, they were angry and devastated at the same time and said to me, "Maybe you just need to take a little break to figure things out and then go back to school."

I said I would think about it, but I didn't go back, at least not right away.

Getting tired of hanging out in the house and on the streets of my neighborhood, I decided one day to look for a part-time job, just to keep my mind occupied and to stay out of trouble. I got ahold of my cousin Jija and asked her if she knew of anyone who was looking to hire somebody on a part-time basis. *I can fight the boredom while getting paid at the same time*, I thought.

She referred me to an office in a nearby neighborhood; they dealt with community affairs in the area and needed some office help. I managed to get an interview and was soon hired as a clerical worker.

Not the ideal job I was looking for, but being so young and not having any educational background to show for it, what more could I ask for?

I was a couple of months into my part-time job, when I became friends with Thomas, one of my coworkers. He was quite a few years older and midway through his college education while working part-time.

One day, we were talking about school. During the conversation, he mentioned that he couldn't wait to graduate from college so that he could become an accountant. He said it was his lifelong dream to get a bachelor's degree, and then hopefully soon after a master's degree in business as well. Being Hispanic, as I was, he told me that the only way to get out of the ghetto and into a better way of life was by getting an education; according to him, there was no other way. He was steadfast in reminding me that an education was my ticket out of the ghetto and a way for my family and me to have better lives as we got older. I could see how passionate he was about what he wanted to do in life and how much he believed in everything he said. I was really inspired.

For whatever reason, he automatically assumed that I was still in school, only to feel kind of let down when I told him that I had dropped out. After hearing my story and all the reasons I had for leaving school, he said, "It's totally understandable," but added that he was really disappointed that I had chosen to take that path in order to deal with my problems. He didn't hesitate to let me know why I should go back to school instead of just hanging out on the streets or working in what he called "a measly part-time job that has no real future and offers no real benefits."

He went on to say, "In fact, you know what? I used to think the same way you're thinking right now when I was younger. But after going through some similar situations myself, I soon realized that there really is nothing out there for me but to get in trouble and waste my time." He then said, "The only true way to really change my life for the better was by getting an education. It's that simple! It's something I believed in then, but more so now that I'm older. Like I said, getting an education is the best and only way to get out of this ghetto environment. And that's the whole truth, man!"

It was the last few words that he said to me that really hit home. "What you need to do right now is go back to school, get an education, and I promise you, you will live a better life, and you will thank me later. Because, honestly, there's really nothing out here but a life on the streets with no real future. I live in these projects right across the street"—pointing to where he lived—"and getting an education, I know, is going to be my ticket for getting out of here and making something of myself."

After the lengthy talk we had, it must have really struck a nerve deep down in my heart and soul because as soon as I left the office that day, the only thing I could think about was going back to school and the impact that decision was going to have on the rest of my life. By the time the next week rolled around, I had made up my mind and said to myself, *This is it. I'm going back to school!*

That very same week, I told my parents, family, and friends about my decision to go back to school. Everyone was extremely happy and supportive of my decision, especially my parents. No one knew the heartbreaks and consequences of being poor and not getting an education more than they did. They lived through it all, and as they said to me, "It's been very hard on us, so we're happy to see that at least you'll have a chance for a better future than we both did."

And with my parents' blessings, by the time September came around in the fall of 1971, I was already registered at my new school, Morris High School, and was soon well on my way!

CHAPTER 45

GETTING THAT SECOND CHANCE

Morris High School, located at 166th Street and Boston Road in the Bronx, was the complete opposite of my former school. DeWitt Clinton was an all-boys school and known citywide for its excellence in sports programs; Morris High School, on the other hand, was a coed school known more for its academic programs than anything else. And although they had decent basketball and baseball teams, sports were always secondary and did not get as much attention as they did at DeWitt Clinton. Nevertheless, my goal for getting back into school in the first place was to concentrate on getting an education and graduating. But more importantly, if I could do all that and also play varsity basketball for the school, then it would definitely be a dream come true for me.

Unlike DeWitt Clinton, where I barely knew anyone and only had a few friends, Morris's environment was completely different. In fact, during this same period of time, one of my best friends from the block, who attended DeWitt Clinton while I was there, decided to transfer over to Morris High School. In doing so, he soon joined me and several of our other neighborhood friends who also attended Morris. These were my lifelong friends, and having them at Morris just made the difficult transition of switching schools easier. Through them, I soon made more friends at the school, and I began to feel really comfortable with the whole new situation and environment.

Although I didn't do that great in my first semester, I knew it would only be a matter of time before I caught up and became the straight-A or B student that I knew I had the potential of being. Well, that was my hope at least!

My old buddies from the block—Orlando "Colon," his brother Angel "Poucho," and Juan "Mono"—were all average students at Morris High School, just as I was; I felt as if I fit right in. Rounding up the cast of my best friends from the block were Misael, who attended a different high school in the Bronx, and finally Eddie, who went to another high school, but became a part of the group years later. Together, we were a tight-knit group of lifetime friends who lived in the same neighborhood.

Starting with Misael, a charismatic individual with a quick wit, a great sense of humor, and the ability to debate and challenge anyone on any subject, he was a good leader. A sophomore at a different high school, he was the oldest and one of the shortest in the group. He was outspoken, and his ability to put up a good fight never faltered, especially when it came to defending his friends and his family. He was one of the sharpest dressers in the group and loved to party and have a good time!

One day while Misael, Orlando, and I were riding our bikes in an illegal dump site on Hunts Point Boulevard in the South Bronx, Misael found this old beat-up fedora inside a hatbox and decided to keep it. Once home, he began to decorate it with all sorts of fake diamond studs, colorful Magic Marker writings, and wild and crazy designs; that really made it stand out. Within a matter of weeks of wearing this silly hat, someone in the group told him he looked like a sheikh with that hat on. That name soon stuck, and it became his new nickname, Sheikh.

That same day, Orlando also found a fedora, but after taking it home and decorated it in his own style, it still didn't come out as nice as Misael's hat, which really stood out!

Next on the list is Juan, or Mono, as we used to call him. He was a sophomore at Morris High School and was the same age as Misael. He was by far the life of the party wherever we went, always clowning around and messing with people he didn't even know. Although he was Puerto Rican, as the rest of us were, his dark skin and the big Afro gave a lot of people the impression that he was Black, not Puerto Rican. This, by the way, led to a few fights when people made racial slurs about him. We used to say that he was the best Black, Puerto Rican friend you could ever have. And just like Misael, he was a very smart, quick-witted, funny, loyal person and the most caring friend anyone could ever ask for.

Then you have Orlando, or Colon, as he liked to be called. He was the one who was with me at DeWitt Clinton High School before transferring over to Morris High School during the same year that I did. Just like Misael and Juan, he was also in his sophomore year when he transferred and was a year younger than both of them. Mr. Slick was the party animal in the group; he quickly made a name for himself with all the ladies he picked up at parties. Somehow, when the weekends came around, he would always have a party or two for all of us to go to and have a great time. Like my other friends, he also had a great sense of humor and was always playing pranks on people. I can't tell you how many times I cried my ass off from laughing so hard at a prank or a joke that he would pull off on someone just for a good laugh. Let's just say he could've had a great career as a comedian if he'd decided to go in that direction.

Ironically, quite a few years earlier, before I even met him, it was I who pulled a mean prank on him when I hit one of his fingers with a homemade slingshot as he stood talking with his stepfather in front of his stoop. I'll never forget how he jumped and screamed in pain while he cursed the hell out of everybody and their mother. And while he was wincing in pain, I, on the other hand, was laughing my ass off at the reaction I got from hitting my target. How little did I know then that this guy, who was hurting and in so much pain that day, would years later turn out to be one of my best lifetime friends of all time.

Shortly after we became friends, one day I finally confessed to him that I was the one who hit him with the metal clip that day. You can imagine the shock and disbelief on his face when the truth was revealed; it was worth a thousand words. He said, "You son of a bitch, how the hell did you do that?" When I told him how it all happened, he said, "Just the thought of what happened to me that day still brings pain to my fingers like it was yesterday!" He continued to curse the hell out of me in a way that only best friends could ever get away with.

Within minutes, we began to laugh as we recounted the whole crazy incident over and over again. Later that afternoon when we told the rest of the guys about what happened, we had an even bigger laugh. Days after the incident was revealed, the teasing and the jokes just kept on coming. But to his credit, Orlando took it all in stride and laughed along with us. In the end, he knew that it was all in good fun. Wow, what an amazing time and memory!

While Orlando was the joker or prankster in the group, his younger brother, Angel, or Poucho, as we used to call him, was the complete opposite. He was quiet and reserved and kept to himself a lot. As one of youngest in the group, just months older than I was, he just basically went along with whatever plans we had for that day or the weekend. He really never complained about anything and was one the nicest and most loyal friends you could ever have, especially when it came to protecting his friends. He was always the first one in line to do battle in any confrontation that would arise in which there was the possibility of a fistfight. Whether it was a confrontation at a basketball game, a party, or just about any event, if any of his friends were involved in a conflict, he had no qualms about throwing the first punch. To him, "That's what friends are for," he would always say. And loyalty to friends and family always came first!

Finally, we have Eddie, who became the last member to join our little group of lifelong friends years later. More on him in later chapters.

In the end, although we had our share of disagreements and discord throughout the years, we always remained the best of friends, despite our ups and down, and never once did we hold a grudge against each other. Instead, we took great pride in knowing that the true measure of a great friendship is always being there for each other through the good times and the bad times. And that, we certainly did!

Now that you've met my friends for life, here's our story...

CHAPTER 46

MY LIFELONG FRIENDS AND HOW IT ALL BEGAN

W e were a bunch of very young teenagers when we met on the block. We had very similar backgrounds and stories that gave us our commonality, both as individuals and as a group. Most of my friends came from single-parent homes, in which the mother was the sole breadwinner of the household and ran a tight ship. While others, like me, lived in a very unhappy two-parent household that was rampant with domestic violence and abuse. All things considered, although some of us came from broken homes, lived in poverty, and were raised in a gang- and drug-infested neighborhood, for the most part I think we all turned out to be pretty decent kids when you consider everything we were up against during those times.

In general, it could be said most of us came from strong disciplinarian mothers who kept us in line by giving us a good slap in the face when we became disrespectful or did something offensive. In short, I think it was that same discipline that we received early on in our lives that became one of the leading factors that kept us from really drifting down the wrong path.

It was this very strong support system we all shared as best of friends that ultimately became the surviving tool we needed as a group when dealing with some of our toughest moments as teens growing up. This is not to say, mind you, that we were all saints. Quite the opposite, as you will see, but it could've easily been so much worse.

Well, that's "us" in a nutshell—as you will see, a young group of Puerto Rican friends with so much in common and with a lot of great stories to tell!

CHAPTER 47

THE SPANISH CAVALIERS

I believe it was in the summer of 1970 when I met Misael. I lived at 586 East 140th Street, and his building was at 599, basically right across the street from mine. One day, it just so happened that we were both hanging out on the streets in front of our buildings when we somehow crossed paths, struck up a conversation, and soon became friends. Misael, by that time, was already friends with Orlando and his brother Angel, who lived at number 595, and John "Mono" who lived right next to my building at 584. It was through Misael that I was able to meet the rest of my friends and to begin what would ultimately become a great journey of lifelong friendships.

As young teens—I was about thirteen going on fourteen; Misael, Orlando, and John were about fourteen going on fifteen; and Angel was about thirteen or fourteen—we were all high-spirited individuals with a lot of energy and tons of crazy, fun-filled ideas on how to have a good time. I would say that one of the first things we all had in common was the fact that we all loved to play basketball. And although we also played other sports, like baseball and street football, basketball always took priority. Soon we got so good at playing as a group that we decided one day to form our very own basketball team. We called ourselves the Spanish Cavaliers.

With no coaches, team jerseys, or money to join a league, we played against every team around our neighborhood that wanted to put us to the test. We played both good teams and bad teams. It didn't matter. So long as we were playing and having a good time, that's all we cared about. And since we never officially entered our team into an organized basketball league, and basically coached ourselves, we played just about anywhere. We played in basketball courts attached to some of the churches, in youth recreational centers, and in even park playgrounds. Wherever there was a good challenge and a basketball court, we were sure to be there. This was especially true if it involved some of the neighborhood teams that wanted to play us just to prove who had the best team on the block. Most of the time, believe it or not, we would fare pretty well against some of the toughest opponents in the neighborhood.

It got to the point we were playing basketball so much that one day we decided to put up our own makeshift basketball hoop, right in our own backyard. To do that, we ventured into different parks, community centers, and even dump sites, just about anywhere in hopes of coming across a basketball hoop.

As luck would have it, one day someone in one of the area community centers ended up giving us an old, but still functional, basketball hoop. With that problem out of the way, all we needed was something to which to attach the rim. So we searched some more.

It wasn't too long before we came upon the site of a recently demolished building, and there were tons of wooden planks scattered all over the place. So we searched the pile until we found planks that were still in good condition. Using a little muscle and sweat, we grabbed one of the approximately fifteen-inch-by-fifteen-foot wooden planks and dragged it all the way back to the cement yard in the rear of my building. Using a hammer and a bunch of rusty nails, we were able to attach the basketball hoop to the wooden plank. Finally, to finish up the last part of our masterpiece, we used a bunch of oversized nuts and bolts, which we were lucky to have at our disposal, and secured the hoop and plank to the giant cinder-block wall that separated my building from two other neighboring residential buildings. After a good couple of hours of putting this thing together, we became the proud owners of what we later called, our own little ghetto hoop. And just like that... a dream was born!

However, not all dreams come without consequences. In our case, it was the approximately four-foot-by-twelve-foot wrought-iron fire escape that loomed just above us, about seven feet off the ground. And because of the proximity to the basketball hoop, twenty feet or so, the hazard of bumping or banging your head while dribbling or shooting underneath the fire escape was always there. But we still played on, regardless of the situation.

In the end, I couldn't tell you how many times we banged our heads on the fire escape, or how many times we sustained minor injuries from crashing into the cement wall on a drive to the basket. Safe to say, there were many! Luckily, the bumps and bruises were never serious enough to stop us from playing the game we loved so much with our best friends.

Although basketball was everything to us, and we played it just about every day, when we weren't playing basketball, we were riding our bikes all over the place. Riding our bikes in and around our neighborhood kept us out of a lot of trouble. This was especially true on a nice summer day when we would grab our bikes and just start pedaling all over the place in a desperate effort to try and get away from our troubled neighborhood... even if it was just for a few hours.

Sometimes our trips would take us around the neighboring blocks, while at other times we would end up in places in the South Bronx and even Manhattan that we had never been to before. "Have bike, will travel" became our mantra for riding and exploring different places with our two-wheelers.

In fact, it was during one of those days, when we found ourselves smack-dab in the middle of nowhere in Central Park West, Manhattan. It was a good hour or so from home, and we really didn't know where the hell we were going. We just rode and rode until we came across a dirt road that we innocently mistook for a bike trail. So we kept on riding just to see where it would lead us. Big mistake!

We were in the middle of a blind turn when we heard what appeared to be a hard pounding noise coming from the ground. It became louder and louder as we continued to ride our bikes on this road.

Thankfully, one my friends, who was lagging way behind the rest of us, yelled, "Get out of the way! Horses... horses... horses!!!"

As soon as we heard that, we immediately hit the shoulder of the road to get out of the way. All of us, that is, except for Willie, John's older brother who'd tagged along with us that day. He either didn't hear the warning or just wasn't paying attention when we yelled, "Move out of the way!"

The next thing we knew, about six horses were barreling down the road at a full gallop, heading straight towards Willie. We screamed in unison from the top of our lungs, "Get out of the way!!!" It must have worked that time because, to this day, we don't know how the hell he was able to get out of the way so quickly and avoid a near-catastrophic pileup between bike and horses.

That day, the incident not only scared the heck out of Willie, but it also scared the shit out of all of us. In the end, it was a lesson that none of us will ever forget. Horses and bikes on a dirt road don't mix, no matter what!

CHAPTER 48

YANKEE STADIUM:
THE HOUSE OF DREAMS

While bike riding as a group was always a great adventure, there were also those times when riding solo was just as nice, and it gave me an opportunity to escape and explore certain areas of our surrounding neighborhoods on my own.

One particular summer day when I was about fourteen years old, I decided to do just that. So I grabbed my ten-speed bike and just started pedaling to another part of the South Bronx, en route to check out Yankee Stadium. Yankee Stadium was located on 161st Street and Jerome Avenue, a good twenty-some-odd blocks from where I lived on East 140th Street. Never having been there before on bike—I had been there twice before by train—I knew this was going to be a challenge.

It took me a while to find my way there, but I made it. Before long, I was staring at this massive white structure with these giant blue letters that said Yankee Stadium. It was about midafternoon, so there was not much action going on in the area. I decided to ride around the outside of the building for a little bit, just to take in all the history that surrounded this legendary place where some of my favorite baseball heroes had once played.

As I made my way back around to where I first started at the main entrance area, I noticed an elderly gentleman wearing a Yankees baseball cap; he was exiting through one of the large side-entrance doors. From where I was standing at the time, I could clearly see a portion of the baseball field behind him as he was about to shut the door. I wasn't sure who he was, but I figured if he was coming out through that door, he must be affiliated somehow with the Yankees organization. So I worked up the nerve to approach this perfect stranger and introduce myself.

He was extremely pleasant and friendly and extended his hand to me as he introduced himself. He said, "My name is Bill Dickey, and I played for the Yankees for many years. What's your name, son?" I told him my name, and he said, "It's a pleasure to meet you," and I said the same.

Unfortunately for me at the time, I had never heard his name before because it was way before my time. So I was extremely curious. I later learned through my father that the nice gentleman I had just met outside of Yankee Stadium was a Hall of Fame legend from the New York Yankees a starting catcher for the Yankees who was involved in some of the greatest World Series Championships ever won by the Yankees.

I was just about to go home when I decided to ask Mr. Dickey if there was any possibility that I could go in and check out the field.

He hesitated for a brief minute, but after giving it some thought, he decided and said, "Sure, why not?" He opened up the door to let me onto the field with my bike in tow.

As I walked through this enormous white side door with Bill Dickey, I soon came upon the famous Yankee dugout. I was instantly in awe. I couldn't believe my eyes or that I was actually standing on the Yankee Stadium playing field. It was absolutely beautiful!!!

Mr. Dickey must have sensed the shock, awe, and nervousness in me right away because he had this great big smile on his face when he said to me, "Young man, why don't you lean your bike up against this rail"—pointing to the rail of the Yankee dugout—"and walk out onto the field a little bit." I was really nervous about doing that and thought I would get in trouble if somebody saw me out there on the field. But he insisted and said to me in a nice calming voice, "Go right ahead, son. It's all right. Don't worry about it. I'm here with you!"

As I started walking towards this beautifully landscaped, enormous field, I began to get goose bumps all over my body. I walked slowly as I inched my way towards the home-plate area. It was here that so many famous Yankees players had produced some of the greatest moments in the history of baseball. I decided to go into the batter's box so that I could take in the enormity of this great moment in my life.

Looking up at the stands from home plate, I found myself being swept away in the euphoria of this unbelievable moment. I began to daydream that I was a Yankees player, playing in game seven of the World Series. It's the bottom of the ninth with two outs and a three-two count with the bases loaded, the Yankees trailing 4–1. With the sold-out crowd standing on their feet and cheering me on, I take one quick swing on the next pitch and hit the ball into the hemisphere to win the game and another championship for the New York Yankees by a 5–4 win. Boy, what a dream…

Anyway, back to reality. Although I was only there for a matter of minutes, it felt like an eternity. And as I walked away from the field of dreams that day and proceeded to take that long bike ride home, I could only reflect on the wonderful memories from that day and the amazing chance encounter I had with this gentleman, Bill Dickey, a true Yankees legend. His kindness and generosity allowed me not only to dream big that day, but also to believe that everything and anything is possible if you just believe in yourself… and never stop dreaming!

CHAPTER 49

PARTY HARDY

Although riding our bikes and playing basketball in and around our neighborhood in those days kept us from getting into trouble on the streets, as we got a little older, our focus and priorities started to change. We matured quickly and found ourselves playing fewer and fewer sports and getting more involved in other things, such as chasing girls, partying, hanging out on weekends, and combining the use of drugs and alcohol for a good time.

It's tough to pinpoint exactly where or how it all started for me, but one thing's for sure: it happened… and it happened fast. One minute it was all about sports and having fun, and the next minute it was about hooking up with girls, partying on weekends, and getting high on drugs and alcohol.

As far back as I can remember, the influence of drugs and alcohol was something that was always around us. On any given day, you could take a trip down our block and see people smoking pot right out in the open. On the street corners, building stoops, and even inside some of the buildings we lived in. Many of us also had family members at home, friends at school, or knew people in our own neighborhood who either smoked it, sold it, or did both. In any case, because drugs and alcohol was so readily available to all of us at the time, it was only a matter of time before the temptation of using both would find its way into our young and vulnerable systems.

As to who was the first one in our tightly knit group to smoke pot? The answer to that question is unknown. But once it got into the hands of one of my friends and he tried it and liked it, it would only be a matter of time before we were all doing it. And that's exactly what happened.

As I recall, Misael, John, and Orlando were the first ones in our group to smoke pot; Angel and I were the holdouts. Since smoking and drinking usually went hand in hand, Angel and I made a concerted effort to just stick to the drinking part of it and skip the weed. Although drinking and smoking weed wasn't something we did every day, it was something we enjoyed doing whenever we had a little spare cash and went out partying on the weekends, or were just hanging out around the block.

"Feeling good," as we would sometimes refer to it, meant getting high on a bottle of our favorite Colt 45 beer; our favorite wine, Boone's Farm or Thunderbird; and last, but certainly not least, our favorite mixed drink, rum and Coke.

Not having a job to provide the money to splurge on our mini vices sometimes made it a bit difficult for us to buy it, but somehow, someway, we always managed. Using money we scrounged from our parents during the week, we would all chip in to buy the drugs and alcohol we needed to go partying and have a good time. Because the liquor stores in our neighborhood never really carded any of us to make sure that we were of legal drinking age, it was a breeze to buy whatever booze we desired. So long as we had what they wanted, which was money, it was never a problem. When it came to buying pot, drug dealers were so bountiful in those days that you could just about buy it anywhere in our neighborhood. So that was never a problem either.

My very first encounter with smoking weed did not take place with any of my buddies from the block, believe it or not. But instead, with my very own brother, of all people. And this is how it all began for me.

One day when I was about fourteen or fifteen years of age, I accompanied my brother when he went to see a friend of his from the neighborhood who had some of what my brother called "good stuff" for him to try. That good stuff, I soon learned from my brother, was pot. Within a matter of minutes, we were there. And it didn't take long for my brother and his buddy to become buried in this cloud of white smoke from a big homemade joint that my brother's friend had rolled.

At the time, I was sitting next to my brother on this living-room sofa when they began to smoke and passed the joint around to each other as if it were no big deal. My brother still had the joint in his hand after taking a big inhale when he turned to me, sporting this great big smile, and said, "Hey, brother, you want a hit?" I laughed nervously as if to say, *Are you kidding me? You know I don't do drugs, bro*, and said no. But the more my brother insisted and said, "Come on, brother. Try it; it's just one hit," the harder it became for me to continue to say no. Finally, the temptation to just take one hit won me over, and I decided to just do it, once and for all. Little did I know then that this one hit would lead to many more hits and mark the beginning of my journey into drug use.

Two or three puffs later, my mind was swirling in all sorts of directions. I was so high that I immediately lost track of time and where I was. I began to laugh uncontrollably at the littlest, stupidest things that my brother and his buddy said to me, even if it wasn't meant to be funny. I felt as if I were in a warped zone, and everything seemed to be moving in slow motion. Sounds and voices appeared to be mere echoes that bounced off the walls at turtle speed. My breathing became a bit more erratic with every increase in my heart rate. I was as high as a kite and feeling very uneasy.

Panic soon started to set in, and I began to feel a bit scared. Scared of the unknown. Scared of being in this different world that I had never been to before, that basically forced me to function and act differently than my usual self. It was really freaking me out. One moment I was scared to death, and the next moment I was on cloud nine and having the time of my life with my brother and his buddy.

This seesawing went back-and-forth for what seemed like a lifetime, until I was finally able to relax my mind and body just enough to enjoy the strange yet wild journey that was overtaking my system. My thoughts weren't bouncing all over the place, as they had been, and I was starting to feel more and more in control of the situation by the minute. My breathing became more even, and my thoughts and worries more relaxed.

My attitude and demeanor quickly changed. I felt carefree and almost worriless. I felt unafraid to be loud, boisterous, daring, and yes, almost problem-free, all at the same time. Which for a somewhat-introverted person like me felt great!

This crazy high lasted for a good two to three hours before things started leveling off, and I was back to the real world. Reality!

CHAPTER 50

WELCOME TO THE CLUB

The events of that day turned out to be some of the wildest and craziest moments of my life up to that point. After the surprise initiation to drugs, I couldn't wait to tell all my friends about it. So instead of telling them one or two at a time, I decided to wait until we were all together on the weekend to break the news.

As we were accustomed to doing, we got together to hang out over the weekend. After we bought our booze and pot, my buddies Misael, John, and Orlando soon rolled a joint, lit it, and began to smoke in the back of one of the buildings in our neighborhood. Poucho was also there, but at that time, he had not yet smoked pot. I knew I didn't just want to come out and say, "Hey, guys, guess what I did last week? I smoked pot with my brother!" Instead, I decided I would surprise them by waiting until they started passing the joint, and then I would jump right in and join them.

I waited until all three of them had taken a hit and were about to pass it around again for the second round. It was then that I surprised the hell out of all of them when out of the blue I came out and said, "It's my turn. Let me get a hit from that, bro," as I extended my hand to reach for the joint.

Their first reaction was naturally to laugh. They thought I was kidding, so they kind of ignored me, thinking I was just busting their chops. One of them even made the comment, "Who the hell you trying to kid, man. We know you don't smoke!" But that was immediately squashed when they saw me take the joint and like an old pro, slowly begin to inhale it. You should have seen the looks on their faces when they witnessed the smoke disappear and then reappear with every inhale and exhale. One or two quick puffs later, and there would be no doubt in their minds that I had become the newest, welcomed member of our little pot-smoking group.

To say they were all shocked would be an understatement. As the night went on and I told them the story of how my brother first turned me on to smoking pot, there was no doubt in their minds that this wasn't just going to be a one-time thing. And it wasn't!

CHAPTER 51

GET OFF THE WALL AND DANCE

P artying on weekends was always a good time for all of us. "Where's the party this weekend?" became our favorite phrase of the week. There were five of us, so it seemed someone always knew about a party or two on the weekend. However, on those days when there weren't parties or places to which to go, we just hung around the block or played sports. Somehow, we always found something fun to do as a group just to keep ourselves busy. Sometimes, in fact, our partying wasn't limited to the weekends, but it included times we were supposed to be in school. But that's another story.

Anyway, back to partying on weekends. Although we had all these parties to go to on a regular basis, there was a bit of a problem. My lack of dancing skills kept me from venturing onto the dance floor. So when all my friends were out and about on the dance floor having a good time, I was busy "holding up the walls," as the saying goes.

In fact, the main reason I wouldn't dance had a lot to do with my still-somewhat-shy personality. A big part of me wanted to be out there on the floor, but when it was time to break away from the wall to ask a girl to dance, I stopped dead in my tracks and made a quick detour. That was just my way of rationalizing my insecurities about, one, being rejected, and, two, embarrassing myself on the dance floor if the girl happened to say yes.

One day, we were all hanging out around the block, smoking a little pot and drinking a few beers, when Misael said his sister-in-law, Magaly, was having a party, and we were all invited. It was about eleven that night when we got there, and all the stuff we had consumed that night was starting to kick in; we were ready to party and have a good time as soon as we got there. I remember how the place was packed with people, and they were playing some pretty good tunes, so I couldn't wait to mingle with the crowd. That night, because

I was feeling a bit daring after all the pot smoking and beer drinking, I made up my mind that this was the night that I would get my butt off the wall and finally go out there and dance.

I figured that if I was ever going to go out there and cut loose, it was going to be to a slow jam, for starters, where the chances of stumbling over my own two feet would be slim. After scoping out the whole place for my very first dance victim, I saw this beautiful girl out of the corner of my eye. She was standing all alone and leaning on the wall, just as I was. It appeared that she was just waiting for someone to ask her to dance.

I remember she was about my age and very attractive; she really stood out from the rest of the girls at the party. She had the most beautiful long, wavy black hair I'd ever seen and a petite body to go with her pretty face. In fact, she was a bit intimidating for a rookie like me. Although she was an all-around great-looking girl, there was one big problem: she was on the shorter side, and I, of course, was a giant.

After giving it some thought, I decided I wasn't going to let anything get in the way of my meeting such a good-looking girl and having a good time. Rather than just go out there and dance to anything, I waited until they played a nice, slow jam that was more my speed. Finally, the right song was playing, and I actually gathered the courage to approach this girl and hit her with these magical words, "Would you like to dance?" To my complete surprise, she said yes and wasn't turned off by my six-two height, versus her little five- to five-foot-two frame. Onto the dance floor we both went.

Well, everything is going great, I thought. I was moving to the slow jam, staying with the beat, and I was really enjoying myself. Although I didn't say a word to her while we danced—because I didn't know what to say—I was still having a great time. Great time, that is, until I managed to catch a reflection of us in this big-ass mirror on the living-room wall.

The ugly image of my hunching over the body of this poor tiny girl clearly spoiled my first dance within a matter of seconds. What I saw in that mirror really scared the hell out of me. God knows what was going through her mind. I mean, I was literally hunched over this poor girl's small frame with both of my long arms awkwardly wrapped around her like an octopus in distress. I looked like the Hunchback of Notre Dame and a giant octopus, all rolled up into one. It wasn't a pretty picture, to say the least.

Immediately I felt as though the whole world was looking at me. I wanted to end the dance right then and there and go back to holding up the wall for the rest of the night. But I decided to stick it out for the remainder of the dance. I straightened out my posture a bit and pretended nothing was wrong, even though I clearly towered over this girl like the Empire State Building.

By the time the song ended I felt really embarrassed. But like a true gentleman, I kindly thanked her for the dance and slowly walked away. I proceeded to make my way through the crowded dance floor until I found my way to the other side of the room, where I met up with all my friends. For the rest of the night, I didn't dare take another girl to the dance floor, for fear that I might screw it up again and be the laughingstock of the party. So I just stayed in my own little world with the rest of my friends, shooting the breeze and talking about the party scene until the party ended in the wee hours of the morning.

That night, I left the party a bit frustrated, thinking about that awful experience on the dance floor. Fortunately, not a single one of my friends made any negative comments about my dancing abilities; that would've really added to my frustration. Instead, it was the complete opposite; they were happy to see me on the dance floor for the first time, and they encouraged me to do it again at the next party. Although I got my friends' blessings for my efforts that night, deep down I knew I had a lot of work to do in order to overcome some of my self-destructive thoughts and boost my self-confidence. In reality, what happened had less to do with physicality, our height differences, and more to do with psychology, my shyness and insecurities.

I just knew that I had to learn how to go into any situation without worrying about what others think or say about me. Because in the long run, it really doesn't matter. As long as you love the person you are, you will be able to tackle any challenge that comes your way. And that's it!

It took me many years to figure this one out, but eventually I did. And I became a healthier person for it.

CHAPTER 52

THE MAGIC IN A SONG

Looking back now, while school played a major role in teaching me some of life's most important skills, it was music that I credit most with helping me through some the biggest issues I had growing up as a young child… and even later on into my teen years.

Music, as it turns out, was my own little way of getting away from it all. A few hours a day in my bedroom, listening to the music being played on the radio, was all I needed to soothe some of the pain and anxiety caused by issues both at home and in school. It was through music that I felt a sense of reprieve that protected me from the rest of the world. It made me feel relaxed, brought me joy, and allowed me to escape from all that was bothering me…even if it was just for a few hours a day. Ironically, music also gave me hope for a better future and a better life.

Over time, things started getting better for me. My self-confidence was at an all-time high. It seemed everything was going so well for me, with the exception of one major problem that kept resurfacing in my life: overcoming my shyness!

When it came to dating, my shyness played a big role in whether I succeeded in getting a date or waited on the sidelines at a party, social event at school, or elsewhere. It seems that when the time came for me to start rapping or romancing, as they used to say back then, some of the beautiful girls I was meeting at parties or at school, my shyness would quickly kick in, and I just didn't know what to say to keep the conversation going and eventually land a date.

Basically, I would freeze and couldn't take it to the next level. Instead, we would exchange phone numbers, the girl would say something along the lines of "give me a call so we can talk," and I would agree to do just that. But when it was time to make that call, I always had a thousand excuses about why I decided not to do it. On those rare occasions in which I struck up the nerve to give them a ring, I was so nervous and uptight that the conversations always ended up being one-sided. The ladies did most of the talking, while I, on the other hand, became an attentive listener. I just didn't know what to say to keep the conversation interesting and moving forward. I knew I urgently had to improve on that if I ever wanted start dating and have a steady girlfriend.

It turns out that it was through the grace of music that I discovered the missing key to many of my dating woes. All thanks to what I can only explain as the magic in a song that came to my rescue in the most unexpected and unique way, all because of the its words. A song that I credit not only with helping me resolve some of my dating issues, but also with assisting me in finally getting my very first official girlfriend. Let me explain…

One day back in 1972, while I was in my mid-teens, I was sitting around my bedroom, listening to some really cool music that was being played on WBLS, which was a very popular radio station at that time. It was known as one of the best rhythm-and-blues stations in all of New York City. That day, they happened to play this one particular song that really caught my attention. It turns out, it wasn't so much the sound of the music that immediately drew my interest, but the words and the message behind the lyrics that were magic to my ears. I had what I can only define as that aha moment! A moment that to this day, I credit with turning my life around and finally launching my dating and romancing journey, something that had eluded me for so many years.

The song was "Love Jones" by the rhythm-and-blues group the Brighter Side of Darkness. While to the average person a song by any other name is, well, just a song, to me it was my savior. For some reason, the words of that song really clung to me and inspired me to write. I began taking notes and repeating the words I was hearing. Words, that I wanted to say to some of the girls I was meeting at school and parties, but had held back because of my shyness.

In the song, the lead male singer is having a romantic conversation with the love of his life; he is expressing openly his heartfelt feelings for his girlfriend and their special relationship. Remarkably, I myself had never been in that kind of serious relationship with any of the short list of girls I had dated up until that point, but I knew I wanted it in the worst way. Because I was so shy, my relationships never really lasted past the second or third date, if I was lucky, no matter how hard I tried. I was always left with the question: why?

Looking back now at those earlier years in my life, I can clearly see why so many of those dates never really worked out. I later learned that a first date without a decent conversation is a failure. If your first date is filled with only feel-good compliments, a little wit, and some laughter thrown in, you've basically ruined your chances at a second date.

After listening to that song, I immediately began to envision myself as the guy on the record, the one with the smooth talk and ease in the delivery of his words. He was exactly the type of person I wanted to be at that point in my life.

Well, as you can imagine, with all these new ideas about romance running through my head, it didn't take long before I decided to take some action. Within minutes, I headed out the door and took off to the nearest record store in my neighborhood. I ended up purchasing not only the record in question, but also a few others that I thought fit the bill to inspire my new plan; for example, "I Miss You" by Harold Melvin and the Blue Notes. As added insurance and to aid me in my new journey, I also picked up a few self-help books like *I'm OK—You're OK* and *Looking Out for #1* from a local bookstore.

That day, I practically ran home with a handful of records and books, really determined to venture into this new territory and accomplish my goals. After listening over and over again to numerous songs from that same genre, reading those books, and taking numerous notes, I began to map out my own personal thoughts and ideas about what I wanted to say on a first date. However, instead of a long list of paragraphs in my own words, I decided to just keep it brief and simple. Instead, I wrote little one-liners and questions on a piece of paper small enough to take on a date and refer to without my date's knowledge.

Prior to a date, I studied the list and rehearsed until my head was filled with a long list of interesting questions in order to get to know my date. If during a date I got stuck and needed a refresher, I simply excused myself, went to the restroom, pulled out my little list of notes, reviewed them, and then, armed with a new set of questions and one-liners, returned to my date. Over time, I continued with this practice until I got so good at it I didn't need to rely on my notes anymore when going on a date.

And the rest, as they say, is history!

CHAPTER 53

THE 1970s DISCO ERA

L ife in the early '70s was a different world. The disco era was sweeping the country and taking it by storm. Bright lights, spinning mirrored disco balls, platform shoes, bell-bottom pants, colorful shirts, drugs, booze, long hair, big Afros, and last but not least, but perhaps the most important—amazing disco music. It set the tone for all the craziness. The loud, rhythmic, heart-pounding, contagious music made you want to get up and hit the dance floor!

While disco fever spread like wildfire throughout the country, the place most responsible for the birth of all this glamour and glitz is the city that never sleeps—New York City. The hype played out big-time in the entertainment industry, with movies like *Dance Fever*, TV shows like *Soul Train* and *American Bandstand*, and disco-music greats like Donna Summer and the Bee Gees. You couldn't help but get all caught up in the whole craze. And that included me and all my friends from the good old South Bronx.

Being a part of the disco era, for us, meant being hip, as we called it in those days. *Hip* was a common term back then; we used it to refer to ourselves as part of the in-crowd. If you were hip, you kept up with the latest fashion trends that were unique to New York City. In our part of the neighborhood in the South Bronx, you could say we had our very own style and flair in the clothes we wore in those days. We knew that dressing hip meant getting invited to the best parties in the South Bronx, setting new trends in our neighborhoods, and most importantly, gaining the attention of the girls in our neighborhood and at parties.

Over the years, we scored plenty of hits with our very own personal fashion style. Some of the things we came up with really drew a lot of attention. For example, the time I decided to buy a used men's black suit jacket and make some alterations to make it look like an upscale version of a waiter's jacket. I took it to a tailor and had her narrow the waist of the jacket to almost half its size, just above the pockets. Then I had her add a thin red trim around the bottom portion of the jacket, the end of each sleeve, the lapels, and even around the edge of the small handkerchief pocket to make it really stand out. Well, let's just say it was a pretty big hit among my friends. And before long, they too were sporting their own personalized version of what I called the waiter's jacket.

Then there was the old army and air force dress jackets that we personally decorated with our nicknames in big, bold diamond-studded sequins on the top right-hand corner of the pocket. It gave the jackets a very unique and fashionable look to them; when we wore them to school, we got a ton of compliments. I decided to change mine up a little bit by adding a thin yellow trim around the sleeves and lapels of the green army jacket, just as I did with the waiter's jacket. It looked pretty cool, I must admit!

All in all, while some of the things we did in those days caught on really well, other things I did were not as impressive. For example, the time I thought it would be a great idea to take a plain white T-shirt and cut out all sorts of different-shaped holes in it, like circles, stars, squares, and triangles. I then finished it off by decorating the edges of each hole with different-colored Magic Markers. Let's just say it wasn't at all the big hit I had anticipated; it turned out to be one of my worst style failures. While I'm the first to admit that cutting holes in that T-shirt was a really bad idea, nothing will ever top my biggest experimental fashion flop of all time: the Marshmallow Glitter Shoes Fiasco!

Marshmallow shoes were a very popular item in the '70s, especially around the South Bronx. They got that name basically from the one- to two-inch-thick bright-white rubber sole that made them comfortable to wear and fashionable. The shoes themselves came in a variety of colors. However, it was that white, distinctive marshmallow sole on the bottom of these hip shoes that made them stand out from all the other shoes on the market. And even though these shoes looked great just the way they were, I wanted to go one step further and add my own personal touch to make them stand out even a little bit more.

One day while I was getting my clothes ready to go to a party the following day, I took a quick look at my all-white marshmallow shoes lying on the floor at the bottom of my bed and decided that they needed a little bit of a makeover to really stand out. I busted my brain trying to come up with something creative that would give my shoes some color and totally change their look. When out of the blue, it hit me! *Why not add glitter?* I thought. *That would really get a lot of attention and make me look like a fashion mogul!*

Not wasting any time, I soon made my way down to the nearest Woolworth's, which was located about three blocks from where I lived, and purchased a white bottle of multipurpose glue and about three large glass tubes of red, blue, and silver glitter. In no time, I was at my dinner table with paper and crayons in hand, etching out a design that would look good on my shoes. With my final design complete, it was just a matter of transferring it to the shoes and applying the glitter.

Within a matter of hours, I had glued and glittered both of my shoes to look just like my drawing. They literally looked out of this world. They were bright, colorful, and most importantly, way different than any other marshmallow shoes out there. So I couldn't wait to wear them for the party.

The next day when my friends saw my latest invention right before we headed to the party, they were in awe. They couldn't stop laughing at the sight of my bright-ass, colorful glitter shoes. And since we were all high on pot, it didn't take much to get them going. So we laughed for hours.

Everything was going great for me that night, and I was really having a good time and enjoying all the attention I was getting as I walked down the street en route to the party. People were literally gawking at my shoes, laughing and smiling, which didn't bother me one bit because I knew I was wearing something special.

When we were a few blocks from the party's location, we couldn't help but notice that with every single step I took, I left a trail of glitter behind me. So much so, that if someone were tailing me, all they had to do was follow the trail of glitter on the street.

As the night went on, and I moved around and danced a little, I started to notice cracks on the surface of my shoes. I assumed it was dried glue. But with every hour that went by, the all-important front and sides of my shoes became more noticeably cracked and ugly. Before long, not only did my shoes have more cracks than I could count, but now, to make matters even worse, they were starting to peel. I had more cracks and peel then a dry riverbed in a sun-filled desert. The shoes basically were falling apart right before my eyes, and there was not one single thing I could do to stop it from getting painfully worse.

My friends and many of the people at the party quickly caught on to what was going on. Soon the laughter started kicking into high gear. I was so embarrassed that I just wanted to get the hell out of there. Somehow, I managed to slip out of the party without too many people noticing, and I ran my ass back home before it got any worse.

Once home, without unlacing them, I took the shoes off so fast that my socks came right off with the shoes. Angry and pissed off at the whole fiasco, I dumped my magical shoes in the garbage can, never to be seen again!

CHAPTER 54

THE RISKIER AND NOT-SO-BRIGHT SIDE OF PARTYING

While wearing marshmallow shoes was a big hit in the South Bronx during the early 1970s, it was what you decided to wear with those iconic shoes that also drew a lot of attention. The use of vintage hats, suits, and baggy pants from the '40s and '50s, became the most recent popular thing to wear in those days. It was the perfect combination for a new trendy style. There was only one big problem with this new craze: where can you buy vintage clothes?

Only a select few stores sold vintage clothes from that era, and it just so happens that none were located in the Bronx. We fell in love with the pants from the minute we saw someone wearing them in our neighborhood, so we knew right away they were something we just had to have in order to be in style and hip.

One day a friend of Misael told him the only place he knew that sold those vintage clothes was a little store located near Flushing Avenue, by the Brooklyn Navy Yard. Having never been in that area of Brooklyn, we were a bit hesitant about going there. But at the last minute, we decided if we were ever going to get our hands on those clothes, especially the baggy pants, we would have to take a trip there. Since none of us had a car, the only form of transportation we had available to us was the subway. So that's exactly what we took.

In was in the early fall of 1973 when Misael, Orlando, John, Poucho, and I decided to embark on our little trip to Brooklyn. We knew right off the bat that it would be a bit of a long ride from our side of town, but we didn't care. We were so psyched about buying those vintage baggy pants to go partying that we even skipped school that day. After taking about three or four different trains, we finally made it to our stop in Brooklyn about an hour or so later. And that was just the beginning, as it turns out.

In order for us to reach the area of the Brooklyn Navy Yard where the vintage clothing store was located, we had to walk another mile or so. Although we weren't thrilled with the idea of having to walk so much, we knew that our biggest obstacle of all still lay ahead of us: finding the little hole-in-the-wall place.

Following the general directions given to us by a friend, all five of us began walking, talking, and joking our way through this quiet, somewhat-desolate residential neighborhood. It didn't take long before we realized just how far we had strayed from our neighborhood and the people we knew. Unbeknownst to us at the time, we were in a Hasidic Jewish neighborhood. Just based solely on our initial observations as we made our way through the neighborhood, it appeared that everything from the culture, religion, language, to even the way they dressed, was completely different than what were used to seeing in our side of town.

Anyway, not that any of this mattered to us at the time, for our only objective was to find the vintage store, buy our clothes, and then head back home to the South Bronx. Well, about ten minutes into our journey, we were walking down this street, minding our own business and not bothering anyone, when suddenly, out of the blue, a white midsize car comes racing down the street past us, jumps the curb, and literally comes to a screeching halt about fifteen or twenty feet in front us, cutting off our path. We didn't know what to make of all of this, but we'd lived in the ghetto long enough to know that whatever was about to happen, it wasn't going to be good.

The next thing we know, four White males all dressed in black suits, white shirts, and black fedora hats bail out of their car and confront us. The front and right-rear passengers were armed with handguns, and the driver and left-rear passenger were armed with baseball bats. Because it all happened so quickly and unexpectedly, we were frozen stiff and could only surmise that they might have been tailing us for a while. Our only guess at this point was that they were probably members of a neighborhood block watch assigned to patrol the area and to keep outside intruders from entering their neighborhood.

Before we knew what the hell was going on, one of the men holding a gun pointed it right at us and started screaming, "Get the fuck out of our neighborhood right now, you… or we're going to fucking kill you," followed by a string of racial epithets. As if that wasn't enough, the two passengers in the car wielding bats came charging right at us to show they meant business. They wanted us out of their neighborhood like… now!

Having one gun pointed at you for no apparent reason is bad enough. But having two guns aimed right at you, a couple of bats ready to clobber you, and a very angry mob chasing you? It's a complete nightmarish, scared-shitless experience.

Scared for our lives, we immediately took off running like bats out of hell, in hopes of getting away from these armed thugs and somehow finding our way back to the train station. About all I remember from this point on is that we were running for our lives in an unknown neighborhood, hoping and praying that we would soon find our way to a safe zone and back to the train station. Like marathon runners trying to make their way towards the finish line, we ran and ran for what seemed like forever. Stopping briefly, only to take a quick look back over our shoulders to see if they were still behind us, chasing us on foot or in their car. Luckily, they were nowhere in sight. About all that went through our minds at this point was staying safe and out of harm's way.

It took us a little while to find our way back to the train station, but somehow, someway, we did. It was the biggest relief I've ever felt in my life. We were all finally safe! We all hugged and made a promise, right then and there, to make it our personal mission to come back in a couple of days and get even! We decided we would take care of this problem ourselves, just as we were accustomed to doing it in our neighborhood, and without filing a police report.

Fighting over territory was nothing new to us. You grow up seeing that; gangs from our block would clash with gangs from other parts of the South Bronx to defend what was commonly known in those days as our turf! What happened that day was not that unusual, especially during the '60s and '70s, when things like that happened all the time. But still, for us, it was the very first time in our young lives that we had ever experienced racism firsthand, and it certainly scared the crap out of all of us.

A couple of days later, still reeling from that encounter, and with an old South Bronx stubbornness about not letting others push you around and about seeking payback in the worst way, we went back. To see what would happen, we decided to take the same path we had taken just days before. This time we were a little bit more prepared than the last time, when we didn't even have a pocketknife with which to defend ourselves against a group of agitators. Armed with several of the popular 007 folding knives and one golf club, we made our way into the neighborhood again.

This time, however, it was a completely different story and outcome. The guys we dealt with during our last trip never popped up again, and we continued on our journey. In the end, we finally made it to that little vintage store and got the clothes we so desperately wanted and risked our lives to get.

But not before getting the scare of our lives for being in the wrong place at the wrong time, for all the right reasons. It's safe to say we never went back there again!

CHAPTER 55

THE COAT PARTY

Partying in that crazy era of the '70s had a lot to do with the type of clothes you wore to a particular house party. But sometimes it wasn't what you had on when you entered the party that got you noticed; it was what you were wearing when you left that got the most attention. Let me explain!

Back in the day, we would go to so many house parties that after a while, it didn't matter who was having the party or where the party was taking place. As long as they provided music, food, and drinks, we were there. And even when we weren't invited but heard about a party in the vicinity, we would just come up with a name, knock on the door, and say we'd been invited by so-and-so. Most of the time, that would allow us to crash the party. While crashing a party is sometimes not considered one of the smartest things to do, and certainly is not recommended, every now and then you take your chances and learn the hard way.

One particular winter weekday at school, a friend from the block heard about this big party that everyone at school seemed to be talking about. The party was taking place in a northwest section of the Bronx, which was a pretty good distance from where we lived in the South Bronx—and a lot quieter, I might add. Well, somehow, someway, he managed to get his hands on the address to this so-called big-ass party, and we all agreed that we would crash it on Saturday.

Not knowing exactly who was going to be there from our school, Misael, Orlando, Angel, Eddie—our newest member of the group—and I decided we would take our chances and just show up. After all, what's the worst thing that could happen to us? They could deny us entry into the party and turn us away at the door. Or they could let us in, discover later that we didn't belong there, and simply ask us to leave. Nevertheless, those were the choices we would be facing come Saturday.

Before long, the day of the party arrived, and we were on our way. Again, since none of us had a car, we had to rely on the good old subway system to get us there. So we hopped on the train, and off we went on our daring journey.

As soon as we arrived in this somewhat-quiet residential neighborhood, something in the air just didn't seem right. We were a bit apprehensive at first as we weren't used to this type of neighborhood. Although everything seemed quiet on the outside of the single-family home where the party was taking place, on the inside, well, that's a whole other story.

Because it was so cold that day, we were all bundled up in our leather jackets. Leather jackets and coats were very popular in those days, and everyone was wearing them. I, for one, was especially thrilled with mine because it was the very first time I was wearing my brand-new red leather jacket to go to a party. I was really excited to be walking around in my new threads and showing the jacket off. *What better place to start than at this party?* I thought.

When the time came for us to make our grand uninvited entrance, we knocked on the door a few times and waited. A beautiful Latina girl answered the door. We immediately gave her a big, friendly smile and told her we were invited by so-and-so from school; I forget what name we used at the time. She asked no questions, let us in, and told us where to leave our coats, pointing us in the general direction.

As we made our way towards the coatroom, we couldn't help but take in all the excitement in the air. The disco music was blasting away, and there were clouds of smoke and the smell of pot everywhere. The colorful, rotating party lights that were reflecting off the walls and ceiling only added to the party mood in the packed house.

As we walked through the dancing crowd, we soon realized that this wasn't the typical house party that we were used to. Among some of the people dancing were members of a notorious South Bronx street gang, the Ghetto Brothers, all dressed in their usual cutoff sleeveless jean jackets and matching jeans, the gang name and insignia on the backs of their jackets. This wasn't good. These gang members were well known to carry guns and knives, and had a big history of violence. And so, at any given moment, anything could happen and we would be caught right in the middle of it.

It didn't take long before we were starting to feel a bit uncomfortable, especially since a few of the gang members started to stare us down as if they knew that we didn't belong there. And although there were plenty of regular-looking people in the mix, somehow it just didn't feel right to us. We started feeling a bit out of place.

We finally made it to the coatroom, which was just a regular bedroom, of course, and discovered that the room was a complete mess. The coats were piled so high on top of each other that they literally created a mountain, leaving us with no other choice but to throw our coats on top of this huge, cluttered bed. Finding our coats at the end of the night would definitely prove to be a true challenge. After throwing our coats on top of the pile, we exited the room and joined the crowd of partygoers hanging out in the living room.

As we sifted through the crowd, trying to blend in, we were able to find a few people who went to our school. Still, somehow deep down inside, we knew that this was not the place for us. In trying to make the most out of a potentially bad situation, we decided that we would socialize a bit and have a few drinks just to kill some time. But unlike what you would normally do at a regular house party—mingle, dance, meet some girls, and maybe get lucky—we instead purposely avoided all of that for fear that maybe the girls were the girlfriends of some of the gang thugs. So we stayed in our own little corner of the room, cautiously bopping our heads to the beat of the music until it was time to go.

Because we weren't having a good time, every second of the clock felt like hours. Time was dragging, and tension was everywhere. Paranoia was quickly setting, and we knew it was just a matter of time before we had no other choice but to make that move and head out the door. In our minds, they were either going to throw our asses out the door for crashing the party, or we could leave peacefully of our own free will to avoid any potential problems. We chose the latter!

We were there for less than an hour when we decided that it was time to grab our stuff and leave before something crazy happened. When we got back to the so-called coatroom, we realized that the pile of coats had gotten even bigger. Our coats were buried somewhere in this massive mess of a pile, and it was going to take a huge effort just to find them. To make matters worse, the room was not well lit, so we knew right away it would be a big challenge.

As we rummaged through this big-ass pile, looking for our coats, it didn't take long before we realized that two of our coats were missing: Orlando's and mine! Someone had actually walked off with our coats and left us coatless on this brutally cold winter night! To say we were pissed off is an understatement.

Confused and lost for words, we basically looked at each other and said, "What the hell are we going to do now? It's freezing out there, and we don't have our coats." That's when Orlando and I came up with the idea that as a payback we would help ourselves to our own choice of leather coats in the pile. We decided we would grab what looked to be the best-looking pair of coats we could find and immediately walk out of the house.

This was a risky and dangerous move on our part because we knew that if someone from the gang actually saw us doing it, they were going to beat the crap out of us. We knew right away that five of us against an army of twenty to thirty gang members wouldn't be a fair fight. So as not to draw attention to the theft, and in case someone in the crowd recognized their coat, we decided it would be in our best interest to just carry them in our hands until we got outside.

As we made our way through the dancing crowd, we once again felt the stares of some of the gang members. We got a bit paranoid and felt as if the guilt of committing a crime was written all over our faces. Fearing the gang members would pick up on it, we tried to avoid eye contact as much as possible and made our way towards the front door as quickly and stealthily as we could.

It was the biggest relief in the world once we exited. However, it turns out that the relief was short-lived because once we were outside the house, we encountered another bunch of gang members who were hanging out in front, drinking and smoking pot. Employing some of our survival techniques from the South Bronx, we proceeded with caution as we made our way past them, trying to avoid sending out red flags that we had done something wrong.

We hit the street and walked briskly towards the train station. One of my friends suggested that we run instead of walk, just in case the coats were discovered missing and they suspected that we were the ones responsible and came after us. *Not a bad idea*, I thought. The next thing we knew, we were running as fast as we could until we made it to the train station.

Out of breath and tired from all that running, we wasted no time in prematurely celebrating our little heist. We were so happy and excited about our close call that we laughed hysterically and poked fun as though we'd gotten the better end of this whole situation. After the laughter died down a little, it was finally time for Orlando and me to try on our new threads to keep warm. And—*boom!*—that's when it all fell apart.

It turns out that in our rush to grab these lovely coats—and I mean that sarcastically—and head out the door, we failed to realize that we had grabbed the wrong merchandise, so to speak. Rather than taking a pair of men's leather coats, we ended up with a pair of women's leather coats instead!

You should've seen my friends' faces when they saw me and Orlando standing there looking like fools, wearing small, tight, and what looked like short-sleeved leather coats that barely went down to our waists.

"You've got to be kidding me," was our immediate reaction. After all that planning, all that risk taking, and finally, all that running we did, and this is what we end up with: two ladies' coats? It was enough to piss anybody off, let alone Orlando and me. In my opinion, we were the true victims of this wild and crazy incident.

For my other friends, this was one of the funniest things they had ever seen. It was really that bad. After a while, even Orlando and I couldn't help but join in on all the laughter about this comedic, once-in-a-lifetime episode in our lives.

In the end, we all had a blast and even learned a lesson or two from it. And that is: Don't do unto others what others do unto you… because sometimes you just never know what you're going to get back at the end of it all!

CHAPTER 56

YOUNG AND STUPID

As the months and years went by, our thirst for the next big thing, in terms of getting high, grew. Soon marijuana was not enough for hitting the party scene. Other drugs like hashish and opium started finding their way onto our city streets and into our young, vulnerable systems. Although this was all part of an experimentation phase for teens in our neighborhood, it was nonetheless just another stupid item to be crossed off our to-do list while growing up in the South Bronx. I, for one, tried it a few times, but didn't quite like the long-lasting effects it had on my system. So I decided to just stick to pot and booze for getting high.

Then along came LSD, lysergic acid diethylamide, one of the most dangerous and potent drugs out there at the time. It was known for its sometimes-long-term hallucinogenic effects on the brain, and the aftermath of what was called a bad trip could affect your life for a very long time. In fact, one particular person we knew from the block during those LSD-craze days was so high on LSD that he tragically ended his young life by jumping headfirst into a giant furnace at the hospital where he worked, killing him instantly.

Many of my friends who used LSD said that the trick to minimizing its effects was that you had to control it, and not let it control you. If you let it freak you out, you could really lose control and have a bad trip. A bad trip meant everything you see, hear, or do being magnified ten times over until you have no control, and you could end up having long, recurring hallucinating episodes for life!

My friends Misael, Orlando, and John "Mono" all tried it and never had a problem with it. But then again, they never abused it or got hooked on it either. It was just one of those things they did once in a blue moon to get high. While Angel and I were the only holdouts again, that didn't last.

One weekend, Misael, John, Angel, and I were hanging out in the block, when Angel and I decided we would finally give in and try LSD for the very first time. I remember so clearly being a nervous wreck when we decided to purchase the LSD tablet on the street. That night, we had no parties to go to or anything like that. We just wanted to get high and hang around the block as we'd done so many times before.

The tablet wasn't in the form of a pill; instead, it was in the form of a tiny square piece of paper no bigger than the size of dime. We were supposed to divvy it up into four pieces so that everyone had an equal amount of the drug. That one-quarter, from what I was told by Misael and John, was more than enough to do the trick, especially for us first-timers.

With our bottle of wine in hand, we headed to Saint Mary's Park, a local park located just minutes away from the block. We stopped near the home plate of the main baseball diamond in the park. It was there where we soon discovered that although all the baseball diamond's lights were on—it was about ten or eleven at night—the place was completely empty with not a soul walking around to deter us from doing drugs or engaging in some other illegal activity. So, it was the perfect place for what we were about to do.

As we stood around in a circle, goofing around and taking turns gulping down some of that cheap Boone's Farm wine, Misael pulled out the LSD tablet and told us to open our hands. He placed on each palm a quarter of the LSD-laced paper. We held on to it until we were all ready to consume it. As the minutes went by, it seemed as though we were standing around for what appeared to be a lifetime, just shooting the breeze. We laughed and talked about this first trip Angel and I were about to take. The tension of taking that giant leap kept building with every second that went by. My heart kept pounding really hard in anticipation of this dark voyage on which I was about to embark. I knew that sooner or later I would have to take that ultimate step: down that magical drug and go on a crazy journey.

Although on the outside I was trying to project that this was no big deal, way deep down inside of me I was a total wreck. It didn't take long before my emotions slowly started to show on my face. My friends, who knew me better than anyone else, immediately picked up on it, prompting one of them to ask me, "So how do you feel about doing this? Are you okay with it?"

My natural response was, "I'm okay, but nervous as hell!" That caused everyone to break into a big laugh.

Finally, the moment of truth arrived. Operating in unison, we each slowly raised the LSD-laced paper to our mouth. My hand was shaking as I began to have doubts that I could actually go through with it. Suddenly, just as I was about to put the LSD in my mouth, I stopped dead in my tracks and blurted out loud, "Sorry, but I can't do this, man!" causing everyone else to come to a sudden stop. I shook my head from side to side as if in disgust and repeated to my friends, "Sorry, guys, but… I just can't do this!"

My friends were all shocked and couldn't believe that I was backing down after all the buildup and trash talking I had done earlier. As much as I wanted to follow through on my own personal dare, deep down inside, my gut instincts told a different story, leading me to back out at the last minute with no regrets…and eventually be able to breathe a big sigh of relief.

Once I convinced myself that I was completely out and wanted no part of it, I took my share of the tablet and gave it back to Misael saying, "Thanks, man, but this shit is really not for me right now. I'll just smoke a joint instead."

Misael and John, although a bit surprised, were completely okay with it and didn't try to peer pressure me into it, which I thought was pretty cool!

Angel, on the other hand, was the complete opposite of me. He said, "Well shit, if he doesn't want it, then give it to me. I'll take it!" Misael and John, being no strangers to this drug, tried to convince him that having a half a square just might be too much for him to handle, especially since this was his first time, but he insisted that he could handle it and wouldn't back down. So, Misael gave in and handed it to him.

Within minutes after taking the tablet, they were all tripping, the street name for getting high on LSD, while I, on the other hand, was content to just get high on that one joint and wine we had brought along with us. After thirty minutes, we were back on our block, having a good time and just goofing on ourselves and the people we came across on the streets. It seemed they were feeling so good that the stupidest things would make them burst out laughing.

By the time midnight rolled around, we were all hanging out in front of John's stoop, enjoying the moment, when all of a sudden my mouth was starting to feel really dry. So I decided to build up some saliva and spit it out right in front of the building, just a few feet from where my buddy Angel was standing. Angel reacted by jumping back aggressively, as though he was trying to get out of the way of a giant boulder that was heading his way. Misael, John, and I noticed what just happened and began to laugh uncontrollably. Angel, on the other hand, wasn't laughing. Instead, he appeared agitated and scared as hell.

We thought he was just clowning around and wanting to get a good laugh out of us. But when I did it a second time, he nearly bolted up the street and begged Misael, "Take me to your house. I'm not feeling well!" When that happened, we knew immediately that this sudden paranoid reaction meant he was having a bad trip. We started to get worried.

Together, we all walked to Misael's apartment, all the while trying to get Angel to calm down. But it didn't seem to be working. As we made it into Misael's apartment, Angel began to cry uncontrollably and pleaded with Misael, "Get rid of those monsters"—referring to John and me—"they're scaring me!" Fearing that things were getting out of control, John and I soon left the apartment and went back to John's stoop to wait for Misael and Angel to come back.

Misael, in the meantime, gave Angel some warm milk in a desperate attempt to dilute the effects of the LSD and bring Angel back down to normal, or at least lessen the effects of the bad trip. About an hour or so later, we witnessed Misael walking Angel home; he stayed with him until Angel had recuperated a bit.

After about a half hour or so, Misael noticed that Angel appeared to be feeling better, so he asked him to poke his head out the window to get some fresh air. Angel was slowly coming around, according to Misael, but the minute he looked out of the second-story window of his apartment and saw John and me standing in front of the stoop, he freaked out again and begged Misael, "Don't let those guys come near me again. Please… please!!!" Misael got Angel away from the window and stayed with him for many hours until he noticed his condition had stabilized, and he was starting to feel better.

It took a couple of weeks before Angel got back to his somewhat-normal self. But his bad-trip-induced paranoia stayed with him for a very long time. It was a horrible experience that none of us will ever forget and one that led him to make a personal pledge that he would never, ever use drugs again!

I'm glad to say that he actually kept his promise and never used drugs or alcohol again! I am so proud of him and the amazing, inspiring person he turned out to be over the years!

CHAPTER 57

THE MOTHER OF ALL BUS PASSES

The first couple of years at my new high school, Morris, were everything *but* what I intended them to be. When I first started at the school, I went in there with an invigorating attitude, determined to get an education and go to college. But a mere two or three months into the school year, I began to slip again and started struggling with all my schoolwork. Part of it, I'm sure, had to do with all the crap at home holding me back. But the other part of it was all on me—cutting out of school to party with my buddies, focusing on the girls instead of schoolwork, smoking weed, and just not focusing on why I decided to go back to school in the first place, which was to finish my schooling and move on to a better life.

The fact that most of my closest friends from the block went to the same school made it easy to ignore school rules in favor of being with my friends. Soon we were putting our books down, skipping school, and hanging out to do a little partying. And since security within the school was a bit lax, cutting out of school was a snap. On many occasions, all we had to do was go to homeroom in the morning for attendance, wait for the bell to ring, and—*boom!*—out the door we went. It was that easy!

Sometimes we hung out within blocks of the school, where we would get together with some of the girls from both our school and neighboring high schools, get high, hang out with friends for a little bit, and then find our way back into the school in the afternoon. It seemed there was always some student who, after a good knock or kick on the metal doors, would open the unsecured doors and let us back into the school building without a problem. At other times, we would just skip school altogether, hanging around neighborhoods outside of our school area until it was time to head back home.

The fact that we didn't have to depend on the yellow school buses to drop us off or pick us up at school made it a breeze! Our only form of transportation came by way of the regular commuter buses or trains, which brought us to within blocks of the school; we would walk the rest of the way. The cost to our parents was just fifty cents for a weekly bus pass, a reduced rate for low-income families like ours. We could use that bus pass to go anywhere we wanted to go in the Bronx, so long as it was during school hours. All we had to do was get on the bus or train, flash our bus passes, and off we went.

These passes, or cards, were issued to us on weekly basis by the school; they came in different colors. Like clockwork, we would get them every Friday so that we could use them for the following school week. To prevent students from sneaking onto the bus with an old or outdated pass, they constantly changed the color of the card and the big, identifiable bold letter and number combination—for example, dark-purple letter-and-number combinations, like N-4, in the middle of a light-violet card. Each pass also had a large, easily legible expiration date.

One day, I was at home, sitting at the dinner table and going through a stack of old, expired school-bus passes that I had collected over the course of the school year, and wondered, *What am I still doing with these old bus passes?* I was in the process of tossing them in the garbage when suddenly I had this crazy idea. That day, I decided to use a regular pencil eraser on a letter of one of the cards, just to see if I could erase it. And it worked! The next thing I knew, all the letters and numbers were pretty much gone, except for a light residue. Right then and there, I knew I was up to something cool. So I decided to tamper with the old cards to create brand-new ones. Now it was just a matter of trying to match the right-colored ink to the color card for the week. If that worked, I would soon have my very own homemade bus pass and could pocket the few bucks my parents gave me every week to buy lunches and bus passes.

Running with this idea in mind, I quickly left the house, stopped by the local Woolworth's that carried all sorts of Magic Markers, and purchased one of each color. Within a matter of minutes of getting back home, I had carefully crafted each letter and number to match almost exactly the following week's school-bus pass. Before I knew it I had my very own free bus pass.

The following week as I got ready to board the bus, I remember being nervous about the whole situation. I knew that if I got discovered, the whole thing would create a big mess for me. On the one hand, I could easily get arrested for it, get suspended from school, and have bus privileges taken away from me for at least a month or two, maybe more. However, on the other hand, the bus driver could just kick me off the bus and tell me not to board his bus again, which wouldn't be as bad as the other punishment. In either case, the stakes for getting caught were high, no matter how you looked at it. But to save a few bucks, I was more than willing to take my chances.

Because there were a lot of students at the bus stop that day, I knew that my chances of slipping through were probably very good. The trick to this whole thing was not to flash the card, which was inside my clear-plastic class-program sleeve jacket, too close to the bus driver's face; that way, he couldn't see the imperfections and call me out on it.

As the line moved along and everyone started boarding the bus, it was finally my time to put my homemade bus pass to the test. I did as planned and quickly flashed my bus pass as I rushed inside the crowded bus. As I took my seat, I breathed a big sigh of relief. It felt great that my little experiment turned out to be such a big success on the very first day.

As the days, weeks, and months went by, I continued my little scam. After a while, I perfected my cards even more, to the point that unless you really inspected them up close, it was tough to tell the difference between a real one and a fake one. Well, at least that's what I thought.

From the late spring of 1972 to the fall of 1973, I not only got on and off the bus without a problem, but I also decided to share my little secret with my best friends from the block and made cards for them as well. Soon they too were boarding buses with my homemade bus passes. That probably was not my smartest decision. The more fake passes floating around out there on the streets, the greater the risk that my scam was going to get discovered.

Well, things were going great for my friends and me until one day when my secret was discovered. I was in the process of taking my usual number-three bus to school when, after my quick flash of the bus pass, the driver suspected something fishy and called me back. "Excuse me, let me see that bus pass again, son!" he yelled out.

I hesitated a little bit, but showed it to him anyway after he called out a second time. Hoping, of course, that the only reason he wanted to see my bus pass was to make sure it was not outdated, I handed it to him.

He did more than check the date. He did a real close inspection of the card and told me, "This is a fake bus pass, son!" He gave me a stern look that spoke volumes. I got a bit nervous and embarrassed and thought he was going to get ahold of the cops and have me arrested. But instead he decided to rip the card into pieces right in front of me and everyone else on the bus. I could tell he was mad as hell, and he showed his anger by giving me a nice lecture on my screwup. He said, "I better not catch you doing this on my route again, because the next time you won't be so lucky, and I'll be calling the cops on you... and have you arrested. Do you understand that, young man?"

I said, "Yes, sir," and apologized, hoping that, now that I had gotten chewed out, he would let me ride on the bus this time around. But no such luck.

He told me, "Now, get off my bus right now, and use a real bus pass next time!"

Humiliated to no end, I shamefully got off the bus and waited for the next bus to come by. And this time paid for it in cash. Well, at least for that one day, of course.

Two to three months after that initial embarrassing incident, I got busted at least four more times by other bus drivers on that route and some of the surrounding ones. My guess was that the word had spread quickly among the bus drivers, and they were briefed by their bosses to be on the alert for this little scam.

After about the fourth bust, I knew it was just a matter of time before this whole thing came crashing down on my friends and me, resulting in one or all of us getting arrested and suspended from school. One day, after constantly stressing out over this whole situation, collectively as a team we concluded that using the free bus passes just to save a few bucks to hang out around the Bronx was truly not worth it. We gave it up completely!

CHAPTER 58

A TRULY SAD DAY IN OUR LIVES

Growing up poor and living in a tough neighborhood like ours is a whole lot easier if you have friends who come from the same background and upbringing. Most of my closest neighborhood friends, like me, were poor and came from households that sometimes had no other choice but to rely on that all-important welfare system, or government assistance program, for help in getting through the tough economic times and hardships we faced growing up. Although some of our parents worked, sometimes their incomes weren't enough to support a family and put food on the table. So, it was a constant struggle to survive. While I had a father who worked and lived in the same household, most of my friends didn't have that luxury and depended solely on their mothers. With three to four siblings each, it was even more difficult to manage.

So, as you can see, the responsibilities of raising a big family can sometimes be a bit challenging, especially when it comes to raising that many kids on your own. Because of that, my friends' mothers had no other choice but to play the dual role of being both the mother and the father. As a result of that, most of the mothers were more heavy-handed and tough, just to keep us in line and prevent us from straying in the wrong direction in this crazy neighborhood of ours.

However, while most of us thought we had it hard in our respective households, none of us, by far, had it harder than John "Mono." For as long as we could remember, John had one of the toughest moms. His mom had so many rules that it wasn't even funny. As one of the oldest in the group, he felt he needed to have more independence and control of his life than his mother was willing to give him. It was so bad at times that even at the age of sixteen or seventeen, he was told that he had to be home way before midnight, no matter what day of the week it was. As the months and the years went by, this internal conflict between him and his mother only got worse.

There were times when we would all sit down together to air out our problems and concerns about our parents, and he would break down and start crying. He felt trapped and cut off from the freedom that he needed and deserved, especially at his age. In particular, he was embarrassed that he couldn't do some of the things we used to do, like hanging out late during the week and partying on weekends. In general, he felt as if he was missing out on a lot of the fun things we were doing; this contributed to giving him an ever-more-consuming feeling of emptiness and sadness that he just couldn't break. In fact, on quite a few occasions, he even told us how he wanted to run away from home because he couldn't deal with it any longer.

As lifelong friends, we really felt for him and tried our best to tell him that eventually things would change, that he just had to have a little patience. But that was a tough sell when you consider that he was the one that had to live with all this drama every single day of his life.

One day, when he was nearing his eighteenth birthday, he brought us all together and told us he was planning on going to Boston to stay with his cousin for a few weeks. If he liked it, he was thinking about staying there for good and never coming back. That was a real shocker to all of us, but knowing what we knew about his situation with his mother, we kind of understood why he needed to make that move, so we kindly supported his wishes. We ended our little discussion that night by giving him an emotional, heartfelt hug, wished him good luck, and said goodbye.

By the next day, he was on his way to Boston. I remember how sad we all were to see him go. Somehow, we all felt that this was probably going to be the last time we saw him for a while. Having one fewer member in the group, especially one who kept us laughing and was always clowning around and in good spirits, was going to be difficult. He was like a brother to us, and we each treated him as if he were a member of our family. He was going to be missed so much that someone in the group even mentioned that without John on our five-man basketball team, we had no team; he was our point guard. A statement like that spoke volumes about how much John meant to us as a member of our tight-knit group.

Well, soon the days turned into weeks, and the weeks turned into months, and John was nowhere to be seen. Maybe he truly did find a new home and made up his mind that he wasn't coming back. How little we knew then, at the time he left us, that it would be the very last time we would ever see him alive. Sadly, he was shot and killed later that year over a heated dispute over a woman.

The news was devastating to all of us. We were all heartbroken to know that someone who was such a special part of our lives was no longer going to be around us… ever again! Let alone coming to grips with the fact that someone so young had been taken from us…just like that… for no reason.

We were all left to mourn the loss of our brother John, who, when he was killed, became the latest victim in a list of so many similar tragedies in our young lives. We love you, John! May God bless you always!

CHAPTER 59

MOVING FORWARD

With the death of John, there was a sudden void in our lives, which took us many years to get used to. What's ironic about the whole situation is that shortly after John left our neighborhood to move to Boston, another young teen and his family moved into our neighborhood and filled the void, so to speak. His name was Eddie. I got to meet Eddie one day, and right away we became friends.

Eddie, it just so happens, moved into the first-floor apartment of my building at 586th East 140th Street, just two flights down from my third-floor apartment. He was about thirteen or fourteen when we first met, but he sure didn't look his age. In fact, I would say he looked older because he already had a light beard and mustache, which added a few more years to his actual age. I, on the other hand, barely had a pencil-thin mustache, never mind trying to grow a beard.

Eddie, just like the rest of us, was Puerto Rican and came from a very big family that included three sisters, two of whom were twins, two brothers, his mother, his stepfather, and his grandmother. They all lived under one roof in a tiny three-bedroom apartment. How they did it, I don't know, but somehow, someway, they managed to make it work for them.

After a while, we became good friends, and I was able to introduce him to the rest of my buddies. Over time, he became one of the most liked and trusted friends of our little group. Or should I say, one of the boys, as we used to refer to each other. He quickly adapted to hanging out with his older, more mature group of new friends. The fact that he didn't go to the same high school—he went to Alfred E. Smith in the Bronx—as the rest of us never really mattered.

Some of the factors that made Eddie fit in so well with our group had to do with the fact that, just like the rest of us, he also came from a tough upbringing and similar family background, and yes, his mother was tough. So he could easily relate to some of the issues and concerns that we all had as young teens growing up in a rough-and-tumble neighborhood like ours.

Although he had the uncelebrated distinction of being one of the youngest and shortest in the group, I'd say it was a toss-up between Eddie and Misael. Eddie never once let his height hold him back from putting up a good fight or speaking his mind when he had to, a common trait in our group. He also had a pretty colorful attitude and a great sense of humor. His sometimes-sarcastic sense of humor was a big hit with all of us, and he had us laughing all the time. This was especially true when it was time to get high on the weekends and hit the party scene to chase after girls. Because he was good at dancing the hustle, a very popular dance in those days, we were never short on getting attention from the girls.

Unlike the rest of us who were pretty good at playing basketball and other sports, Eddie's thing was the dance floor, not the basketball court. Whenever we played a game of basketball, we used Eddie to rough up some of the opposing players because of his aggressive and sometimes a bit out-of-control playing style. He intimidated some of the people we played against, for fear of getting hurt. But that was his style. He played hard and never quit hustling after the ball.

Regardless, our friendship was not based on how well we played on the court, but on how much we cared for each other off the court. The trust and respect that we had for each other as brothers—that's what mattered the most. If you ever had a fight or any type of confrontation with anyone on the streets, it was nice to know that your brothers always had your back and were always right there for you if you ever needed them… every single time. So, no matter what you did or where you went, it was a great feeling to have.

It didn't take long for that camaraderie to be put to the test in perhaps one of the biggest life-altering moments of my life! It happened on a crisp, hot summer day in 1973.

I remember it clearly. The streets were packed with people just hanging out and enjoying this beautiful day. As usual, whenever there are lots of people congregating in a one-block area, there's always the potential for trouble. In a volatile block like ours you must always be prepared for the unexpected! One thing I'd learned from all the years I lived in my block was that sometimes it doesn't take a lot for a fight or a battle to erupt. Sometimes all it takes is a simple dirty look, a stare in the wrong direction, or even a rumor or gossip about a person, for a fight to start up and get out of control. One of the unwritten rules that came along with living on our block was to never let your guard down, and always be ready for whatever might come your way!

Such was the case on that hot summer day. I was with Eddie, Poucho, and Chuito, another friend from a different neighborhood. We were hanging out on the block in the early afternoon and decided to take a walk out of our neighborhood, do some window shopping, and hang out on 138th Street and Brook Avenue. That was where most of the big retail stores in our neighborhood were located.

We were out of the area for no more than a couple of hours when we decided to call it a day and started heading back. Once we made it to the block, Eddie invited us to his home to grab a bite to eat before we hit the streets again. That day, since we were all so tired and hungry, the timing couldn't have been better. At least that's what we thought.

That afternoon, as soon as we entered Eddie's home, we heard a loud commotion coming from the living room. Once in the living room, we soon realized that something bad had happened to Eddie's mother and sister Julie. They were both extremely upset and crying.

Eddie was very close to his mother, and to see her in this state really pissed him off, especially when he noticed that they both appeared to be a bit bruised; it looked as though someone had beaten them up. When Eddie saw this, he wanted to know right away what happened and who was responsible for attacking them.

Evidently, shortly before Eddie got home that afternoon, they were hanging out across the street with some friends when Julie and one of the younger twin sisters got into an argument over something stupid, a rumor that was running around the block. The dispute quickly escalated into a fistfight between the two girls. When Eddie's mother tried to stop the fight, they were both jumped from behind and beaten up by a couple of the twin brothers for no apparent reason. She gave Eddie the names of the two brothers responsible for the assault and mentioned that these two brothers, after they beat up the women, walked away as if nothing happened. From what they said, the two brothers appeared to get a kick out of what they did, were even laughing as though it was a big joke as they left.

The twins' family was a big one consisting of at least four grown adult males, three young sisters, including identical twins, and their parents. They all lived in a four-bedroom, ground-level apartment located near the corner of Saint Ann's Avenue and 140th Street. The building, which was five or six away from ours, had two concrete walk-up steps that went from the street, right up to their apartment doorway, making for an easy access to both the apartment and the street below.

The family was known to everyone on the block as a troublesome clan. All four brothers were grown men already, and they had bad reputations for getting drunk and picking fights with people on the streets. In addition, they were also known to carry weapons. Because of that, it made them an even bigger threat to anyone having to confront them.

However, on this day, their bullying went a little bit too far when they decided to pick on Eddie's family and then thought they could just walk away from it without any consequences. Boy, were they wrong!

After hearing everything that happened to Eddie's mother and sister, we were all pissed off and felt that something had to be done to straighten these brothers out. That's when Eddie, without skipping a beat, gathered all of us together and said, "I'm going to have a talk with these fucking assholes to see how tough they really are."

Fearing the unknown and to be on the safe side just in case they happened to be armed, Poucho suggested that maybe we should prepare ourselves for the worst and get some protection, just in case something crazy happened. Within minutes, Poucho and I left Eddie's home and ran to our respective apartments to get whatever we could to protect ourselves. Without hesitation, I ran upstairs and picked up my 007 folding knife, which had a five-inch blade, and put it in my pants pocket. While Poucho, on the other hand, ran home and grabbed a golf club and a .22 caliber handgun he had secretly stashed away without his mother's knowledge.

In less than five minutes or so, we were back at Eddie's home. Eddie and Chuito quickly grabbed folding knives, and we began to devise a plan. In the discussions that followed, we decided that it was best that we give Eddie the gun just in case anything crazy happened. That way, he would be prepared to defend himself should the twins come after him with a weapon. Without skipping a beat, Eddie grabbed the loaded .22 caliber pistol from Poucho's hands and tucked it underneath his waistband, concealing it with his T-shirt.

The plan from the very beginning was to have a peaceful talk with these idiots about what they did wrong. But more importantly, to give them a good stern warning about the consequences of continuing to harass, threaten, or fight with any of us or our families. They would get a beating. It was that simple!

It just so happens that at the time of this incident, Eddie was still trying to come to grips with the sudden death of his beloved stepfather. Just a couple of months earlier, his stepfather was caught in an ambush, and was shot and killed by a pair of armed junkies during a street robbery. Eddie's emotions were still raw. And now, having to deal with this incident, we all knew that it was going to be an extremely challenging situation for Eddie.

Within minutes, we were out of Eddie's apartment and on our way to pay the twins a surprise visit. Although we were all aware of the potential dangers that awaited us, we were all so angry that day that we really didn't care! We were ready! We walked fast and kept our focus. But as we got closer, we noticed that although none of the twins' family was outside their apartment, as they usually were, the front door was wide-open, leading us to believe that someone was still at home.

We decided that it would be best for Eddie to walk quite a few feet ahead of us; that way, it would make it look as though he were walking all by himself, just in case they happened to see him approaching. While Eddie was walking towards their apartment building, Poucho with a golf club in hand, Chuito and I, armed with knives in our pockets, trailed behind and stayed out of sight with the idea of positioning ourselves just to the left side of the building, by their front entrance. Once in position, we waited patiently for something to happen as Eddie slowly inched his way to the front of the building.

By the time Eddie got to the front steps of the twins' doorway, he noticed that one of the culprits he knew by name was milling around inside the apartment. He immediately called him by his name and calmly asked him to step outside so they could have a few words about what happened. But the culprit refused to even acknowledge Eddie's presence and acted as though Eddie weren't even there. This lack of respect truly got Eddie pissed off. That's when he called the culprit every Spanish curse word in the book in order to coax him to step outside of his apartment. But even that didn't work.

Finally, Eddie was so fired up that he decided to go for the jugular and basically challenged his manhood by yelling out, "So you like to hit women, you fucking piece of shit. Why don't you just come out here like a real man and try to hit me too, you motherfucker!!!" He then added, "What, are you scared I'm going to whip your ass, you fucking pussy?"

It was those last few words that really got under the twin's skin, and he decided to go after Eddie. What happened next still sends chills up my spine. When I think of the consequences of how this one single incident could have changed my life forever…

Infuriated, the culprit charged Eddie like a raging bull going after the red cape. He came at Eddie with only his fisted knuckles as he readied himself for serious battle. But just as he exited the front door, Poucho came from the side of the building and struck him once, right across the center of his chest, with his golf club. That slowed the culprit's momentum and nearly knocked him off his feet. But somehow, he managed to regain his balance and went after Eddie again.

This time, however, Eddie was going to give the culprit the biggest surprise of his life. Eddie just waited as the culprit tried to go after him again and came to within several feet of him. That's when Eddie, operating on pure instinct, reached into his waistband, grabbed the pistol, and instinctively began firing away without any hesitation. This sudden turn of events took us all by complete surprise, for we never expected anything like it to take place without any warning or reservation. But Eddie's adrenaline was in full swing, and all his built-up anger just exploded right before our eyes.

I soon found myself in this dreamlike state of mind, in which everything just felt so unreal, and every movement appeared to be taking place in slow motion. I remember it ever so clearly—the fire, the smoke, and even the smell of the gunpowder coming out of the muzzle of the gun with every squeeze of the trigger. I also remember the distinctive loud noise of the gunfire exploding in our ears with each round that Eddie fired, numbing the moment even more.

We all froze momentarily and didn't know when or how to intervene in order to stop this whole incident from getting any worse. Without skipping a beat, the culprit did what anybody in his shoes would have done: he ran for his life as he tried desperately to dodge the barrage of bullets and the threat coming his way. He hopped; he jumped; he did whatever he could on the spur of the moment to save his life and run like hell out of Eddie's sight.

Then, just as fast as the rounds were fired, there was this quiet pause. The firing had stopped after a barrage of three or four quick shots because Eddie's gun unexpectedly jammed and stopped working just as he was about to enter the apartment to pursue the culprit. This break in the action, gave us the perfect opportunity to jump in and forcibly drag Eddie out of there before things got any worse. Without hesitation, we grabbed him and pulled him out of there.

Within seconds of pulling Eddie away from this near-tragic situation, we were off and running up our street. From that point on, it took only minutes before our block was swarmed with cops who responded to the call of shots being fired. As the cops were busy looking for us, we were hiding in a friend's house, quietly watching all the action take place from a window several stories above the street below us. It took us a little while before our nerves finally started to calm down a bit, and we decided to return to our respective homes for the evening after the cops left the area.

Up until that time, we did not know how serious the situation was or if anyone had gotten hurt in the incident. Not seeing an ambulance at the scene was a good sign that possibly no one got hurt or injured by one of the bullets. However, it wasn't until later, after all the chaos died down, that we discovered just how drastically this incident was going to affect our lives. That's when the panic really started to kick in as we began to ponder how this nightmare was going to turn out and where it would go from here.

Miraculously, the twin brother somehow managed to escape unharmed from this crazy ordeal that could have easily cost him his life, or at least seriously injured him. It took a few days before the cops could piece together what happened and make an arrest. In the end, Eddie and Poucho were summoned to court on juvenile charges— Eddie for attempted assault with a deadly weapon, and Poucho for the assault with the golf club. However, all those charges were later dropped when the twin brother decided that he did not want to pursue the charges. The case was later dismissed with no further adjudication. Chuito and I, on the other hand, were never charged, as the twin brother never pointed us out as being involved in the incident.

To this day, when I reflect back on that fateful day in 1973, I realize just how truly lucky we all were that no one was killed or seriously injured in that wild incident. Otherwise, my whole life would have been a completely different story.

PHOTOGRAPHS

Me at 3 months of age with my beautiful
mom, Gloria, way back in 1956.

My dad, Calept, in 1962 at
my uncle's home.

Acting like the CEO of my own
home taken during the early 60's!

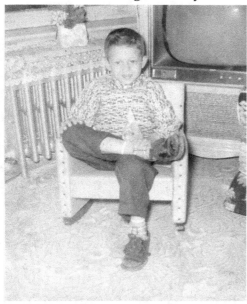

As an extremely shy kid in elementary school who very rerely spoke
in class and got bullied... until the day I learned how to box.

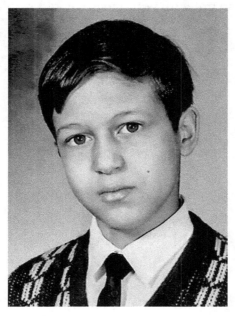

In my mid teens, hanging out with one of my
best friends, John. Who sadly, a few years
later ended up getting shot and killed.

Here's a photo booth picture of another one of my best friends,
Misael, who grew up with me in my old neighborhood.

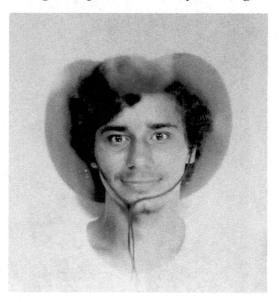

In my "Disco Room" getting ready for my Morris
High School basketball game, back in 1974.

Graduating from Morris High School in June of 1974.

Picture of two more of my best friends from the block (right to left, me, Eddie and Orlando), taken right after I graduated from H.S.

Making my dream come true, after graduating from the Hartford Police Academy on April, 3rd 1980.

Sustaining a serious injury to my neck, after running into a wire that nearly sliced right through my neck, during the execution of a search warrant at a drug house.

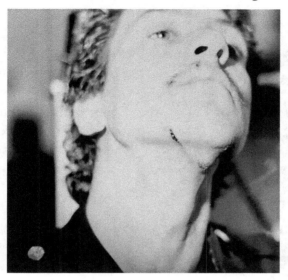

Dreaming it, and making it happen! As a kid dreaming of one day becoming a crime fighter like my tv idol, "The Lone Ranger."

Me and Alex "The Wonder Horse" competing in The National Mounted Police Equestrian Competition, that took place in October of 1998, in Hershey, Pennsylvania.

One of the most memorable days of our lives…the day of our engagement!

Surprising my fiancé with a portrait of us on
the 2nd Anniversary of our engagement!

Celebrating our one
year engagement
with this surprise on
3-30-94 !

The day I was blessed to
marry the love of my life,
on May 14th, 1994!

Celebrating our love and vowel renewal on our
25th Wedding Anniversary, on May of 2019.

Enjoying one of our many wins, as Aladdin and
Jasmine, during our yearly Halloween Costume
Contest from the 1990's into the 2000's!

Winning the Mr. Latino Bodybuilding
Championship of Connecticut, in 1991.

One of my very first modeling jobs for "Men's Passion
International Hair Magazine", in the early 90's.

Another one of my early modeling
pictures from the early 90's.

The rejection letter (from one of the top modeling agency
in NYC) that fueled my passion "to never give up!"

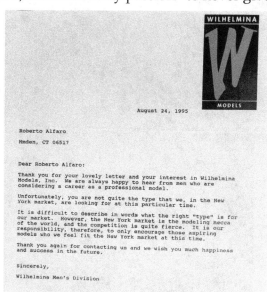

Selected as one of the top 10 models, in the "Buscando Estrella Con Budweiser" ("Star Search") National Model Search Competition, in 1993.

Selected as one of the 10 models in the National Latina Magazine, "Papi Chulo" Contest, in 2001.

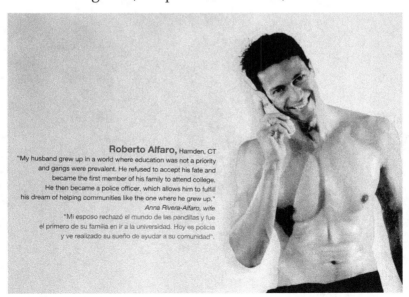

Roberto Alfaro, Hamden, CT
"My husband grew up in a world where education was not a priority and gangs were prevalent. He refused to accept his fate and became the first member of his family to attend college. He then became a police officer, which allows him to fulfill his dream of helping communities like the one where he grew up."
Anna Rivera-Alfaro, wife
"Mi esposo rechazó el mundo de las pandillas y fue el primero de su familia en ir a la universidad. Hoy es policía y ve realizado su sueño de ayudar a su comunidad".

Story on my acting and modeling career, by the
Quinnipiac University's Chronicle Newspaper.

Growing up in a rough area in the South Bronx, Robert Alfaro dreamed of either being a police officer or on TV. But now Alfaro, a Public Safety officer, is doing both.

Alfaro, who began working at the university in July of last year, is also a former member of the Hartford Police Department, a professional model and actor, mounted police instructor, salsa instructor, personal trainer, competitive bodybuilder, writer, inventor and motivational speaker.

But Alfaro's most recent triumph was an appearance in Showtime's "Billions." He has been acting and modeling professionally for the past 24 years. He has had roles in shows such as "Orange is the New Black," and "Law and Order."

Robert Alfaro

"I've done tons of movies, shows – nothing major. I've been in quite a few independent movies and commercials," Alfaro said.

The poster I used during my "Never Stop Dreaming"
speaking engagements!

Photo of Me and Sgt. Bob Vignola, during a "Coffee With A Cop Day" with the students from Quinnipiac University.

Story in the Quinnipiac University Chronicle, about my invention "Hooked on Baby: The Lifeline To Your Baby!"

Me and my beautiful family (from left to right, my kids Bobby, me, my wife, Christian, and Brianna) celebrating a family wedding, in 2021. Missing from this picture is our beautiful daughter, Bianca who was in California, with her family.

Hanging out with all four of my kids, at my son's (Bobby's) birthday party!

Having a great time in the park,
with our oldest grandson, Niko.

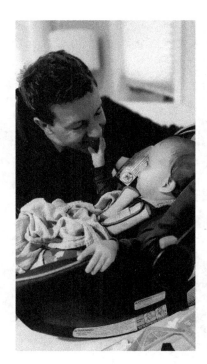

Enjoying a quiet, bonding
moment with my youngest
grandson, Noah.

A short poem dedicated to my beautiful
wife, Anna, on a date night!

The beauty of your gorgeous smile...
So pure, so loving, so captivating
In a million ways and more...
For you're the fiber of my every being...
My majestic Queen...My Forevermore!!!

I Love you with all my heart and soul Babe!

-Roberto-
xoxoxoxo

Having a great time with my Queen at the Hartford Police
Department, Hispanic Officers Association Christmas party!

Me and my oldest brother, Valentine (aka "Flaco") and
my oldest sister, Mercedes, hanging out at home.

Me and my older sister, Esther, taken during
a trip to the South Bronx to visit the family.

One of my last photos taken at Quinnipiac University,
just weeks before my retirement, in 2021.

The words that I use to keep me motivated
and inspired every single day!

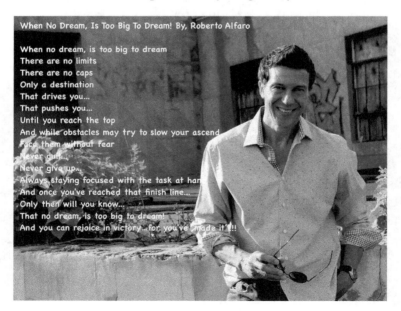

When No Dream, Is Too Big To Dream! By, Roberto Alfaro

When no dream, is too big to dream
There are no limits
There are no caps
Only a destination
That drives you...
That pushes you...
Until you reach the top
And while obstacles may try to slow your ascend
Face them without fear
Never quit...
Never give up...
Always staying focused with the task at hand
And once you've reached that finish line...
Only then will you know...
That no dream, is too big to dream!
And you can rejoice in victory...for you've made it!!!

CHAPTER 60

MY SCHOOL BUST

After that very close call with Eddie and the rest of my friends, I did some deep reflecting on my life. Specifically, on where I was now and where I wanted to go. In fact, so much had happened in my life in such a short period of time, that I knew I had to make changes once again. Or else, who knows what could happen to me in the next ten to fifteen years. I just knew that, right then and there, I wasn't feeling good about the direction I was heading. For one thing, I was aware that I needed to work on myself right away to avoid any further slipups that could ruin my life forever.

One day, I was going through my desk drawer at home, looking for some paperwork that I had misplaced two weeks before, when I came across this high school report card from my freshman year at Morris High School. It was a report card from the fall of 1971 that was marked in big bold letters with the word *UNSATISFACTORY* across the bottom in the comments section of my report card.

The day that happened, I got busted by school security for cutting out of school without permission. At the time, I couldn't have cared less about a simple blemish on my record that described my careless behavior and attitude towards school. I was in another frame of mind then, and all I wanted to do at the time was skip class, hang out with my friends, and have a good time. That's all! But now, with everything that was going on in my life, that one little word splashed across my old report card spoke volumes to me about my character and my future. *If only I had listened*, I thought to myself at the time.

Suddenly, it all came back to me, and I started thinking how different things might have been had I been willing to listen to the advice I got from Mr. Shapiro and the assistant principal. As I recall, the incident that culminated in the *UNSATISFACTORY* occurred on a day I decided to skip class. So after attendance was taken in homeroom that morning and I was marked present, I left the building to go hang out with some of my friends in the park.

As I have mentioned before, cutting out of school back in those days was really easy. Security was so poor that it almost appeared as though you were given an unlimited pass to come and leave as you pleased. Since there were so many exits in the building, you could literally pick and choose the door of your choice, then simply walk out of the building without a problem.

That particular day, after spending the whole morning with my friends, I decided it was time to call it a day. I headed back to the school right before noontime. My friends, on the other hand, decided to stay in the park. Within minutes of getting to the school and not seeing any of the security guards in or around the school grounds, I decided to make the bold move of trying to enter the school through the front entrance, instead of using one of the side entrances where there was less of a chance of getting caught. As it turns out, that was not the smartest move in the world!

I had only made it past the first set of double doors when I was confronted by one of two security guards who wanted to know where I thought I was going. When I responded that I was on my way to my classroom, the guard laughed and said he didn't think so. He then grabbed me by my left arm and escorted me right into the assistant principal's office. Once there, both guards sat with me until Mr. Willmer got back to his office.

He got there within minutes and wasted no time in telling me how stupid it was to get busted for cutting out of school. I sat there quietly listening to his lecture. I had no other choice but to admit that I was totally wrong and was willing to take the punishment. Luckily, because this was my first time getting busted for skipping school, I was let off the hook with just a permanent mark on my report card that read, "This student has been marked UNSATISFACTORY in citizenship on his permanent record because he left the building without permission." It was signed, "Mr. Willmer." But it didn't end there; he threatened that if I got caught again, I would be suspended from school right on the spot!

This one incident hit me like a ton of bricks. For it was the very first time that anything like this had ever happened to me, and unfortunately, it was now on my permanent school record. Although it was a quick lesson learned, it was what Mr. Willmer told me next that really got to me.

He said, "Do you realize there are not too many students that get a chance to graduate at the age of seventeen? Young man, you have an opportunity of a lifetime here, so why mess it up by doing stupid things like this?" He added, "Your job right now is to focus on your schoolwork and get good grades so you can go to college, earn a degree, and get a good job down the road...and that's it! So why ruin this chance of a lifetime?" He took a long pause, shook his head, and said nothing else. I could tell he was really upset, didn't believe I would heed any of his heartfelt advice, and knew I would eventually end up back in his office. He then had the security guards escort me back to my last class of the day.

Once again, I had someone in my life who cared enough to step in to tell me that everything I was doing was wrong, and that I needed to get my priorities in order if I wanted to be successful one day. This was the third time—Mr. Shapiro in eighth grade, my former coworker Thomas, and now Assistant Principal Willmer—a mentor came into my life and basically told me, "You better straighten out your life now, or you'll be just another statistic who never made it in life!"

That sound advice was still ringing fresh in my ears as I looked at the report card. After analyzing every single word Mr. Willmer said that day, I finally concluded that he was absolutely right! If I had listened to what he and the others had been telling me all along, I wouldn't be stressing now over all these near misses and second chances.

The incident with Eddie, along with the fake-bus-pass debacle, I guess, turned out to be a wake-up call for me in 1973. I just knew that if there was ever a time when I had to make changes in my life, this was the time to do it, and do it fast. So that day, I made a strong commitment and promised myself to start anew and get back on track before it was too late! And I'm so proud to say that's exactly what I did!

Refreshed, and with a whole new mindset, I slowly but surely began to turn my life around. Starting with school, I took my schoolwork more seriously and focused more on improving on my grades and my attitude towards school. By the time I entered my senior year, I was a totally different student. My grades had improved dramatically. So much so, that I even managed to get a few academic awards, which was a big incentive for me and boost to my self-confidence. But more importantly, since I wanted to graduate on time with some of the other students in my age group, I even decided to go to night school, in lieu of summer school, each semester of my senior year in order to graduate with my class in June of 1974.

CHAPTER 61

MY SENIOR YEAR IN HIGH SCHOOL

E ntering my senior year in high school was like a brand-new start for me. It wasn't until my senior year that I really started to realize the importance of getting that high school diploma and going to college. Something that, up until that point in my life, no one in my family had ever done. My accomplishing that would be such a huge milestone for my family, and I knew that everyone would be so proud of me.

Aside from my new goal of graduating from high school and going to college, I also started thinking of other things to do to keep myself on track. In the coming days and the weeks that followed this renewed mission to better my life, I found myself interested in trying out for the varsity basketball team at my school, something that I had ignored in the past because I was too busy hanging out. I had loved playing basketball since the age of thirteen, when I learned how to play the game in my junior high school for the first time. Although I was a bit clumsy at first, over time I got better and better at it. And since I was still growing, I knew that one day I would be tall enough to make a difference on a team.

By the time I was sixteen years of age, I was already six two and had the uncanny ability to jump high, up to thirty-eight inches in a vertical leap, and dunk with ease. I was also a very good rebounder who could score both from inside and outside the paint. In my neighborhood, I played on a few good teams, including the Spanish Cavaliers, a team that my friends and I put together to play in several recreational leagues against some of the toughest teams in our area. Although our team was small, we were quick, talented, competitive, and always played our hearts out, no matter how tough our opponents.

One day, they announced over the school intercom, that the varsity basketball team was having tryouts after school that day. By the time three o'clock came around, I was one of the first students in my school gym to sign up for the tryouts. With the dozens of other students who also waited anxiously for their turn to be called up for the big tryout, I waited patiently on the sidelines for my name to be called by the head coach, Coach George Mattes.

Similar to any young teen with big basketball dreams, mine was to make the varsity team, do very well, hopefully get noticed by a college team, and get a full scholarship to play for their school. But my dreams went beyond that; for deep inside my heart and soul, my ultimate goal and dream was to one day be the very first Puerto Rican to get drafted into the NBA and play professional basketball. I guess you could say I had some really big hopes for my future in basketball. But first, to realize those dreams, I had to do well in the tryouts and most importantly, make the team.

Well, the day went better than what I had anticipated. After going through some rigorous competition, numerous rounds and eliminations, and some nervous, heart-pounding moments, I made the final cut and became a Morris High School Bulldog, a varsity basketball-team player!

We had a total of twelve players who made the team. Out of those, only one and I turned out to be the tallest on the team at six two, while the shortest player stood at five six. This meant that it was going to be a very challenging season, when you consider that some of the other teams in the league had much taller players, according to what the coach told us during our first meeting. We knew right from the jump that we were going to have a really tough road ahead of us.

Back home, making the team was like a dream come true. Especially when you consider all the tough challenges I had gone through up to that point in my life. This was positive, and it highlighted a big accomplishment in my life that gave me the confidence and push that I so desperately needed to start thinking of a better future.

To my best friends from the block, this was a pretty big thing. It was the very first time that someone in my inner circle of friends got a chance to play basketball at the varsity level. They were all so proud and happy for me. As for my family, they too were happy for me, just not in the same way as my friends were. For one thing, they really weren't sports fans and probably couldn't tell you the difference between a basketball and a football! So let's just say I had to do a lot of explaining to help them understand the significance of what I had accomplished. As for me, it meant the world to me, and I couldn't be prouder!

Once the season started, we lost more games than we won. And by the time midseason arrived, we had a record of 4–7. Not a happy season for our veteran coach, who according to the *Daily News*, "had three consecutive top-notch winning seasons in a row." He didn't get there by being a slouch. During both practices and games, he was one tough coach who had a reputation for being quick-tempered, often losing his cool during games.

That was something I witnessed firsthand when, during one of the games, an official made a bad call on one of our players. Coach responded by grabbing a chair and throwing it in the direction of the referee who made the bad call. He was subsequently tossed out of the game. In another game, when one of the referees made repeated bad calls, Coach got so pissed off that he charged at the referee and took a swing at him. Luckily, he missed, but he was tossed out of yet another game.

But just as he demanded the game be played fairly on the court, during practice he did not hold back when we screwed up. But at the same time, after practice he was one of the nicest guys around. He used to love to joke around and make us all laugh with his dry sense of humor. He was also a mentor to all of us, frequently lecturing us on the fundamentals of why getting an education was so important.

He believed in education so much that one day, when he found out that the best player on our team was failing in his classes miserably, he dropped him from the team right away. In doing so, he set an example for all of us to follow. We knew the consequences. "If you can't keep up with your schoolwork and you're failing your classes, I don't want you on my team. It's that simple!" Coach said. We all had to maintain a B average or better...or risk being kicked off the team.

As for me, it was perfect. I needed to have that kind of pressure and discipline in my life to force me to do well in school, graduate, and hopefully get a college scholarship. This was the ticket to a better life that I had been waiting for. It was the chance of a lifetime that not only allowed me to play in a sport that I love, but also gave me an amazing opportunity to get a great education.

Since I was a senior, I knew I only had one chance to prove myself and to get noticed. Overall, I started quite a few games and came in as a sixth, and sometimes seventh, man off the bench; I didn't get the playing time I really needed as a first-year varsity athlete. My other teammates had all been there from their freshman year, which made me the new man in town, so I had to settle for whatever playing time I got from the coach. And because I was one of the tallest players on the team and had good jumping ability, I was forced to play the center position against many taller opponents on some really tough teams.

Although we finished the year with a losing record, overall I think we did pretty well, considering we were probably one of the smallest teams in our conference. My total stats for the year were five points a game and an average of about six to eight rebounds per game during the fifteen to twenty minutes of playing time I got. Not bad, I guess, considering that with my height, I should've been playing forward, instead of center.

In the end, by the time I finished playing my last and final game for my school, I left the school with just one partial scholarship offer to play at Pratt Institute of Technology in Brooklyn, New York. It was an offer that I contemplated for a few months before I decided to turn it down in order to try my chances at playing professional basketball in Puerto Rico.

So right after graduation, I packed my bags and headed to my family's home in Arroyo, Puerto Rico, where a relative with connections to the owner of a professional basketball team in the next town over, Guayama, was looking for Puerto Rican basketball players coming from the US. It was the opportunity of a lifetime, and although it didn't pay much, at least they provided the players with housing and living expenses. At the time, there were not too many tall Puerto Rican basketball players in the league. So they were really hoping to improve their competitiveness and talent rosters by adding tall Puerto Rican players coming from the US.

Well, everything was all set to go, and I was in the process of making arrangements to meet up with the owner, when during a pickup game just couple of days before meeting the owner, I landed on the foot of another player during a rebound and immediately broke my left ankle. As I lay there in excruciating pain, about all I could think about was how my dream of playing professional basketball in Puerto Rico was abruptly coming to an end before it had even started.

I was immediately rushed to the hospital, where my ankle was placed in a cast, as I watched in disappointment and contemplated my options, now that I could no longer make the team. A few days after the incident, I decided that it was best for me to head back home to the Bronx. And although I was invited by the owner to come back the next season to play, by the time the next year rolled around, I had already made my decision not to go back in order to pursue other options.

CHAPTER 62

THE GRADUATE

Up until that point, graduating from high school was going to be the biggest thing that had ever happened to me. So to know that I was going up on that stage, to finally receive my diploma, was absolutely a dream come true! Hard to believe that just a few years back I had dropped out of high school and was weighing my options on what to do next with my life. So much had happened to me that at times I thought, *How is this all possible?* But here I was, just weeks away from graduating and looking forward to a better, more rewarding future. I was super, super excited!

Although I was moving on, deep down inside of me I knew that saying goodbye to all my friends, classmates, and teachers was not going to be easy. I had so many good friends that I used to hang out with at school and on weekends at some of the many parties I used to attend, but most of them did not live in my neighborhood. So the chances of seeing them again were slim. This is especially true since some of my friends were going off to colleges out of state, while others were either joining the military or moving out of the area and going straight into the work force. So sadly, graduation day was probably going to be the very last time I would ever see them.

There were two exceptions: Orlando and his brother Poucho. They were two of my best friends for life, and they not only attended and graduated from Morris High School, but also lived in the same block and neighborhood that I did; neither had any immediate plans to leave the neighborhood. Another one of my best friends from the block, Misael, in the meantime, had decided to join the United States Air Force and was soon heading to boot camp. But overall, I knew I was going to see my friends from the neighborhood on a regular basis in my block, so that wasn't going to change.

However, the closer and closer I got to graduation day, the more and more nervous I got. For the very first time, I felt that even though I had reached this big moment in my life, there was always that fear of failure looming in the background trying to hold me back from moving forward. That's when I knew that I had to constantly stay positive and convince myself that getting over this big hurdle was going to do wonders for me and my future.

Luckily, my grades had never looked better. I had an overall grade point average of B+ in my senior year. A huge improvement when you consider all the other disappointing years I had in high school. So I was really proud of myself. I even got a few certificates of excellence to go with my good grades!

Yet even though I had all these great things going for me, deep down inside of me I was scared. Scared of the unknown, scared of what I wanted to study in college, and finally, scared of failing in college and not being able to handle another disappointment. All this, after having busted my butt in school for the past year and a half just to bring up my grades and graduate on time. I was stressed to the point that I felt I needed take a bit of break from school in order to figure out what my next career move would be after graduation.

So, in June of 1974 when the big day finally arrived, I was super excited and couldn't wait to get that diploma in my hand. Yet, I was also a bit disappointed because, on the biggest and probably one of the most important days of my life, my parents were nowhere to be found in the crowd. For whatever reason, they never made it to graduation that day. Instead, I had to rely on my oldest sister, Mercedes, to be there to congratulate me and take a few pictures of me in my cap and gown.

In an instant, my biggest accomplishment had come and gone. And I finally had that long-awaited high school diploma in my hand. So many of those painful moments that I experienced while growing up somehow disappeared, at least for the moment, as I relished the joy of reaching such a huge milestone in my life. A milestone that just a few years ago was just a distant dream of my imagination. As I proudly declared, "I made it!" I knew the reality of it all was that I still had a long way to go, and life for me was just beginning!

Well, as I mentioned before, shortly after graduation I headed straight to Puerto Rico in pursuit of my longtime dream of playing professional basketball. But unfortunately, my dream quickly vanished when I got hurt during a pickup game in preparation for the big tryout for the team. A week later, I was back at home in the Bronx, still thinking of plan B for my next career move: finding a nice, decent job.

It didn't take long for me to realize just how tough it would be to find a well-paying job with just a high school diploma. After exhaustively searching everywhere for what I thought was that dream job, and not finding it, I decided to take a job at a clothing factory in the garment district of Manhattan. Boy, what a rude awakening that turned out to be.

As soon as I started working there, I was miserable! It took me less than one week before I quit. About a couple of months later, I ended up taking another job at a fast-food joint, Arthur Treacher's Fish and Chips, and worked there for a couple of months before deciding to move on and go back to school.

In the end, I applied and got accepted into Lehman College in the Bronx. My plans were to get a bachelor's degree in sociology and to play varsity basketball for the school. I wanted a career in which I could use all the hard-knock lessons I had learned to help others in similar situations find their way. A career in law enforcement, I decided, would eventually be the perfect choice, following in the footsteps of my Puerto Rican grandfather who served as a state police officer on the island. All and all, I was really super excited about this new journey I was about to embark on. But more importantly, by going to college, I wanted to serve as an inspiration to my family, as an example that anything in life is possible, no matter the hardships you've dealt with in your life. That is something I soon proved on the day that I stepped onto the college campus as a freshman and became the very first person in my family to ever go to college! It was truly an unbelievable feeling!

CHAPTER 63

MY NEXT JOURNEY INTO THE WORLD OF LOVE AND INTIMACY

Still pumped up, I was literally on a roll. I was in college, had a career path in mind that I was trying to pursue, and I was dating. And while that shy side of me was still present at times, it was nothing in comparison to those early years of dating. By this time in my life, I was going to parties, dancing, and meeting girls as never before.

The fact that I was no longer intimidated about asking a girl out on the dance floor made things so much easier for me when it came to meeting girls and going out on dates. In fact, it was during a wild date that one day I also lost my virginity to a much older girl—she was about twenty years old to my sixteen years of age—from my neighborhood, shortly after meeting her through a friend. And that's when things really started changing for me; it opened up a brand-new chapter in my life.

In the months ahead, things were literally starting to happen so fast that it seemed, with every passing day, I was maturing. So much so, that it almost appeared as though I was trying subconsciously to make up for all those lost years. Here I was, a young man enjoying this new life. This new horizon. This new experience. Wow, what a turn of events!

Looking back, I remember one day, while in my senior year of high school, I set my eyes on this very pretty girl in my English class. She was relatively new to the school and at first glance appeared to be a bit shy. We sat a couple of seats away from each other in the third row, and every now and then I would catch her giving me this flirtatious look, as though she was interested in meeting me. Although I later found out through some of my classmates that she was a junior and a bit younger than I was, I was not going to let that stop me from meeting her and chatting.

After class one day, I approached her and introduced myself. She told me her name was Ana. I decided to escort her to one of her classes just so we could talk some more. During our brief conversation, I found out that she had just recently arrived in this country from Honduras and was still trying to adjust to her new life of living in the United States. While her English was not the greatest, and she spoke with a heavy accent, we were still able to hold a decent conversation; however, it was mostly in Spanish. That, as it turns out, was a minor problem for me. Being a Nuyorican from the South Bronx, my Spanish was not the greatest. I struggled at times with understanding her very distinct dialect, or what I used to call that perfect Spanish, from her home country. But somehow, someway, she managed to understand my Spanglish, a combination of Spanish and English blended together to make a word. And I, her Spanish.

As the months went by, and we moved on to other classes, I started seeing less and less of her at school. While we both showed interest in each other, somehow we never really took that extra step to go out on an official date outside of school. And because I was already dating a few girls, I didn't really go all out to pursue the friendship.

By the summer of June 1974, I had already graduated from high school and was pursuing other interests, including trying to play professional basketball in Puerto Rico. But as I mentioned before, we all know how that ended.

Almost a year to the day after graduating from high school, Eddie and I were hanging out around our neighborhood with some other friends when we got a little bored and decided to go elsewhere. As we were accustomed to doing, when there was nothing exciting going on in our neighborhood, we went to other neighborhoods, just looking for something new to see or explore. That day, we decided we'd walk to 149th Street and 3rd Avenue in the South Bronx, just to do some window shopping and to kill some time at this little strip mall, which was located about twelve long blocks from our neighborhood.

I remember it being an early Saturday afternoon, and the streets by this time were packed with people shopping. Eddie and I walked up and down the strip mall a few times, and after not finding anything of interest to see or buy, we decided to call it a day. However, just as we were heading towards 149th Street on our way back home, I noticed this very attractive young lady making her way through the crowd and heading right towards us. It took me a little bit before I finally realized that I thought I knew her. As she got closer and closer, it soon hit me. The girl that was walking in my direction was Ana, the same girl I had met in my English class last year, except she looked completely different.

Her hair was no longer in a bun or ponytail, as I was accustomed to seeing her in school. Instead, her hair was long, wavy, and loose, and it was flowing back freely with the breeze. I even noticed that her style of dressing had changed. She had gone from a very simple and conservative style of dressing, to a very high-fashion and trendy look. I must say, overall, she looked completely different from the person I got to know as Ana back in Morris High School.

She recognized me and gave me a great big smile. Surprised to see each other after a year's time, we stopped and talked for only a few minutes before we said our goodbyes. As it turns out, she was in a bit of a hurry to get back to work after a short lunch break from her job at Miles Shoe Store in that same strip mall. However, before saying our goodbyes, we decided to exchange phone numbers and keep in touch.

On our way back home, I remember telling Eddie how excited I was about bumping into Ana and how much she had changed in appearance since the last time I saw her. In addition to her looks, I was also surprised at how well she had mastered the English language in such a short period of time. Although she still had a little bit of an accent when she spoke, this time around, her English was great. I could easily understand every single word she said to me without a problem.

I told Eddie the whole story of how we met in class and later became good friends. I wasn't really in the right position to push the friendship to the next level because I was already dating a girl at the school and didn't want any problems. Ironically, as it turns out, that relationship was short-lived. Just a few months after we both graduated from high school, we broke up and decided to go our separate ways.

Eddie, after hearing the whole story, thought it was pretty cool and suggested I give Ana a call soon. About week or so later, that's exactly what I did, and we went on our very first date!

Our first date went better than either of us imagined. We had such an awesome time and got along so well that we decided to go on another date. Eventually, that date led to many more meets, and before we knew it, we had officially become boyfriend and girlfriend.

As two very young—I at 18 and she at 17—inexperienced pups entering into their first serious relationship, we quickly fell in love. In fact, we were only three or four months into the relationship when we started talking about marriage and having a family. Yes, things were starting to move at lightning speed, and neither of us ever thought about slowing it down and just enjoying the time as boyfriend and girlfriend before taking it to the next level. Instead, we decided to stay the course and continue on our fast-track journey towards matrimony. And just like that, literally almost six months to the day after we started dating, we took the leap and got married on December 23, 1975.

Looking back now, unlike the average couple who get married, live in their own place, and make a life of their own, ours was a bit different and a little more complicated. For starters, neither of us had money. It wasn't as if we'd taken the time to save money and plan for all the expenses involved in a wedding. We had none of that. We were both poor, and literally lived on a day-to-day basis at home, each of us with our respective families.

At the time, I was a full-time student at Lehman College in the Bronx, trying my best to get my degree in sociology and fulfill my long-time dream of being the first one in my family to get a college degree. Financially, I really didn't have much money. In fact, just to make a few bucks, I worked a part-time job in the school's periodicals section of the library. During summer break, I found a full-time job working as a field supervisor for the Neighborhood Youth Corps. The Neighborhood Youth Corps was a citywide agency, established through Federal grants, to keep kids off the streets during the summer months by providing them with activities and trips to take within and beyond the city limits. Ana, on the other hand, was working part-time for a shoe store in the heart of the Bronx while attending classes at the Barbizon Modeling and Acting School, trying to pursue a career in modeling.

On the day of our wedding, we had no limo, no big expensive catering hall, and no large group of invitees. Instead, we used the car of her older brother, Omar, to go to and from the church…and hours later, to our reception. In addition, to keep the cost down, we decided to use her brother's apartment for our wedding reception. And since it wasn't a big apartment, it quickly filled to capacity with more than sixty people whom we'd invited. We danced and partied all night in the limited space we had available to us. Although it was a bit tight, we still managed to have a great time.

After the party was over in the wee hours of the morning, her brother once again gave us a ride to an affordable hotel in Midtown Manhattan, where we stayed until later that morning when, after breakfast, we took a cab to the bus terminal and hopped on a Greyhound Bus to Boston, Massachusetts. Once there, we checked into a downtown hotel, did a little sightseeing, and dined that night. The next morning, we continued on to the home of my father's brother, Uncle Heriberto, who lived just about an hour or so from Boston in a town called New Bedford. We decided on New Bedford, Massachusetts, for our honeymoon because my uncle had lived there for many, many years. He always said that it was beautiful and a good place to get away from it all and have a great time.

Not much excitement happened during our stay in New Bedford, but we did get a chance to be interviewed live on the air during a community segment that my uncle hosted during the week at a local radio station. It turned out to be a pretty cool experience for both of us since neither of us had ever been interviewed as a guest on a live radio show. During the interview, we talked about a variety of things, from how we met, to how it felt getting married at such a young age, and even about our plans for the future. We stayed with my uncle for just a few days before going back to our home turf in the South Bronx.

Unlike the typical honeymoon in which a couple gets to experience a breathtaking trip to a tropical island with white sandy beaches, crystal-clear ocean waters, and a nice, warm tropical breeze, ours was quite different. We did none of that. But for us at the time, it was memorable!

The long hours on a coach bus made for interesting conversations along the way, as we traveled from state to state, enjoying the roadside sites and watching people walk city streets as they went about their daily lives. Considering the small amount of spending money we had saved up over the span of a few months for this trip, it was just perfect. In the end, we had an awesome time!

Once the honeymoon was over and we were back in the Bronx, reality quickly set in. Not only did we have to plan our life together as a married couple, but also we had to work on the next chapter in our lives and start a family.

CHAPTER 64

OUR TEMPORARY HOME

B efore we were married, we each lived under our parents' umbrella; they supported us throughout most of our respective lives. And as a result, we never had to worry about anything because they were always there to provide us with whatever we needed. But now, as a married couple, we had new responsibilities.

And therein, lies the most difficult part of this new chapter—being independent! This was especially true for two young teens, with no experience of any kind, facing all the new demands and responsibilities.

Our first concern was having a place to stay while we garnered enough money to live independently. We made the difficult decision to move in with my parents for a little bit, buying us enough time to save up some money so we could find a place of our own and start planning a family. As you can probably imagine, living with one's parents is not the easiest thing to do. It is a most difficult situation that in the long run, can interfere with a marriage and a way of life. But it was a chance that we were both willing to take in order to save up some cash for our future plans as a married couple.

So, by January of 1976, just a month after we got married, we moved in with my parents.

CHAPTER 65

THE NEXT CHAPTER IN OUR MARRIAGE

By late February of 1976, we received the greatest news that any newlywed couple could ever dream of, or hope for, when they're planning on having a family. Yes, after several months of trying, we got word that we were going to be parents!!! It was, by far, one of the happiest moment of our lives! A true blessing!

While we could not wait for the birth of our child, we were a bit apprehensive about all the new challenges that lay ahead, especially for two young teens with absolutely no experience in life, but with all the responsibilities that come with being first-time parents. Regardless, we were still beyond thrilled and looking forward to this new journey.

Now that we were expecting our first child, we knew that we had to make some big changes, starting with finding new jobs with better pay and benefits. And second, finding our very own place in which to live and raise a family. Luckily, about a month or so after we got married, Ana left her job at the shoe store and found a full-time job working for Finnair, which was located in Lower Manhattan. While I, on the other hand, took a leave of absence from school and started working full time for a research company in Manhattan, the Conference Board, as a stock clerk in the mailroom. And while it wasn't the greatest job in the world, and the pay was horrible, at least I was blessed to be employed!

However, when it came to my fellow coworkers, they weren't the nicest people in the world. In fact, on quite a few occasions, we ended up in some heated arguments that almost led to fistfights. I was truly miserable, but over time I learned how to keep my cool in order to avoid getting into a physical altercation and losing my job. Something that I certainly could not afford to do, especially now that I was going to be a first-time dad. In other words, I really had no other choice. It was either work and deal with all the negative crap, or leave and take my chances trying to find a new job. I chose to stay!

Finding myself in such a difficult position just pushed me to think really hard about my future goals and where I wanted to be in five or ten years. I was inspired to think beyond what I was doing at that point in my life. It was because of this mindset that I kept dreaming of a better life for me and my family. In essence, that was the driving force that I clung to in order to keep going and stay optimistic. For I knew, deep down inside my heart and soul, this was only a temporary phase. No matter what, I had to stay positive through each and every challenge.

CHAPTER 66

THE START OF A NEW LIFE FOR ME AND MY FAMILY

Approximately six months or so after living with my parents, we had saved up enough money to find our very own apartment. After looking around for weeks for a suitable place, we finally found something in the northwest section of the South Bronx. We settled on a one-bedroom apartment on Valentine Avenue. While it wasn't the greatest place to live—there was a lot of crime and drug activity—it was a lot better than shacking up with my parents. We finally had the privacy for which we had longed.

By this time, I also owned my very first car. I bought it a few months before moving out of my parents' home. It was an old 1968 Oldsmobile Cutlass that my brother-in-law sold me for a mere $350. Although it wasn't in the best shape, and it needed some minor repairs, at least we could get around easier and didn't have to constantly depend on mass transit anymore.

I considered myself pretty lucky to be driving a car, let alone own one, based on our financial situation. Prior to owning the car, I had never driven, or even taken a driving lesson. How I convinced my brother-in-law to sell me the car is beyond me. But I told him that if he sold me the car, I would put it in my father's name and would only drive it once my father taught me how to drive. He thought about it for a minute and then agreed, but only under those conditions. As it turns out...I wasn't completely honest!

Less than a week after buying my car, I got this crazy urge to take it out for a spin and invited my wife to come along for the ride. Since this was my first time behind the wheel of a car, I wasn't planning on going too far; I thought I'd just drive around my parents' neighborhood. Mind you, this was without ever being taught to drive and without a driver's license. A part of me said, *Be patient and wait for Dad to teach you to drive.* But the other side of me just egged me on to take a chance and not wait until it was convenient for my father.

Looking back now, it was far beyond a risky thing to do. It was outright dangerous, especially since it was about eight o'clock at night and I would be driving with a pregnant wife in the car. I know, what was I thinking? My wife thought I was nuts and wasn't sure if she should chance it. However, at the very last minute, she decided to join me and go along for the ride.

I soon learned that pulling out from in between two parked cars was probably the hardest thing to do for a first-time driver like me. In fact, it didn't take long before I realized just how big of a challenge this was going to be. I got into the driver's seat and tried to figure out all the intricate mechanisms involved in making the car move. *How the heck do I get out of a parking spot using all these options?* I asked myself. It truly was an overwhelming experience, but I was determined to see it through, no matter how long it took to finally hit the road!

Upon putting the car in Reverse, I bumped into the car behind me pretty hard, which left me a bit startled for a minute. I then switched gears and ran into the car in front of me. It didn't take long before I felt as though I were riding in a bumper car at the local amusement park. With each back-and-forth movement of the car, I continued to make hard contact with the two cars boxing me in. While it was a nerve-racking experience, I never gave up and was determined to stay the course! It took me a while, but somehow, someway, I managed to get out of that parking spot. And off we went!

That night, I remember holding on to the steering wheel so tight that my hands were starting to get a bit sore. I prayed that no one would dart out in front of me, or cut me off with their car, and force me to slam on the brakes unexpectedly. At the time, I was probably driving about ten miles an hour, if that, all along making sure I was making my turns with ease and braking without any issues.

As the minutes went by, my confidence was slowly starting to soar. I was thinking to myself, *I got this; this is no big deal.* I hadn't experienced any issues, so I was really getting into it. In fact, I was starting to get a little cocky... that is, until I hit the major intersection of University Avenue and 170th Street. These are two main roads. University

Avenue is known for its massive two-car lanes and cars that zoom by traveling at speeds that appear to be more than forty to fifty miles per hour, in a twenty-five-mile-per-hour zone.

I found myself stopped at a stop sign and facing this menacing roadway. I froze. But I had nowhere to go, no place to turn, no way to avoid the intersection. It didn't take long before a line of cars started to build up behind me. Anxious drivers soon took to their car horns in desperation, angrily trying to put pressure on me to cross into the intersection and get it over with. Feeling the stress, I decided to take a deep breath, find the nerve to meet my challenge, and go for it!

Within seconds of entering the intersection, I nearly caused several accidents, cutting off speeding cars that nearly hit us. The combination of the loud beeping horns and screeching tires scared the crap out of me and my wife. Although we had a few close calls, somehow we made it through without any other problems!

I decided to drive for a little while longer before calling it a night and heading back home to our block. Luckily, once on the block, I managed to find a parking spot in an open space near where this crazy journey first began. Once parked, I had the biggest sense of relief!

After that hair-raising experience, you would think that I would've just given up on driving on my own until I took the proper driving lessons from my dad or from a driving school, but instead I did the opposite. It fueled an interest in me to keep on driving until I mastered it and the fear.

In the weeks that followed, I started getting a little bit more daring, to the point where the more time I spent driving around my neighborhood, the more I wanted to branch out to other sections of the Bronx, both to put in more time on the road and to cover greater distances.

Slowly, but surely, I was getting the hang of it and feeling really comfortable behind the wheel. The more I practiced, the better I got behind the wheel and the more confident I became as a driver. After a few months, I got my driver's permit. But it then took me nearly a year before I finally got my driver's license. Hard to believe that I drove for nearly a year with just that driver's permit, and without the accompaniment of a licensed driver by my side. My dad wasn't too thrilled about that. However, in the long run, he had enough confidence in my driving skills to trust that I would do the right thing and not get stopped by the cops for breaking any traffic laws.

It all was going great for me until one day I got stopped by the cops for going through a red light. At that point in time, I had been driving without a license for approximately six months. When they asked me for my license, I gave them my permit. They yelled at me for driving without a license. I told them that I'd borrowed the car from my father while he was sleeping so that I could run an errand. They believed me and let me go with just a verbal warning. And off I went!

That turned out to be the scare I needed. Approximately six months or so after that traffic stop and stern verbal warning, I'm proud to say I finally got my license!

CHAPTER 67

ONE OF THE GREATEST MOMENTS OF MY LIFE: BECOMING A FIRST-TIME DAD

Almost a month to the day after my twentieth birthday, I became a first-time dad!!! It was, by far, one of the greatest feelings in the world and one that I will never, ever forget! That day, I rushed to Lincoln Hospital in the Bronx, and hours later my son, Robert Jr., was born.

While I celebrated this amazing moment in my life and felt as if I were the proudest dad in the world that day, so many other feelings were going through my head at lightning speeds. Mainly, how do two young, inexperienced parents provide a rich and fulfilling life for a newborn when they are both financially strapped for money and living paycheck to paycheck?

It took a lot of prayers to God, accompanied by many positive thoughts, to get us through this new chapter in our lives. And while there were times when we questioned ourselves about how we were going to get through it, we never gave up!

Within a few months of the birth of the baby, we decided to put all our pride aside, and we sought help via a federal-government assistance program geared to help lower-income families in need. It was called the WIC Program, which stands for women, infants, and children. It was through this program that we were able to supplement our family's basic nutritional needs. WIC provides needy families with items such as milk, eggs, cheese, and cereal—just to name a few of the food items—in order to help them care for their families.

To us, this was heaven-sent. It was the assistance we desperately needed as we moved forward as a family. And it helped us tremendously!

After approximately three months of maternity leave for my wife and a couple of weeks for me, we started to think a great deal about our plans for the future and how we were going to improve our financial situation. By the fall of 1976, I made the decision to go back to Lehman College on a part-time basis at night, while still working full time during the day. In my eyes, I saw getting an education as the only way to improve on our living conditions and hopefully the path to a better life. And while I knew it wasn't going to be easy, I was determined to stay the course and to finish my degree in sociology.

Nearly a year and a half into my quest, things at work started getting very difficult. And while I was still doing well at school, I knew it was going to take forever to finish my degree by just going to school on a part-time basis. I was starting to get a bit anxious.

One day in the summer of 1977, I got into a real big argument with my boss at work. He and I had never seen eye to eye, so it was only a matter of time before I'd had enough and decided I didn't want to work there anymore. Approximately two weeks after our disagreement, I quit my job and never looked back!

After talking it over with my wife, I decided that the only way I was going to finally finish school and get my degree was to go back to school on a full-time basis. I would supplement our income by working on a part-time basis at the school and full time during the summer at the Neighborhood Youth Corps.

CHAPTER 68

ANOTHER MOVE, ANOTHER CAREER

I was extremely happy and excited to be back at school. I honestly felt, that in the long run, getting my degree was going to provide the bridge and foundation I needed to get out of poverty and hopefully provide a more fulfilling life for my family.

Most of my focus was geared towards getting a degree in sociology and eventually becoming a police officer just like my grandfather. As a kid, my father used to tell me stories about my grandfather's years of service, and how later in his career he became a motorcycle cop in the traffic division. Those stories only served to pique my interest to be a police officer even more.

Aside from my grandfather and his influence on my career choice, more than anything I just wanted to make a difference in the lives of others. This is especially true, after all that I had gone through while growing up and after seeing so many lives destroyed due to drugs and violence.

During the fall semester, I decided to try out for the school's basketball team and made it on my first try. It was definitely another dream come true, especially since, just three years before, I almost played professional basketball in Puerto Rico straight out of high school. The fact that I made the basketball team at the age of twenty-one was truly a big accomplishment and proved that anything is possible; you just have to dream it and make it happen!

While juggling school full time, working part-time, and playing basketball for the school's team was challenging, I knew that nothing would ever compare to all the duties and responsibilities that came along with being a young dad and husband.

By the end of the fall semester of 1977, my grades weren't the greatest, but I finished the term with a 2.84 grade point. Not bad, I thought, considering I had been out of school for nearly two years.

By the summer of 1978, the neighborhood was starting to see a steep rise in both crime and urban decay. We finally made the decision that it was time to leave the area and relocate to a nicer and safer neighborhood. Luckily, a couple of longtime friends of ours, Jorge and Mini, had moved out of the Bronx and into a very nice neighborhood in Flushing, Queens.

Unlike the apartments we were both used to in the South Bronx—row houses usually five stories high, multiple families living on each floor—this particular housing development, located at 7504 150th Street, in Flushing, Queens was less traditional. It was a community of three-level, brick row houses with only three families living on each floor. In complete contrast to the cement walkways of the Bronx, these buildings actually had grass all around them, something we weren't used to seeing. Overall, the neighborhood appeared to be very nice and tranquil, and it gave us the feeling that this would be a great place to live and raise a family. We signed up for one of the wonderful apartments and moved in as soon as we got approved.

For a little while, I commuted to and from school in the Bronx every day. But over time, that got a bit tiring, and I decided to switch schools. I applied and got accepted into Queens College, which, like Lehman, was part of the CUNY, City University of New York.

This turned out to be the perfect place for me. It was less than a mile from home, within walking distance. Upon switching schools, I had to say goodbye to all my coaches and teammates from the Lehman College basketball team, all great people whom I truly enjoyed being around, both as teammates and good friends on and off the court.

Thankfully, I left on good terms, and my head coach put in a good word for me with the head coach at Queens College, so I was able to continue with my basketball career. The only stipulation was that NCAA rules mandated at the time that I sit out for a whole year before playing for another team. That was perhaps the hardest part about switching schools. But then again, if I wanted to play at another school, this is what I had to do. And after a while, I was okay with it.

While taking classes and waiting for my eligibility to kick in, a few unexpected things happened in my life that really had me wondering if moving to this new neighborhood was the right thing to do.

One day, I got up to go to school, and instead of walking, I decided to drive. As I was making my way around the corner from my building, to where I usually parked my car—by this time, a 1972 Pontiac Grand Prix—I noticed it wasn't there. For a quick moment, I thought my mind might be playing tricks on me, so I decided to walk around my whole block one more time, just to satisfy my curiosity that this, in fact, was the place I had parked my car the day before. As I looked around, I noticed fragments of glass where my car once stood. I immediately knew, right then and there, that my car had been stolen!

I later learned, from neighbors in my building, that this was the typical way thieves stole cars in our neighborhood. They broke the small rear-passenger window and unlocked the door. Once inside, they ripped the vehicle's ignition right off using a car dent puller and got the car started by using a screwdriver to turn the ignition. And off they went!

This truly broke my heart, for I had only had that car for two months before it was stolen. I'd bought it after my Olds Cutlass broke down, and I had no other choice but to sell it to a junkyard for $40. That left me in debt at the time and forced me to borrow money from several family members just to buy another used car, the Grand Prix, to replace my Oldsmobile. Now I was carless again!

A few months later, having no car to move me and my family around, I ended up borrowing money from my Dad to replace the stolen car with a used 1970 Chevy Malibu. That put me in the hole for $1,500, which took me a long time to pay back. I eventually did and got plenty of miles out of the Malibu...for many years!

The other incident that really had me second-guessing if this area was better than the place we had been living in, in the Bronx, happened about a year or so later.

One sunny afternoon, I stepped outside my building to pick up something that I'd left in my car the day before. Immediately after stepping onto the sidewalk, I took notice of a suspicious-looking vehicle occupied by two White males. It was parked right in front of my building. Suspecting these two characters might be looking to either buy or sell drugs in my building, I gave them a stern stare.

The right passenger in the vehicle apparently took offense to my staring them down with suspicion and decided to say something about it. "Hey, you got a problem?"

I said, "No, do you?" Probably not the smartest thing to do on my part, especially since I was by myself and I was challenging two individuals who, unbeknownst to me, could've been armed. This is especially true when it involves drugs.

The next thing I knew, this individual gets out of his car and decides to confront me face-to-face. Once again, he repeated what he'd said before, "Yo, what's your problem, man?"

I again replied, " I don't have a problem. Do you?"

It was then that I realized I had just committed one of the biggest no-no's that's engrained in you from a very young age when you grow up in the Bronx: never, ever let anyone come to within an arm's length of your face before stopping the threat. That day, I let my guard down. When this individual was about to confront me, I should've just knocked him on his ass before he had a chance to get right up in my face.

The next thing I know, this guy takes a solid right hook to the left side of my face, at the eyebrow; it really rocked me! The impact immediately opened up a one-inch cut on my left eyebrow. There was blood everywhere! But I never went down. Within seconds, I was able to regain my composure and put up a really good fight. Suddenly, my punches were landing all over his face, and I was getting the best of him. Before I knew it, he broke loose from me and took off running towards his car. He immediately jumped in, and the car sped off. I never saw this idiot or his crony ever again!

That night, I went to the emergency room; it took several stitches to close up the gash. It was a tough lesson learned that I still carry with me to this day. I will never, ever let someone get to within an arm's length of confronting me again before taking action to defend myself.

In the end, it was this last incident that truly inspired me to go after my dream and become a cop!

CHAPTER 69

A NEW CAREER AND THE BEGINNING OF A NEW CHAPTER IN MY LIFE

B y January of 1979, I was in full throttle and had finally made the decision to go after one of my biggest lifelong dreams: becoming a police officer!

It just so happened that around the same time, the NYPD announced that they were recruiting police officers for the next class and that applications would be available in every police precinct throughout the city. I wasted no time and picked up one of the applications in one of the precincts near my home. I quickly filled it out, turned it in, and waited for the test-date notification.

Within a matter of months, I received a letter in the mail notifying me of the test date and location. Coincidentally, the place I was to take the test just happened to be in my old high school, DeWitt Clinton, the place where I once had big dreams of becoming a star varsity basketball player and the first Puerto Rican basketball player in the NBA. But as you already know, after I broke my ankle, that dream was never realized.

After taking the test, a few months went by before I was notified that I had passed the written portion and would be moving on to the next phase of testing. When I got the news that I had passed the initial test, I was super excited and couldn't wait for the next challenge.

In the meantime, while I waited patiently, one day I got a call from my cousin Jija, who lived in East Hartford, Connecticut, at the time. She'd found out about my interest in becoming a police officer and wanted to tell me that the Hartford Police Department in Connecticut was hiring cops. In all my years of living in New York City, I had never once ventured out to the neighboring state of Connecticut. So, this was going to be a totally new challenge for me, but one that I was willing to take if it meant making one of my lifelong dreams come true!

My two other cousins, Wilfredo and Orlando II, in New York City, were also thinking of becoming police officers. As it turns out, when my cousin Jija informed me that Hartford PD was hiring, she also told them about the job openings.

By the time June of 1979 came around, all three of us had taken the written test and passed with flying colors. Because Hartford PD was in dire need of cops, due to retirements and attrition, the testing process actually moved along pretty fast. Everything from the physical-agility test, medical examination, oral boards, background investigation, psychological evaluation, and finally, the interview with the chief of police—it all happened so fast!

And finally, on November 5 of that year, my cousins and I got acceptance letters in the mail that all three of us were hired! The letter went on to say that we should "report to classroom 2, room 2205, Hartford Police Headquarters, on November 26, 1979, at 07:45 hours, to begin the Police Recruit Training Program!"

When I got that letter, I was beyond ecstatic! I couldn't wait to yell out loud to all my family and friends and tell them that my dream job of becoming a police officer was now well on its way!!! It was a day that I will never, ever forget! Because from that day forward, my life and my world were going to change forever; all the hopes and dreams that I had for myself and my family were going to be realized!

CHAPTER 70

THE HARTFORD POLICE ACADEMY

D ay one in the police academy felt as if it were my very first day in college. I was in a large classroom filled with some forty-seven other police recruits. And while I was never in the military, I can only imagine that this is how it must feel on your first day of basic training. Everyone was dressed the same—khaki pants, khaki shirt, black tie, black belt, and black shoes—and neatly groomed. More importantly, everyone was nervous as heck in anticipation of what was expected of us as the next group of newly minted police recruits.

That day, we all sat there quietly in our chairs as the academy instructors, dressed in their police blues, stood in front of the class with serious and intimidating looks on their faces that spoke volumes. This only added to the tension in a room that was already so quiet and intense that you could literally hear a pin drop.

I later learned that this was all part of the program aimed at toughening us up as we entered into this new, stress-filled police career. A career that is considered one of the toughest, most stressful, and dangerous jobs in the world, one in which making split decisions becomes an everyday part of your life. Decisions that can make the difference between life and death, going home to your family at the end of your shift or not. Hence the reason everything you learn during those six months of training in the academy is geared towards not only learning about enforcing the laws of the land, but also protecting your life and the life and property of others, no matter the risk at hand. No matter the cost.

That is not an easy concept to absorb, especially when you realize that every time you go out there on the streets of Hartford, there's no telling what will happen from one call to the next. That is what makes this career unique, yet so unpredictable and risky at the same time!

The tension was finally broken when the commander of the police academy, Sergeant Kelly, introduced himself and the rest of the instructors—Sergeants Lewis and Garrett and Officers White and Officer Goodrow—whose responsibility it would be to ultimately make us full-fledged police officers by the end of the six-month training period. After they each introduced themselves and briefed us about their respective careers and training as instructors, it was our turn to introduce ourselves and to tell the class a little bit about ourselves.

One by one, we all stood up and introduced ourselves. Some had prior law enforcement and military experience, while others worked as loss-prevention security officers in department stores. Then, of course, you had those, like me, who had absolutely no experience in the field of law enforcement, other than having a lifelong dream of becoming a police officer. My introduction was brief, and I said something to the effect that I was a married father of one from the South Bronx, New York, who'd always wanted to be a police officer just as his grandfather had been.

Throughout this intense training, we learned everything from the laws of arrest, elements of search and seizure, criminal-investigation procedures, defensive driving techniques, report writing, firearms training, accident-investigation protocol, and first aid, to learning hard-core, hands-on training in defensive tactics, boxing, running, and even working out every single morning in order to build up our strength, energy, and stamina.

Midway into our training, we became the last Hartford police class in the department's history to be sworn in just three months into the academy, which essentially made us police officers. We were all given badges and guns, and assigned to a field training officer (FTO) for two weeks of actual hands-on training and experience while working on the streets of Hartford. The purpose of this was to acclimate us very early in our training about what it's like to be a police officer.

My FTO was Officer Anderson, a great cop who had been on the job for more than twenty years. He was well respected within the department as someone who had just about seen and done it all during his twenty-plus years of service with the Hartford Police Department. During those two weeks, even though we were still wearing our khaki uniforms, we basically had all the tools and equipment that any regular police officer on the streets would have, including badge, gun, and handcuffs.

I quickly learned that one of the most important survival techniques on the streets is to never let your guard down and most importantly, to always keep your eyes and ears open to your surroundings. In short, you're trained very early on to always expect the unexpected! This was ingrained into all of us right from the very beginning for the sake of our personal safety and well-being as police officers.

In those two weeks I was out patrolling on the streets of Hartford, we went on a few domestic-dispute calls, recovered a couple of unoccupied stolen cars in the projects, took a few armed-robbery complaints, and even conducted a couple of accident investigations in which no one was injured.

While you're in FTO training, the initial case incident reports are always written by your FTO; you, as the trainee, watch and learn. Later in your field training, you're given the reins, and it is up to you to investigate every complaint, under the watchful eye of your FTO, of course. That is, until you feel comfortable enough to do it all on your own from start to finish.

After it was all said and done, it was by far one of the greatest feelings in the world for me, and truly reaffirmed my decision as to become a police officer. Shortly after those two weeks on the streets, we returned back to the academy and had to surrender our badges and guns until we completed the course. From that point on, it would take a total of three more months of classroom training before our last and final day in the police academy, which was scheduled for April 3, 1980.

CHAPTER 71

A DREAM COME TRUE: I'M FINALLY A COP!!!

April 3, 1980 was one of the biggest moments of my life! It was on this day that my lifelong dream came true, and I officially became a police officer. I had dreamed of this moment ever since I could remember. And now, at the youthful age of twenty-three years old, I could finally say, "I made it happen! I'm a cop now!!!" But more importantly, for the very first time, I'm in a profession in which I have a title attached to my name: Officer Roberto Alfaro. A title that carries so much responsibility, so much expectation, so much respect, and so much pride! By graduating, I also became the latest member in my family to become a police officer, following in my grandfather's footsteps, those of the late Esiquell Alfaro.

At the graduation ceremony, my wife, son, dad, mother, and a few other family members from the South Bronx were there to cheer me on and congratulate me after I walked onto that stage in my proud blues. It was truly a symbolic moment when finally my badge was pinned on my shirt, and I officially became a full-fledged Hartford police officer!

Joining me on this momentous occasion were my first cousin Wilfredo Rivera and distant cousin Orlando Allende, who also became police officers. It was one of the biggest moments in our family's history. That day we laughed, we cried, and we celebrated loudly as one super proud and happy family!

After graduation, we all headed to my home in East Hartford, Connecticut, to celebrate some more. One of the funny things that really sticks out vividly in my mind from that day was my cousins and I going shopping at a local supermarket in full uniform, just to pick up a few things for our celebration. We couldn't help but notice the look on everyone's faces as we shopped in our uniforms. But we didn't mind! We didn't care what others were thinking. We just knew that we wanted the world to take notice of how a family of three cousins from New York City had finally made their dreams come true!

I guess we just wanted to share publicly how excited we were about our new careers in law enforcement. We knew the struggles that we had all endured, growing up poor and coming from tough and impoverished neighborhoods, to be where we were at that moment in our lives. And while life was surely tough growing up in the South Bronx and New York City in general, we were now at the start of a brand-new chapter in our lives. We knew that we had all finally made it!!!

CHAPTER 72

TIME TO HIT THE STREETS!

Three days after graduating from the police academy, it was time to hit the streets of Hartford and ultimately put to work everything we were taught. As in every police department, the start of the eight-hour shift usually begins as soon as you report to roll call, where sergeants, lieutenants, or captains brief the squad on all the important issues affecting the police department and the City of Hartford. These roll-call briefs include everything from the types of crimes being committed on that particular day, to the names and/or descriptions of the suspects, vehicles, and weapons involved in the commission of these crimes. At the end of each roll call, we were usually reminded to "be safe out there and make sure to look out for each other!"

Normally, there are three shifts in a police department. They rotate around the clock twenty-four seven; the day shift is A-squad; evening shift, B-squad; and finally, the midnight shift, C-squad.

As a brand-new rookie reporting to work for my very first assignment, I was really excited and was looking forward to it. As most rookies are, I was bit apprehensive about what to expect and about how my first day on the streets was going to turn out. Aside from that, I wanted to make a good impression by looking very sharp my first day on the job. This was my way of showing how much pride I took in wearing the Hartford police uniform, while at the same time paying homage to all the history and respect that came along with being a Hartford cop. That day, my shoes were shined to the max; they had a glassy appearance, and you could almost see your reflection in them. My uniform was cleaned and crisply ironed, without any wrinkles or flaws to diminish my appearance as a true professional in this amazing career. And finally, my eight-point police hat was perfectly aligned on my head, the bill just shadowing over the bridge of my nose.

In roll call, I tried to portray a cool and calm demeanor on the outside, but on the inside, my heart was beating at a mile a minute in anticipation of dealing with the unknown once I hit the streets. That first call over the radio. That first emergency call. That first high-risk call. That first of everything that I would have to respond to and investigate on my own. For I knew that as a matter of protocol, no matter how complex or involved the call or situation might be, if my patrol-car number was the first one called on the radio by dispatch, I owned it. Additional units might be sent as backup, depending on the type of call. If the call was deemed to be active, such as a robbery in progress, it would mean even more units being dispatched to the scene.

Regardless, if the case was assigned to you, it was your responsibility to respond to the location as quickly as possible, assess the situation, and determine whether or not a crime had been committed—and if so, by whom—before taking the appropriate action necessary to resolve the threat, intervene on the crisis, or investigate further. Therefore, in those instances when you discovered information on the suspects and/or vehicles, it was your responsibility to relay it to all units in the area via your police radio as soon as possible, giving a detailed description of the wanted vehicle and/or suspects.

One thing really stands out in my mind about my very first day of working the evening shift. It happened just minutes into roll call and really took me completely off guard. After you graduate from the police academy, the on-the-job training with your assigned field training officer, or FTO, continues for an additional three or four weeks or so.

But that night, as I waited anxiously to hear my assigned area of patrol from our squad leader, the lieutenant, I did not hear whom was assigned to train me. So I decided to ask the lieutenant, "Excuse me, sir, but do you know who's my FTO tonight?"

He paused for a moment and smiled before answering me, "I'm sorry, kid, but you're on your own. You have no FTO," and threw the keys to car 54 right at me.

I caught them and briefly looked at them before responding, "Thank you, sir," as I left roll call and headed out the door to find my patrol car. It was truly a surreal moment. One moment I'm in the police academy, and the next I'm on my own, patrolling the streets and dealing with the unknown. It was unexpected, but I knew I had no choice but to push through it and do the best I could with the little bit of street training that I had under my belt—two weeks with my FTO in the academy and one week on the day shift. That was it!

During that period of time, the department was so short on cops that they needed bodies out there to cover as much of the city as possible with the little manpower they had. Tying up two men in one car just wasn't cutting it. That meant that a few of us would be without a field training officer for the start of our careers. I, unfortunately, was one of them!

Fending for myself and just trying to learn as much as possible from some of the veteran officers on the streets wasn't going to be easy, especially for a brand-new rookie with very little street experience. In addition, up to that point, I had only lived in Hartford for about seven months. So the streets were still foreign to me, and getting to learn them, I knew, was not going to be easy.

However, as someone who had lived in one of the worst drug- and gang-infested neighborhood of the South Bronx, I wasn't about to quit, no matter how difficult things got for me. I took this as just one more challenge that I had to overcome in my life in order to be successful in my brand-new career. I was determined to learn as much as I could without a field training officer. That meant watching and observing some of the veteran officers in action, while mentally trying to put myself in their shoes and to see how I would handle each and every situation. I asked a lot of questions and made as many mental notes as I could while working with those seasoned officers.

Luckily, I had the golden opportunity to learn from some of the best cops on the streets of Hartford over the weeks and months that followed. They became my mentors and taught me as much as they could from all their personal years of experience on the job.

It didn't take long, after my indoctrination into this whole new world as a public servant, before I had to make my first arrest. It all happened about three weeks after hitting the streets, while the *Hartford Courant* was riding with me. They were doing a story on the "New Policemen on the Beat," covering the lives of two brand-new rookies, my classmate Darlene and me, as we patrolled the streets of Hartford. That night, I got a call about an elderly homeless man who needed medical attention after a long night of binging on alcohol. Upon arriving at the scene, I noticed that the homeless man was sitting on the edge of curb, his body leaning up against a light pole. The man was still conscious, but clearly extremely intoxicated. I immediately called for an ambulance to be dispatched to the scene, and the man was later transported to St. Francis Hospital for detox and treatment.

Shortly after finishing up with this call, I got another call about a possibly intoxicated female slumped over the wheel of car, the vehicle still running. It just so happened that that incident was right next door to our first call, so my backup unit and I decided to just walk there. Once there, the female driver was found, as reported, slumped over the wheel of her car with the keys still in the ignition and the motor running. Somehow, someway, we managed to wake her up, and it soon became clear to us that she was so visibly intoxicated that there was no way she was in any condition to drive her car. As a result, a field sobriety test was administered, but she failed it miserably and was subsequently placed under arrest for driving under the influence.

This was my very first arrest since hitting the streets; it made me feel as though I was making a difference in a big way and had possibly saved a life, that of either the driver or an innocent hit by her. That night, we had one less intoxicated person to worry about on the roads. And one more life saved and given the chance to see another day.

A few days later, on May 4, 1980, a big spread in the Sunday newspaper documented the incident with a full-page write-up, along with a host of photos from that memorable day in my life. The first arrest of your career is one that you will never forget, one that marks the beginning of many, many more to come!

CHAPTER 73

MY FIRST CLOSE CALL

Just months after the start of my new career in law enforcement, I had my very first close call on the job. There would be many others after that, but this day I came to within a foot or so of getting shot.

It happened on a quiet evening in the southeast section of the city. My partner, Carlos, and I were enjoying a nice dinner break at Comerio, a restaurant located at 158 Park Street in Hartford, when a volley of about four to five gunshots rang out during a drive-by shooting that took place right in front of the restaurant.

We were sitting at our table, which was set near the front glass window and entrance, when we heard the shots fired and quickly realized that one of the bullets had gone through the restaurant's window, narrowly missing me and my partner by a mere foot in either direction. There were loud, piercing sounds, which were caused by the bullets hitting the glass and creating almost-nickel-sized hole, piercing the glass in numerous places.

We instinctively drew our weapons to confront the threat, but it appeared that the drive-by shooter had sped away from the scene. We later learned that we were not the intended targets; we were just in the wrong place at the wrong time and nearly paid the price for it. It turns out that it was a drug- and gang-related dispute, which led to the driver taking potshots at his intended victim, who happened to be standing right in front of the business.

In the investigation that followed, we discovered the identity and whereabouts of the suspected shooter and arrested him without incident, right in his apartment. He was charged with a host of crimes, including numerous counts of criminal attempt to commit assault in the first degree and reckless endangerment with a firearm. This, as it turns out, was my first exposure to the dangerous gang violence in Hartford.

In the end, it was a close call that neither my partner nor I will ever, ever forget.

CHAPTER 74

GANGS, DRUGS, AND DRIVE-BY SHOOTINGS, ALL IN THE MIX

The era of the '80s and '90s marked the worst troubled times that the City of Hartford had ever faced. Gangs, such as the Latin Locos, the Bachelors, the Ghetto Brothers, the Nomads, the Latin Kings, and the 20 Love Gang, roamed the city streets and created chaos for so many of its residents and the police officers on the streets.

With the gangs came disputes over control of territories for drug peddling, drug use, assaults, and murders. And with the number of weapons running rampant among the gangs on the city streets and in the projects, drive-by shootings became the norm. So many innocent people paid with their lives under the onslaught of these reckless and violent assaults on their community.

It seemed that every car you stopped, or every street corner you cleared of gangbangers, you were bound to find a cache of drugs and guns. With the rise in gangs came the rise in crime. A record number of homicides—fifty-eight alone in 1994—assaults, and robberies raised the crime rate in the city to an all-time high. So much so, that the police department decided to create a gang task force, and at times enforced curfews, in their desperate attempts to put a dent in the crime rate, and hopefully put an end to, or at least slow down, the rise in gang warfare and the street violence affecting the city.

It didn't take long for me to realize that working in Hartford was not going to be, as they say, a walk in the park. Instead, it reminded me so much of some of the tough neighborhoods I grew up around during the '60s and '70s, where shootings, violent assaults, and drug issues were regular occurrences.

In the end, it was these same conditions that ultimately inspired me to become a cop in the first place; I hoped one day to make a difference in the lives of others and to change lives!

CHAPTER 75

FIGHTING FOR MY LIFE

By 1981, so many great things had happened to me. For starters, after more than a year on the job, I was getting really comfortable with my new and exciting police career. In addition, I was now able to navigate through the streets of Hartford with ease, even though at one point it had seemed so foreign to me. It was also during this time that I was slowly, but surely, starting to build up my experience as a street cop, having made dozens of arrests for everything from armed robberies to burglaries, larcenies, and everything else in between. In fact, I even managed to get involved in quite a few stolen car chases during that time. It was all far more than I had ever expected as a rookie cop.

While I accomplished so many of my goals as a cop, two milestones in particular clearly stood out from among the rest. The first one, exactly one year after graduating from the police academy, I passed my probationary period without any issues. Reaching this milestone afforded me the opportunity to join the Hartford Police Union. This was a goal that every rookie on the job strives to achieve in order to get union protection and representation and to ensure job security.

The second one, and most important of all, I was now a dad for the second time! And I couldn't be more excited or grateful for this amazing blessing! My beautiful daughter, Bianca, was born in January of 1981, and it was truly a dream come true. That day, I remember I cried, I jumped for joy, and I wanted the whole world to know how happy and thrilled I was to have my beautiful little princess in my life. Something that, for many years, I had hoped and prayed would one day happen in our lives.

Looking back now, it was sometime in the early spring of 1980 when we finally got the word from the doctor that my wife was pregnant. The excitement and joy in our hearts and faces were truly priceless! And we will never, ever forget it!

Everything was going so well. I had a steady job that I loved, a beautiful family who meant the world to me, and I finally had the means to buy so many things in life that I couldn't afford to buy when I was a young, struggling dad trying to make ends meet while living in the South Bronx. I felt truly blessed!

One day, this beautiful life, which I was enjoying so much and for which I felt so blessed, almost came to an end when I found myself fighting for my life. It became another wake-up call that would change my life forever!

It happened in the wee hours of the morning, around 3:00 a.m., on a quiet weekday during my midnight shift. That morning, I got a call from my dispatcher to respond to a silent burglary alarm at a small mini supermarket located at 175 Farmington Avenue. The call had come in from the monitoring team of a SONITROL security system; they reported hearing glass breakage coming from this business. SONITROL, at the time, was one of the few alarm systems that equipped businesses with a sensor able to pick up any noise or disturbance that might result from someone trying to break into a business.

By this time on the force, I had been to many false alarms from systems monitored by SONITROL. Their sensors were so sensitive that any movement, even that of a rodent, would be enough to trigger the alarm. After a while, you start taking it for granted that each alarm you're dispatched to might be just another false alarm.

That night, I did something that I swore I would never do: I let my guard down and became complacent. I remember pulling up in front of the business while my backup partner, Officer Jon Fox, covered the back of the building. This was protocol when dispatched to an active scene such as a tripped burglar alarm. I immediately assessed the situation and determined that it appeared that no entry had been gained.

I noticed, however, that the front glass window had an extensive crack in it. I also saw a men's ten-speed bike on the ground, right in front of where the damage to the business had taken place. It was clear that an attempt had been made using the bike as an instrument to gain entry. Unfortunately, it appeared that the suspect had left the area before our arrival at the scene. I advised dispatch of what I had found and told her to notify the owner so that we could investigate further.

While standing in front of the business, out of the corner of my right eye, I saw what appeared to be a dark, shadowy figure rushing towards me. By the time I turned my head to see the threat, the suspect had swung at my head in full force with a broomstick, but he missed me. Somehow, I managed to fend off the impact just in the nick of time, blocking it with my right forearm. I immediately fought for control of the stick, disarming him rather quickly, but it was the aftermath of this ensuing battle that soon found me in the struggle for my life.

The dangerous suspect and I were in a hand-to-hand battle when I noticed that he had turned his attention towards my gun. He lunged and tried desperately to get control of my gun by attempting to force it out of my holster. The battle intensified as we both fell to the ground. I was trying everything I could to push the subject off me. But the more I fought back, including by punching him in the face, the angrier and more determined he got to take my gun and end my life.

It appeared to me that the suspect was immune to pain. Wearing just a pair of shorts, no shirt or shoes, I knew this individual was either a complete nutcase or high on some type of super-potent drugs, or a combination of both. He seemed impervious to my commands to stop and attempts to arrest him.

My radio had fallen out of its case during the struggle, and I was not able to reach it to call for help, making matters more desperate. I thought about my family and how much I needed to survive this battle to be there for them. I was quickly losing my strength. As I was fighting on my back, I felt my gun slowly being pulled out of my holster, but I fought hard as heck not to let that happen. I prayed to God that I could somehow muster enough strength to fight my way out of this one, or that help would soon arrive to get me out of this life-or-death situation; my prayers seemed to be falling on deaf ears.

Just as I was losing hope, an alert dispatcher tried to raise me numerous times on the radio. And when she got no response from me, she decided to ask my backup unit, Officer Fox, to check on me to make sure I was okay because I was not answering my radio. When I heard that on the radio, it was the biggest relief of my life! I knew that help was definitely on the way.

The next thing I remember was hearing Officer Jon Fox's hurried footsteps running towards me and joining me in the melee. Officer Fox's quick, lifesaving actions made a huge difference in my life. He was able to wrap his nightstick around the suspect's neck and somehow pull him away from me at just the right time. As the suspect continued to put up a fierce battle, violently trying to use his fists and feet to strike us both, we fought to bring him under control and hand-cuff him behind his back. It took all we had to subdue the suspect, but we finally got it done!!! Thanks to Officer Fox and an alert dispatcher who came to my aid, my life was saved! That day, I was extremely blessed to have won the battle and make it safely home to my family!

After it was all said and done, we put the suspect in my car and took him to the station, where he was booked on a variety of criminal charges, including several counts of assault on a police officer, interfering with a police officer, and attempted burglary. We later discovered that the suspect was wanted for escaping from a mental institution, Cedarcrest Hospital in Newington, Connecticut, and was considered extremely dangerous, thus explaining his violent behavior!

As it turns out, this was the first of many close calls I would face as a police officer!

CHAPTER 76

GUNS, GUNS, AND MORE GUNS

Perhaps one of the biggest problems affecting the high crime rate in the City of Hartford during the turbulent '80s and '90s was the vast number of illegal guns being carried around by gangbangers, drug dealers, and drug users. I soon learned that guns were literally everywhere. Just as so many of my brothers and sisters felt while fighting this epidemic of gun violence on the streets of Hartford, I just never knew when it would turn out to be my turn to get into a gun battle with one of these brazen, hard-core criminals.

During my twenty-one years of dedicated service, I had numerous encounters with armed subjects, any of which could've ended with being shot, wounded, or killed. In many of these incidents, the subjects were armed with firearms used in the commission of a crime or for self-protection from other desperate criminals trying to infringe on their drug territory. In all, I estimate taking more than twenty loaded firearms—everything from revolvers, automatic handguns, long rifles, sawed-off shotguns, to a MAC-10 machine gun—off the streets of Hartford during my many years of service. You name it, and they were out there. Most, if not all, were taken from gangbangers prior to or during a gang fight. And those are only my statistics. Many of my fellow officers did their part and took just as many, if not a lot more, firearms off the streets than I did during those very turbulent years of the gang wars.

It is said that for every gun taken off the streets by police officers, one or more lives are saved, and it has a domino effect on an entire generation of families just from that one life being saved. The opposite is also true when a life is painfully taken away from a family because of gun violence. That is something that so many of us in my blue family truly believe because we see it every day. In the long run, it serves to inspire us to take off the streets as many of these illegal and dangerous firearms as we can in order to make a difference. And in doing so, we risk our lives every single day to save the lives of others.

Not all armed subjects are involved in gangs; some carry guns to protect their drug-peddling business from hard-core junkies who roam the streets of Hartford, ripping off drug dealers, businesses, and the average person on the street just to support their addictions. Dealing with one such case nearly got me and my partner shot one day when we unintentionally walked into an active robbery while on another call.

It happened approximately four years into my career on a cold, wintry late night in December. Another patrol officer, Rick G, and I were dispatched to a domestic dispute involving several family members on Ashley Street in Hartford. At the time, we were still dealing with the aftereffects of a snowstorm that had dropped about eight to ten inches of snow on the ground just a few days before. The sidewalks still had snowbanks that measured nearly a foot in height. The streets were eerily quiet, not much vehicular or pedestrian traffic at all in the area.

Luckily, this complaint did not involve any physical confrontation or threats, just a family involved in a domestic dispute that required our presence in order to resolve the issue. However, these are situations that we never take lightly, for more cops are killed or seriously hurt during domestic disputes than on any other call for service. For this reason, we usually approach these situations with a lot of caution. We know firsthand how a call for domestic intervention can quickly go from bad to worse within a matter of seconds.

That night when we arrived on this call, we were met by the complainants who were standing right in front of their house, still arguing over an unknown issue. There was no evidence of violence; it appeared to be just a big disagreement between a husband and wife. The screaming and the shouting could be heard a mile away; the husband and wife appeared ready to go at each other physically at any given time. We immediately separated them to quell the argument and prevent its escalation from a verbal confrontation to a physical one.

After a few minutes, things appeared to be calming down, and we were making progress. In the meantime, a neighbor from a house across the street yelled, "Officers, there's a fight going on right down the street!" She pointed in the direction from her third-floor window, from which she could apparently see two combatants duking it out on the side of the road.

Still dealing with the domestic dispute, I radioed the dispatcher and reported the status of our call and advised her of the new situation. I requested backup and told the dispatcher that we would head up the street to break up the fight, but would stand by until the backup arrived. We explained the situation to the complainants in the domestic dispute and asked them both to walk with us while we dealt with the situation at hand. They agreed and walked behind us as we headed towards the fight.

We made our way from Ashley to Huntington Street. Under the dimly lit streetlamps, we could see what appeared to be two shadowy figures that stood out among the white snowbanks covering the city streets. The poor lighting from the streetlamps, only added to the eerie feeling of that night.

As we closed in, we saw these two individuals rolling around in a snowbank, embroiled in what appeared to be a physical altercation. We were less than thirty yards away when suddenly the individual who was getting the crap beat out of him somehow broke loose and started running right down the middle of the street in our direction. The individual still on the ground jumped up and began firing numerous rounds right in our direction!

Before we could react, the rounds were literally whizzing right by us and over our heads. The loud popping noise of the gun echoed through the empty street, as the bright-red muzzle flash from the revolver lit up the street with each round fired. Within a matter of seconds, we were in the line of fire and quickly found ourselves ducking for cover to keep from getting hit. Somehow, we and the two individuals from the domestic dispute managed to take cover behind the rear of a nearby unoccupied parked car. We quickly drew our weapons on the armed subject, forcing him at gunpoint to drop the weapon or risk being shot and possibly seriously injured or killed. Thankfully, he decided to cooperate and was immediately disarmed and handcuffed at the scene by me and my partner.

We later discovered during the investigation that the armed individual had tunnel vision and was so focused on taking down the assailant that he actually never saw us walking towards him during the fracas. It turns out that the individual who had run right past us was in fact the bad guy who was trying to rob the other guy at gunpoint. It was an attempted armed robbery that went wrong.

According to the victim, he had picked up the suspect in his cab somewhere in the downtown area of Hartford, with the intent of dropping him off somewhere in the west end of the city. It was nearing this unknown location that he felt a gun being pressed to his temple by the armed suspect, who demanded that he stop the car and give the suspect all of his money. Fearing for his life, the cabdriver decided instead to hit the gas and purposely crash his yellow cab into a utility pole. The impact was so powerful that it tossed the armed suspect into the front seat with the victim. A desperate and intense struggle for possession of the weapon soon began.

Somehow, someway, the suspect managed to open the front passenger's door and started running. But he didn't get far before being chased down by the cabdriver, who tackled the suspect on the snow as they both struggled to gain control of the gun. During the struggle, the suspect managed to break free, but not before the victim was able to disarm him and fire four or five rounds at him as the suspect ran for his life.

In the interview, the victim admitted to us that he never saw us approaching and only fired the gun because he didn't want the suspect to run away and rob somebody else. With the description of the suspect, a search ensued by assisting units in the area, but unfortunately he was never found and ultimately got away with it. No clear, identifiable finger prints were found on the gun.

While the victim's taxicab was totaled from the crash into the pole, he was extremely happy to walk away from it with only minor injuries. All things considered, he could've easily been charged for recklessly firing of the weapon, a .22 caliber long revolver that nearly got us killed. Luckily, after we talked it over with our sergeant at the scene, he decided that "the guy's had a really rough day as it is…so why punish him any more by arresting him?" We all agreed!

CHAPTER 77

THE (SOMETIMES) HIDDEN DANGERS OF POLICE WORK: HERE'S MY STORY

B y this time in my career, I had faced many close calls involving bad guys armed with everything from handguns, knives, and a host of other potentially dangerous weapons that could've easily cost me my life. However, never in my wildest dreams did I ever imagine encountering a situation such as this one that could've ended my career in law enforcement at HPD and left me seriously injured.

This incident happened on January 4, 1985. That night, I was assisting members of the vice and narcotics squad in the execution of a search warrant for narcotics. This warrant was aimed at a group of illicit drug dealers who were selling narcotics right out of their single-family home in the northern section of Hartford. As soon as we arrived at this location, with my adrenaline running at full throttle, I took off running to cover the northeast side window of this particular house, completely unaware that in the very dark, unlit alleyway was an uncoated metal wire as thin as a fishing line, which was tightly secured and ran from the side of the house to the top of an approximately five-foot metal pole. I hit it head-on.

Before I knew it, I was lying on the ground, temporarily unconscious, and bleeding from a cut to the jaw, as well as suffering from a few other injuries to my neck and head, all sustained when my body crashed hard to the ground. About all I remember was opening my eyes and seeing a handful of my fellow officers surrounding me and asking me repeatedly if I was okay. But unfortunately I wasn't. I felt my head spinning in circles. I was dazed and confused and couldn't figure out what the heck had just happened to me. One moment I was running to cover the side window of the house, and the next moment

I was on the ground and suffering from multiple injuries. It was literally that quick!

Shortly thereafter, my team of brothers and sisters helped me to my feet and rushed me to St. Francis Hospital for treatment. Once there, I was examined by an ER doctor who treated my injuries before releasing me later that night. Preliminary results showed that I had suffered a deep laceration all the way to the bone on the right side of my chin; it required several butterfly stitches. I was also diagnosed with a neck strain and slight concussion as a result of my head hitting the ground.

In the end, the attending physician remarked, that I was extremely lucky. Another half inch lower and the wire could've easily sliced right through my neck, killing me instantly. It was a surreal experience for me, and one that is still fresh in my mind. Bearing the visible scar on my chin constantly reminds me of the what-ifs.

That day after leaving the hospital, I thought about how truly blessed I was that my jaw had taken the brunt of the impact. In fact, there is a phrase in boxing, "leading with the chin," which means you've left a vulnerable point unprotected. But in my case, that is exactly what I truly believe saved me!

CHAPTER 78

AN OPPORTUNITY OF A LIFETIME

O ver the years that followed, I continued to patrol the city streets as a veteran officer who, at this point, had five and a half years of experience under my belt. During that time period, I did a few stints as a recruiting officer for the department, but mostly spent the early part of my career walking a beat in the projects, or in a cruiser patrolling some of the toughest, crime-ridden areas of the city.

Towards the latter part of 1984, an announcement was made that applications were being accepted for newly created positions in the department's brand-new mounted unit. I had never been on a horse, or even seen one up close in the South Bronx, but this was definitely a lifelong dream come true, and I couldn't wait to jump at the chance to be a mounted police officer!

You see, as a kid growing up in the South Bronx, I used to be glued to the television set after school as I watched one of my favorite TV shows of all time, *The Lone Ranger*! It was a half-hour adventure involving a masked Texas Ranger known as the Lone Ranger. His crime-fighting partner was Tonto. This dynamic duo fought crime on horseback, chasing after the bad guys in the Wild, Wild, West! Being a huge fan of the Lone Ranger from a young age, I was always in awe of how cool it would be to chase bad guys on horseback. To me, there was nothing I wanted to do more than be just like the Lone Ranger!

One day, I got this awesome Christmas gift from my uncle, who knew I was a huge Lone Ranger fan. When I opened it up, I literally got the shock of my life. Inside this big box was a full cowboy outfit, gun belt and all, minus the mask. While it wasn't exactly the TV Lone Ranger's outfit, to me it didn't matter. For in my imagination, I was the Lone Ranger. I wore the outfit proudly as I strapped on my gun belt and put on a makeshift eye mask, making the transformation complete. And while I didn't have a horse to ride while chasing the bad guys when I played cops and robbers with my friends, it didn't matter. I always had a great time making the best of what I had, and my imagination was limitless!

Now, fast forward to many years later, and I couldn't believe that I was in the position of possibly making another one of my dreams come true by becoming a Mountie! I wasted no time in submitting my application. While I had no experience whatsoever, I was hoping that my dedicated record as a hardworking street cop would give me a chance to be selected as one of the lucky eleven mounted officers for this brand-new unit.

Within a couple of months of submitting my application, a background review was conducted. That was followed weeks later by an interview with the chief of police, which I thought went pretty well. Then on April 17, 1985, I finally got the news that I had been dreaming about all this time. I received an interdepartmental memorandum from Chief Sullivan, congratulating me on being selected for the mounted police program. That same day, transfer orders were cut that advised me I was to begin training on May 13, 1985.

I was beyond excited and couldn't wait for the training to begin! I was the very first Hispanic ever to be selected for the mounted unit! A true blessing and an unbelievable honor!

On the morning of May 13, I reported to training for what was supposed to be a six-week basic equestrian skills course at the Governor's Horse Guard facility in Avon, Connecticut. Once there, I learned that, like me, most of my fellow selectees had very little to no horseback-riding experience. Knowing that I wasn't the only non-rider gave me a little more confidence. I later found the department chose nonriders on purpose because they didn't want anyone with bad riding habits going through the course. This made total sense to me, and I could clearly see why they would go that route.

After the first full week of equestrian training, I was sore in muscles that I never knew existed! The training was beyond tough! Especially during those hot and humid days when we would ride around in circles inside a riding ring. Heat coming off a hot and sweaty horse made matters even worse and only added to the discomfort that came from training on a hot day.

As far as riding equipment was concerned, we did all our training on McClellan saddles, a traditional saddle used by the army' cavalry back in the day, and one that to this day is still being used by the Governor's Horse Guards during parades and other special events. It is a saddle that was specifically made for the comfort of the horse, not the rider. And believe me, after riding on these saddles for days on end, you really start to feel the pain in your buttocks.

As the weeks went by, we went from riding in a saddle without the stirrups in order to strengthen our legs, to riding bareback while using different gaits—walk, posting trot, and canter—and learning to incorporate balance and control during all sorts of challenging riding situations. Through it all, it was the best boot-camp equestrian training that any of us could have ever imagined. And while the training lasted more than the six weeks it was supposed to, in the long run it was well worth it! We all managed to pull through and learn how to ride the correct way. All this hard-core training eventually gave us the riding confidence, discipline, and training we needed to work on the city streets.

On June 30, 1985, we finally graduated from the equestrian course and became full-fledged Mounties! A few months after our graduation, we moved into our brand-new stable located in Keney Park, in the northwestern section of the city. The newly constructed stable came fully equipped with everything we needed: twelve horse stalls, a bathing area for the horses, plenty of rooms for all our equipment and saddles, three training/turnout paddocks, a hay loft, a feed room, a male and a female locker room, and an office for the head of the mounted unit, our sergeant. We also had two horse trailers, and a marked and an unmarked unit for transportation and patrol work, for those days of inclement weather when the horse couldn't be used on the streets. Our new mounted uniforms and helmets arrived soon after, and our unit was off and running.

On Tuesday, December 4, 1985, the mounted unit was officially introduced to the residents of the City of Hartford during a large ceremony that took place in Bushnell Park. It was attended not only by the general public, but also by city officials from the mayor's office, department heads from the Hartford Police Department, representatives from the state of Connecticut, and finally, media outlets from every news channel and newspaper in the state. It was definitely a great turnout in celebration of this special day for both the City of Hartford and the Hartford Police Department!

I remember that day as being one of the coldest days of the year; the windchill was below freezing. We were freezing our butts off and couldn't wait until it was all over so we could finally go back to the horse trailer and head back to the stables to warm up!

Once all the fanfare was over, the reality of it quickly set in. From that day forward, we were officially ready to hit the streets and city parks to continue making a difference in our community… only this time on horseback!

The main objective with the new mounted unit was to be proactive in fighting crime. This was done by maintaining a high visibility in the crime-ridden areas of the city, where we hoped that our presence alone would serve as a deterrent to crime in the City of Hartford. Our main goal as mounted officers was to make people feel safer while walking on the city streets and in the city parks. And from day one, that became our mission each time we suited up and went out there in the communities. This soon led to many accolades and positive feedback from the city residents in some of the most crime-ridden neighborhoods of the city.

The mounted unit soon became a public relations machine that everyone, especially the kids, looked forward to seeing in their neighborhoods, schools, and even at special community events and festivals. I, along with all my fellow brothers and sisters in our unit, was truly enjoying it and loved the feeling of working the streets and being appreciated.

However, as the days and the months went by, I personally wanted more out of the unit, besides just being a public-relations tool. So, one day I decided that the unit could do much more than just be visible and patrol the city parks and surrounding streets. While I knew that standing on a street corner was great and served its purpose in putting a dent in crime, I wanted to take a more proactive approach to fighting crime in the neighborhoods that we patrolled. With that in mind, I decided that by taking a more hands-on approach to fighting crime, starting with motor-vehicle enforcement and clearing the street corners of loiterers, we would hopefully have an even bigger impact on the communities we served.

During the initial phase of working in the city, each member of the mounted unit was assigned to one of the many parks and its surrounding streets. Sometimes we would work in pairs, but for the most part, we were working on our own and riding solo. All told, as a unit we would ride five to six days a week, logging six to seven hours a day per rider. One of my first assignments was patrolling Colt Park, located in the southeastern section of the city, and the surrounding streets, including the projects. It was a fairly good-sized area, and I had a lot of ground to cover each day.

One day, I decided to park myself right in the middle of a three-way-stop intersection at the corner of Stonington and Groton Streets to initiate traffic enforcement on seat-belt violators, expired emissions stickers, and unregistered motor vehicles. Over time, with some of the legal stops and investigations that I initiated, I discovered that some of the drivers were also wanted on an arrest warrant from either our department or another police department in the area. As each car came to a stop at one of the designated stop signs and intersections, I would approach the car with my horse, Bobby at the time, take a quick glance at the vehicle's windshield and its driver, and if everything checked out, they were allowed to proceed through the intersection without issue and go off on their merry way. However, those motorists in violation of any motor-vehicle law were quickly instructed to pull over to the side of the road, shut their car off, and produce their license, registration, and insurance card.

Well, before long, this approach soon led to other things. At times, the operators were found to be driving under suspension, driving an unregistered motor vehicle, or a host of other motor-vehicle infractions. Sometimes the motor vehicle stop led to more serious offenses, such as the vehicle's operator being wanted on an active warrant. At other times, I pulled the car over, only to discern the strong odor of weed, which typically led to a complete search of the car and the arrest of the driver for the possession of marijuana and a host of other drugs that might have popped up during the search of the vehicle. Last, but certainly not least, sometimes I pulled over a car, only to find that the driver was in possession of a stolen plate on the vehicle, which resulted in the operator being arrested for the stolen property and issued a slew of tickets for motor vehicle infractions.

Then there were those more dangerous stops, in which the operator was driving a stolen car or was wanted on a felony charge; for example, an armed carjacking. In most of those cases, the suspects took off and headed into the housing projects or other neighborhoods just to avoid getting arrested. These were high-risk situations because you just don't know if the driver or passengers were armed.

This type of enforcement, over time, led to many car chases. In those situations, I gave chase just to keep the suspects in sight, while calling in their descriptions and direction, in hopes that any patrol units in the area would pick up the chase, stop them, and make an arrest.

In the end, I'm proud to say that while a good percentage of these chases led to an arrest, none of it would've been possible had it not been for the amazing work and dedication of my brothers and sisters on patrol who were always there for me during so many of these encounters! I owe them a lot of thanks and gratitude for making my job so much easier. Although some of these bad guys did manage to get away, it wasn't for long. Sooner or later, just like my hero, the Lone Ranger, the good guys always win in the end!

CHAPTER 79

SOME OF MY MOST NOTABLE CHASES AND ARRESTS ON HORSEBACK

Some of my most memorable chases and arrests, during my incredible fifteen-year career in the mounted unit, involved just being in the right place at the right time. I could say it was just pure luck, but a lot of it involved trying to do something inspiring to make a difference in the lives of others. Over the years, every time I went out there, I wanted to show that the amount of good police work a mounted unit member could do is immeasurable. I think this type of mentality is what kept me going. I always performed with the attitude of giving 110 percent, of making a difference. I wanted to prove that being on a horse doesn't stop you from being a cop and doing your job effectively, with complete honor and dedication to the job you love!

Case in point, back on April 3, 1987, I had been on the streets approximately two years and was assigned to my first horse, Bobby. Coincidentally, this just happened to be my nickname on the job as well. I always joked that when one of my coworkers yelled, "Hey, Bobby," my horse and I both turned around and looked. Aside from having the same name, I think what I really enjoyed about this horse was his amazing speed and his dependability; he was always there for me when I needed him the most.

Bobby was a towering horse whose lean body, height, and demeanor were always intimidating to the average person on the streets. But more importantly, he was perhaps the fastest horse we had in the mounted unit. This was mostly due to his type of breed; he was classified as a Thoroughbred-Standardbred mix; that accounted for his lean body and quick speed, just like a racehorse. Bobby was blessed with amazing speed that always came in handy, especially when I had to chase down bad guys on the streets of Hartford. Although he was also a bit skittish at times, which made for some unpredictable and scary moments, somehow I managed to tolerate it in hopes that over time he would eventually overcome some of these episodes of fear and finally settle down.

That particular day, we were on routine patrol of the southeastern section of the city, Wethersfield Avenue near Colt Park, when a call came in over the radio. A citizen had seen an individual operating a stolen car in the rear of 159 Wethersfield Avenue. Several of our patrol units in the area were dispatched to this location, but by the time they arrived, the suspect had fled the scene in the stolen car. What made matters even worse was that the suspect was bragging to his friends that he had stolen the car on March 22 and had not been caught yet.

After listening to the second or third call and hearing that the suspect had fled the scene without being caught, I decided to get together with one of the responding units, Officer Jimmy Doyle in Unit 23, to set up a trap to capture this brazen and elusive criminal. It just so happens that, directly behind this particular parking lot, there was a huge tree that I thought would serve as great cover for me and my horse. I suggested to Officer Doyle that he stay in the Wethersfield Avenue area while my horse and I took cover behind the tree. I would let Officer Doyle know if the suspect pulled into the back lot. Officer Doyle thought this was a great idea, and we decided to put it into action.

Approximately fifteen minutes or so after hiding behind the tree, I saw the stolen car pull into the driveway and head towards the rear of the parking lot. It appeared that the suspect was so focused on driving into the lot to meet up with his friends that he never saw me. Instead, he parked the stolen car and started walking towards his friends.

I notified Officer Doyle, and he immediately stationed himself in front of the building, right next to an alleyway in between the two buildings in question, in order to block the suspect's escape route. I quickly moved in on the suspect and at gunpoint ordered him not to move as I made my approach.

He tried to distract me by asking, "But, Officer, what did I do?"

I told him not to move as I holstered my revolver and immediately grabbed him around his jacket collar to make the arrest. But instead of complying, he broke free from the hold and took off running. I was in hot pursuit chasing him through the alleyway. During the chase, I caught up with him. And when I reached out and grabbed him around his jacket collar once again, my helmet accidentally struck some sort of metal pipe that was attached to the building, putting a good-sized dent in my helmet from the hard impact. Luckily, I sustained no injuries in the accident, and my horse stayed in control during the whole chase.

With the impact, the suspect was able to break loose from my grasp for the second time and kept running. Unfortunately for him, he didn't get too far. For as soon as he hit the street in his last-ditch effort to escape, Officer Doyle was right there waiting for him; he quickly tackled the suspect to the ground and arrested him after a brief struggle. That day, in addition to being arrested for the stolen car, the suspect was charged with possession of narcotics and drug paraphernalia.

In the end, the good guys had the last laugh, and the bad guy was hauled into booking while wearing a nice pair of fashionable matching bracelets around his wrist... courtesy of HPD!

CHAPTER 80

ANOTHER WILD INCIDENT

About a month or so later, I was in the process of using my lead rope to tie Bobby to a pole in front of Comerio Restaurant when a call came over the radio. There was a robbery in progress on Cedar Street, near Park Street. When the call came in, I advised the dispatcher that I was only two blocks away and could easily be there in no time. Following that transmission with dispatch, I immediately hopped on my horse and started galloping towards that location.

I arrived within seconds, and as soon as I made the turn onto Cedar Street, there it was. Right in the middle of the street were four young males beating up on another young man. The victim was on the ground, trying to shield himself from the barrage of hits to his body by these four young adults, two of whom were armed with baseball bats. While two were whaling away at the victim with their bats, the other two were trying to hold him down on the ground and forcibly remove his money and wallet from his pants pocket.

Upon seeing this, I immediately took off after them, spooking them. As they ran in different directions, I focused my attention on one individual who'd taken off through an open field near a housing project. My horse and I galloped after him. As he was running, he managed to take a quick peek behind him to see how close or far I was, only to discover that this huge horse was mere steps behind him and quickly gaining. The look on his face said it all; he was scared shitless!

As we neared the end of this open field, he made a sudden left turn toward these two-level housing projects that were located in between Cedar and Wadsworth Streets. It was there where he somehow disappeared, and I momentarily lost sight of him.

That's when a female who was standing right outside her home frantically pointed to her dwelling and screamed, "Officer, he ran inside my house!!!"

I dismounted and tied my horse to a fence in front of her house. Dispatch was immediately notified, and backup units were soon sent to assist. Since the home was still occupied, the woman's young children still inside, out of fear that their lives might be in danger from this violent intruder in their home, I decided to enter the home before backup units arrived. As I made my way into the house, several of the woman's children ran past me and met up with their mother. A room-by-room check of the house subsequently led me to the suspect's whereabouts. I found him hiding underneath a bed in one of the children's bedrooms. The suspect was subsequently forced out at gunpoint, handcuffed, and taken into custody after a minor struggle.

In the end, the suspect was arrested on numerous felony charges, including attempted armed robbery, assault, interfering with a police officer, burglary for forcing his way into an occupied dwelling, and several counts of risk of injury to a minor. The other suspects involved unfortunately got away and were never arrested.

CHAPTER 81

THE SAD ENDING OF A GREAT PARTNERSHIP

During the four years I worked with my horse, Bobby, we got involved in numerous other chases and arrests. I also experienced several close calls in which something would spook him, and he would take off on me unexpectedly, putting my safety and his at risk.

One particular day, we were taking a little break in an open grass field by an elementary school. A young student, trying to make his way into the open field by cutting through a row of bushes behind us, accidentally scared the living daylights out of Bobby, and he took off running at a full gallop. Because I was relaxed and wasn't expecting something like that to happen, the reins, which more or less work like the brakes on a car, were resting loosely on the front of the saddle. With the reins loose, it gave Bobby the lead, allowing him to take off running with nothing to hold him back.

It immediately felt as if he'd broken out of the starting gate at the racetrack and was running to the finish line. Somehow, I was able to grab hold of the reins and pull back in my desperate attempt to get him under control. However, just as I was trying to get him to stop, my saddle started slipping. I was practically riding sideways, trying to regain my balance, while attempting desperately to bring my body and saddle back to the upright position. I literally felt myself falling off his back and bracing for a big fall to the ground.

I was just about to lose hope when suddenly Bobby came to an abrupt stop, his nose still flaring and his heart still pounding out of control from being so scared. It was the biggest relief in the world, and I thought, "Okay, this is it."

However, just as I was trying to bring my leg over to the other side of the saddle to be fully balanced, the kid who had originally, unintentionally caused Bobby to bolt came over to apologize. Unfortunately in doing so, he once again scared the crap out of my horse, who immediately took off running once more. Right after that, my left ankle snapped in the stirrup. I instantly felt the pain and knew it wasn't good!

While in excruciating pain and off-balance, somehow I was able to turn the reins tightly to the left, forcing Bobby to go in circles briefly, before finally coming to a stop. Then I was able to bring him back under control.

That day, I was taken to the emergency room by one of my coworkers in the unit. X-rays revealed I had suffered a small fracture to my left ankle; it left me in a cast for six weeks.

After coming back from my injury, I had a lengthy conversation with the stable manager and my sergeant about Bobby. The decision was made that for safety, both for the rider's and the horse's, Bobby would no longer be a part of the mounted unit. A few months later, he was retired from the mounted unit after nearly four years of dedicated service. A good family who owned a farm somewhere in Connecticut adopted him, and he was able to live a nice, comfortable life with several other horses.

Shortly after my partnership with Bobby ended, I was assigned to another beautiful horse by the name of Ashley, that had just been donated to our mounted unit by a nice family. Like Bobby, he was a Thoroughbred cross, a big horse. If he worked out, Ashley would turn out to be a perfect fit for me and the unit.

After about a month's time working with him in the ring and training him on the streets of Hartford, we decided to give Ashley a shot. He actually did so well during the initial evaluation and street training that he was able to make the cut and become a probationary police horse. If at any point, during the next three to four months, we discovered issues that could undermine the safety and well-being of either the rider or the horse, he would be returned to the owner without a problem. But for now, at least, Ashley was considered a member of the mounted police unit. And while he wasn't perfect, for he was skittish at times, I hoped that over time he would overcome his nervousness and finally feel comfortable enough to work on the city streets every day.

As the months went by, I was able to do many of the police functions I had done with Bobby, including traffic enforcement, making arrests, and appearing in community events and at neighborhood schools. In fact, on September 23, of 1990, we actually competed in the National Police Equestrian Competition in Wilmington, Delaware. It was there that we took third place in the Best Dressed Uniform competition, receiving both a ribbon and a plaque, out of a field of more than twenty-four competitors from throughout the United States and beyond; one representative from Toronto, Canada, also competed.

It was not a complete surprise, considering that Ashley was such a beautiful horse with great stature and a nice, shiny black fur coat that really made him stand out from the other competitors. My blue mounted police uniform had a yellow thin stripe down the side of the pants, which was complemented by a yellow handkerchief around my neck and a campaign police hat that blended perfectly with Ashley's commanding presence. It was truly an amazing experience, not only for me, but for our whole mounted unit. This was the very first time in our mounted unit's history that we had competed at the national equestrian competition, and we'd come away with an award. So for our mounted unit and our department to achieve this honor was truly a big deal!

Ashley was coming along pretty well and was making a really good adjustment to working on the streets until one day when everything sadly changed for him. While being turned out with one of the other horses in our paddock, he was kicked really hard in his left knee by one of the other horses; it caused extensive damage. Immediately after the injury, he was taken off the line, and our veterinarian was called in to examine him and treat his injuries.

After numerous exams and treatments, the vet determined that because Ashley's injuries were so severe, he would no longer be able to perform his services as a police horse; he would have to be retired. A few months later, Ashley was retired from serving in the mounted unit and would spend the rest of his life as a pleasure horse. Sadly, this ended a very short but good career.

Thankfully, Ashley was able to recover enough to be adopted by another family, and he happily served the rest of his life on a farm surrounded by other horses.

CHAPTER 82

MEET ALEX THE WONDER HORSE

Shortly after I got the bad news on Ashley, I found myself without a horse. Little did I know then that the horse that would later go on to become the greatest police horse in the history of our mounted unit was just doors away from me, relaxing in his stall and yet to be assigned to a rider.

Ann Marie, our stable manager, approached me to ask if I'd like to try a horse that had come into our unit a week before. I took one good look at him and immediately said yes. I remember being outside his stall when this conversation took place. He came right up to me and gently gave my shoulder a big nudge, as if to say, "Thank you for selecting me to be your next partner."

Alex was a stunning quarter horse with a bay, shiny coat that truly made him stand out among the rest of the police horses at the stable. He really caught my eye. Similar to my two previous horses, he was tall, but a lot wider and a bit heavier. Yet, something about this beautiful horse quickly clicked with me from the moment we met. His friendly and gentle demeanor truly made him shine.

I remember how when I first started to pet him on his forehead, he would nudge my arm if I stopped. It was as if he was saying, "Why are you stopping? That feels really good!"

I also remember just standing there, staring at him, and thinking to myself, *This is going to be the perfect horse for me.* I couldn't wait until the next day to start riding and training him in the ring.

Early the next morning, I groomed him, saddled him, and then walked him to one of the paddocks to begin our training. From the onset, his gait at a walk, trot, and canter was smooth. He was a bit out of shape, but I knew that I could have him back in shape in no time. And sure enough, after a few weeks of training in the paddock, we got to know each other really well, and he was ready to move on to the next level. For that part of our training, I took him into an open field in Keney Park.

That morning, after riding Alex for about thirty minutes in a series of warm-up exercises, he did so amazingly well that I decided it was time to move on to the next challenge: a control canter. Unfortunately, things didn't turn out as planned after I gave him a good squeeze using leg signals to ask him for a controlled canter.

He started off really well, but then he somehow switched gears and tried to throw me off his back. He jumped and kicked back with such power that I immediately felt as though I were competing in a rodeo. I was trying to hang on for dear life. It seemed that the more I tried to hang on, the more he bucked. Finally, after trying for what seemed like minutes, when in reality it was just a few seconds, I flew right off his back.

Thankfully, I was able to brace for the fall before landing on my back in the tall, thick grass, which I credit for cushioning my fall. Luckily, I didn't sustain any serious injuries in this fall. I just had some minor soreness to my lower back.

I watched from the ground as Alex took off running and headed back in the direction of the stable, which was nearby. I immediately got on my police radio and advised the people at the mounted police stable to open the gate. Before I knew it, Alex was safely back at the stable and had been led back into his stall. Within a matter of minutes, I arrived, just a little bruised and dirty from the fall, but more than anything, a bit embarrassed that I'd gotten thrown off his back.

Not letting Alex get the best of me, I jumped right back on him and rode to the exact spot where he'd thrown me. Our training sessions began once again! He tried to pull the same stunt, but I wasn't falling for it, no pun intended. I quickly put a stop to his bucking by steering him around in tight circles until he just got exhausted and gave in. Minutes later, I was running him up and down that open field with no other issues. I think he finally got the message that I wasn't going to give in to his antics and finally decided to get with the program and stop horsing around!

Over the weeks that followed, we continued to train hard and then began the next phase: overcoming certain obstacles that might spook a horse on the streets of Hartford. Much to my surprise, he did amazingly well! Much better than I ever expected for a brand-new horse in our unit. To paraphrase a certain term that's used by mounted police officers everywhere when describing an great horse that nothing seems to bother, Alex was bombproof! No matter what scary items or obstacles he was exposed to, nothing affected him.

During our tough obstacle-training segment, we walked on a blue-plastic tarp containing water that many horses just hate because of the noise it makes when they step on it. Their perception is that they might be stepping into a giant hole on the ground. He did fantastically well! As part of the training, he was also exposed to a large collection of colorful balloons, the sudden opening of an umbrella, exploding firecrackers, and a host of other obstacles. And once again, he performed awesomely! I even managed to shoot numerous simulation rounds off his back with my firearm, and he didn't even flinch. That's how great he did in this part of the training.

In the final segment of our training, we actually hit the streets in order to expose him to a variety of challenges, from exposure to motor vehicles, pedestrian traffic, and noisy construction sites, to barking dogs and a host of other regular, everyday noises. Among them were the honking of car horns, loud music, and everything else in between. In fact, when we weren't walking, we also worked on just standing still at an intersection, observing the traffic and people.

In the end, he passed with flying colors every single test he was given! It was from that point on, that I realized just how great a horse Alex was going to be. I knew that, together, we would have a long, amazing career as crime fighters in the mounted unit.

Over the years, Alex became such a vital part of the mounted unit that before long I decided to call him Alex the Wonder Horse! And you'll soon see why!

CHAPTER 83

ALEX EARNING HIS REPUTATION AS A GREAT POLICE HORSE

During the weeks that followed, Alex performed so satisfactorily that it was time to put him to the test as a working police horse. On our first day of ticketing parked cars, he did so well that I decided to take it to the next level and see how he would do during the traffic enforcement of moving violators. I picked a four-way intersection located at Affleck and Ward Streets. This particular spot gave me the greatest visibility for monitoring the intersection, while at the same time, because traffic was so light, it was the perfect scenario for conducting traffic stops in a safe manner, especially for a brand-new horse like Alex.

The first car we pulled over to the side of the road was a motorist who rolled through the stop sign without coming to a complete stop. As I pulled alongside the driver's side window, I told the operator why he was being pulled over and asked him to produce his license, registration, and insurance card. The motorist was very cooperative, and when he reached over to hand me his yellow registration form, the unexpected happened!

Before I could reach out to grab the paper from the driver, Alex intercepted it, probably mistaking it for a snack, and in one big bite, he ate the whole damn thing, right in front of the stunned motorist and me! About all I could do at that time, was watch helplessly as Alex chewed away on the driver's registration paper. I couldn't stop him since I was still on his back.

"Officer, what am I going to do now?" asked the stunned driver.

I felt really bad about the whole incident and politely apologized. I explained to him that he should go to the motor-vehicle department the next day and tell them that a police horse ate his registration; hopefully they would be able print out a new registration form without any issues. The driver was really upset, but seemed a little relieved when I told him that I would let him go without giving him a ticket for rolling through the stop sign.

It turns out this wasn't the only embarrassing thing I would have to deal with while working with Alex in the many years ahead. There was another time when I tied him to a pole in front of a mini-mart while I went inside to grab a snack. The next thing I knew, some lady came running up to me to tell me that Alex had just grabbed on to some lady's purse, and he wouldn't let go. I quickly ran outside, only to witness Alex holding on to the lady's wicker-type purse and trying to pull it away. The lady was desperately pulling in the opposite direction, but clearly unsuccessfully.

I never imagined in my wildest dreams that my horse would one day become a purse snatcher, but it happened!

I immediately jumped into action, put my thumb into the side corner of Alex's mouth, and pressed down on his tongue, causing him to release the purse. I apologized, but the lady said she understood why the horse went after her purse, especially when she was so close, trying to pet him. It was truly another one for the books; I'll never forget it.

And lastly this one! As far back as I can remember, Alex always had this incredible fascination with big buttons on coats and sweaters. Because of that, I always tried my best to warn people not to get too close to him, especially if they had big buttons on any part of their clothing.

Well, one day, Officer Al Jardin and I were about to load our horses onto a two-horse trailer, when a lovely couple from Germany asked if they could take a picture with our horses. Of course, we said yes, and as the lady stood in between the two horses for the picture, we stood alongside them, dismounted and on the opposite side.

Just as her husband was about to take the picture, Alex quickly turned his head towards the lady as if to reach for something. Unbeknownst to me, Alex had just spotted a couple of big buttons on the lady's sweater and instinctively decided to go after them. Before

I knew it, he'd managed to bite one of the buttons. However, in doing so, he also accidentally clamped onto the lady's left breast!

As you can only imagine, the lady immediately started screaming for help in her German accent, "Ouch... Officers, Officers!" She yelled, "He's got my tit; he's got my tit," as she winced in pain!

I jumped into action right away and forced Alex to release his grip. Luckily, I was able to get to him in time, before he pulled away and unintentionally seriously injured the poor lady! Embarrassed by this whole incident, I apologized numerous times as I explained to her that my horse had a strange fascination with big buttons.

To my surprise, she wasn't upset whatsoever. She insisted, "It's all right, Officer. I completely understand. Please don't worry about it! I'm okay!" And to my relief, other than seeing her a bit shaken up, she did appear to be okay!

After finally taking the pictures, we shook hands with the friendly couple and said goodbye. On our way back to the stables, Al and I couldn't stop laughing. Her reaction was truly priceless, and it gave us a moment that we'll always remember.

This was just another great story in the archives of Alex the Wonder Horse! The greatest Hartford Police Department mounted police horse ever!

CHAPTER 84

ALEX THE DRUG-SNIFFING POLICE HORSE

Alex the Wonder Horse was my partner in the mounted unit for an amazing ten years, from 1990 to 2000, the longest service by any horse in the history of the Hartford Mounted Police. During this time, we were involved in the investigation of just about every imaginable street crime you could think of, including tons of chases.

Alex was dependable and fearless, a true warhorse on the streets. Although he wouldn't hurt a fly, his size and stature were enough to scare the heck out of anybody that didn't know any better. In reality, he was really a gentle giant and always brought a great big smile to the face of every kid and adult he met. He was definitely one of a kind, and the stories we made together as a team will forever be a part of my life and that of the Hartford Mounted Police. Here's just one of the hundreds of memorable situations we encountered over the years.

One day, we were patrolling in a high-crime area of the city; it was known for illicit drugs and gang problems. We came upon an individual who was hanging around this particularly troublesome corner, which was a known hot spot for criminal activity. As we got closer, the man appeared to be getting a bit jittery and uneasy with my presence. Suspecting he might be up to no good, I called him over and asked to see some identification.

The man was standing about two feet or so from Alex when he began to rummage through his wallet, desperately looking for his ID. You could easily tell how nervous and scared he was around Alex as he quickly quipped, "He's not going to bite me, is he, Officer?"

"No," I said, "not unless you do something stupid. You'll be fine."

Alex, always the curious horse looking for treats, innocently began to sniff about the suspect's body. As he got closer to the suspect's pants pockets, he became a bit more aggressive, to the point of actually nibbling on the edge of the suspect's left side pocket.

The suspect by now was a complete nervous mess and suddenly blurted out, "But, Officer, why is he trying to go into my pockets?"

My response was, "He's a drug-sniffing horse trained to sniff out all types of drugs on people. Well, is he right?"

Shocked and in total disbelief that the horse, or so he thought, had actually detected something illegal in his pocket, the man came clean and admitted in his audibly shaken tone of voice, "Yes, sir, I gotta be honest with you, Officer. I had some pot in my pocket, but I smoked it a few minutes before you got here!"

Moments later, after searching him and finding no drugs, I walked away with a great big smile on my face. For I just knew, from that day forward, that man would tell all of his drug-dealing buddies about Alex. They'd all think twice before ever coming in contact with Alex the Drug-Sniffing Police Horse ever again! In the end, he did smell grass; it was just not the legal kind that he was used to eating!

CHAPTER 85

ALEX THE CRIME FIGHTER

With every passing month, Alex was getting more and more used to being a police horse. Ticketing illegally parked vehicles, conducting motor-vehicle traffic enforcement, and clearing loiterers from street corners became second nature to Alex. And by the way, do you remember the first car I stopped with Alex, the one where he ate the driver's registration paper? Well, I think the incident must have left a really bad taste in his mouth because he never did it again after that embarrassing motor-vehicle stop.

During the weeks and months we worked together, we made just about every imaginable arrest, from issuing summonses for a host of motor-vehicle infractions, to misdemeanor arrests involving low-level drugs, like marijuana, possession of stolen car plates, and loitering, just to name a few. But up until that point, there were no felony arrests. However, that all changed one day when we happened to be at the right place, at the right time.

It was a bright, sunny summer day, and Alex and I just happened to be enjoying this beautiful day in the sunshine. As I was accustomed to doing, I would randomly pick an intersection where Alex and I could just relax, but at the same time maintain high visibility in the area. This particular day, we were stopped at the corner of Washington and Webster Streets, observing motor vehicle and pedestrian traffic.

When a lady exited a bus right behind me and screamed at the top of her lungs, "Help!!!" I immediately turned Alex around and approached the lady to see what was the matter, and she yelled, "Officer, that man"—pointing to an individual who was running southbound on Webster Street—"just stole my necklace as I got off the bus!"

With the suspect still in sight as he ran down the street, I took off with Alex at a full canter. When the suspect saw me running towards him and gaining ground, he slowed down from exhaustion, and I was able to catch up to him. I quickly grabbed him around his shirt collar and immediately placed under arrest him, without incident, on several felony counts, including a robbery charge. In fact, the gold necklace that the suspect had ripped off the lady's neck was still clutched in one of his hands when he was arrested.

To say the lady was ecstatic is an understatement. She thanked me for making the arrest and for returning her jewelry. And although the necklace would need some repairs after being violently taken from her neck, she didn't care one bit, so long as she got her necklace back. She stated, "My husband gave it to me a long time ago; it means so much to me!" An emotional value that you can never put a price tag on. Glad it all worked out for her that day!

One thing that I learned about Alex during that pursuit was how he maintained control in a stressful situation. I just knew that composure would come in handy during some of the many tough challenges that lay ahead. I soon grew to love that about him because, along the way, Alex and I encountered numerous other chases, most of which involved vehicles used in a host of felony offenses, including stealing cars.

Because I was approximately ten feet off the ground while sitting on Alex's back, I had an advantage that most police officers on the street don't have. That being said, whenever I stopped at a street corner to observe traffic, usually at a four-way-stop intersection, I could literally see any type of illegal activity taking place inside a car. This was especially handy in identifying a stolen car. From my vantage point, I could clearly see if the ignition was popped or missing, and if the operator had used a screwdriver to start the vehicle.

One day, Alex and I were at one of our usual spots, at the intersection of Putnam and Park Streets, when this vehicle pulls up to the intersection and stops at the red light. It was occupied by males, and I quickly observed that the vehicle's ignition switch was missing; in its place was a screwdriver. I immediately ordered both suspects, at gunpoint, not to move and to keep their hands where I could see them.

Instead of complying, the occupants of the vehicles decided to do the opposite; the driver shoved the car in Reverse and took off northbound on Putnam Street, Alex and I galloping right behind them in hot pursuit.

We chased them for nearly a whole block. Right before we hit the corner of Russ and Putnam Streets, I saw that the occupants had opened both doors and were looking to bail out while the vehicle was still in motion. This is a known tactic used by many suspects involved in car chases; It is done to get an extra jump in their desperate attempt to elude apprehension.

Somehow, the driver managed to bail out of the vehicle without hitting the brakes, leaving the lone passenger to fend for himself. Just as the passenger tried bailing out of the slow-moving car, the door slammed into him, immediately knocking him right to the street. The front right tires just barely missed running over his legs as he lay there motionless. The hard impact had taken the wind out of him and left him momentarily unconscious, only to reopen his eyes and find me and Alex standing right above him, my gun pointed directly at him.

I immediately dismounted, placed him in handcuffs, and arrested him without incident for the stolen vehicle. However, the same could not be said about the driver who took off running and was never located. For the passenger's sake, he was lucky that the unmanned vehicle struck a curb and was forced to a sudden stop before hitting the intersection. Otherwise, an innocent bystander or motorist could've been struck and seriously injured by the out-of-control vehicle.

I was really fortunate to have a hand in this arrest from start to finish; that's not always the case. During most of my car chases, I try to keep the suspect in sight while I radio in a description of the vehicle and the direction of travel. On many occasions, units in the area spot the suspects' vehicle and engage them, hopefully forcing them to come to a stop. The suspects are then handcuffed and detained or arrested on the spot. Sometimes, the subjects are brought back to me, as the initiating officer, for the official arrest, while at other times, they are arrested at the scene, later taken to booking and booked on the criminal charges.

That was exactly what took place a few years after this last incident. That particular day, I was heading towards my police trailer to take a break on a hot summer day, when a bunch of shots rang out in succession from what sounded like an automatic handgun. At the time, my police horse trailer was parked on Niles Street, which was less than fifty feet or so from where the volley of shots were fired on Marshall Street.

I immediately took off on Alex, running towards the gunfire. And just as I was about to hit the corner, a vehicle occupied by two males came racing around the corner, from Marshall Street onto to Niles Street. With my gun drawn, I quickly summoned them to pull over. They completely ignored my command and instead took off down Niles Street towards Woodland Street at a high rate of speed.

With my gun in one hand and the police radio in the other, I gave chase to the suspects' vehicle, which was traveling westbound on Niles Street. While in pursuit, an unmarked police vehicle, which happened to be in the area with several plainclothes officers, thankfully took over the chase and pursued the vehicle onto Woodland Street. The suspects ultimately lost control of the vehicle and crashed right into an office building. They barely managed to duck down just in time, right before their vehicle struck a raised corner of the building. This quick reaction by the suspects prevented them from being decapitated on contact as the car slid under the building. The crash completely destroyed both the driver's and passenger's sides of the vehicle on impact.

The suspects, who were lucky to sustain just minor injuries in this incident, were subsequently placed under arrest on numerous criminal charges, including several counts of first-degree reckless endangerment with a firearm, after firing numerous rounds from a 9mm handgun and striking an occupied apartment dwelling, as well as a parked car. Luckily, no one was hurt during this drive-by shooting incident.

In addition to these charges, the suspects were also found to be in possession of a large amount of cocaine, which resulted in additional criminal charges for possession of narcotics with intent to sell.

All and all, it was another pretty exciting day in the saddle with Alex the Wonder Horse! And another one for the books that I will never, ever forget!

CHAPTER 86

A SUBSTITUTE HORSE STEPS IN FOR ALEX ON HIS DAY OFF!

As a member of the police force, horses get top-notch treatment and training. The treats are bountiful, and they get incredible amounts of personal attention and nurturing. Everything from having regular physical exams and cleaning their teeth, which is otherwise known as floating, to making sure that their vaccinations are up to date and that they are eating top-quality foods and maintaining a good diet. The horses are given the greatest of care as they carry out their daily duties as police horses.

About every four to six weeks, horses also have their shoes replaced by a farrier, or blacksmith. Because most police horses work primarily on pavement, they have to have special horseshoes that are specifically made to garner good traction, in order to prevent them from slipping on the asphalt. These special horseshoes are called borium cleats, and they work wonders during situations in which you are chasing someone.

When certain horses are off duty for whatever reason, a spare horse is issued as a substitute for the day. On May 28, 1997, it was Alex's turn to get his brand-new borium cleats, and so they gave him a day off and assigned me Tootsie, a horse whose regular rider was off that day. This happened to be my very first time on Tootsie, after nearly ten years of riding Alex. But, just like Alex, this horse had a reputation for being very fast and a good horse to ride. Tootsie, too, was a very tall, muscular horse that was in tip-top shape and bombproof. I suspected that he was going to be a great ride for patrolling the streets, especially in the heavily populated areas.

That particular day, Tootsie and I were assigned to patrol the downtown area of Hartford. We rode all over the place, and I had a great time just enjoying the beautiful, sunny afternoon. Sometime during that quiet afternoon, a call was broadcasted over the radio about a wanted vehicle containing two suspects who had just committed an armed robbery of a lone victim in the northwestern section of Albany Avenue. The victim had been pistol-whipped and subsequently robbed of all his money and jewelry.

I was only a few blocks away from the lower section of Albany Avenue, so I decided to take a position at the corner of Albany Avenue and High Street, hoping that the suspects might try to make their way into the downtown area. Within minutes of the broadcast, I spotted their vehicle traveling eastbound on Albany Avenue; it came to a stop behind two other vehicles at a red light.

I immediately advised the dispatcher to give me the air, and I announced that I had spotted a vehicle that fit the description; it was stopped at the light at Albany Avenue and High Street. With my gun drawn, I pointed it at the driver and passenger and yelled, "Shut the car off right now, and let me see your hands!!!"

The driver hesitated and tried to distract me by saying, "But, Officer, what did I do wrong?." After which, he put the car in Reverse and took off westbound on Albany, still in reverse.

Once again, as in so many of my felony chases from the past, I had my gun in my right hand, and the mic and control of the reins in my left. The clippety-clop of my horse galloping down Albany Avenue could be heard a mile away, I was later told by dispatch. The suspect was able to outrun me as he had a good lead. However, just as he came to an abrupt stop and tried desperately to make a 180-degree turn to go down Chestnut Street, his vehicle stalled. As he struggled to get the car restarted, I was quickly gaining on him… and eventually managed to catch up to the vehicle.

Once again, I yelled at the driver and passenger not to move and to let me see their hands. Instead, the driver ignored my commands, managed to crank the car, and took off down Chestnut Street, towards the westbound entrance ramp to I-84.

As I was galloping after them, two ICE agents, who happened to be in the area in an unmarked federal vehicle, spotted me chasing the vehicle and decided to give chase. Once on I-84, the suspects tried to outrun the agents while traveling at a high rate of speed. Before long, a number of our Hartford Police units joined in the chase. After several miles, the suspects got off on one of the exits in West Hartford. Soon, the chase went from one pursuing officer who initiated the chase, to more than twenty cop cars, including the Hartford and West Hartford Police Departments and the state police, all trying to capture these two armed-robbery suspects.

The more-than-thirty-minute chase, which ran from Hartford into West Hartford, finally came to end when the suspects bailed out of their vehicle. However, thanks to the efforts of the canine unit, the suspects were soon found hiding in two separate car garages and placed under arrest after brief struggles.

Once the scene was secured, the officers were able to locate near the suspects' car a .22 caliber Luger handgun, the money, and all the jewelry taken in the armed robbery. Both suspects were charged with a host of criminal charges, including armed robbery and assault for pistol-whipping the victim and forcing him to give up his valuables. The victim, who sustained minor injuries, refused to seek medical attention for his injuries.

After it was all said and done, just knowing how it all turned out was the greatest feeling in the world. One misstep in either direction, from start to finish, and things could have gone the other way. The bad guys could've gotten away with it, and gone on to commit many other serious assaults and robberies. But not today!

CHAPTER 87

ALEX STEALS THE SPOTLIGHT WITH THE KIDS

As the months and the years went by, Alex soon became a seasoned police horse and received so many accolades as one of the best police horses in the history of the mounted unit. By this time in his career, he had been involved in just about every imaginable situation. From chasing after bad guys involved in some serious, hard-core crimes, to the other extreme, making numerous officer-friendly visits to the elementary schools and special events throughout the city. Namely, places where kids would have a great time petting Alex and admiring his friendly presence.

And while this was going on, it allowed me to take advantage of that precious and valuable time and talk to the kids about saying no to drugs and being aware of stranger danger.

Alex soon became a big draw for the kids wherever we went. They loved being around him and the other horses, and we were always invited to come back. As a way of saying thank you, each visit included tons of carrots and apples for the horses. The children took a lot of joy in hand-feeding and petting them. After a while, it became really tough to tell who was having the most fun. Was it the kids feeding and spoiling the horses? Or the horses that didn't want to go back to work? In either case, it was a great day for all involved.

CHAPTER 88

ALEX GAINS ATTENTION IN THE NATIONAL POLICE EQUESTRIAN COMPETITION

U p to that point in my career, I had competed only once in any of the national or regional mounted-police equestrian competitions that took place in different states every year. As you may recall, in the uniform national competition, I came in third place with Ashley in 1990. That was the closest I had ever been to competing against some top, elite police horses and riders from throughout the country. At that competition, I was tempted to compete in the obstacle course, which tested a police horse's ability to handle scary and extreme situations, but I never did.

I think a part of it had to do with having the right bombproof horse that would be able to handle some of the extreme challenges. With my two horses before Alex, I just didn't feel confident that they could perform well in these tough circumstances; I was afraid they would bow out after the first few obstacles.

As a unit, my fellow coworkers had already competed in numerous competitions over the years, and had won quite a few ribbons, but never the big one as the top police horse. That is, until October 22, 1995.

That year, our department decided to be the host city of the Ninth Annual New England Mounted Police Equestrian Competition. It would include thirty-four riders from mounted police units from Connecticut, Massachusetts, Maine, and even as far away as Toronto, Canada, all competing in two major events. One was the equitation class, which showcased the riders, their horses, and their showmanship in all three gaits: the walk, trot, and controlled canter.

The other major event was the obstacle course, which presented a series of ten challenges for the horse and rider. For example, in one challenge, there was a loud, noisy jackhammer chiseling away on cement blocks; another challenge was to enter the arena through an area of dense smoke; another, chasing a fleeing felon; another, ticketing a parked car; and a host of other situational challenges.

To host this large event, the city used Riverside Park, a very popular park located in the northeastern section of the City of Hartford. Because the event was open to the public and the media, it was expected that there would be a large turnout to see the city's very first New England Mounted Police Competition. As the hosting city that year, everyone in our unit was scheduled to compete, including me in my very first equitation and obstacle skills course ever!

Right from the onset, the pressure for this event was at an all-time high. In addition to the pressure of displaying your talents in front of a large crowd of people as the hosting unit, you also felt as though you had to win in order to show everyone—from the people in your department to the residents of the city we served—just how much talent existed in our mounted unit, whose members at the time included Sergeant Robert Ratches and Officers Massicotte, Abbatiello, Gerent, Jardin, and me.

At the start of the competition, it was raining. That added to the difficulty of handling a horse in wet, muddy, slippery, and other hazardous conditions all around us. The downpour made each event just that much more difficult to execute,

In the equitation ring, there were several judges whose job it was to rate your performance in controlling your horse through all three gaits: walk, trot, and canter. While on the obstacle course, field judges were positioned at each of the ten obstacles of this very challenging event. They rated on a scale from one to ten, based on how well you and your horse performed on each challenge.

By the time the competition was over, we didn't do too badly as a team, considering the tough riding conditions; we were awarded two ribbons. Officer Gerent and her horse took first place in the equitation part of the competition, while Alex and I came in tenth place in the obstacle course. That night, at a ceremony that marked the end of the competition, Kelly and I were each awarded a ribbon for our efforts in this wonderful event. A true honor for both of us!

I was super proud of the amazing job that Alex had done in the competition that day! But more importantly, he showed me his true grit as a police horse when he did such a great job against some extremely difficult and challenging situations. Hazardous conditions that made so many other horses and riders quit midway through. Yet Alex marched through the course like a true champ, and really showed me just how lucky and blessed I was to have such an incredible horse as my crime-fighting partner on the streets of Hartford.

After that amazing experience in Hartford, I felt as though we were ready to compete on the national level against some of the best mounted police horses in all of the country. That national event was scheduled to take place on October 17, 1998, in Hershey, Pennsylvania.

In preparation for that big event, I decided to compete in another New England Mounted Police Equestrian Competition that was scheduled to take place that same year, on August 22, 1998, this time on the grounds of the University of Massachusetts in Amherst, Massachusetts. This was similar to the event that took place in Hartford, just with a few more competitors than the last time. And just as in Hartford's competition, this one would include an equitation event and an obstacle course as part of the program.

However, unlike like the last one, this competition took place on a really nice, sunny day. Throughout the course of the competition, Alex and I did very well. However, not well enough to place among the rest of the riders in the event. In fact, it was bad all the way around for our whole mounted unit. That day, we headed back home without a trophy or a ribbon to show for our efforts. What the events of that day did for me, however, was provide insight as to what Alex and I needed to work in order to get ready for the big competition in Hershey, Pennsylvania.

On October 16, we arrived at our hotel in Hershey, Pennsylvania, for the big event. The next day was the actual competition. You can imagine the nerves and anticipation we were all feeling as we saw so many mounted police competitors from throughout the nation. More than 125 competitors were scheduled to compete on that day.

As in the previous events, the equitation portion on the program came first, with the obstacle course due to follow right after that. I remember the excitement that ran through me as we prepped for the big event that morning. This was our version of the Olympics, only this one involved competing against some of the best mounted police horses from throughout the US, the best of the best! So this was really a big deal for not only for me, but for everyone taking part in this, including all my fellow teammates from Hartford.

Finally the day of reckoning was here. One by one, they called our names and numbers. They had us wait in line before entering a huge riding ring filled with obstacle stations everywhere. When my name was called, Alex and I entered from the side of the ring, where a giant type of beach ball was blocking our path. The object was to have the rider and his horse push this giant beach ball out of the way until the path was clear so that they could enter the ring.

This was a timed event; you had less than thirty seconds to execute this challenge before moving on to the next event. In those cases in which your horse refused to perform, you were allowed to move on to the next obstacle, but points were deducted from your score.

Alex breezed right through it without a penalty. Additional obstacles included chalk-drawn boxes on the dirt; you had to stay inside the lines during each exercise you were given to execute in those areas; for example, a man spraying a fire extinguisher right at your horse's legs. Other obstacles involved a very noisy, bouncing toy on the ground, a man suddenly jumping up from a park bench and opening his umbrella to see if your horse rears up and takes off. In addition, you also had a man who fired about four rapid gunshots right behind your horse while you tried to keep him calm and inside the box. That is just a small sample of some of the really tough challenges that these police horses and their riders had to face in this tough competition.

Midway through the course, we were doing so well that we actually placed within the top ten riders. Our team was super excited. But as the afternoon went on, we soon lost our place in the top ten. Finally, by the time the competition ended, we finished in twenty-fifth place out of the more than 125 competitors. Although not what I was hoping for, I had to remind myself that we did finish in the top twenty percent of a field filled with so many competitive riders. I left there with a big sense of accomplishment. Proud to have done so amazingly well with Alex, even though neither he nor I had a great deal of experience competing at an elite level. A truly great job once again, Alex!!!

CHAPTER 89

ONE OF MY MOST INSPIRING EXPERIENCES EVER AS A POLICE OFFICER!

Back in 1984, I was making my rounds in my marked unit when I observed and arrested a young local-gang member who was peddling drugs on a street corner well known for its illicit drug and gang activity. On the way to booking, I realized that the young man, whom I had just arrested and placed in the back seat, was sobbing uncontrollably. So I asked him, "Hey, what's going on, man? Why are you crying so much?"

He paused momentarily before telling me his story. "Officer, I am really sorry about this, but you have no idea what I'm going through right now. My parents don't want me at home. I've been trying to get out of the gang, but I'm really afraid, and I've been kicked out of school because of my poor grades and absences. I really don't know what to do anymore?"

As police officers, we hear similar stories all the time. Criminals who lie and tell you what they think you want to hear, in hopes of getting a break, pity, or leniency. But something in this young man's story really struck a chord with me. For some reason, I thought that maybe, just maybe, he was telling the truth. Against my better judgment, I decided to give him some advice, in hopes that maybe it would help him turn his life around!

"It's never too late to turn your life around, young man!" I told him, "So why don't you go have a talk with your parents and tell them how sorry you are, how you're willing to change. Then, go back to school, get out of the gang, and most importantly, stop messing around with these stupid drugs! Because one day it's going to catch up to you, and you'll either end up dead, or you'll spend the rest of your life in jail!"

He appeared to be bit surprised that I took the time not only to listen to his story, but also to give him some sound advice. He thanked me, and I wished him well as I led him into booking and booked him on the drug charges.

Fast forward fifteen years later to the summer of 1999, and this time I'm on Allyn Street in Downtown Hartford, patrolling the streets with Alex the Wonder Horse. Out of the blue, I hear a male's voice yelling, "Officer, Officer, Officer," as he ran towards me and Alex. I immediately came to a stop, thinking that maybe this guy was running over to report a crime or in need of some urgent help. But I was wrong!

Instead, I got one of the biggest surprises that I've ever gotten in all my years as a police officer! He extended his hand to shake mine. "Officer, I know you probably don't remember me, but you arrested me fifteen years ago on drug charges. And I just wanted to stop you, just to say thank you for changing my life! You might not remember this, but at the time I was involved in gangs and was having all sorts of issues at home with my parents, in school, and with drugs. That day, you took the time to show me that you cared about my life and that I mattered. I will never forget how you gave me some great advice that really changed my life forever! Officer, since that day, I have turned my life around completely! I am now happily married with a great wife, three beautiful kids, and work two full-time jobs to support my home and my family...and all thanks to you!"

That amazing moment, truly left me speechless. But more than anything, it really warmed my heart just knowing that I was able to make a difference in that young man's life at a very difficult point in his journey! As police officers, we rarely get a chance to see how many lives we've touched during our careers, or even the difference that one little encounter can make in the lives of others... unless you have that golden opportunity to hear it right from them. I felt amazingly blessed for this wonderful experience. It became one of the proudest moments of my career, and one that will be with me forever.

That day, I thanked the young man for making a difference in my life with his story! A story that I'm hoping he has shared with others as he hopes to make a change in their lives. And in doing so, pays it forward!

CHAPTER 90

MY DAYS OF WORKING IN PLAIN CLOTHES

One of the added bonuses that I enjoyed about being in the mounted unit was having the opportunity to work in plain clothes. Those opportunities usually came around during really cold, wintry days when conditions weren't favorable for riding safely on the city streets. Safety always took priority over any riding assignment. That's because, during those snowy or icy days, there was always the possibility of one of the horses sliding on the ice and getting hurt, along with the rider. Or worse yet, a car sliding into a horse and seriously injuring both the rider and his mount.

Other conditions that also prompted strict adherence to the safety protocol had to do with the temperature outside during the winter months. Severe weather conditions could prevent us from carrying out our regular duties as mounted officers; therefore, in order to protect both the officers and the horses from working in frigid conditions, the police department developed a parameter whereby, any time the temperature or windchill dipped below 32 degrees Fahrenheit, we wouldn't ride. Instead, we were allowed to carry out our patrol duties in plain clothes using an unmarked unit, as a supplement to the patrol division in high-crime areas of the city.

One particular day back in August of 1990, I was heading back to the stables after a long day of working in my assigned area in the north end of the city. Just as I was pulling up to a stop sign near the corner of Charlotte and Garden Streets, I observed a Black male running with sawed-off shotgun in his right hand. At the time, he had just cut right in front of my unmarked police vehicle, which apparently he had not noticed. The individual was sweating profusely and breathing hard.

There were two possibilities: either he was running away after shooting someone, or he was on his way to shoot someone. Regardless, he had no business walking around with an illegal sawed-off shotgun in his hand in broad daylight.

I quickly exited my car, drew my weapon after identifying myself as the police, and ordered him to drop the gun. The suspect hesitated for a moment, but decided to comply with my demands to drop the weapon on the ground. I ordered him to hit the ground after I kicked his weapon to the side, and I was able to handcuff him without incident. Backup units soon arrived, and the weapon was subsequently unloaded and secured.

Upon further inspection of the weapon, we discovered that one spent shotgun shell was still in the chamber, an indication that the shotgun must have been recently fired. Our conclusions were right on. We later learned the accused suspect had just shot at another armed individual during a heated argument, one that culminated in both subjects trying to shoot each other. And while no one was hurt in the incident, the potential was surely there. Several bystanders later interviewed at the scene of the shoot-out said they had to duck for cover to prevent from getting hit with one of the stray bullets.

Following the investigation, the accused subject was placed under arrest on numerous felony charges, as was the other individual involved in the shoot-out. However, that weapon was never located, and he proved to be very uncooperative during the whole investigation.

It was just another day of being in the right place, at the right time, in this challenging world of police work!

About a year or so later, in December of 1991, my partner at the time, Officer Jardin, and I were patrolling in our unmarked vehicle in the southwestern section of the city when the dispatcher put out an all-points bulletin on a vehicle wanted in numerous towns for close to a dozen armed robberies, including some of which had taken place right in our city.

Shortly after that APB, all-points bulletin, was put out to all units, we were traveling southbound on Zion Street, and I was driving. I noticed a vehicle fitting the APB's description: 1986 Olds Delta 88, color gray, with a White-male operator. It was traveling in the opposite direction, northbound on Zion towards New Britain Avenue. We immediately made a U-turn and proceeded to follow it at a safe distance, so as not to blow our cover. Seconds later, the suspect was seen getting out of his car and entering a grocery store located at 408 New Britain Avenue. We waited to get confirmation on the wanted vehicle's license-plate information and suspect.

While we kept an eye on the suspect, it appeared that he may have intended to rob yet another store, but somehow felt uneasy and quickly left the store without making a purchase. The suspect walked towards his car in the parking lot. He looked a bit nervous, so we weren't sure if he had made us or not. Just before he grabbed the driver's door handle to enter his car, we decided to move in and take him down at gunpoint. We immediately placed him in cuffs and detained him until further information could be received and the suspect was positively identified as the serial-robbery suspect.

With the suspect now safely secured, we decided to take a quick peek inside his car. Right there on the back seat, in plain view, we spotted the ski mask, the jacket, and the weapon, a tool shaped in the form of a gun, all of which were used in the robberies. Minutes later, detectives from our department, along with some from those neighboring towns affected, all arrived at the scene. The suspect was positively identified as the serial robber involved in a multi-town armed-robbery spree and was subsequently placed under arrest.

We later learned that in all the cases, the suspect's modus operandi was to enter the store, look around for the right opportunity before approaching the store clerk to announce, "This is a robbery!" In one of the cases, the suspect was quoted as saying, "I've got a loaded .25 caliber gun in my pocket. You won't get hurt if you give me some money!" After getting the money, the suspect calmly walked out of the store and took off in his gray Olds Delta. During his multi-town crime spree, the suspect was believed to have absconded with thousands of dollars. Until the day he decided to test the waters once too many times and got busted by two Mounties…just without the horses this time around!

Another memorable case took place back on January 13, 1994, as Officer Harry Satterfield and I were working in plain clothes and assigned to patrol the southeast section of the city, considered by crime stats to be a high-crime area of the city known for its illicit gang violence and drug use.

That day, at about 1:20 p.m., we were driving southbound on Broad Street when I noticed that the vehicle directly in front of us, a brown Olds Delta 88, fit the description of a vehicle possibly wanted in connection with a homicide that had taken place earlier that same day. This vehicle, which was occupied by three Hispanic males, had been lurking around the area for quite some time. In fact, they had already made several turns around the block without stopping, raising red flags that they were probably looking for a target in order to carry out a drive-by shooting or pull off a robbery. This was a common practice d in drive-by shootings during those days.

Without waiting any longer and risking the chance that the suspects might try to leave the area if they noticed that they were being followed, we decided to light them up with our red lights and siren. We made this felony stop right around the area of 87 Madison Street.

Immediately after being pulled over, all parties in the vehicle suddenly exited their car just as we were approaching with our guns drawn. We quickly grabbed the driver and held him at gunpoint, while the other two suspects started slowly walking away in the same direction, northbound on Broad Street, while mumbling some incoherent words that were directed towards us. We yelled at them to put their hands up in the air and to come back to their car. But they refused to comply and took off running.

With the driver now handcuffed and secured with my partner, I took off running after them. I was able to catch up with one of the suspects and managed to tackle him down to the ground, and handcuffing him after a brief struggle. I then brought him back to the scene of the felony stop and continued with our investigation. The third subject managed to get away and was never located.

We soon learned that the vehicle that we had stopped was not the one being sought for the homicide. However, we questioned ourselves, if this wasn't the car that was wanted in the homicide, why would they run from us? Well, it didn't take long before that question was answered.

It turns out that right underneath the driver's seat, in plain view, was a fully loaded MAC-10 machine gun, an extremely lethal weapon that's made to take out a large number of people within seconds. Upon inspecting the weapon further, we found that it was fully loaded with twenty-two Winchester Black Talon .45 caliber rounds in the magazine and one in the chamber... ready to go! Upon searching further, no other weapons or contraband were found to be inside the vehicle.

That day, we counted our blessings, for we both knew how things could've easily taken a turn for the worst had the suspects decided to shoot it out with us. Going up against such a powerful assault weapon would've been tough with only our .45 caliber Smith and Wessons... but not impossible. And while they had more firepower than we did, we would've never backed down.

In the end, this is just one example of what cops are up against on a daily basis in our line of work. One that's filled with so much uncertainty and unpredictability. That day, thanks to God's blessings, we were able to go home safely to our families. While the bad guys went to their temporary home as well. But this time around, their home was a six-by-ten cell surrounded by iron bars!

CHAPTER 91

WORKING A SPECIAL PROTECTION DETAIL WITH CELEBRITIES

Some of the most unforgettable moments of my career as a police officer didn't happen chasing bad guys, but working on special details as part of a security team protecting celebrities who came to visit the City of Hartford.

These special assignments, called "private duty," involved a number of different enterprises that hired off-duty but fully uniformed Hartford police officers for the purpose of protecting an entity or a person, business, or structure. Some of those off-duty jobs included hiring police officers at construction sites in order to reroute traffic and keep the construction workers safe from vehicular traffic. These subcontractors would then pay the city a fee for our services, and the balance was paid forward to the officer who worked the job, after the city took its cut, and was added to the officer's regular weekly paycheck.

These private jobs can vary in the type of work, depending on the circumstances. The gamut of these jobs can run from hiring a police officer for construction sites, to hiring them for a host of department stores within the city. The reason, of course, is to cut down on theft. Finally, you also have companies that hire police officers for crowd control during concert venues, sporting events, parades, and even marathon races, just to name a few.

Personally, some of my favorite private-duty assignments involved working at concert events. This was especially true if a very popular artist was performing at either the Civic or XL Center, which is an indoor arena that seats about 16,000-plus people. Or at the Meadowlands or Xfinity Theatre, which serves as both an indoor and an outdoor arena and can hold a capacity crowd of over 30,000 people. To me and many of my coworkers, these private jobs give us a chance to earn a little extra cash, while at the same time, they allow us to watch a great concert or special event. That is, of course, assuming there are no major issues in the stands or at the concert venue, such as a big fight that requires quick police action…and possibly an arrest. However, for the most part, those incidents happen very few and far between.

Luckily, though, that wasn't the case on the night I had the golden opportunity to work on the Michael Jackson Bad Tour on March 30, 1988. I was selected by our bosses to be a part of his security team!

As a kid growing up in the South Bronx, I grew up listening to his music, both as a solo artist and when he was a member of the Jackson 5. During that period of time, they were dominating the airways, as well as the *Billboard* charts, with one huge hit after another and were selling out concert venues wherever they performed.

Over time, as I grew older, I became a big fan of his music as a solo artist. Over the years, I ended up buying many of his hit singles and albums. In fact, during some of my short stints as a DJ at random house parties, I remember playing many of his hit songs. As it turns out, I wasn't the only one. Many of my best friends from the neighborhood were also big fans of his music and used to play and dance to his music all the time. So for me to finally get a chance to see him in concert as an adult was truly an awesome experience!

On the day of the concert, I reported to roll call at about 7:00 p.m. to work alongside about another sixty to eighty officers who would be assigned to work inside the coliseum. That day, we stood at attention, five to six rows deep, in the inside corridor and waited for our duty assignments to be given to us by the captain in charge of the event. As our captain went through the list of names, I noticed that he had called nearly everyone's name on the list, but not mine or those of three other officers.

The captain, before dismissing everyone to their assigned posts, said, "And after roll call, I want to see…" and mentioned my name along with the other three officers who were not called during the initial roll call.

After everyone was dismissed, the three other officers and I approached the captain to get our instructions for the night's concert. He then told us that we had been assigned as part of Michael Jackson's security team that night, and we were to go downstairs and meet up with the head of his security team, where we would be given further instructions. Still a bit shocked and surprised, we immediately acknowledged his commands and quickly proceeded down the stairs.

One of the things that sticks out most about that moment was the excitement we were all feeling on being selected for that special detail. Just knowing how lucky we were to be chosen out of the more than eighty cops who had reported for duty that day. The captain had said that we were hand selected for the detail. I remember clearly we were sporting the biggest smiles on our faces as we gave each other high fives as we went down the stairs.

Once there, we met up with this gentleman, a really cool and friendly guy, who introduced himself to us and ran over some of the details of what was about to take place that evening. He said, "Michael will be here shortly, and what I'm going to need from you guys"—pointing to me and Bryan—"is for you guys to line up right here, where you will be walking shoulder to shoulder with Michael"—I was on his right, and Bryan on his left—"as he heads towards the stage. While you two other guys will line up directly behind them"—again pointing to me and Bryan—"All we need from you guys as a team is to escort Michael right up to the stage, and then once he's done after each set, to meet him back on the edge of the stage, and escort him back down to his dressing room." After we went through all the details and rehearsed it a few times with his security manager, we all looked at each other in disbelief. And just smiled.

The entrance to the stage, was less than one hundred feet away from us. As we got into position and waited for Michael, we heard the boisterous chant, "Michael, Michael, Michael," coming from the audience. Accompanied by the loud and in-unison sound of feet stomping on the floor. The noise was so loud that it echoed through the corridor of the staging area like thunder. The closer we got to showtime, the louder the noise got.

Then, with just minutes to go before the 8:00 p.m. scheduled concert time, here comes Michael Jackson, escorted by several members of his security team and his manager. They stayed with Michael right up to where we were all standing, and, one by one, we all got introduced to

Michael and shook hands with him. He seemed a bit shy and reserved, but smiled and took the time to thank us and tell us how much he really appreciated our being there and helping out. A film crew from his own production company had set up right before showtime, and they covered the whole interaction between Michael and us.

As the chants got louder and louder, we all lined up, just as we had practiced, shoulder to shoulder, with Michael smack-dab in the middle. The next thing I remember is Michael turning around to face us and asking if we were ready. A few seconds after we all said yes, we were walking in sync towards the stage. The intensity and the adrenaline of screaming and foot-stomping fans took on its own life, and we all felt as though we were a part of the show. When we finally escorted Michael right up to the stage, the place went berserk. The fancy lighting and the loudness of the music, only added to the excitement in the arena. It was truly a moment to remember. And one that I will never, ever forget!

Throughout the concert, we must've escorted him back and forth from the stage to his dressing room at least three or four times throughout the evening. About two hours or so later, this amazing concert was over, and we escorted Michael back to his dressing room for the last time.

As we waited outside his dressing room, I decided to ask his manager if there was any way that Michael could sign a couple of autographs for my two kids, Bobby and Bianca, before he left. He said he'd check with Michael. To our surprise, a few minutes after that request, Michael emerged from his dressing room and autographed two ticket stubs that I found on the ground after the concert; he then headed back into his dressing room.

That night, Bryan and I stayed behind to escort Michael to his personal van that would take him back to his hotel. When Michael exited his dressing room, he stayed with us for about five minutes or so as we waited for his van to arrive through the rear loading-dock area of the Civic Center. While standing there, we chatted for a little bit, and I complimented him on his amazing performance that night. He thanked me for the compliment and then thanked us once again for assisting him. Moments later, the van showed up and he was whisked back to his hotel. He had to rest up for part two of the concert that was taking place the very next day.

Early that next day, his management team reached out to our department with a special request from Michael. They wanted to know if there was any way that they could use the mounted unit's officers to escort Michael's van, starting from the loading dock's entrance ramp in the rear of the Civic Center and ending at the corridor. The department agreed.

By that evening, three other members of the mounted unit and I were doing just that, escorting Michael's van into the Civic Center. This time, however, in order to allow Michael's van to get through the crowd, our detail was required to cut a pathway through the large crowd of screaming fans gathered by the entrance ramp.

As soon as Michael's van made its way through from Asylum Street to Ann Street, escorted by the Hartford Police motorcycle unit, we joined in and got right in front his van. We moved in unison to slowly part the sea of die-hard screaming fans right down the middle. The huge crowd of excited fans quickly began banging on the van as they screamed out Michael's name. Somehow, someway, we managed to work our way through this boisterous crowd without a problem. All thanks, in part, to our amazing police horses and officers who did an awesome job, considering the pandemonium that surrounded all of us.

Somehow we made it happen, and Michael was able to perform the second leg of his concert! That evening, after all was said and done, we put our horses on the horse trailer and headed back to the mounted unit's stables for a well-earned break. An article about the experience was published in the *New Haven Register* on July 3, 2009, under the title "Remembering Michael: Ex-Cop Shared Adrenaline on the Security Detail at '88 Concert."

About a year or so after the concert, I was watching a one-hour Michael Jackson TV special covering his Bad Tour, and I managed to catch a quick glimpse of our mounted unit in action as we escorted Michael's van past the throngs of screaming fans. Thanks to his production company, who did a great job of capturing some of the most exciting moments of Michael Jackson's world tour!

Finally, over the years, besides working with Michael Jackson's personal security detail, I also had the pleasure of getting assigned to other celebrities like Alfonso Ribeiro from *The Fresh Prince of Bel-Air*, famed basketball player Patrick Ewing from the New York Knicks, the Reverend Jesse Jackson, Football Hall of Famer Roger Staubach, and a host of others, including President George H. W. Bush, and later working on the presidential detail of President Bill Clinton when he came to Hartford.

CHAPTER 92

FACING A NEW
CHAPTER IN MY LIFE

As the years and the months went by, my career was really flourishing, so much so, that I used to look forward to going to work every single day. There was never a doubt in my mind that this was what I was born to do. My calling!

During my career I had achieved so many milestones. I couldn't be more grateful for all the blessings that came my way, from receiving numerous medals, awards, letters of commendations, and a host of other accolades, to serving in different capacities within the police department, becoming a veteran police officer on the force, and last, but certainly not least, even making third on the sergeants' list before it expired. All possible because I had big dreams and never let those tough times of growing up poor in a very difficult environment interfere with everything I wanted to do in my life and career.

Yet while I was doing so well in my career as a police officer, at home my marriage was slowly falling apart. Looking back now, I attribute so much of what we went through to the pitfalls of getting married at such a young age and everything that's involved in raising a family.

Shortly after getting married, we decided to have a family and right away took on all the difficult responsibilities that came along with running a family and a household as very young parents; it was challenging! But nevertheless, we marched on and tried to make the best of it with the little bit of experience we had, both as a married couple and as parents.

After about four years of marriage, we left Queens, New York, and moved to Connecticut. I became a police officer, and Ana found a job working as a receptionist at Shepherd's Park, a housing complex for the elderly in Hartford. Having left all our friends and family behind in New York City to start a new life became an extremely difficult task. So much so, that within a year's time of being in Connecticut, we became homesick. We found ourselves in a whole new life and environment, without our tight-knit group of lifetime friends and family that were a part of our lives for so many years. After a while, it truly felt as though we were rebuilding our lives from scratch. A new life, a new place, new jobs, and a whole new set of friends, all of which took some time and adjustment to get used to.

But more than anything, I noticed, that as the years went by, we were starting to grow, and not just as a young married couple, but also as individuals. Things were slowly starting to change in our marriage, and we soon started to realize that we were not the same people we were when we first got married. And with this change came the problems and difficulties in our relationship. Alternating heated arguments and periods of trying to talk things through and compromise soon became a major issue and continued to get worst over time.

As years went on, cracks in our marriage became more apparent. We were growing apart emotionally, and the tension of it all soon created a big separation between the two of us. Heated arguments and disputes continued to erode a marriage in trouble, slowly chipping away at all that we had built as a couple over the years. It got to the point that a simple fun night out to a club or a house party with friends would quickly turn into a heated dispute, which sadly sometimes even happened right in the presence of our friends and family. At times, a woman's simple glance or stare in my direction at a house party or a club would result in an all-out verbal altercation, which quickly put an end to a great night out of dancing and hanging out with friends. The arguing would often continue once we got home. This was soon followed by a night of silence afterwards, which would last well into the next day, or for even days or weeks.

Dealing with all this stress at home and in my line of work as a police officer wasn't easy. At times, getting away to hang out with some of my friends from work was a nice reprieve. It allowed me to have a couple of cold beers or drinks to relieve some of the anxiety about issues that I was dealing with both at work and at home. On the other end, my wife was doing the same things I was doing, going out with some of her best friends from work and enjoying some time to herself.

However, with every year that passed, we started slowly creating more and more distance between us as a married couple. In fact, on many special occasions, like birthdays and anniversaries, we would go on without any major celebrations or even acknowledgments. Sometimes just going out to dinner for a little relaxation would turn out to be awkward, with not much conversation at our dining table.

While we were having our personal difficulties at home, we tried our best to always shield the kids from the problems and issues we were having as their parents. Instead, we would do the complete opposite, by showering them with lots of love and giving them the best of everything life had to offer in order to foster their mental and emotional well-being. Looking back now, I think that the main reason we stayed together for as long as we did was clearly for the love of our kids who mean the world to us.

With the emotional distancing getting worse over time, we were starting to feel as if we were two perfect strangers living in the same household and sharing the same space, but only in an effort to support the household and our children. This ultimately led to a lot of resentment and disappointments in our marriage. Before long, we started seeking from elsewhere the love and attention we once found in each other. And when that happened, our relationship was basically over.

Extramarital affairs on both sides of the relationship only added to an already-fragile union. In fact, one day I discovered that she was having a long-term relationship with a jeweler she met in New York City sometime between the years of 1989 to 1990. On the day I found out about it, I immediately confronted her, and she never denied it. She admitted that it was true and gave me a host of reasons for the affair. All in all, the bottom line was that her main reason for the affair at the time was that she had fallen out of love with me.

My first reaction was shock, but not surprise, considering all of issues and problems. But more so because this wasn't her first time going down that road. And neither was it mine, for that matter. By this time in our relationship, I had already been involved in a few affairs. Her affairs and mine were an all-out indication of the troubled state of our marriage and the direction it was heading on this dark path. In the months that followed, we both agreed to end our affairs and the discord in our personal lives in order to focus on trying to save our crumbling marriage through counseling.

Through it all, on at least three occasions in our marriage, we actually sought marriage counseling to try to work things out, all in desperate attempts to try to get things back to where they used to be. But that also failed. In fact, within a matter of years, I must have packed up my bags and moved out of the house on at least two separate occasions, all under the assumption that maybe we just needed to take little bit of time off in order to work on ourselves... and our situation.

While at first things appeared to be working out as we tried to patch things up, months later, it was back to the same old stuff and the same old problems.

CHAPTER 93

ONE OF MY DARKEST DAYS

A nother day that contributed greatly to the demise of our troubled marriage took place just a few years earlier, before all the intense bickering, quarreling, and affairs entered into the picture. It happened on July 21, 1987, one the darkest days of my life!

About a week or so prior to this date, my wife approached me to ask if I would be willing to take a trip with her to visit two of her half brothers, Jose and Beto, who lived in Montreal, Canada. I told her I would think about it and let her know in a few days. Up to that point in my life, I had never met any of her brothers, but had heard about them during numerous conversations with my wife and her family in the Bronx.

According to my wife, they both left their country of Honduras, in search of a better life in Canada. Beto, the younger of the two, had been in Montreal, Canada, for quite a number of years. He was going to school and working under the umbrella of a work-study visa program that allowed him to both work and go to college at the same time, with the possibility of maybe one day being granted a Canadian citizenship down the road.

Her other brother, Jose, on the other hand, had a totally different set of circumstances that resulted in his emigration to Montreal, Canada, under a temporary work visa. Jose and his family were living under extreme poverty conditions back in Honduras. With a wife and several kids, he was the sole breadwinner in the household. Just months before emigrating to Canada, he lost his job at a factory and was really having a tough time trying to make ends meet. So one day, out of pure frustration and desperation to find a job, he decided to take a chance and headed to Canada, in hopes of finding a job somewhere in a foreign land to feed and support his family.

Somewhere around the middle of July 1987, my wife talked to her aunt about her brother's condition. It was during that conversation, that her aunt asked if there was any way my wife could take a trip to Montreal, Canada, and bring Jose back with her into the US. If my wife was successful, Jose would stay in our home until he found a job and could provide for his family. My wife agreed to help, but said she would not be a hundred percent committed to that plan until she was able to discuss the situation with me.

About a week or so before our trip in early July, my wife asked me if she could talk to me regarding her brother's situation and her plan to go up to Canada and bring Jose back into the US. When she first told me about this plan, I shut it down right away. I didn't want any part of it because of all the potential risk involved. But she was persistent and told me that, according to her aunt, if he was stopped at the border, the worst that could happen was that he would be sent back to Montreal, and we would continue driving back home.

The more and more I thought about Jose and his dire situation, the more I felt the pressure to take a chance and try to help him. Just days before our trip, however, I was having second thoughts about it once again. I decided to put it on hold until I could give it some more thought. In the interim, we decided to take a trip to her aunt's house in the Bronx to discuss it further.

Once in the aunt's home, she begged us to help get Jose into the US. She added once again that the worst-case scenario was his being turned back at the border. After a few more pleas and assurances, she was able to convince us both, and we decided to take this journey.

So on Saturday, July 18, my wife, our two kids, a niece and nephew, and I packed our bags and headed to Canada. About six hours later, we crossed the Canadian border, and headed to our hotel in Montreal. The next day, we planned to have a great time visiting her brothers and to take some time out to see and experience some of the great tourist attractions in Montreal.

When we finally met with her brothers that afternoon, they were ecstatic to see us. That day, we spent a great time as a family. We decided to head back home after spending a long, fun-filled weekend with them. That afternoon, we discussed with Jose our plan for heading back to the US; he was beyond thrilled and couldn't wait for that day to arrive.

On the morning of July 21, at approximately 1:00 a.m., we pulled up to the US Border and were met by a customs agent who greeted us kindly and asked us some basic questions about our trip to Canada. Most notably, he wanted to know if there was anything illegal that we were bringing into the US. We said no.

He decided to take a quick look inside the car, and soon became very suspicious when he saw Jose in the middle of the back passenger seat. Jose really stood out because, unlike my wife and the rest of her family members, Jose had really dark skin and didn't blend well with the rest of the family in our car. When the agent began to ask Jose a few general, probing questions about our trip, he couldn't answer them because he couldn't speak a word of English. This quickly aroused the suspicion of the border patrol agent; he asked us to pull over to the side of the road and told us he would be right back.

We did as instructed. As the minutes passed, and we saw no sign of the agent, we began to get a little bit nervous and worried. After about five minutes or so of waiting, we noticed the agent approaching our car; he was accompanied by a couple of additional agents. The minute we saw this, we knew it was not a good sign; we might be in trouble.

Upon approaching our vehicle, the agents asked us to step out of the car and to walk with them inside the Border Patrol building. Once inside, they split us up into different rooms. We quickly surmised that they thought my brother-in-law was not related to us, that he was just a stranger we had picked up in our travels, and that we were trying to bring him into the country illegally.

After about twenty minutes of interrogation and verifying some of his legal documents, they finally came to the conclusion that we were telling the truth, and that Jose was in fact a family member. At that point, they decided to let us go, but not before charging me and my wife with one misdemeanor count each of allowing a person to attempt to gain entry into the US without proper documentation. They also impounded our car until we reported to the court the next day with a lawyer, to plead guilty in front of a judge to that one charge, which carried a fine of $200. Jose, on the other hand, while he did have a work visa from Canada to work in their country, he did not have a passport and was charged with one misdemeanor count of attempting to enter the US without proper documentation. He was later released to the Canadian authorities after paying a fine in the same amount, and ultimately deported back to Honduras.

Throughout this whole process, I was under the impression that once I pleaded guilty to the one misdemeanor charge, my car would be released back to me without a problem. Unfortunately, that wasn't the case. It took me nearly two months before I was finally able to get my car back. In the meantime, my other brother-in-law, Julio, was kind enough to let me borrow one of his spare cars until mine was returned.

After this incident took place, I was a total mess. I was embarrassed, heartbroken, and truly depressed over this whole situation. A situation that could've easily been avoided had I not given into my wife's and her aunt's pleas to help them out with this family issue. Instead, I let my heart, my emotions, and my willingness to help someone, in this case a family member, cloud my vision of the right thing to do.

Looking back now, I should have listened to all these questions that kept popping into my head: *What will happen if things don't go as planned? How will this affect the job that I love and serve with so much dedication? What happens to that job if I get in trouble?* All these question proceeded to circle in my mind, only to be overruled by the humanitarian side of me that was trying to help a family member in need of assistance.

As a cop, I always took so much pride in the job that I did, a job that I had dreamed about ever since I was a young child. Inspired by, most notably, my grandfather who was a cop back in the day in Puerto Rico, other family members on the police force, and finally, a few police officers whom I met during my many years of living in the South Bronx.

In the days that followed, I had sleepless nights. I worried about the status of my job and having to confront my police chief with this situation. I thought deeply about the punishment I would face for my poor judgment and indiscretion. I also thought about the many people I let down and how they would feel once they find out what happened to me. But most importantly, I feared for the welfare of my kids, and what would happen if I lost my job?

That day, I prayed long and hard to God for His help in getting me through this process as I met with Chief Sullivan in his office on that Friday morning, July 24. The union president was also there with me, not only to discuss my case with the chief, but more importantly, to try his best to keep me from losing my job.

Throughout the meeting, they discussed that in my eight years in the department I had been an "exemplary officer" with "numerous commendations for great police work." He also added that "throughout his many years of dedicated service with the police department and the City of Hartford… he has served a life of distinction, commitment, and professionalism throughout his career."

That day, after giving the matter much thought and consideration, the chief decided that the best course of action at the time would be to suspend me for two weeks without pay, under the condition that any other indiscretions would be met with an even more severe and harsh punishment.

I gave him my sincerest apology, promised that I would not let him down, and that I would do everything within my power to never embarrass him or my department ever again! This was a promise that I would not have a problem keeping, and instead, would use as a motivating factor to continue to bring pride to my department and my fellow peers!

Looking back now to that turning point in my career, he could've easily fired me, given me a longer suspension time, or lastly, booted me right out of the mounted unit and transferred me back to patrol. But in the end, he did none of that, for I'm sure he believed in me as an honest person and most importantly, as a driven cop who would do the right thing from that day forward and not make him regret that decision. And I never did!

Ultimately, as the months and the years went by, we became really good friends. But more than anything, he became one of my biggest mentors and supporters ever! Over time he went on to become the best police chief we ever had in the history of the Hartford Police Department! Someone who was loved and admired by everyone who had the honor of working under his amazing leadership and command. He was, and will always be, someone whom I truly respect and admire!

For he believed in me and gave me that second chance to continue to serve in the career that he knew I truly loved, and that meant so much to me! It is for that reason, and so many more, that I want to take a moment to say, "Thank you, Chief Sullivan, for making such a huge difference in my life! You are truly the best!!!"

CHAPTER 94

A NEW LIFE... A NEW BEGINNING

After that nightmarish experience, I held a lot of resentment towards my wife because of what happened to me. On that horrible day in my life, I did the unthinkable and let my heart dictate what I should've known all along was a really bad decision on my behalf, one that I wholeheartedly regret and took full responsibility for. In the end, I came to the decision that I wasn't about to let that one little asterisk in my life dictate how I was going to live the rest of it going forward. That's when I made the conscious decision to hold my head up high and continue being the best person, father, and police officer I could be, no matter what challenges lay ahead!

While this one incident certainly didn't end my marriage that year, it added to the cumulative frustration of everything that was going wrong in our relationship. As months went by, we went on with our troubled marriage in hopes that somewhere along the line things would work themselves out, especially for the sake of our children. But unfortunately, that never happened.

The heated verbal disputes and arguments continued without any resolution. With each confrontation, our relationship just grew further and further apart. In fact, it got to the point of no repair, the point at which not even the presence of a marriage counselor could make a difference in saving our marriage. The communication and intimacy that usually bonds a loving couple together was no longer there.

It soon became clear to us that this situation wasn't working out. And that the only reason we were still together was because of the love and care we had for our children, not wanting to hurt them in anyway. But we both knew that wanting to be there for the love of our kids alone was not enough to hold a family together. And in the long run, it would be detrimental for all involved.

As the kids got older in age, however, they were starting to sense the distance and the tension between the two of us. The lack of closeness and communication that once existed between the two of us was no longer there. They knew right away that something was definitely wrong. This was especially true when they witnessed firsthand some of the heated arguments that took place right in front of them.

And then, of course, there was all the drama and masquerading that took place behind the scenes to protect their feelings. We created a façade that in the long run became a very unhealthy and unstable environment for both the kids and us. We both knew we needed to make changes soon! A divorce was imminent!

CHAPTER 95

1991: THE YEAR THAT MY LIFE CHANGED FOREVER...

By the time I welcomed the New Year of 1991, I had already made up my mind that this was going to be the year to make big, permanent changes in my life. I could no longer continue to live under the stressful and unhappy conditions at home that were making my life miserable. I just knew that I needed to start taking the right steps forward, not only for the sake of my own personal and mental well-being, but also for the kids, whom I wholeheartedly recognized needed to grow up in a mentally safe and happy environment, not in a place filled with so much turmoil and discontent.

By 1990, our marriage had hit its lowest point ever. We were in shambles. Triggered in part by numerous heated arguments, and aggravated by our multiple marital affairs. And by the end of 1990, there was no doubt in my mind that it was only a matter of time before our marriage would end in divorce. Because of that, I knew I had to prepare myself financially for all the challenges that lay ahead: a marital separation followed closely by a divorce.

As part of my New Year's resolution, I made it a priority to try and save as much money as I could, in order to ultimately move out of my house and move into my own apartment. With that in mind, I knew I needed to save up enough money to not only support my personal living expenses, but also all the expenses that came with a marital separation. Especially, when there are children involved.

And while this inevitable separation was looming in the background, we managed to continue to live our separate lives, while still sharing the confines of our home and honoring all our own personal obligations to our home and our family. In essence, we were living no differently. Our main focus remained taking care of our children's personal needs while making sure to continue to provide them with the same unconditional love and support that they'd been accustomed to getting all along.

The dim prospect of splitting up and going our separate ways was something that had been brewing in our lives for many years. I was extremely unhappy at home, and I just couldn't envision myself living the rest of my life under those highly contentious conditions. I wanted to be happy in the worst way. But at the same time, I also wanted Ana to be happy. I just knew that we could not be happy together.

One thing I think we can both agree upon is that while we both gave it a valiant effort over the years, somehow we just couldn't make our marriage work, no matter how much we tried. And it was finally time to step back and to start thinking of ourselves as two different people, with two totally different personalities, who tried our best to keep our marriage alive, but we just couldn't save it!

I just knew that 1991 would be the year that I would be entering a new chapter in my life and in my marital status: becoming single once again!

One unforgettable day in 1991, after another heated argument and confrontation with my wife, I made the decision that was it; enough was enough! That night, I quickly packed my bags and moved out of my house for the final time! At the time, I literally had no place to go, neither did I have any idea what my next move would be. However, two things I knew for sure: first, I didn't want go back to my home, and second, I needed to start a new life.

Thank God, that I had a loving, beautiful niece, Cindy, and her awesome husband, Nano, who lived in East Hartford, the next town over, with their wonderful family. Once I asked them if there was a possibility that I could stay in their home until I could find my own place, they were more than welcoming! They invited me into their home with open arms and without bestowing any negative judgments or reservations about my decision. Instead, my niece supported me all the way because, as she said, she was a true believer in always being there for my family, no matter what!

That was a day in my life that I will always remember! For it was on that day, that my niece opened her heart to me when I needed it the most!

CHAPTER 96

DESTINY

Back near the end of 1990, just about seven or eight months before moving into my niece's house in East Hartford, Connecticut, I remember waking up earlier than usual on a Tuesday morning, after not being able to get a good night's sleep the night before. That morning, I was feeling emotionally drained and tired from everything that was going on in my life at the time. A period magnified by a lot of ups and downs that were really starting to take a mental toll on me. At times, I felt as if I were walking on eggshells, not knowing when the next big argument or dispute would take place.

That day, as I sat on the edge of the bed, thinking about my problems at home, I came to the conclusion that maybe what I really needed right then and there was to give myself a little break just to get away from it all. A mental break. A place where I could find a little peace and tranquility and have some fun! And after thinking about it some more, the number one place that kept popping into my head was New York City! The city that never sleeps. The place where I was born and raised. The place that holds so much history for me. But more than anything, the place that has the best salsa clubs of anywhere in America. *Salsa* is Spanish for sauce, as in hot sauce, and that's what salsa music and dancing is. And if you're looking to have a good time, there is no better place than old New York City!

As a lifelong enthusiast of this genre of music, I used to love going to the clubs in New York City from time to time, just to do a little salsa dancing and have some fun with some of my closest friends and family.

Salsa music, whose original roots can be traced back to the islands of Cuba and Puerto Rico, came to the United States way back in the 1940s, where it eventually gained great prominence and popularity over the years. To this day, it remains more popular than ever! Coincidentally, it was through salsa dancing that my parents first met while partying at the old Tropicana nightclub in New York City back in the late 1940s, according to my father. So it's no surprise I too would grow up loving salsa just as much as my parents and siblings did back in the day. That's why I've always said to myself, that my love and appreciation for salsa music has lived in my blood since as far back as I can remember!

Fast forward to today, and you will find that New York City is considered by many as the mega capital of salsa dancing. The place where some of the best salsa dancers in the world can be found taking over the dance floors and showing off their best moves with their partners. This is where my oldest brother, Flaco, and sister Mercedes, both known for their dancing prowess, became amazing *salseros*. It was also here where many years later they would teach me some of their greatest moves, allowing me to add *salsero* to my dancing repertoire.

When you talk about some of the best salsa dance clubs in New York City, perhaps none earned that distinction better than the iconic Copacabana nightclub! Recognized in all of New York City as the best of the best! A place whose history can be traced as far back as the 1940s, a place that provides the best entertainment in all of New York City. Where you can find not only great salsa bands performing live, but also an amazing dining experience. All of which took place at the famous Copacabana nightclub, located right in Midtown Manhattan, at 10 East 60th Street, between Fifth and Madison Avenues.

However, it wasn't until the mid-1970s that the club went from being known as the Copacabana nightclub to the Copacabana disco. This was due, in part, to the rising fame of salsa dancing that was really catching on and quickly spreading throughout the city. And from that point on, it became known as the place to go for a great night out of salsa dancing and having a great time!

At any rate, getting back to my trip to New York City. That night, I made it to the Copa, short for Copacabana, just after 7:00 p.m. It was one of the Copa's After Work dance-party nights, which meant that they were open for business right at 6:00 p.m. to start the party! Admission was free for everyone on Tuesdays and Fridays, so long as you showed up between the hours of 6:00 to 8:00 p.m. that night. And there was even a free buffet.

By the time I got there, the music was already jamming, the bar was open, and a few people could be seen milling around the dance floor, while a few others danced on the open floor. Because it was still very early in the night, people were just starting to arrive right from work or home. As I started making my way towards the buffet table, I happened to take a quick glance towards the dance floor, and I noticed this very attractive female who really caught my eye.

Standing there all alone, right near the entrance to the dance floor, stood this tall, stunning brunette, who literally lit up the room. She was about five eight or five nine in height and had a glowing olive-skin complexion. She was also dressed to impress, wearing this very elegant yet sexy dress that complemented her very impressive, curvy figure perfectly! Her hair was long, slicked back, and tied up in a ponytail, which gave her what I call a very "distinctive Puerto Rican / European combo look" that made her stand out among all the other beautiful women in the club that night.

Within seconds, I had worked my way towards her, having decided to ask her for a dance. She hesitated a bit, but gave me a quick smile before saying, "Sure!" Right about that same time, the DJ played a great salsa song, so the timing couldn't have been any better! As I escorted her to the dance floor and we began dancing, we matched each other's steps precisely while dancing in rhythm to the music's every beat. We finished dancing to one song, and we got along so well on the dance floor that we decided why not go for another one!

During our second dance, we talked briefly and exchanged a few smiles. Everything appeared to be going so well until an individual who appeared to have drunk one too many nearly ran right into us several times while dancing with his partner. I tried to keep my cool and just kept an eye on him, hoping that eventually he would move to another part of the uncrowded dance floor, or step off the dance floor completely. But unfortunately that didn't happen.

We were having such a great time when I noticed that this same guy appeared to be stumbling all over the place. At one point during our dance, this guy completely lost his balance and ran right into my dance partner, nearly knocking her down.

I immediately lost my temper, grabbed him around his shirt collar, and yelled, "What the hell is wrong with you, man? You almost knocked her down!" I pointed to my partner. He was lucky that my dance partner and his date quickly intervened and prevented this incident from getting into a physical altercation.

After all was said and done, he ended up apologizing before leaving the dance floor, and possibly the club, with his partner. As he was leaving, my dance partner and I looked at each other and shook our heads in amazement, as if we couldn't believe what had just happened.

Shortly thereafter, we both walked off the dance floor, and I asked her if I could buy her a drink. She said yes, and I went to the bar to order them. After I brought over the drinks, we got a chance to talk some more while standing on the outskirts of the dance floor. It was at this time that we finally got a chance to formally introduce ourselves. And when she told me her name was Anna, it took me back a bit because, as it turns out, she and my wife share the same exact name, even though they are spelled differently—one has an extra *n*.

What are the chances? I thought.

I made no comment as to the coincidence in names, and we continued to talk and enjoy each other's company over a few drinks. Later on, I even got a chance to meet some of her best friends who met up with her later at the club.

Throughout the night, we never talked about anything personal regarding our relationship status. Instead, we talked about our love of salsa music, dancing, and work, along with a few other general things that we had in common. We ended up dancing a few more times throughout the evening before we realized that it was almost 12:00 a.m., and we both had to work the very next morning. So we called it a night.

Before leaving, we exchanged pleasantries, shook hands, and expressed how much we enjoyed meeting each other and dancing that night. And while we didn't exchange numbers or make any dates to meet up down the road, we ended the night by saying something to the effect of it having been a "true pleasure meeting you and, hopefully we'll see each other again sometime!"

After exiting the club that night, we both went our separate ways, not knowing if we would ever see each other again.

CHAPTER 97

DESTINY: PART TWO!

O ver the weeks and months that followed, I couldn't stop thinking about her, no matter how much I tried. Maybe it was her charm and personality that truly left an indelible mark in my mind that evening. Or maybe it was her unique beauty that made her stand out among the crowd of women at the club. But whatever it was, she certainly left me intrigued, and I definitely wanted to know more about her.

Over the next three months, I managed to go to the club a few more times in hopes of seeing her again, but it didn't happen. After those last two visits to the club, I kind of resigned myself to the fact that maybe our timing was bad, and it just wasn't meant to be. But as the saying goes, maybe the third time would be the charm. So with that in mind, I decided to give it one more shot a few weeks later!

It happened on Saturday, March 30, 1991. I was scheduled to work the evening shift, 3:00 p.m. to 11:00 p.m., at the mounted police stables. That day, I remember feeling in the mood to go dancing and having this unexplainable urge that maybe I should take a trip to the Copacabana right after work. The more I thought about it, the more I realized that driving to New York City after work at 11:00 p.m. would certainly be a big challenge for me, especially since commuting to New York City from Hartford at that time of the night was at least a two-hour ride. I probably wouldn't get to the Copacabana until about 1:00 a.m., which was a bit too late to go out dancing in New York City. Nevertheless, I decided to pack some clothes just in case I changed my mind later on that evening.

As the hours went by, the more I thought about it, the more this inexplicable drive kept pushing me to go for it! And so by the time 6:00 p.m. came around, I'd finally decided that I was going to the Copa! That night, instead of waiting until 11:00 p.m. to head to the city as I had originally planned, I decided to take four hours of compensatory time off, which would give me plenty of time to really enjoy the night. So by the time 7:00 p.m. rolled around, I was already out the door and well on my way to New York City!

As I drove to the city, I had my salsa music in the car playing at full blast, and was truly enjoying singing along to some of the best classic salsa beats playing in my car's cassette player. This made the mood for the long ride into the city really upbeat and exciting, all in anticipation of having a good night out!

While driving, I also started thinking that maybe, just maybe, this would be the night that I might bump into Anna again. But then again, the last two times I'd gone there with the same hope, only to leave a bit disappointed when it didn't happen.

About two hours later, I arrived at the Copa, and the place, by this time of the evening, was starting to get packed in both the upper level, which was considered the freestyle section, and the salsa section on the lower level. I picked up a drink at the bar and then a few minutes later had my first dance.

I was heading towards the outskirts of the dance floor when there she was. Our reactions and the looks on our faces clearly revealed mutual pleasure at our meeting again. They showed how happy we were to finally see each other after three long months! She had the biggest smile on her face and looked absolutely beautiful! After giving each other a nice, warm embrace, we soon started a conversation to catch up from where we were when we'd last seen each other.

It turns out that she had also come to the Copacabana on several occasions, just as I had, in hopes of bumping into me again. But unfortunately, we must've missed seeing each other by a couple of days during a period of several weeks. And while the timing was off then, on this night, we finally got it right!

Throughout the night, we got a chance to get to know each other a little bit more. We shared many laughs and also managed to dance quite a few salsa dances on the crowded dance floor. We had an awesome time as the night just seemed to fly by. Once again, it was getting late, and I knew I had a long drive ahead of me. And she was a bit tired from all the dancing we did that night. So we mutually agreed that maybe we should call it a night, and eventually we did.

I escorted her to a taxi. However, before leaving, we managed to exchange phone numbers and told ourselves we'd stay in touch! I closed the door to her taxi and waved goodbye as it slowly drove away.

Driving home that night, I kept thinking about her as I blasted the salsa music in my car. My smile stretched a mile long, as I thought about the wonderful time we had and how happy I was to finally have a chance to see her again after all these months.

Over the weeks and months that followed, we frequently talked on the phone, and we got to know each other a little bit more each time. During our chats, I opened up about my current situation at home and all the problems in my life. But more importantly, I was sincere about how I was planning to rectify those issues going forward by moving out of the house and finding my own place. I also explained to her that the separation and eventual divorce had been coming on for many months, if not years. It had nothing to do with finding someone new, but rather with how extremely unhappy, frustrated, and stressed I'd been for a very long time and how desperately I needed to make changes in my life. I needed happiness. I needed to be loved. But more than anything in the world, I needed to have the peace of mind and tranquility that had been missing for such a long time. Going to work with all this pent-up stress was detrimental in my line of work as a police officer, but it was also harmful to the well-being and happiness of my children.

After sharing my story, Anna was a bit taken back and certainly had reservations about even continuing these conversations as friends. But I assured her that whatever plans I made had nothing to do with meeting her or anyone else, reiterating that it was something that I needed for my own personal mental health and well-being, and that of my family.

As the months went by, we continued to talk on the phone and eventually got a chance to see each other again about two months down the road. By then, I was in the final stages of moving out. Over the next couple of months that followed, I would eventually move into my niece's house, and my wife and I legally separated sometime in

August of 1991. It was shortly thereafter that Anna and I formally began dating. And by the end of the year, we'd become a couple!

Like me, Anna was from the Bronx. She worked in the accounting department of a real-estate development company in Manhattan. She was also of Puerto Rican descent, both of our parents having been born and raised on the island of Puerto Rico. But in addition to that, we also had so many other things in common, from our taste in music, food preferences, and travel, to staying healthy, working out, and living a good life in general. Yet most importantly, we both had big dreams for the future, including advancing our education, and our life goals, and landing that dream career.

Personalitywise, we got along so, so well. We laughed a lot and complimented each other on just about everything. But more than anything, even in the initial stages of our relationship, we could both sense that there was something really special here. Something that neither one of us had ever felt before in our previous relationships.

Although there was difference in age—she is eleven years younger—we never let that become an obstacle in our quest to build an amazing relationship based on the many things that made us happy!

On a sidenote, besides meeting this amazing woman, 1991 also turned out to be a great year for me for another reason!

In retrospect, that scary incident in 1981—the one in which I almost lost my life when I was ambushed while investigating a possible burglary in process—was a turning point in my career!

Before joining the police force, I was in decent cardio shape from all my years of playing basketball, but I had never lifted a single free weight to gain muscle strength. I weighed in at about 150 pounds soaking wet. While attending the police academy, I did a lot of calisthenics, running, light combat fighting, boxing, and a little bit of strength training using the universal gym. Yet, through it all, I never really prepared myself for the strength training that I needed to survive the city streets during close combat when making an arrest. That is, until I found myself fighting for my life on that fateful morning in 1981. That incident turned out to be a huge wake-up call for me to get in better physical shape!

It was shortly after that incident that I started training heavily in the police gym. It is there that I learned so much about weight lifting and bodybuilding while working out with a group of seasoned police officers on a regular basis. Besides the police gym, I also decided to join one of the best and most recognized gyms in Hartford, the East Coast Gym. Soon after signing up, I learned so much about eating right and working out to gain muscle mass by speaking to some of the bodybuilders who worked out in this gym, including the owner. After eight years of dedication to improving my health and fitness, I started noticing some big changes in my physique. I had definitely gained weight and muscle mass.

It was also in 1991 that Chuck, the gym's owner, approached me and asked if I would be interested in competing in a bodybuilding contest that was being sponsored by his gym. According to Chuck, he thought I would do very well, and even stood a good chance of winning, if I decided to compete. Inspired by what he told me that day, I went home, gave it some thought, and then came back the very next day to tell him that I would give it a shot!

Now that I'd decided to compete, I had to work out even harder than usual and dedicate more time to the gym, especially since the competition was only a couple of months away. A friend of mine in the gym, Miguel, who'd actually won the Mr. Puerto Rico bodybuilding championship a few years back, was nice enough to give me some really great pointers on prepping for the competition. He showed me some of the routines and posing techniques that he'd used over the years, valuable techniques that I would practice on a regular basis in preparation for the big day.

On the day of the Mr. Latino Bodybuilding Championship of Connecticut, I was in the best shape of my life. That day, I entered the competition feeling a bit nervous, but at the same time confident that I would do well, based on all the hard work I had put in to ready myself for the competition. As a rookie in this field, I knew right from the minute I walked into the building that it was not going to be easy. Just looking around at all the experienced bodybuilders whom I would be going up against that day, I recognized the big challenge for me as a first-time competitor.

However, once it was my turn to go up onstage, I tried to hit every mark and pose that I had learned from the former Mr. Puerto Rico himself. After a whole slew of routines and poses onstage, I was blessed to make it to the final cut. Making it that far surely boosted my confidence; perhaps I had a chance of winning this light heavyweight class in which I was competing against two highly experienced bodybuilders.

The final posedown occurs just before the results are announced. The top-three competitors are asked to take the stage together, then the final posedown begins. The competitors basically show off for the judges, running through their best routines so that the judges can compare competitors side by side and select a winner.

After my final posedown and several deliberations by the judges, I was totally surprised when I was declared the winner!!! I was super excited and couldn't believe that I had actually won my first bodybuilding competition ever!

But just when I thought it was all over, they called me back onstage to compete against the winners of the other two weight classes, middleweight and lightweight. Now I knew I had to go all out, not only to please the judges, but also to win over the crowd of spectators who'd come to see the event and root for us!

After what appeared to be five minutes, I was selected as the overall winner of the Mr. Latino of Connecticut competition at the age of thirty-four! That day, I was awarded two big trophies to go along with my title! More importantly, I was super proud of the tireless work I had done to get to that point. A long journey inspired by that near tragic event back in 1981!

Many years later, I decided to enter into another bodybuilding contest at the age of forty-five. To my surprise, I came away with a third-place finish and a trophy! After my competitive bodybuilding days were behind me, I became a certified personal trainer and was able to train a few bodybuilding hopefuls.

CHAPTER 98

THE START OF A NEW LIFE AND MANY CHANGES!

By the spring of 1992, so many changes had taken place in my life. My soon-to-be ex-wife served me with divorce papers, which turned out to be the beginning of a long, drawn-out court journey that lasted for over a year before it was finally settled. Our divorce was final in February of 1993.

But the second biggest thing that happened to me in the spring of that year was that my girlfriend, Anna, decided to leave her new job at the United Nations to join me in Connecticut. I was already in the final stages of moving out of my niece's house after nearly a nine-month stay, and was really looking forward to moving on to a different chapter in my life with my girlfriend. We were taking our relationship to the next level by moving in together.

In just a matter of weeks after making that decision, we found a beautiful apartment in North Haven, Connecticut; it had its own little duck pond, overlooked by the apartment complex, Whitewood Pond Apartments. It is there that we eventually started our new life together as a loving couple.

In hindsight, her leaving the Bronx and moving in with me was a really big move, considering that she had lived in the Bronx all her life. Moving away from her family and friends was going to be a big adjustment for both her and her family. I completely understood and could certainly relate because I had made a similar transition when I decided to leave the South Bronx and move to Connecticut back in 1979.

But by this time in our relationship, we were in love. Having a long-distance relationship was extremely difficult, taxing, and not conducive to maintaining a healthy relationship. One thing we both knew for sure was that we missed each other to no end and just wanted to be together in the worst way. So after numerous talks, by the early part of the spring of 1992, she said yes! And we finally moved in together!

That day, I remember feeling extremely happy and excited when Anna finally broke the news to me that she was moving to Connecticut! We both celebrated that special moment by toasting to our love and to this new journey!

A few weeks later, after working her last day in New York City, she took the Metro North train to Connecticut, where I was waiting for her with a big surprise of my own—a beautiful bouquet of flowers and the most oversized arrangement of helium-filled balloons you could ever find—as she arrived at the train station that evening. As you would expect, she was a bit embarrassed as many passengers in the crowded train station quickly took notice and were curious to know what was going on. While she knew how much I loved surprising her, this one truly took her by complete surprise! Her reaction, coupled with the big smile on her face, was priceless! And she immediately gave me the biggest hug and kiss ever as I welcomed her to her new home! By two weeks' time, she had completely moved out of her old apartment in the Bronx and into our new home in North Haven, officially marking the beginning of our new life of together in Connecticut.

Looking back now, one of the things that I clearly remember, from the numerous conversations we had about moving to Connecticut and starting a new life, was talking about her future and her biggest dreams. One was to be happy and find her lifelong love. The other one was to go back to school to get a bachelor's degree in accounting. At the time, she had an associate's degree.

We were deeply in love, so that part of her dream had come true. But making her other dream a reality would take a little lot longer. A little while later, after an extensive search and a host of interviews along the way, Anna finally found the perfect place that would eventually help her further her education! In less than a year, not only did she find a job at a well-known university, but also, over the ensuring years, she earned both a bachelor's and a master's degree in business. These degrees eventually led to an amazing job in the finance and administration division of another university in Connecticut.

Anna finally accomplished a lifelong aspiration she'd dreamed about for many, many years! A true blessing! A true believer! And a dream maker! I am so, so proud to call her my beautiful, loving girlfriend!

CHAPTER 99

OVERCOMING SOME TOUGH OBSTACLES ALONG THE WAY

On February 26, 1993, my long-awaited divorce battle in court was finally settled. The judge granted us joint custody of our two children. Included in this settlement, he awarded my ex-wife alimony for five years and child support. The child-support agreement consisted of monthly payments for each child, until each reached the age of eighteen or graduated high school, whichever came first. Also, as part of the deal, we were each responsible for the one child's college tuition payments until they graduated.

At the time, my ex-wife and I agreed to divide our assets. She was granted full ownership of our house in Windsor, Connecticut, as well as a three-family investment home we owned in Hartford. While another three-family home we owned in Hartford was split evenly between my ex-wife, a business partner who'd helped us purchase the house, and me. We each received a one-third interest in the property.

The purchase of those multi-family homes turned out to be horrible investments. The once-potentially-lucrative investment soon turned sour when the previously quiet neighborhoods became riddled with crime and drug activity, forcing all of our great, responsible tenants to leave the area out of fear for their safety and well-being. Property values plunged and left us with many apartments vacant. Because of that, we were forced to pay out of pocket in order to maintain the mortgages.

Before long, the bills started piling up and cutting into our regular income and savings, which created a serious hardship for me. The stress of keeping up with my child support, alimony, large credit card debts, car payments, and regular day-to-day living expenses soon took its toll on my financial situation. One day, seeing no relief in sight,

I was left with no choice but to file for bankruptcy. This really hit me hard and left me feeling truly frustrated and drained.

At work, there was not much overtime, which made it all the more difficult to remedy my financial problems. I did the best I could with what I had. Thankfully, I had the support of my girlfriend throughout this crisis, and she really helped me to stay strong and never lose hope that things would get better in the coming months and years!

CHAPTER 100

A NEW AND UNEXPECTED CAREER

After winning the Mr. Latino Bodybuilding Championship, I continued to stay in great shape by working out on a regular basis. One day a reporter by the name of Shana from the *Hartford Courant*, was going to different fitness centers around the Hartford area, scouting for a male model in great shape to take part in a fashion ad for the newspaper. Her travels ultimately led her to my workout gym, Bally Total Fitness in West Hartford, where we met, and she asked if I would be interested in posing as the model for a *Hartford Courant* ad. She said that the job was a paying gig for a feature in the *Hartford Courant*'s "Style and Fashion" section of the newspaper.

Not having any modeling experience whatsoever, I was a bit hesitant about saying yes, but I asked her to let me think about it. That night, I told my girlfriend all about this great news, and she was really excited for me and told me that I should definitely go for it! She thought it might be a once-in-a-lifetime opportunity that could lead to other things. While I'd always thought about one day trying to get into the modeling industry, I just didn't know where to begin. But at least this job offer would give me the chance to see if I had what it takes to pursue this amazing second career.

The very next day, I called Shana and told her I was definitely interested in doing the ad! She gave me all the details and reiterated that it would be for a full-size ad in which I would be modeling Victoria's Secret men's silk boxer shorts while shirtless. When she told me that, I got a really good laugh, just knowing that once my brothers and sisters at the police department got ahold of this ad, they were going to post it in the squad room. Who knows what kind of hilarious stuff they'd write on it? So I couldn't wait for this day to arrive and have fun with it. About a week or so after I agreed to do the ad, we shot it at the *Hartford Courant* photography studio.

It took several weeks before the ad actually came out in the fashion section of the Sunday newspaper on August 28, 1992. Just as Shana had said, it was a full-page ad. This being my first photo shoot ever, I wasted no time in purchasing at least six to eight copies of the newspaper, some of which I kept. The rest I gave to family members in the South Bronx. Seeing myself in this ad was truly an awesome feeling. Never in my wildest dreams did I ever imagine that something like this would ever happen to me. Was it luck? Or was destiny once again putting me in the right place, at the right time? Whatever it was, it was certainly a true blessing!

A few days after the ad came out, someone in my department cut out the page and placed it in the roll call squad room, just as I predicted. Before long, all sorts of hilarious comments were written on the newspaper clipping. Comments that weren't mean or negative, but all in good fun. As expected, I got a really good laugh out of it and truly enjoyed the moment. But more than anything, I was just super happy and excited that I decided to go for it!

One particular cop—Ian, a great friend of many years; he had seen the ad in the squad room—approached me one day to ask, "Have you ever thought about doing some modeling professionally?"

"Many times, but I never knew where to go, or who to see to get into the business," I said.

As luck would have it, it turns out that Ian had been modeling professionally for many years; he was registered with Visage Models, Inc., an agency in the Hartford area. He said, "I think you have a great look; you'll do very well with our agency."

I immediately responded, "Yes, but unfortunately I don't have any other pictures to show, other than this one ad I did in the newspaper."

He said, "Don't you worry about it; that will do. I'll talk to my agent, Yana, tomorrow, and I'm pretty sure she will want to sign you up."

About a week later, I went to see Yana with my one newspaper ad and got signed! She was super nice and actually said to me, "I think you have a lot of potential in the industry, especially because of your great ethnic look!" Her inspiring words immediately struck a chord with me when she added, "In fact, there are very few tall, Hispanic male models in this industry, so I'm sure you're going to do amazingly well!" Her words boosted my confidence and inspired me to jump-start a future in the modeling world.

A series of photo shoots later to build up my portfolio, and I had my first professional modeling job for Macy's, a department store in the West Farms Mall, as a runway model. From there, I did a few more runway shows before getting my very first commercial print job. It was for a beauty salon by the name of Sheer Artistry; they hired a handful of male models for a photo shoot that was going to be featured in a well-known hair magazine by the name of *Passion International Men's Hair Magazine.*

It took close to a year before the magazine hit the beauty-salon circuit. But when it did, it was all over the place. Friends and family who didn't even know I had done that shoot called to tell me they had just spotted me in the magazines in their salons. It was the greatest feeling in the world and something that kept me inspired to keep following this dream!

As the months went by, my modeling career continued to grow. I was booking print jobs on a pretty regular basis. It became a really nice part-time gig for me. One day, my agent approached me and told me that she thought I was ready for the next level; she encouraged me to sign with different agencies in different states, while still remaining with her in Hartford. I decided to take her advice and started scouring the *Yellow Pages* for other modeling agencies in the tristate area.

But before seeking representation out of state, I decided to try and join one of the biggest modeling agencies in Connecticut, the Johnston Agency. Besides Connecticut, they also represented models from both New York and New Jersey. In the spring of 1993, I met with the owner, Esther, and she gladly agreed to represent me. On the day I signed with her, Johnston Agency represented only one other Hispanic male model. Before long, I was getting booked on commercial print jobs all over Connecticut and even a couple in New York City.

One day in August of 1995, I decided to give New York City a shot, in hopes of landing a modeling contract with Wilhelmina Models. At the time, they were considered one of the biggest agencies in the city, representing models from all over the world. I gave them a call one day, told them I was seeking representation in New York City, and asked what I needed to provide in order for them to consider signing me. They told me to send them a cover letter, along with a short resume and photos of my modeling work. I sent everything right away and waited to hear back.

About two weeks later, I finally got a letter from them in the mail. I was a bit excited, but nervous at the same time, not knowing what to expect. However, when I opened the letter and read their response, I was extremely disappointed and deflated. More than anything, I was really upset at the wording in the rejection letter: "Unfortunately, you are not quite the type that we, in the New York market, are looking for at this particular time!" The letter went on to say a few other negative things. To say this was not what I expected from a well-known agency like Wilhelmina would be an understatement!

But thankfully, what this rejection letter did was inspire me to go out there and prove them wrong. I was not going to allow this bump in the road to discourage me from moving forward and being successful in the modeling industry!

Shortly after this rejection letter, I started off on a personal mission to seek representation in some the largest and most well-known agencies in Massachusetts, Model Club Inc and Maggie Inc.; Rhode Island, Model Club Inc and Donahue Models and Talent; New Hampshire, New England Models Group; New Jersey, Meredith Models; and yes, even New York City, Cunningham-Escott-Slevin-Doherty, one of Wilhelmina's competitors. All in hopes of landing at least one or two agencies in that bunch.

But to my surprise, during a matter of a few months, I walked away getting signed by every single agency with which I interviewed. That, coupled with my two other agencies in Connecticut, gave me a total of nine agencies representing me. It turned out to be better than I ever dreamed or expected; it was the perfect opportunity to really get my name out there and continue to build on my new and exciting career!

Signing up with all these agencies couldn't have come at a better time, especially after filing for bankruptcy, which had left me struggling and wondering how I was ever going to recover from this tough financial situation. But, thanks to God's blessings once again, I never lost hope and kept dreaming that things would get better with time! And they eventually did!

CHAPTER 101

THE BIG COMEBACK: BACK IN THE FIGHT AGAIN!

As in my two agencies in Connecticut, every other agency with which I signed had either no Hispanic male models or only a few. So the timing couldn't have been any better. Before long, I was booking jobs, including both national and regional ads, and traveling from state to state, from city to city, slowly building my portfolio as a working professional model. I was blessed to work with some of the biggest clients in the modeling industry. Over time, my jobs tallied more than 350 ads with major companies like American Express, Aramark, Ames Department Stores, Bob's Stores, Fruit of the Loom, Healthy Choice, Mastercard, Western Union, Holiday Inn, UPS, and a host of others. I even managed to land on the cover of a romance novel by Silhouette. During this time, I was also doing a lot of runway shows in different cities, modeling brand-name fashion lines. Thankfully, I was able to manage my modeling career while still working full time as a police officer. By working on my days off, juggling my schedule around, switching days off, and lastly, using my accrued time in the books to take days off as needed.

The fact that there was a big demand for Hispanic male models meant that companies were aware of the buying power that existed in the growing Hispanic population in this country. This trend contributed to my flourishing career and kept me in demand. With the influx of work, I was slowly, but surely, starting to get out of debt. Everything that was happening to me at the time was beyond my wildest dreams. Especially when you look back at all the challenges that I faced as a young man growing up poor in a household filled with domestic violence and living in one of the worst drug- and gang-infested neighborhoods of the South Bronx. For that same boy to now be a working model representing products that I either used or saw in magazines and newspaper ads was truly unimaginable!

One day during the summer of 1993, I heard about a national model search that was taking place in New York City. They were looking for male models to compete on *America's Top Hispanic Male and Female Models*, a program that was to be nationally televised on Univision, the Hispanic network. Models for the show were being auditioned throughout the country, and even Puerto Rico! At the time, they were only looking for eight male and eight female models to represent Budweiser, Anheuser-Busch's beer. The competition was called *Buscando Estrella Con Budweiser*; it was basically the Hispanic version of the hit TV show *Star Search*, but sponsored by Budweiser.

I decided to head to New York City with my girlfriend to give it a shot. At the time, about all I knew about the model-search contest was that all potential male models had to "bring a bathing suit and have great presence onstage." That was it! As soon as I got there, I noticed that the line was out the door; more than 200 potential male models were waiting in line for a chance to compete. The auditions had been highly advertised on La Mega, one of the biggest Spanish radio stations the New York City area.

Upon seeing the long line, I knew right away that this was going to be one tough competition, especially because it was happening right there in New York City. While waiting, I tried my hardest not to let this dissuade or discourage me from competing. With that in mind, I entered the building with a positive attitude and a desire to get selected so that I could move on to the next level of the competition.

After registering and waiting my turn, I was interviewed by the host in front of a panel of Hispanic celebrity judges. It was these same judges who would determine the overall winner, based on the contestant's overall stage presence, physique, and physical appearance in a bathing suit. After the interview, I got a nice round of applause from the audience members in the crowd just as I exited the stage.

As soon as I got off the stage, Ilene, one of the talent executives for the show, thanked me and said I would get a call if I was chosen. I thanked her, we shook hands, and before long, I was on my way back home, hoping that I did well enough to make the cut.

About a week or so later, I got home from work, and on the answering machine was a message from Ilene, that same talent executive I met in New York City. She said, "Hi, Roberto, I have some great news to share with you. Just wanted to let you know that you were selected as one of the eight finalists that will be competing in the nationally televised show of *Buscando Estrella Con Budweiser* at Disney/MGM Studios in Lake Buena Vista, Florida. We will be in touch with you with some more information in the coming weeks."

When I heard this message, I jumped up and down with excitement and couldn't believe that I got selected out of so many competitors. My girlfriend, who was right there with me when I got the news, was just as excited and congratulated me with a big hug and a kiss! That night, we decided to go out to dinner and celebrate this huge moment in my life!

Approximately two weeks later, I got an official letter in the mail from the sponsors, congratulating me once again, advising me that they would be sending me some additional information regarding my one-week, all-expenses-paid trip to Florida, and telling me what to expect once I got there.

I arrived in Florida with my girlfriend about a week or so after receiving my letter. A shuttle bus took us right to the resort, and we unpacked. I made contact with the talent executive, Ilene, with whom I had been in contact for the past couple of weeks. She welcomed me to Florida and gave me a quick rundown of what to expect over the next few days.

The very next morning I met up with her and some of the other finalists in the contest. We signed a ton of paperwork, releases mainly, and then got fitted with the clothes that we would be using on the show. They also gave us a list of some of the questions the host of the show—who we later found out was a famous Mexican singer by the name of Mijares—might be asking us in front of a panel of judges, a live audience, and the cameras on national TV. They also gave us credentials that would allow us free admission to all the rides at MGM Studios. In addition to that, they supplied us with an unlimited food-and-beverage stipend that we could use at any of the restaurants in the park. The whole experience truly felt like a dream come true for me, and I couldn't wait to see what would happen next!

On our second day, I had a chance to go up on the *Star Search* stage to rehearse and read from a teleprompter. It was here the eight male-model finalists were paired with the eight females. I was paired with Diana, a Venezuelan model who now lived in the US. As male and female spokesmodels, our job was to introduce a number of variety acts that were also competing in their particular categories from singing to dancing. The judges would then grade us on how well we did in front of the cameras and in introducing the acts. We would also be judged on videos that we were scheduled to shoot later that day, highlighting our personalities and physical appearances—shirtless for the men and bathing suits for the women. Last, but not least, we would be rated on how well we did onstage while being interviewed by the host of the show.

They were recording four shows per day, two male and two female spokesmodels for each show, for a total of 16 models overall. At the end of each show, only four male or female models from each show moved on to the next step in the process. The others were eliminated and sent home. I was scheduled to be on the very first show, going up against Renaldo, a male model from Puerto Rico.

That day, I remember being extremely nervous just thinking about being in front of such a large live crowd, and about being in front of the camera on a program that was scheduled to air in the homes of millions of television viewers in both the United States and Latin American countries. By this time in my career, I had been in front of big crowds before while doing tons of runway shows, but this was way, way bigger and had a lot more at stake. More than anything, I was going up against some super-tough talent who spoke fluent Spanish and represented countries like Columbia, Peru, Mexico, Cuba, and a few others. While my Spanish was pretty good, theirs was better because Spanish was their main language. I, as a native New Yorker, spoke a little more of what I call Spanglish, a combination of Spanish and English!

On the day of the actual performance, while answering some of the questions being asked by the host, I had a difficult time with certain Spanish words. By the end of the show, the host brought both couples back before the judges for one final look. It was then that the judges made the final decision as to who was moving forward to the next level of competition. Moments later, after all was said and done, Renaldo was selected as the winner by a small margin, and he moved on to the next level in the contest.

The next day, he competed and was eliminated by the model who ended up winning the whole contest at the end of the series. As for the female model I got teamed up with, Diana Franco, she won top female model.

After six great days in Florida, coupled with a few anxious moments, I returned home to Connecticut. Shortly after getting back to work the next day, I got a call from a reporter, Cindy, from the *Hartford Courant*; she had heard about my appearance on the show and wanted to write a story about my journey and experience in the contest. Within a couple of days, the newspaper story hit the newsstands. I was really excited when I got a bunch of congratulatory phone calls and messages from so many of my friends and family who watched the show and got a chance to read the pretty cool article!

In the end, while I didn't win, just the fact that I made it that far as a finalist, out of thousands of other hopefuls, was truly an amazing experience for me that I will never, ever forget!

However, to my surprise, it didn't end there, not quite yet!

CHAPTER 102

MODEL SEARCH: ROUND TWO!

A few years after my last competition in 1993, I was driving home from Massachusetts, after finishing a modeling job for a uniform company in Boston, when I heard an announcement on the radio; Bacardí Limón was having a National Model Search contest at a local club in Boston that same night. I quickly pulled over and wrote down the name of the club where this event was taking place. As soon as I got home that evening, I gave them a quick call and got more details. Within about two hours' time, I took a shower, ate dinner, got dressed, and was out the door, heading back to Boston.

I got there about two hours later, just minutes before the contest was about to take place; I'd even brought my niece Michelle along to cheer me on. As soon as I got there, I noticed it was very similar to the competition two years before, *Buscando Estrella Con Budweiser*; there was a line out the door. This one, however, was not as long as the other one; nevertheless, you could tell from the onset that it was going to be a big challenge. I registered right away and waited until the call went out for the start of the contest.

One by one, each of us was called in front of a panel of judges, who took notes on our appearance, dancing ability, and last, but not least, our interview with one of the organizers representing Bacardí Limón. After all was said and done, they called out the three finalists, and I was one of them! At the end of it all, with a little assistance from the crowd, and of course my niece, who applauded when we were each called out by name, I was selected as the winner! Wow, once again I was feeling truly blessed to have been picked as a finalist in two national model-search competitions within a matter of two years! The host and the judges all congratulated me and gave me a designer jean jacket by Bacardí Limón, a gift for becoming a finalist.

However, the biggest surprise of the night came when the host detailed exactly what I had won. I was awarded another all-expenses-paid trip to California for five days, with a chance at winning a cash prize and making several TV appearances. She also told me that the whole event was for a great cause: raising money for pediatric AIDS research and treatment. Just as in the previous competition, the panel of judges in California would include several well-known celebrities.

About two weeks or so after winning the contest, I flew into California with two other models representing New York City, one female and one male. Once there, a shuttle bus was waiting for us at LAX; it took us to the famous Beverly Hilton Hotel. We checked into our rooms, and later that evening we had a meeting with the host and the rest of the male and female models taking part in this awesome event, all twenty of them. I was told that we were selected from ten cities across the US: Los Angeles, San Francisco, Miami, New York, Denver, Dallas, Atlanta, Boston, New Orleans, and New Jersey.

At the meeting, as we filled out a bunch of paperwork and signed waiver releases, they gave us each a rundown of what to expect. They also give us some credentials to carry around during our stay at the hotel and for various functions that we would be attending throughout the length of the event.

After our second day, we got a chance to rehearse in the International Ballroom, known as the place where the Golden Globe Awards ceremony is held every year. Naturally, we were all excited to be there and to be taking part in such a great cause!

The whole experience was truly amazing! In my private thoughts, I once again started thinking back to the many struggles I endured while growing up in a tough environment, and all challenges I had to overcome in my life in order to be standing in the International Ballroom! This was one incredible journey that was beyond anything I could've ever imagined in all my wildest dreams!

On the day of the contest, as we were lined up behind the stage, waiting for our names to be called by the host, I decided to take a quick peek through the curtains to check out the audience. I noticed that the place was packed, and there were a ton of recognizable celebrities. Among the crowd, you had Nia Peeples, Jamie Foxx, and Mark Curry,

David Chokachi, Tim Robbins, and even "Downtown" Julie Brown, just to name a few. They all showed up to support this good cause.

Directly in front of the runway was a long table with ten celebrity judges who would be judging us not only on our fashion style and look, but also, in their words, on our attitude and charisma onstage as we strutted our stuff on the runway. Finally, they were judging on our overall stage presence and our interview with the MC and host of the event, Josie Bissett, from *Melrose Place*.

My fashion look consisted of a leather vest I wore shirtless, a black pair of jeans, and a pair of low-top black construction boots. We were also fitted with a second look from the latest collection of famed fashion designer Mark Eisen.

As the night went on, we all got a chance to be interviewed onstage by our host, who asked us a series of questions regarding our careers and choice of fashion. After that, each of the twenty models got a chance to strut their stuff on the runway before the judges picked their final top male and female models for the event.

After all the votes were tabulated, I didn't win, but just the fact that I made it that far was a huge accomplishment and a true honor! Especially at age of thirty-nine and for a competition in which I had the proud distinction of being the oldest model, male or female, by quite a few years.

At the end of the contest, we were allowed to mingle in the crowd of attendees, have some drinks, eat from a huge buffet, and even pick up a few souvenirs and celebrity autographs! It was truly a one-of-a-kind, memorable experience that will be with me forever!

Two days after the event, I was back home with my family and celebrating another special moment in my life!

And just when I thought my competition days were behind me, years later my future wife decided to enter me in a national magazine contest that was looking for Hispanic male models to be crowned as the *Papi Chulo*, Sexiest Man of the Year!

The contest was being sponsored by a very well-known Hispanic magazine by the name of *Latina*, a monthly fashion and entertainment magazine loaded with inspiring stories about health, fashion, and people making an impact in the Hispanic community in the US and Latin America! A couple of days after seeing the article in a *Latina* magazine, Anna decided to enter me in the contest. She sent them a shirtless photo of me talking on the phone, accompanied by a short write-up on why I should be selected as the next *Papi Chulo* contest winner.

About a month or so later, she got a letter in the mail addressed to me; it stated that while I wasn't selected as the winner, I was picked as a runner-up. They added, "we combed through thousands of entries but yours had *algo muy especial*." Something very special. "Your story is a true example of a complete *Papi Chulo*! Congratulations!!!"

As a runner-up, I got a bunch of goodies, including a T-shirt from the magazine and a write-up with my photo, which appeared in the February 2001 issue of the *Latina* magazine! I was super proud of my future wife for this amazing gesture and show of love!

This one really turned out to be my last model-search competition! All told, it was an incredible journey that involved three contests over a period of nine years! Feeling truly blessed!

CHAPTER 103

THE REASONS THAT SPARKED MY LOVE FOR WRITING POEMS

As a young man growing up, I really never had an affinity for writing or reading. Looking back now, I guess that lack of interest can be traced back to the many days I spent absent from school in my earlier years due to all the reasons you've read about in the preceding chapters. As the years went by, and I grew older, the traumas of my past subsided, and my chronic asthma attacks also slowly ceased. However, it wasn't until way later in life, that I started to show interest in reading and writing. I then had to do a lot of catching up in order bring my reading and comprehension skills up to par.

Over the years, I started reading everything I could get my hands on, from short stories in books, to newspaper and magazine articles. Anything, just to learn about the storytelling and writing skills of others. Up until the time I met my girlfriend, I very rarely wrote about anything. However, once I started dating my girlfriend, and we became seriously involved as a couple, that's when I suddenly discovered writing.

It started with small love notes every time I would surprise her with a bouquet of flowers just to say, "I'm thinking of you," and slowly progressed into writing short paragraphs for birthday celebrations and our anniversaries. Over time, one or two lines would turn into three or four lines of romantic love notes in which I would dig deep into my heart and soul and just let the words come out naturally. By allowing love to speak freely and the words to flow out without hesitation from the heart.

One day, I decided to surprise her with a poem. For as long as I can remember, I have always been intrigued about how people write poetry and tell a love story in a poetic format. But I just never had the inspiration to write a poem until the day she came into my life.

After my first poem, "What is Love?", I could see the immense happiness it created. At times, my poems were emotional and brought the biggest smile to her beautiful face, a clear indication of how much it really touched her heart. I realized from that moment on, how a collection of heartfelt words composed in a poetic tone could evoke so much love and happiness. More importantly, how something that simple could bring a smile to her heart and a whisper of passion into her soul! For as I once told her, "some the greatest moments of my life are the ones that I spend thinking of you!"

Before long, I was hooked! I started writing love poems and letters on a regular basis. Every greeting card was accompanied by either a short poem, short story, or sometimes a combination of both. This is something that has been a very special and mutual part of our lives ever since we got together and fell in love. She also writes me some of the most romantic and inspiring love poems and letters that I have ever read. They leave me feeling so truly blessed and happy to be in this amazing and loving relationship we share together as a couple!

Besides love, I also started writing inspiring poems and short stories about police work, current events, and life in general, many of which were shared with hundreds and hundreds of police officers and others nationwide. To this date, I have written hundreds of poems and short stories covering a variety of topics.

Thinking back in time, I have surely come a long way since my days when reading and writing were things I hoped I would one day do, but never thought it would become a reality. Sometimes you just never know the blessings that are in store for you later in life. So long as you continue to believe in yourself and never, ever stop dreaming, you can make anything happen!

CHAPTER 104

SURPRISE AND MORE SURPRISES

Since the beginning of our relationship, I've gotten a big kick out of surprising my girlfriend. Birthdays, Valentine's Day, anniversaries, and other holidays—all present an opportunity to bring a great big smile to her face. It truly makes my day to know how much each surprise means to her and how much it contributes to the growth of our loving relationship.

For her birthday one year, I made dinner reservations at a popular restaurant in Milford, Connecticut. Prior to making reservations, I made a personal visit to this well-known restaurant and sat down to talk to the manager about the birthday surprise I was planning for the love of my life. After our talk and learning about what I had in mind, she gave me a big smile and told me how happy she was to know that out of all the restaurants in town, I decided to select hers to pull off this wonderful surprise.

My love is a huge fan of Kenny G, and I thought, *What better way to surprise her than by having someone play one of her favorite songs, "Going Home" by Kenny G, right in the middle of the two of us having a nice romantic dinner?*

It wasn't easy to pull this off. I had to search for just the right talented saxophone player who could play that particular song. I looked just about everywhere, but couldn't find someone who fit the bill. I was about to give up when I picked up a local *Variety* newspaper that listed musicians for hire to play at weddings, events, or special venues. After going through the long list of musicians to pick from, I decided to call this one gentleman whose ad really stood out from the rest. And while he was a jazz saxophonist, he admitted to me that he had never played any of Kenny G's songs. However, he said that if I gave him the name of the song and a couple of days to research it and rehearse it, he should be able to pull it off. I agreed, and he said he would get back to me and let me know either way.

After a few days, he called me back and said that he'd found the song and would be ready to play it in a couple of days. That was great news to hear, especially since he was probably my last hope of finding someone to make this thing happen. While I was really excited, deep down inside I was also a bit nervous. Suppose this guy is an amateur and his playing sucks, then what? But after weighing all the options I had left, which was really none, I decided to take a gamble and hired him on the spot. After our phone conversation, I gave him all the details about my surprise, including the location, date, and time, as well as when I wanted him to walk in and start playing.

And about a week later, he made his entrance just as planned, midway through our dinner. The timing couldn't have been better! The place lit up with this amazing music coming from one saxophone player. For a quick moment, it sounded as though it were really Kenny G who had just walked into the restaurant to entertain us with his wonderful tones. I was in awe of how great he sounded, especially for someone who, in all his years as an entertainer, had never played a Kenny G song before.

At first look, she thought the restaurant had live music that night and commented about how cool it was to have a jazz player entertain the guests as they dined. But then she realized that the song he was playing was one of her favorite songs of all time. As the saxophonist slowly inched his way towards the back of the room to where our dinner table was situated, she gave me this surprised look, which I captured on video, as if to say, "Like, wow, it looks like he's heading to our table!"

And she was absolutely right! It was at that exact moment that I had the biggest grin on my face as I said, "Happy Birthday, babe, this is all for you!!!"

She blushed, and immediately covered her mouth as though she couldn't believe what she was seeing right before her eyes! The closer he got to our table, the more nervous and excited she became. In fact, with all the commotion, even the restaurant patrons got in on it and applauded! The look on her face was priceless and truly made for the perfect birthday surprise that neither she, nor I, will ever forget!

To top it all off, somehow the saxophone player was able to segue from playing the Kenny G song, right into "Happy Birthday," without skipping a beat. Before long, all the waitresses and waiters in the restaurant joined in a circle to sing "Happy Birthday!" After one of the waitresses presented her with this beautiful cake that I had delivered to the restaurant earlier that day, she slowly closed her eyes, made a wish, and blew out the candles…highlighting the celebration of this great moment in her life! That day, the smile and happiness on her face spoke volumes. And marked a birthday celebration that we will both remember for a very, very long time!

And while there were many, many more surprises over the weeks and months ahead, one of the biggest ones of all had yet to happen. Our engagement!

CHAPTER 105

PULLING OFF THE BIGGEST SURPRISE OF MY LIFE

By the spring of 1993, we had been dating for nearly two years, and our anniversary was fast approaching. I wanted to do something really special to celebrate this memorable day by asking her to marry me! About two months into my preparation, I walked into this well-known jewelry store in Hartford, Connecticut, in search of the perfect ring for this wonderful day in our lives. I must have looked at dozens and dozens of rings before I settled on this one particular engagement ring that really wowed me, and I knew she would love! Without giving it a second thought, I ordered it right on the spot. Thankfully, I had her ring size in advance, so that saved me a lot of time and sped up the process.

Approximately two weeks after placing the order, I picked up the engagement ring and hid it in a really secure place in our home, so she wouldn't find it. I then reserved a white limo for the occasion and later made restaurant reservations for the big day. In the meantime, I also wrote a short speech for the proposal and put together a twenty-seven-inch-by-forty-seven-inch poster with words written in big, black, bold letters, which read: *Happy Anniversary, Babe!!! Will You Marry Me?* The poster was decorated with several white-paper wedding bells and other wedding decorations.

Finally, I selected what I thought would be the perfect song for the occasion—"This Is for the Lover in You," by the group Shalamar. The general theme of the song revolved around the engagement of a couple, who are symbolically united forever in love by the blessings of the ring! The perfect song for the perfect moment!

The day finally arrived! The limo showed up just a little bit before 11:30 a.m. I went over all the plans, which included attaching the poster to the right side of the car and giving the limo driver the cassette with the engagement song. We also talked about the timing as to when he was going to emerge from the limo in front of my future fiancée's job, the engagement song blasting from the limo's stereo, just as I got ready to propose.

After we talked it over, I left my apartment with rings in hand, hoping that everything would go as smoothly as I had planned it! No one in my future fiancée's job had any idea what was going on. I kept it under wraps for fear that someone would slip and mess up the whole thing. About all my fiancée knew was that it was our anniversary, and I was taking her out to lunch to celebrate.

We arrived just about ten minutes before noon, and limo driver waited on the side of the building, out of view from everyone in her first-floor office. I entered into her office, and she was all smiles, just happy to see me. She quickly introduced me to a bunch of the coworkers in her new job. Then, she said to me, "Babe, I'll be right back. I'm going to get my coat in the office."

The situation couldn't have worked out any better. I took the opportunity to whisper to everyone in her office that I was going to propose to her, and I asked them if they could step outside just as we were leaving the office, to be there for the big moment.

They all agreed! The smiles on their faces said it all, and they couldn't wait to see her reaction when I proposed. Just as I stepped outside the building with my future fiancée, the limo slowly approached with the theme song blasting, while showcasing my makeshift poster. It was at that moment that she finally realized what was happening, and she got really emotional.

Moments later, with all her coworkers witnessing what was about to happen, I got down on one knee, pulled out the engagement ring, recited my speech, and then asked her if she would "do me the honor of marrying me."

And without hesitation, she said, "Yes!!!"

When that happened, everyone started applauding, while some even wiped away tears. We hugged and kissed for what seemed like an eternity, and sealed the moment with a mutual "I love you, babe!"

Shortly thereafter, we said goodbye to everyone before hopping in our limo and heading to a restaurant. Once inside the limo, we popped open a bottle of champagne and toasted this wonderful moment in our lives! From there, it was off to celebrate our engagement at an awesome restaurant, Jalapeno Heaven, in Branford, Connecticut! Wow, what a truly amazing day we had!

CHAPTER 106

DISCOVERING A "WHOLE NEW WORLD" AS ALADDIN AND JASMINE

One day back in 1993, about two to three weeks before Halloween, we were watching the animated version of *Aladdin* at home when the craziest idea came into our heads. How about if we dressed up as Aladdin and Jasmine for Halloween? And not just the characters, we thought, but the whole ensemble, complete with the flying carpet, the genie, and Abu the monkey.

Within a week's time, we had laid out the whole plan. I would design and build the flying carpet, while she would design the outfits and put them all together. That week, I remember going to Home Depot with the idea of finding something that was light yet sturdy enough to serve as the flying carpet. I looked around everywhere until I came across a one-inch aluminum insulated panel; it measured approximately thirty-six by ninety-four, which turned out to be the perfect size for a flying carpet.

Once home, I laid it out on the floor and cut two round holes right in the middle of the panel, about ten inches apart. The holes were big enough for each of us to fit into them comfortably.

My fiancée, on the other hand, had the most difficult part of this whole project. Using images, she was able to make the layout of the carpet look just like the one in the movie, down to the right colors and shapes found in the movie's flying carpet. She also bought the material to use for our outfits and designed, cut, and sewed all the clothing to match those worn by Aladdin and Jasmine, to every exact detail. And lastly, because we would be standing inside the cutouts, she added fake legs for each one of us, giving the illusion that we were really sitting on the carpet and flying through air, our fake legs stretched out in front of us, on top of the carpet. Also, in order to cover our real legs and keep them from being seen, she draped the whole flying carpet with a black cloth all around it, making it look as though the carpet were floating on air!

After everything was in place, we went to Toys"R"Us and found a replica of the magic lamp with the blue genie. We also found a plush toy of Abu that we thought we'd use with his hands, held together by Velcro, wrapped around my neck. While my fiancée, on the other hand, would hold the magic lamp, with the genie halfway out of it, on her lap. In addition to the above, we also bought all the accessories that went with each character, such as the tiny purple hat worn by Aladdin and the earrings and necklace worn by Jasmine. With everything complete, we were ready for a good night out to have some Halloween fun.

About two weeks after we assembled everything, we decided to go out to a bar-restaurant by the name of Harbor Park, in Middletown, Connecticut; they were having a big Halloween party and costume contest. That night, we couldn't wait to get there, just to see the reactions on people's faces once they saw Aladdin and Jasmine on a flying carpet. But more than anything, we wanted to go out and have a great time on Halloween!

Immediately after arriving at the restaurant, they asked us if we wanted to take part in the Halloween contest they were having. Of course, we said yes. They quickly took down our names and gave us a number that the judges would use to pick out the best costume. Hours later, when it was time to compete, they told everyone to line up, and when our numbers were called, we were to march in front of the judges.

One by one, we all took turns going in front of the judges and the partying crowd. Before we knew it, they called out our number and announced our costume. Right away, the crowd went wild, and they started applauding and cheering us on. My fiancée and I looked at each other and couldn't believe the reactions we were getting. After everyone had gone in front of the judges, they picked the three finalists. We were one of them.

Now it was up to the audience to pick the winner. And once again, when the MC pointed to us and announced us, the place went crazy with people chanting, "Aladdin, Aladdin, Aladdin!!!" And since we received the loudest ovation, the judges declared us the first-place winners! The award was a $500 gift certificate to Becker's Jewelers in Hartford.

We had the most amazing time with people coming up to us to congratulate us and to take pictures. It was an incredible experience, and the timing couldn't have been better. We were getting married the following year, and this was a nice down payment on our wedding bands, so it was truly a great blessing all the way around. A couple of months or so later, we took a trip to Becker's Jewelers and purchased our wedding bands!

After that rewarding experience, we were hooked. For the next ten years or so, we traveled all over the tristate area to compete. Wherever they had the biggest prizes, we were there with our award-winning costume, Aladdin and Jasmine and the Flying Carpet. One thing we made sure of was to never return to a place at which we'd already competed and won!

Over the years, we were blessed to win two separate all-inclusive vacations, including round-trip airplane tickets, one to Florida and the other to the Bahamas. In addition to the trips, all told, we won about $8,000 in cash and prizes. A truly amazing experience for something that started out as just a fun night out at Halloween party!

In fact, years later after hanging up our outfits and our flying carpet, we decided to come out of retirement to compete in the *Regis and Kelly* Halloween Costume Contest; the overall winner would be awarded a $20,000 cash prize.

When we arrived outside of the *Regis and Kelly* studios, there must have been at least 200 people dressed up in all sorts of creative costumes. Prejudging took place right outside, in front of the studio. After a few hours of waiting, we were super excited to hear that we got selected as one of the top-twenty-five contestants. The twenty-five semifinalists were then invited inside the studio, backstage, where more judging and eliminations took place.

Moments later, the judges came around again with a narrowed-down list of the top-six finalists. To our surprise, we were selected as one of the top finalists! Not long after, just before show was to go live, they brought all six of us finalist inside the studio where we had a meet and greet with Regis, Kelly Ripa, and Carrie Ann Inaba, a guest judge, who would select the winner of the grand prize. After we were all introduced, one by one, to the audience and after all the fanfare on TV, the judges decided to select a couple dressed as the Verrazano Bridge as the grand-prize winners!

Although we didn't win, the fact that we were picked as a finalist out of so many tough competitors was good enough for us! Best of all, so many of our friends and family got a chance to see us on TV as Aladdin and Jasmine and the Flying Carpet for our very last time competing! It's safe to say, we retired for good after this last competition!

CHAPTER 107

OUR SECOND-ANNIVERSARY ENGAGEMENT SURPRISE!

For our anniversary as an engaged couple a year later, I wanted to surprise Anna with something really special! I decided to hire an airbrush artist, who had painted hundreds and hundreds of portraits during his many years as an artist. At the heart of it all, I wanted him to use a picture of the two of us, which we had taken a few years back when we first started dating, and convert it into a life-size airbrush painting. In addition to that, I asked him if he could paint a smaller version right above that one, except this time around have the two of us dressed in our wedding outfits and standing next to a white Excalibur limo in the background.

He said, "No problem! Just give me a couple of weeks, and I'll have it ready for you!"

When he said that, I got super excited and couldn't wait to see the finished product. The whole meaning behind this portrait was that I wanted Anna to have a vision of how we were going to look in our wedding outfits the following year... to set our wedding dream in motion!

Two weeks later, the painting was completed as promised, and it looked amazing! Even more incredible was how he was able to dress us up in our wedding outfits, from a four-by-six photo that we took back in 1991, ultimately to make what I envisioned in my mind a reality. Once I had the portrait in my hands, I decided to go back to the restaurant where we first celebrated our engagement the previous year, and once again speak to the manager about my idea and surprise!

She was so welcoming and happy that I would once again use her restaurant to celebrate yet another special day in our lives. I asked her if it was possible to seat us at the same, exact table, with the portrait hanging on the wall directly behind us. She didn't hesitate to say, "Yes, by all means, do whatever you want! It's your day!"

That morning, on the exact same day of our engagement anniversary, I went back to the restaurant to work on my surprise. I hung the portrait right behind our table and placed a big purple bow and ribbon that went from one corner of the portrait to the next. I then decorated the table with a purple tablecloth that matched the bow and ribbon. Lastly, I decided to add a beautiful bouquet of white and purple flowers to go along with the rest of the theme, which incidentally matched the dresses the bridesmaids were scheduled to wear on our wedding day. Once everything was all set, I left, only to return for our 6:00 p.m. dinner reservation.

That night, we entered the restaurant, and as the waitress was leading us to our table, Anna saw the big surprise waiting for her. She was totally speechless and had the biggest smile on her face; it truly brightened up the room! It was one awesome moment that really touched her heart and soul. Still shocked and surprised at the display of love and affection that stood before her, about all she could say at that moment was, "Wow, babe, how the heck did you this? This is amazing!!! I absolutely love it!!!"

I wished her "Happy Anniversary," and we sat down for dinner. Soon after, the owner, a few of the waitresses, and even a couple of the patrons who were sitting near our table stopped by to congratulate us and to wish us a happy anniversary!

That night, we had a nice, romantic dinner and talked about our pending wedding. But more importantly, about how that one portrait of us mirrored exactly what we envisioned our wedding to be. Capturing all the heartfelt feelings that brought us together as a loving couple. With that, we raised our wineglasses and made a toast. "Here's to us on our anniversary...two hearts, one love, and one very special moment! I love you, babe!!!"

CHAPTER 108

OUR WEDDING DAY

Nearly a year and half later, after we exchanged our vows at the Cornerstone Christian Center in Milford, Connecticut, on May 14, 1994, we officially became husband and wife! It was truly a dream come true for the two of us!

It was the most amazing day ever, sharing our special day with about one hundred of our closest and dearest friends and family. We danced the night away and partied like never before. Each song meant so much to us, including our wedding song by none other than Luther Vandross, "Here and Now!" It was truly an evening to remember! The memories we shared on that night as husband and wife are etched into our hearts and souls forever!

The next day, we left on our honeymoon to the Sandals resort on the beautiful island of St. Lucia! Once there, we stayed for five awesome days, enjoying the sun, the white, sandy beaches, wonderful island dishes, and tropical drinks. In fact, we were having so much fun that we even decided to take part in a bunch of cool games and activities designed for newlyweds. All in all, we had the most incredible time ever! This time, however, as a newly married couple... Mr. and Mrs. Alfaro!

Almost twenty-five years to the day, we celebrated our twenty-fifth wedding anniversary by renewing our vows in front of about one hundred family and friends once again! And just like our first one, we danced and celebrated the night away in a big way, with lots of love, lots of laughter, lots of kisses, and most importantly, lots of amazing memories that will last a lifetime!

On February 14, 1995, approximately nine months after getting married the first time, we were having a nice, quiet romantic dinner at September's in New Haven, Connecticut, when my beautiful wife decided to surprise me with the greatest Valentine's Day gift ever.

That day, she handed me a gift box, and once I opened it, I discovered the most amazing gift any husband could ever hope for in his life. Inside the gift box was a small baby onesie with a message that read, If You Think I'm Cute, You Should See My Daddy!

I immediately jumped up with excitement and gave my wife the biggest hug and kiss ever! I was so excited that I even drew a little bit of attention from some of the patrons having dinner at the restaurant. Almost immediately, they all stood up and applauded the moment while sending out well-wishes and shouts of congratulations.

That day, I thanked my wife, from the bottom of my heart, for surprising me with the most amazing Valentine's Day gift ever…one that I know will be tough to top! But knowing my wife as I do, you just never, ever know what other wonderful surprises she might have in store for me down the road!

CHAPTER 109

MY ACTING BUG: DISCOVERING A WHOLE NEW CAREER AS AN ACTOR

U p until this point in my life, I had never ventured out to try and tackle another career besides my main job as a police officer and my side job as a professional model. Life was great, and I couldn't be happier.

One day back in July of 1995, I got a call from my agent, Christy, at Model Club Inc in Boston; she wanted to know if I had any acting experience because she had an acting job in mind.

"No, not really," I said. Other than a few public service announcements that I had done for the police department, I really had zero experience in acting.

"Well," she said, "I just got this casting call, and they're looking for actors to be in a short movie. Would you be interested in giving it a try?"

I paused briefly before saying, "Sure, why not? I'll give it a shot!"

"Wow, that's awesome Roberto. Please take down this info on the casting. You will be auditioning for the main character in this short movie. You'll be playing the role of a photographer," she said.

I was excited about this great opportunity, but at the same time, a bit nervous, not knowing what to expect. But then I said to myself, *What the heck? I really got nothing to lose by trying. I'll just go out there and give it my best, and see what happens.*

The next day, I showed up at the casting bright and early, only to find a long line of potential actors waiting to audition for the role. I felt a bit intimidated, seeing all these actors with their scripts in their hands, rehearsing their lines. While I, on the other hand, just looked over the script and tried my hardest to envision myself in that role and executing it in my audition, hopefully impressing the director and the producers enough to land the part.

Once inside the studio, I met up with them, and they proceeded to give me a quick recap of the scene and what my character's role would be in the movie. I took a deep breath before they yelled, "Action," cueing me to start my scene.

In the scene, I was photographing a high-fashion model and directing her on what actions to take in front of the camara. "Okay, now let me see that beautiful smile... Awesome..." I said as I moved around the room, taking different angle shots while I talked her through the scene.

The scene was a short one, and before I knew it, I heard the director yell, "Okay, cut. Thank you so much for auditioning. You'll be hearing from us soon if you got the part."

I said thank you and left the studio feeling relieved that the audition was finally over. Now I could finally relax!

A few days later, I got a call from my agent with some really great news. She said with lots of excitement in her voice, "Guess what? They loved your audition, and they would like to meet up with you for a quick lunch before they make the final decision tomorrow."

My immediate reaction was to yell, "What, are you kidding me," before jumping up and down with excitement and anticipation of hopefully landing the role once I met up with them!

The very next day, I met them at a restaurant in Newton, Massachusetts. We had a great conversation, and they showed me the complete script of the short movie. "Do you think you might be interesting in doing this?" they asked.

"Absolutely!" I said.

"So then, be ready to shoot next week," they said, "because you got the part! Congratulations, Roberto!!!"

I was beyond excited to land my first role as an actor on my very first try! In my wildest dreams, I could never have imagined something like this happening to a kid from the South Bronx. Now here I was, starring in my first role as an actor. Who would've ever thought this would be possible? What a true blessing...thank you, God!!!

On July 18th and 19th, after signing a Screen Actors Guild (SAG) contract, we started shooting the short film. There were two very long fifteen-hour days of shooting and working with several actresses in numerous scenes. We finally wrapped the movie after an exhausting second day of shooting!

It was truly an amazing experience, and one that I learned so much from after working numerous hours in front of the camara. As we ran scene after scene, and take after take! All the while, I tried to make sure to take direction well, in order to make the scene believable. In fact, during the filming, I even got a chance to ad-lib some parts, which the director loved and decided to keep in the movie. The film aired about a year later in numerous film venues and events.

After this experience, I suddenly had the acting bug, and I knew there was no turning back! I badly wanted to explore how to work my way into landing a small part on a TV show, or even a feature movie. How little did I know then that that opportunity would come way sooner than I ever expected!

About a few months after filming this short movie, I was working a modeling job with a model by the name of Luz. Luz and I were working for the same agency, the Johnston Agency, but had never worked together as a couple until that day. After we finished the shoot, I asked Luz if she did anything else besides modeling.

She said, "Yes, I'm also an actress."

Intrigued by the acting world, I decided to ask her, "So what kind of TV shows have you been on?"

And she said, "Quite a few, but *New York Undercover* has been my regular gig."

Shocked and surprised that she was working in one of my favorite shows, I said, "Are you kidding me, *New York Undercover*? I love that show. I watch it every week. Wow, how I would love to be on that show. Just curious, do you have any connections or anyone that you could refer me to?"

She said, "Why, yes, absolutely! Here"—she wrote it down—"just send your headshot and resume to my friend Milton. He's the casting director for *New York Undercover*. Tell him I referred you to him, and hopefully he'll call you and book you on the show."

I said, "Thank you so, so much, Luz. I will definitely do that!" I was feeling pretty excited about hopefully getting a call from Milton after mailing him my headshot and resume.

Days went by, and I hadn't gotten a response from the show. Finally, approximately three weeks or so later, I received a call at home from Milton Cruz with some really great news to share.

He said, "Hi, this is Milton, casting director for the TV show *New York Undercover*. I went over your headshot and resume, and I wanted to know if you would be free on Monday, October 2, to do some background work on the show."

"Absolutely!" I said without hesitation.

"Great, then all you have to do is call this number on Sunday night, and all your booking information will be on that recording."

I thanked him and was all smiles as I looked forward to working on one of my favorite TV shows of all time. Once I hung up the phone, I couldn't wait to tell my wife this awesome news! She was almost as excited as I was when I told her about my chance of a lifetime to be on one of our favorite shows! She immediately congratulated me and gave me a big hug!

I showed up on the set of *New York Undercover* bright and early that Monday morning. I was in awe, just being there and admiring the entire set. The same exact set that my wife and I would consistently watch on TV on a weekly basis. When I arrived on the set, there must have been at least sixty other background artists who'd also shown up to work on the show that day.

My role on the show was to portray a business man getting off the elevator with one of the principal actors of the show. During the rest of the day, I also did a few other background crosses in front of the camera at the police precinct. The best part of the day came when I actually got a chance to meet and talk to one of the stars of the show, Michael DeLorenzo, during one of the breaks in between scenes. He was really cool, and I even got an autographed Polaroid picture with him before we started shooting the next scene.

Other than meeting Michael, working on the set that day was nothing to brag about. Each scene was crowded with a bunch of background artists, so I knew the chance of being seen among the crowd of actors was going to be really slim. But I really didn't care. I was just happy to be there and to finally get my foot in the door.

While there, I introduced myself to quite a few of the background artists to learn as much as I could from each of them. Among some of the background artists were a number of people playing the role of NYPD cops. Their uniforms and equipment were similar to mine as a real-life cop in the Hartford Police Department. Out of curiosity, I asked one of the actors—after introducing myself and telling him that I worked as a real cop in Hartford, Connecticut—where they'd gotten the uniforms and equipment.

"I actually got it all at Schlesinger's Police Equipment and Uniforms, located on 18th Street in the city," he said, "and if you have a law enforcement background, all you have to do is go in there, show them your badge and ID, and you can order a badge set and a complete uniform."

I thanked him for the information. The reason that I inquired was that I wanted to play a cop on the show, and hopefully be able to use some my actual police experience in some of the cop roles. One thing I'd noticed over the years was that playing a cop always got you more exposure in front of the camera than the other actors doing background work. Or as some of the background artists who played cops on a regular basis would say, "You get more airtime." More of a chance that your family and friends see you on the small screen.

About two weeks later, I stopped by Schlesinger's, ordered my hat piece and badge, and picked up four sets of NYPD patches for my uniform. I really lucked out in that regard because, as it turns out, NYPD had the same exact dark-blue uniform that we used in Hartford. It was simply a matter of switching the patches over to those of NYPD. Since I already had a gun belt and all the police equipment needed from the Hartford Police Department, it made the whole transition so much easier.

After picking up my badge set, I called Milton, told him about my background as a real cop, and advised him that I had the complete uniform ready to go if he needed me to work as a cop on the show.

"Wow, that's cool, Roberto! Okay," he said, "then be prepared because I'll be calling you soon to play a cop on the show!"

He kept his word, and before long, I was working pretty regularly on the set. Soon I started getting better parts near or around some of the main characters in the show. I even had lots of friends, family, and even members of my department, calling me to say, "Hey, I just saw you on the show *New York Undercover*!" It felt so great just being on the show and having fun! I was really inspired to continue working in this new career and to better myself as an actor. I even decided to take acting classes, which helped me tremendously. I soon qualified to join the Screen Actors Guild and joined right away.

One day, after being on the show for about three years, I showed up to work on the set and heard that one of the actors who was slated to play an officer who commits suicide showed up with a different look from what the director expected when he was cast for the role. The actor had cut off all his hair.

Needless to say, director was furious! As luck would have it, I happened to be standing right next to the director at the time. During his outburst, he looked in my direction, paused for a moment, and said, "Sir, are you in the union by any chance?" After I said yes, the director said, "Okay, guys, this is what we're going to do here. This gentleman is going to take his spot...and will be playing Officer Vincent. We need to get him ready right now for the next shot!"

The next thing I knew, I was whisked away to the hair and makeup department to be prepped for the scene. During preparations, the assistant director walked into the room to talk to me about the scene. I took this opportunity to introduce myself and told him I was a real cop in Hartford, Connecticut.

He said, "Okay, being that you're a real cop, how would it look if someone shoots himself and commits suicide at point-blank range?"

I explained to him, "The area around the wound should show signs of powder burns from the impact of the bullet being fired at close range!"

He said, "Great, thanks so much. I'll let the director know!" He also told the makeup artist to "prepare the bullet wound to look just like he explained it to me."

Once I was brought on the set, I even assisted them in the position of how one would fall if they committed suicide on the edge of the bed. They were extremely grateful for my assistance, and even included the part about the powder burns in the script.

Everything was moving so fast. I just couldn't believe how quickly it all evolved. One moment, I'm standing there observing a heated argument between the director and this actor. The next thing I know, I'm replacing him for the role. More importantly, the whole story line of this episode revolved around Officer Vincent's suspicious death and the effects it had on his family. It was definitely a great role for a newly minted actor. It was definitely pure luck that I was in the right place, at the right time. Another amazing blessing!

When the show aired about six weeks later, all my friends and family got a chance to see me in this featured role as an actor. Unfortunately, because my character was killed on this episode, it would also turn out to be the very last time I would appear on my favorite show. I knew right then and there that it was time to move on to other acting projects.

As the years went by, I started working on other shows, playing roles mostly as a police officer, FBI or Secret Service agent, and even a few stints as a detective. Mostly, all were law-enforcement related. The longer I worked on some of these shows—like *Law and Order*, *Blue Bloods*, *Elementary*, *Person of Interest*, and a host of others—the more networking I did. Sometimes the director or assistant director would use me because of my law-enforcement background in scenes that required someone in the field who knew what they were doing, someone who didn't need any type of training to make the scene look realistic. Like handcuffing, escorting someone during an arrest, pulling out your weapon to take down an armed suspect, or standing by one of the principal actors to move the scene along. Most of these scenes were considered featured roles, which means you will be working alongside a principal actor, especially when there is an arrest to be made during an intricate part of the story line.

After a while, I also had a strategy that I would employ, especially on any new show or movie set, in order to get a featured role or a small speaking part. I even came up with a name for it—hustling on the set! Here's what I would do! On the day of the shoot, before my actual call time, I would show up really early in the holding area. This is where all the background artists show up to check in with the production assistant, or PA. Once you check in, they tick off your name on the roster and give you a voucher, which you fill out with all your personal information, so you can get paid. PAs on the set also have what they call sides, which is basically a breakdown of the script; it details for the principal actors all of that day's scenes and dialogue.

It is during those early arrivals in the holding area that I would ask the PA if I could take a look at the sides. Most of the time, they're okay with that, and they share them. Once I have the sides in my hands, I try to get a breakdown of every scene and what scenes in particular involve some type of physical police action. Scenes in which they might need the presence of a real cop to carry the scene along and make it look real, especially if a principal actor is getting arrested.

That's exactly where my hustle comes in. I go to the PA, identify myself as a real-life cop, and advise the PA that I'm available if a real cop is needed for a particular scene. It doesn't work every single time, but about eight out of ten times, the PA relays the message up the ladder to the assistant director, and before I know it, I'm called to the set to do the scene.

One day, I auditioned for the part of Richard Gere's limo driver in the movie *Arbitrage*. While I wasn't playing a cop, the fact that I had been trained as a police officer in defensive-driving tactics won me the role with the director, Nicholas Jarecki. He would later tell me that they needed an "excellent driver to drive a Maybach," which I found out was one of the most expensive luxury cars by Mercedes-Benz. I managed to work on this movie set for close to two months, two to three times a week, with an award-winning actor. I also had an amazing time in the role of Ramon the Limo Driver.

Over the years, I've been blessed to have many opportunities to work in minor roles with other famous actors, including Richard Gere, John Leguizamo, Michael J. Fox, Jaimie Alexander, Edie Falco, Paul Giamatti, Damian Lewis, Danny Aiello, Lauren Vélez, Michael DeLorenzo, Jesse Martin, Robin Williams, Jackie Cruz, Harry Lennix, and a host of others.

I also had the golden opportunity to work in featured roles on the popular daytime soap opera *All My Children* for nearly four years, on and off, thanks to a great friend and fellow actor, Omar, who referred me to the casting director, who then put me in numerous episodes playing the role of a police officer.

Locally and closer to home, over the years I've had the chance to work as a principal actor in numerous commercials, everything from playing the lead actor as a dad and a husband on *"Prudencia,"* a Spanish soap-opera-style TV commercial, to playing the dad of a teenager in a local commercial for St. Mary's Hospital, and many other Connecticut commercials.

Wow, what a truly amazing time and journey it has been for me!

CHAPTER 110

WORKING WITH MICHAEL J. FOX

By this point in my acting career, I had worked on many sets and had met some truly amazing actors along the way. Yet perhaps none was as nice and inspiring as Michael J. Fox, a legendary actor. One day back in 2010, I got cast to play Michael J. Fox's limo driver on the set of *The Good Wife*. During the two weeks I worked with him on the set, I found him to be one of the nicest, kindest, and most down-to-earth actors you will ever meet!

While working on one of the scenes, we had a nice conversation going, and he asked me, "Roberto, besides acting, what else do you do?"

I told him, "I'm actually a retired cop from the City of Hartford, where I retired after twenty-one years of service."

And he said, "Wow, that's awesome! Thank you so much for your service!"

During our conversation, I also mentioned to him that my family and I were big fans of the *Back to the Future* trilogy! And how we loved watching the movie series as a family.

He said, "That's pretty awesome! Thank you so much for being a fan!" But it's what he said to me next, out of his own free will, that truly shocked me. He said, "Roberto, if you bring me the box set next week, I'll be more than happy to sign it for you."

When he said that, it took me by complete surprise because I really didn't want to bother him for an autograph. But out of the kindness of his heart, he actually volunteered to do such a good deed for me and my family. I was beyond grateful!

About a week later, as soon as we wrapped up the last scene, he said to me, "Roberto, did you bring the box set with you today, by any chance?"

"I sure did, Michael," I told him, quickly pulling it out of my backpack and handing it to him. He immediately autographed it, wishing me and my family, "All the best," and handed it back to me. He then shook my hand and said, "It was so great working with you, Roberto, thank you so much! Take care!"

I said, "Thank you Michael, it was my pleasure!"

His act of kindness and generosity truly made my day! A true gentleman!

CHAPTER 111

1995: ONE OF THE MOST INCREDIBLE YEARS OF MY LIFE

While I have experienced many big milestones in my life over the years, 1995 would turn out to be one of the largest! For not only did I discover acting for the very first time in my life, but also I got my first acting gig in a short film. Only to top it off months later, by landing an acting job on *New York Undercover*, one of my favorite TV shows during that time period.

But it didn't stop there; the blessings continued when I entered and got selected as one of the finalists in the Bacardí Limón National Model Search contest. And just when I thought that year couldn't possibly get any better, it did!

For 1995 was the year that God blessed our family with the birth of our beautiful daughter, Brianna, who was born in September of that year! Seeing my beautiful daughter being born was truly this father's dream come true! Becoming a father for the third time was one of the most fulfilling and most life-changing experiences I could have ever imagined as a parent.

Everything you do in life from that day forward is for the love and greater good of your kids and their future. Always hoping and praying that as they grow up and mature, they know that everything they want to do in life is possible. So long as they believe in themselves and never give up on their dreams, it can happen! For there is one thing I know for sure, and that is that I would never want my kids to experience any of the tough challenges I had to endure as a young child growing up.

My beautiful daughter grew up so fast, it seemed. One moment, she was crawling along in her diapers; the next moment, she was running and talking up a storm. By the age of two, I discovered that she loved taking pictures and smiling for the camera. A talent that we soon picked up on and thought she might be great as a baby model. A few test shots here and there with an amazing photographer from my agency, Steve Prezant, and we knew right away that it was something she truly enjoyed doing, especially posing in front of the camera.

Within a matter of weeks after taking those test shots, she was signed by my modeling agency, the Johnston Agency, and started booking jobs in both regional and national ads for the likes of a Carter's baby-clothing line, Ames Department Stores, and a handful of other companies.

One day, we submitted a modeling shot that we had taken together as a father-and-daughter team to Johnson and Johnson's national Baby and Me photo contest. To our surprise, we won, taking home first prize and winning a $500 savings bond. We couldn't be prouder of her for all of her accomplishments at such a young age.

As the years went by, she continued modeling, but the older and older she got, the less of an interest she showed in wanting to continue modeling. One day, she told us she didn't want to model anymore; she just wanted to do sports, and that's when everything changed. A few months later, she started playing basketball, baseball, and taking karate lessons, all sports that she flourished in until her teen years.

As parents, we couldn't have asked for a more inspiring daughter; she was never afraid to go after her dreams and have fun! Daughter, we are so, so proud of you!

CHAPTER 112

BECOMING A DAD ONCE AGAIN

Nearly two years after the day my wife surprised me on Valentine's Day with the amazing news that I was going to be a dad, she surprised me again. However, this time it was on Christmas Eve. We'd decided to stay in, instead of going out to a restaurant. It was the perfect way to celebrate our love: a nice, romantic candlelit dinner in the comfort of our own home.

After dinner, we sat down on the living room floor to eat some chocolate candy and to exchange a few gifts. For some reason, my wife wanted me to open up my gift first. It was a big box, the type you would put a shirt or sweater in. When I had it in my hands, it felt really light, as though nothing were in there. I quickly unwrapped it, only to see a bunch of wrapping tissue. That led me to believe that the box was empty, and she was just playing a joke on me. So I laughed out loud, as though to say, "You got me!"

I remember her having the biggest smile ever when she said, "Are you sure there's nothing in there? Look again!" And when I did, I came across this little white-plastic box that was probably about two inches by two inches in size. I was intrigued and wondered what it could be.

That's when she turned it over on the other side and asked me, "So what do you see?"

There, right in the middle of this box, was a blue line that said, "You're pregnant!" I immediately said, "What??? Are you kidding me???"

And she said, "No, babe, this is real. We're going to have a baby!!!"

All I remember at that point is the two of us getting all emotional, crying, hugging, kissing, and celebrating with pure joy and happiness! Once again, she pulled off one of her biggest surprises, without me ever having the slightest idea that we were going to be parents for the second time. This was an unbelievable moment, and we could not wait to share the great news with all our friends and family, especially our little girl, Brianna, and her two other siblings, Bobby and Bianca. This was yet another magical day in our lives, and one that will stay with us forever!

In October 1997, we welcomed a beautiful baby boy, Christian, into our world. We were beyond happy and excited at the birth of our son and our growing family, which now included two boys and two girls. We simply couldn't be happier! That same day, I brought my little girl, Brianna, to meet her little brother. I remember that on the way to the hospital, all she would talk about was seeing her baby brother.

Once at the hospital, she gave her mother a big hug and kiss, and waited anxiously to see her little brother. As soon as we showed her the baby, she sported the most amazing smile and gave him a big kiss on the forehead while holding him in her lap. You could easily tell how happy she was, yet curious at the same time; she finally had someone to play and have fun with at home.

Babies grow so fast! And before we knew it, Christian was crawling and doing a lot a baby talk. In the months that followed, that crawling quickly progressed to walking and talking. Seeing Brianna and Christian together and playing in their own little way was really something to marvel and smile about. How fast they bonded as siblings!

Although there was a bit of an age difference between them and their two older siblings, they all loved each other just the same. I knew that one day they would all grow up to be adults, and the age gap wouldn't matter anymore. In time, all four of my children would be doing things together as loving brothers and sisters, and having a great time.

It didn't take long before our son Christian started getting into sports. He loved playing basketball and baseball every chance he got. Soon, he was playing on teams in multiple sports, but leaning more towards baseball, which eventually became his favorite sport.

In his early years of playing baseball, Christian was doing amazingly well, especially in the seven-to-eight age group. So much so, that when the Pepsi decided to sponsor the Pitch, Hit, and Run contest, he dominated in his age group. First winning the overall for our town of Hamden. Then winning the regional competition in the tristate area of Connecticut, New York, and New Jersey. Then, as a semifinalist, he was invited to compete—in McCombs Park, right across the street from Yankee Stadium in the Bronx—against kids in his age range from other states. The winner in this last competition received a trip to the All-Star Game in Pittsburgh, Pennsylvania, to field balls during the Home Run Derby.

On the day of the competition, Christian missed winning the whole thing by just one pitch that was deemed out of the zone, or target area, and had to settle for second place. Although he was a bit disappointed with the outcome, it didn't last long.

All the competitors from that day were later invited to be on the field at Yankee Stadium in order to be honored for taking part in the contest. Minutes before the start of the New York Yankees game against the Florida Marlins, all the participants were lined up in front of home plate. One by one, each kid was introduced by Mr. Bob Sheppard! It was the most surreal moment for us as parents, but even more so for our son Christian as he stood there in awe of all he was witnessing, while the fans packing the stadium applauded the kids and cheered them on!

He later said that his biggest thrill that day didn't happen until after they were honored; walking off the field, as he passed in front of the Yankees players' dugout, Derek Jeter and Bernie Williams, two of his favorite players on the team, both waved at him. It was truly a dream come true, not only for him, but for us as well!

For his participation in the Pepsi challenge, he received a nice T-shirt and baseball cap that represented the Pitch, Hit, and Run contest and was awarded a wonderful plaque in the shape of home plate, that read: Pitch, Hit, and Run, 2004 Team Championship, Second Place!

In the years that followed, he continued to play baseball and became one of the best pitchers, hitters, and outfielders in his league. Until one day, after graduating from high school, he decided to give up playing baseball in order to focus solely on his education and getting a degree. Four years later, after obtaining his criminal justice degree from Quinnipiac University, he became the last one of his siblings to earn a college degree, joining his older brother and sisters—Bobby, Bianca, and Brianna—who all had degrees from their respective universities.

As a dad and as parents, we couldn't be prouder of all our children's academic accomplishments, especially when you look at some of the highlights! Besides those already mentioned for my two youngest, Brianna and Christian, my oldest son, Bobby, after playing varsity football for Windsor High School, went on to play football at the University of Connecticut. A few years later in 2002, he applied to work as an NFL scout for the Tampa Bay Buccaneers and got the job. It was in that same season that they won the 2003 Super Bowl. They celebrated it in a big way, awarding every single member of the Tampa Bay team, including my son, a Super Bowl ring for their efforts! That day, not only was it an amazing moment in my son's life, but also for our whole family. We were all so proud of him!

And then there is my oldest daughter, Bianca, who, years after getting a BA degree in communications from Quinnipiac University, decided to become a nurse. She went back to school full time while still holding down a full-time job. Truly inspiring and proof that anything and everything is possible. With a little bit of determination and hustle, you can accomplish anything you want in life, regardless of the challenges at hand! Years later, she got married to an amazing man, Alby, and they gave us two of the most adorable, beautiful grandkids, Niko and Noah, that any grandparent could ever ask for! We are all so proud of her and her wonderful family!

Finally, you have our daughter Brianna, who decided to follow in her older sister's footsteps by getting a degree in public health from Southern Connecticut State University. Just months after graduating, she began working a full-time job as a clinical assistant, while still going to school part-time in pursuit of a master's degree in public health.

To say we all are so proud of her and the rest of our kids is an understatement! We love and admire them all for who they are and for their inspiring achievements in life!

CHAPTER 113

RETIRING FROM THE JOB THAT I LOVE!

By the year 2000, I made one of the most difficult decisions I had ever made in my life: retiring from the police force after twenty-one years of dedicated service to the department and the community. Throughout most of the prior three or four years on the job, my side work as an actor and a professional model had really taken off. So much so, that there were many times when I couldn't book a job because of my work obligations with the police department.

Being a police officer is all I ever dreamed of, all I ever wanted to do with my life, ever since I was a young child growing up in the South Bronx. And having a grandfather who was a state police officer in Puerto Rico just inspired me even more to pursue a career in law enforcement. It was this same drive that in 1979 propelled me to go after my dream when I joined the Hartford Police Department and became a police officer. Throughout the years, I was blessed to work in a variety of patrol positions, from being assigned to a walking beat in Stowe Village, one of the toughest projects in all of Hartford for nine months—with two amazing partners, Ernie and Joe—to working in a patrol car in the same general area. Years later, I also got a chance to work plainclothes assignments, and later, to become a member of the recruitment team that was geared towards finding qualified candidates to become police officers.

But throughout it all, my proudest moment happened when I was selected as one of twelve members of the newly formed mounted police unit. And in doing so, became the very first Hispanic in the history of mounted patrol. It was in this unit that I truly shined, and I used to look forward to getting to work, hopping on my horse, and going after the bad guys. Which is why, when I finally made the decision to retire, I knew right away it was going to be one of the most difficult choices I'd had to make in all my many years as a police officer. For retiring meant parting ways with my amazing horse and best partner—Alex the Wonder Horse!

Throughout the ten years we worked together, we got involved in and investigated almost every imaginable crime and situation you could think of, including getting car chases and even galloping after criminals trying to get away on foot. But more than anything, he was just such an amazing, gentle horse that was loved and admired by everyone within our unit, the police department, and even in the crime-ridden areas we worked in as a team for so many years. So saying goodbye to him, I knew, wasn't going to be easy! However, I left content, knowing that the memories will always be a part of me and will be with me forever!

In the ten years from 1990 to 2000 that I had the honor and pleasure of working with Alex, we issued a total of ninety-six citations, 439 summonses, and made a total of 203 arrests. Truly astounding, when you consider that to do that on horseback, you need an amazing horse that always keeps himself under control, even during very extreme and dangerous situations. This was especially true when we were engaged in chasing a wanted person or a car that had been involved in a serious crime. During all those years, thank God, we never got hurt, and Alex never came up lame while working the streets.

My very last day of work turned out to be very emotional for both Alex and me. I think he was going to miss me, just as much as I was going to miss him. As a final farewell, I gave him a big hug, gathered up his last pair of horseshoes, and took them home with me. I later painted them gold and stored them with all the other memories and pictures that I collected of him over the years. I will miss him dearly, and so will my family and our two kids who used to ride him on a regular basis, usually on Sundays. They always spoiled him with his favorite treats of carrots and apples!

The one really great piece of news relative to my retirement was knowing that Alex was also retiring and going to a great new home on a farm in Franklin, Connecticut. My family and I still get a chance to visit him from time to time, and even take him for a short ride around the paddock.

After saying my last goodbyes to my partner, it was time to go off the line with our police dispatcher for the very last time. Ironically, my cousin Maureen, who had been working with the Hartford Police Department dispatch center for many years, was on the line on my last day. She wanted to do me the honor of putting me off the line for the last time. As you can imagine, when the time came to make that last announcement to all the units in the city, it was a really tough and emotionally driven situation for both of us. I was really going to miss not working with her after all those years!

After the announcement was made, the congratulations and "good luck" sentiments came pouring in from all my brothers and sisters on the force. And that's when it really hit me. Retiring on that day meant not being able to hear their voices again on the radio or go on calls with them. And last, but certainly not least, not being able to have them around for backup whenever I got involved in a chase or a struggle with someone during an arrest. All of that, I soon realized, was about to come to an end!

With tears in my eyes, I said, "Unit 96, I'm going off the line for the last time. Thank you all so much. I will miss each and every single one of you guys. Please stay safe, and may God bless you all always!!!"

I shut off my police radio for the final time!

CHAPTER 114

COMING BACK AFTER EIGHT YEARS OF RETIREMENT

About a month after I retired from the force, the mounted unit was disbanded because "the city could no longer afford to keep the horses and maintain the mounted police stables." This started a big petition by numerous organizations, city residents, and supporters from surrounding towns. They loved the horses and strongly believed that the mounted police were a deterrent to crime, making them feel safe in their neighborhoods and communities.

Despite the petitions and outpouring of support to keep the mounted unit going, the city had already decided their fate and did away with the mounted unit. During the closing phase, they donated all the horses, saddles, and equipment to different organizations, including other mounted police units in Connecticut. The Ebony Horse Women were given the mounted police stables, along with a host of other equipment for their organization. The mounted unit was now history and a thing of the past!

However, back in 2007, a drive to restart the mounted unit was soon in the works. And by 2008, the mayor and city council all agreed to bring it back. A great friend of mine for so many years on the force, Sergeant Eddie Resto, was selected to lead the new mounted unit. He was tasked with putting it all together and with having the mounted unit ready to hit the streets by the year's end. A building right next to the old mounted stables—that was once used to house the Parks and Recreation office and equipment in Keney Park—was going to be gutted and made into the new mounted unit's stables.

Things were moving really fast. Soon a team of six mounted officers—Officers Marcel, Debbie, Todd, Gena, and months later Jamie—and one sergeant, Sergeant Resto, was put together and assigned to the Governor's Horse Guard in Avon, Connecticut, for training. The

Governor's Horse Guard is a volunteer, military-type unit comprised of retired military officers; they specialize in riding horses for all sorts of events, including parades.

It was there that the new group of Hartford mounted officers were trained on all there is to know about horses. From learning how to ride them at different gaits and under a host of challenging conditions, to riding them bareback and without stirrups, for the purpose of establishing good balance, control, and mutual trust while riding your steed. Half of the trainees had experience in riding, while the other half were just starting, and every aspect about learning to ride a horse was new to them.

Because the unit, up to this point, did not have their own horses, they had to borrow the Governor's Horse Guard's horses for their training. While everything that you needed to know about horses and the training required to ride at a proficient level was taught by the Governor's Horse Guard personnel at their stables, learning to ride and work on the city streets requires a totally new set of skills that the riders needed to learn before becoming certified mounted-patrol officers.

It was then that Sergeant Resto reached out to me one day to ask if I would be willing to come out of retirement to train the new mounted unit. And without hesitation, I said yes. A few weeks later, I was hired to train the recruits in the tactics and procedures needed in order to work on horseback and succeed in a very difficult urban environment. Basically, I was getting them ready in a program that I developed and called Street Ready!

As the most tenured mounted patrol officer in the history of the mounted unit, with a total of fifteen years' service, I had all the training and experience needed to be an instructor. From handling the most challenging and unimaginable situations that a mounted police officer can experience on the city streets, to the numerous equestrian competitions and training that I'd taken part in over the years, I was prepared to teach the new officers. So yes, I was eager to take on this new challenge.

By the time I committed to training the new mounted unit, they had already purchased a handful of horses. So they were off to a very good start. During the training, we worked on everything, including issuing a ticket on a parked car, enforcing motor vehicle traffic laws, conducting a two-officer felony stop, arresting an armed suspect, going after and chasing down a suspect, searching for drugs, maintaining officer safety, controlling crowds, and a host of other situations mounted officers would encounter on the streets while in the performance of their duty. We trained for several months in and around Keney Park before we moved on to the next phase. Street training!

On the streets, we put some of what we learned during training into actual practice. We also worked on exposing the horses and riders to the elements of traffic and weather and took them through obstacles they would encounter on the streets, things that might make the horses spook, jump, bolt and/or shy away at a critical time in law enforcement. For example, construction sites, crowds, and places where sudden loud noises were likely. All the while, I taught the recruits how to overcome these types of situations and encouraged them to slowly inch their horses towards whatever obstacle was making them nervous.

After four months of training, the horses and riders did such an incredible job that they all graduated with flying colors. That day, we had a small ceremony in which they received their certificates for successfully completing the course. I couldn't be prouder of the amazing mounted officers they all turned out to be over the coming months and years!

Sadly, eight years later, the city council voted to do away with the mounted unit because they claimed it "was too costly to maintain!" In 2016, after much public debate and protest, the mounted unit was disbanded for the second time in a span of sixteen years. This, after all that training, the purchasing of those amazing horses, the equipment, the horse trailers, and a wonderful stable, only to put it all to the wayside! History repeated itself yet again, and the mounted unit is no more! A truly sad and heartbreaking ending to a great and valuable program!

CHAPTER 115

ONE OF THE BIGGEST HIGHLIGHTS OF MY CAREER!

It was on April 24, 2014, when I got a random email, from the Hamden Arts Commission, telling me that they had some "wonderful news to share!" In part, the email stated that I had been selected by their commission as one of the latest Hamden Notables inductees, a veritable Who's Who of Hamden. This was definitely a total surprise to me; it came out of nowhere! I never, in my wildest dreams, expected this to happen!

It all started sometime back in June of 2013 when I received an email from a member of the Hamden Arts Commission, telling me that she had some great news to share. Her email went on to say that someone had nominated me for consideration as one of the latest inductees into the Hamden Notables for the City of Hamden. According to the email, this was a distinction that "identifies and honors individuals who have made significant contributions to the cultural arts (architecture, art, dance, film, literature, media, music, theater, and photography)." Past inductees included "a host of other great artists that either live or lived in Hamden."

Some of the Hamden Notables recognized on their website are: Academy Award-winning actor Ernest Borgnine, actor Dwayne "The Rock" Johnson, Pulitzer Prize-winning author Debbie Applegate, Rock and Roll Hall of Famer and lead singer Fred Parris, from the song "In the Still of the Night," among many others.

I accepted this tremendous honor without hesitation. I felt extremely lucky, honored, and grateful to even be mentioned in that list of amazing Hamden Notables. So to be inducted into their Who's Who of Hamden was totally unexpected and definitely felt like a dream come true!

This was truly one of the biggest highlights of my career and once again, one that I will never, ever forget!

CHAPTER 116

THE DAY I MADE AMENDS WITH MY DAD BEFORE HIS PASSING

It happened on April 28, 2015. That's the day I got a call from Dad's doctor at the nursing home; my dad had passed away in his sleep. When I got the call on that Tuesday morning, I was truly heartbroken and immediately started calling all my family members to inform them of his passing. And while I was shocked at this sad news, I was not totally surprised.

During the last few days of his life, my father's health had been declining rapidly. I kind of suspected that it was only a matter of time before his body could not take all the pain and suffering he had been going through since being diagnosed, a few years back, with colon cancer and a weak heart, among a list of other ailments that were attacking his frail body.

While I was in a lot of emotional pain from his passing, deep down inside my heart and soul, there was peace. Peace because he was no longer suffering, but also because we had finally made amends before his passing.

As most of you know from what I have shared about my father's troubled past, my family and I suffered immensely from all the trauma, heartbreak, and pain he caused all of us due to his violent, alcohol-driven, and out-of-control behavior that went on for many, many years. Sober, he was the nicest and quietest person you could meet. But once that alcohol got into his system on those Fridays, Saturdays, and at times Sundays, he was a totally different person. Not the person whom I used to know, not the one who would take me out to all sorts of places, from rowing boats in Central Park, to trips to the Bronx Zoo and even amusement parks. He would spoil the heck out of me with candy and toys whenever he had extra money that he wasn't spending on booze. Most of these activities would actually take place during the day. But once the sun went down, and he hung around with his friends on the weekends, our whole world turned upside down when he got back home in the wee hours of the morning.

On so many occasions, purely out of fear for our lives and for our safety, we ran out of our home and sought safety at a family member's house, or at those of a number of close friends who lived in the South Bronx. This routine went on for years and years, until one day when he suffered a heart attack that nearly cost him his life. It was then, and only then, acting on the advice of his doctor, that he was forced to get sober. He stayed that way for the rest of his life.

About two years prior to his death, I gave my father a call one day. Just to let out all the hurt and pain that had been brewing inside my heart and soul for decades. I said, "Dad, I've been holding back this pain for so many, many years now, and I just have to tell you how much hurt and pain you put us through because of all your drinking."

At first, he said that what happened back then was in the past and he really didn't want to talk about it.

Then I said, "But you have to talk about it. I need to know why you inflicted so much heartbreak and pain on all of us?"

Suddenly, there was a big pause on the line, and I could sense that he was getting a bit emotional and wanted to say something. But he just didn't know how. Finally, he said, "I know this has been difficult for everyone. Yet I want you to know that I've had to live every single day of my life with regret because of my selfish and out-of-control behavior. But alcohol really took full control of my life, and made me do things that I feel really bad and ashamed for doing to my family. I am really sorry for all this pain. Can you please forgive me?"

After hearing this come out of his mouth, I felt the biggest relief I had ever experienced in my entire life. That was all that I had been waiting to hear from him after all these painful years. And while crying emotional tears, I said, "I forgive you, Dad. Thank you so much for coming clean with this!"

It had been a long wait for this confession from my dad. I'm just glad that we finally made amends before his passing. May you rest in peace, Dad.

CHAPTER 117

OTHER HEARTBREAKING MOMENTS WITH MY FAMILY

B esides my dad's passing away in April of 2015, we also had three other prominent family members die between the years 2001 and 2020. Sadly, those three family members all passed away unexpectedly and in tragic ways. The first of the three to pass away was my mother, Gloria, who died in 2001. Then it was my brother, Valentine "Flaco," who died in 2016. And lastly, my oldest sibling, Mercedes, who passed away in 2020. Here's how it all happened.

Back on December 12, 1999, my family and I went to visit my mother and dad, who lived in the Bronxdale Projects on Watson Avenue. That day, my mother seemed to be her old happy self, but was complaining of a backache that she said had been bothering her for the past few days and wouldn't go away. At the time, we all thought that maybe she'd either slept in an awkward position or pulled a muscle while lifting something. After spending a few hours visiting, before we left, I told my dad to please keep me posted and let me know if things worsened.

Two days later on December 14, I got a call from my dad saying that my mom was being rushed to the hospital by ambulance because her condition had gotten "really bad," and she needed medical attention. That same day, he kept me abreast of her condition by calling me every couple of hours. Each time, he said she was still in extreme pain, and her condition was getting worse by the hour. He was really ticked off because she'd been in the emergency room for hours and had yet to be seen by a doctor.

The next morning on December 15, I got a frantic call from my dad. My mother had suffered a massive heart attack and had been put on a ventilator. I rushed to the hospital immediately after that call, doing about a 100 miles per hour just to be by her side. I made it there in less than an hour's time; it usually took me about seventy minutes when driving at the speed limit.

As soon as I got there, I ran to my mother's bedside, crying uncontrollably at seeing her in that state. My father, along with a few other family members, were also there at the time. We called a meeting with the attending physician and wanted answers. He told us that they found that my mother had a large kidney stone that was blocking her urinary tract; it subsequently infected her blood and forced all her organs to fail, including her heart.

We later found out that all of this could've been prevented had the hospital medical staff taken immediate action to dislodge the stone with a surgical procedure. Instead, she was left lying in a hospital bed, with no one taking appropriate action to correct her medical emergency.

My mother went into a coma and never recovered. She lived in a vegetative state for approximately a year and half. On June 11, 2001, at the age of 84, she tragically passed away in a nursing home.

Our family was devastated, and we hired an amazing law firm to investigate the tragedy and to sue the hospital. It took more than six years in civil court before the wrongful death suit came to an end. The defendants in the case—hospital doctors, nurses, and their representatives—all agreed to settle out of court when it was determined their odds of winning this negligence lawsuit were going to be extremely poor. Thankfully, we won the case!

To lose our mother in this way was beyond heartbreaking. But hopefully, by suing the hospital and winning the case for their egregiously negligent treatment of an elderly person, we have prevented another family from experiencing the horrible pain that we all went through on the day we lost our mom because of the negligence of others.

Another sad passing, which really hit me and my family hard, happened on the day my loving brother, Valentine, died. He passed away on November 11, 2016, after an approximately four-year-long battle with emphysema, otherwise known as COPD, that truly destroyed his active way of life.

For as far back as I can remember, my brother loved salsa dancing and having a great time at house parties and salsa clubs throughout

New York City. That is where he was the happiest, where he felt at home, and where it brought joy and smiles to all those around him while watching his awesome salsa moves. In fact, it was because of him and my sister Mercedes that I learned how to salsa dance as a young man. Something that I still enjoy doing to this day, thanks to my two siblings!

On the downside, during his younger days, he also picked up a cigarette habit and over the years got hooked on smoking, at times going through at least one pack of cigarettes a day. During his heyday, it seemed that drinking, smoking, and partying came with the turf. He would go out dancing with his friends, who also smoked, and they would drink and smoke while partying. Smoking soon became a way of life, and he couldn't go anywhere without puffing on a cigarette. It became like a drug that he couldn't put down, one that sadly continued to be a part of his life for many, many years.

One day, while in his forties, he developed a strong cough that he couldn't get rid of, and decided to have it checked out with his doctor. A quick examination and a few X-rays later revealed that his lungs were so corroded with tar and nicotine that the doctor finally told him, if he didn't stop smoking immediately, he was going to die at an early age. That is all my brother needed to hear. The next day, he quit cold turkey and never picked up another cigarette.

Twenty years later, he developed that same nagging cough. This time, however, the news wasn't good. It took my brother by complete surprise when the doctor told him he had early-onset emphysema. Over the years, this affected his breathing so badly that he had to carry around an oxygen tank to help him breathe. When that happened, it immediately took away something that had been dear to his heart and soul for decades: his ability to salsa dance with his loving wife, Fela, of more than twenty years.

As things worsened over the years, something truly unbelievable happened to him. He finally got to meet his long-lost daughter, whom he had never met, but always hoped to see one day before he died.

Back in the day, during the early 1960s, my brother was involved in gangs, running around and meeting girls all over the place. He was in his late teens when he met and got involved with an underage female.

They soon began a consensual relationship that lasted for some months before she became pregnant. When her parents found out, they immediately called the police. My brother was arrested, and he served a few years in prison for having sex with an underage female. It was during this time, while my brother was serving his time in prison, that her parents left the neighborhood, never to be seen again. As the years went by, he learned that the girl he had been involved with had given birth to a baby girl, but their whereabouts were still unknown.

Fast forward more than fifty years, and that same young girl whom he had never met was now a grown woman with kids of her own, and even grandkids. Like my brother, she had been searching and praying all these years that, hopefully, one day they'd cross each other's paths so that she could finally meet her long-lost dad. That beautiful soul is Maria.

It turns out, that one day she decided to join Ancestry.com, in hopes that maybe she could find a DNA match to a family member of her dad. As luck would have it, immediately after joining, she found a match with one of my cousins, Ray, who carried the same DNA. She decided to reach out to him, and before she knew it, she was thrilled to learn that her father was still alive and living with his wife in Ponce, Puerto Rico.

After talking at length over the phone with Ray, he decided to give her the telephone number to his uncle, her father, and she called my brother right away to surprise him with the news. Their hunt for each other was finally over after all these years! That day, they talked for over an hour. It was the surprise of a lifetime for the two of them. They cried, talked about the past, and caught up on so much of what they had missed over the years.

After their long and emotional conversation, Maria quickly made plans to go see my brother. She took her daughter, Khadijah, my brother's granddaughter, and her aunt Yolanda; they flew to Puerto Rico less than a week after that first call. They were both extremely nervous and emotional when they finally got a chance to meet in person. According to my niece Maria, that day they hugged and cried for what seemed like an eternity. It was a perfect reunion that had been in the forefront of their minds during an amazing journey that lasted for so many, many years.

Sadly, on the very next day after meeting her father for the first time, he suddenly landed in the emergency room with an emphysema attack that made it difficult for him to breathe. Maria immediately rushed to the hospital with her family and stayed with him in Puerto Rico for about a week until he got better. During the time she was there, she spent every single day she could with him, just getting to know each other and trying to make up for lost time. They shared many stories about their lives and caught up on so many of the special moments they'd missed. So many questions were answered about their respective journeys that had brought them together after more than five decades.

One of the discoveries that came out of this long-awaited reunion with her dad was that Maria also had two half brothers, Valentine Jr. and Abel. She also learned that in addition to Valentine and Abel, she had another brother, Rene, from my brother's previous marriage. While talking with her dad, Maria found out that one of her brothers, Val, actually lived in a town in Florida just minutes away from where she lived. So she was really looking forward to getting ahold of him once she got back home.

The days quickly flew by, and before she knew it, it was time to say goodbye and head back to Florida with her beautiful daughter and aunt. Shortly thereafter, her dad started feeling better, was released from the hospital, and sent home. However, just about two weeks or so after meeting her dad, Maria got the frightening call that her dad wasn't doing well and had just been admitted to the emergency room at a hospital in Ponce. A few days after receiving that message, she headed back to Puerto Rico to be by her dad's bedside.

A couple of days after hearing this news, I also jumped on a plane with my family. We flew to Puerto Rico to be there for my brother and to pray by his bedside. Other family members soon joined us in Puerto Rico. By the time we all got there, my brother's condition had stabilized, and he was no longer in critical condition.

Once we were all together at the hospital, we finally got a chance to meet the newest member of our family, the one whom my brother had talked about for all these years. Being there to witness this wonderful reunion was one of the greatest feelings in the world for all of us, especially for my brother. And one that we never, ever imagined would one day happen.

That day, there were smiles, laughter, and even tears of joy everywhere as we welcomed our beautiful niece into our wonderful family with open arms, hugs, and kisses! And ironically, her resemblance to our family was truly amazing. So much so, that we even noticed she had my brother's charm, looks, and infectious, outgoing personality that made everybody smile. She was truly the perfect fit for our family, and we couldn't be happier!

But perhaps one of the biggest surprises of all happened when my brother got a chance to finally see at least two of his children, Maria and Val, together in one room. An amazing moment that he had only dreamed would one day happen…if he ever got a chance to see his daughter. Seeing the look on his face that day, you could easily sense that he was experiencing one of the greatest moments of his life, right there in front of us. Even while he lay in bed connected to an oxygen tank, trying to fight this long and exhausting battle with emphysema that was draining away his energy, he was still able to laugh and smile in our presence.

It was truly tough to watch, but all we could do as a family was pray our hearts out that his situation would get better with every passing day and that he would hopefully get back to living a somewhat-normal life. However, deep down inside we all knew that since there wasn't a cure for emphysema, the chances of his surviving this and being the same person we once knew and loved were very slim. But one thing's for sure; we never, ever lost hope!

With his condition showing signs of improvement by the day—and the doctor explaining to us that he might be discharged within the next few days—we decided to head back home and keep in phone contact with his doctor for updates on his condition. About a week or so after landing in the intensive care unit of the hospital, my brother's condition had improved so much that he was discharged from the hospital and sent back home to continue with his recovery. When we heard this news, we were all extremely happy and just kept praying daily that his condition would continue to get better with every passing day.

Sadly and unfortunately, about a week or so after being released, he was rushed back into the emergency room in critical condition. This time, we were told by his doctors that his chances of surviving did not look good. And less than three days after being admitted into the hospital, I received a dreadful phone call from his stepson and was told that my brother had passed away during the night.

When I got the news, I was a total wreck and couldn't believe that my brother had passed away just a week after I saw him in the hospital and thought he was doing better. That morning when I broke the news to our family, they were completely devastated and heartbroken. Especially his daughter, Maria, who had waited all these years to finally get a chance to meet her father, only to lose him once again after just one month since their amazing and long-awaited reunion.

Within a couple of days, we were all back in Puerto Rico. About two days after that, we all said our last goodbyes and buried my brother in a tearful and heartbreaking ceremony in a cemetery near his home in Ponce. During the next few days, we spent the time with each other, sharing family stories about him, especially talking about the fun times that made him so special and loving to every single one of us. Once again, we laughed and cried as one big family as we reflected back on his memory. He was someone who meant the world to us all, and he'd touched our lives in so many, many ways.

Just last year, on March 24, 2020, we were dealt another painful blow when my sister Mercedes, at the age of eighty-two, unexpectedly passed away from heart failure brought on by possible complications of COVID-19. The news of her dying was extremely upsetting and heartbreaking for the whole family. That day, we lost the matriarch and leader of our family. She meant the world to all of us.

To me, she was like my second mother who always tried to look after me in every way possible in order to keep me safe. So when my nephew Ray called me that night to inform me of her sudden death, it really broke my heart and left me in a state of shock.

As a kid, she was my hero! One day, while crossing the street in our old neighborhood, the driver of a vehicle was backing up into an open parking spot when he struck me on my right pelvic area. Had it not been for my sister Mercedes's quick actions, the right rear tires of the vehicle would've definitely run over my legs. Thank God, at the time, she was holding my hand as we were crossing the street and was able to pull me out of harm's way just in time. Otherwise, I would've sustained some serious injuries to both of my legs. That day, I was lucky to walk away with just minor injuries from the impact. The driver claimed he never saw us and apologized. Because the injuries were minor in nature, we never called the police and just accepted his sincere apologies for his actions.

It was also through my sister that, years later, I would learn how to salsa dance. She and my brother, Flaco, actually took turns showing me how to dance. And while it took a long while before I was able to finally get the dance moves down pat and ultimately become a salsa dancer, it was definitely worth the wait. Over the years, I continued to improve on my dancing, and eventually I got really good at it.

Ironically, it was this love for salsa dancing that one day led me to meeting my beautiful wife at the Copacabana in New York City. It was a true blessing that brought us together as a couple, thanks in big part to my sister's determination to teach me how to dance. In fact, years later, my wife and I would also become salsa dance instructors. Something that we truly enjoyed doing together as a couple for many, many years!

The memories and the good times that we had while growing up in the South Bronx will forever be with me. For not only was Mercedes always looking out for me and spoiling me with her amazing cooking talents, but also she was always there for me with her motherly advice and wisdom when I needed her the most!

Sadly, because of COVID restrictions, none of us was allowed to see my sister during her final days. And she passed away without any of her family members being there for her. That was the most heartbreaking and painful of all.

A few weeks after her death, the family decided to have her body cremated. From that point on, it took nearly a year before we were able to have a memorial in her name at my sister's home church in the Bronx. That day, I did her eulogy and had the most difficult time just trying to get through the reading because I kept breaking down and crying. But thanks to my loving family's support, I was able to make it through and finish my personal tribute to my beautiful big sister!

CHAPTER 118

IN CONCLUSION...

O ver the years that followed, I continued acting and modeling. I even went back into the public-safety arena when I was selected as a public safety officer for Quinnipiac University, retiring in 2021, after more than five and a half years of dedicated service.

During my journey I also ventured out to explore other dreams and projects that had been on my mind for many years, ones that I never quite pursued until later in life. I became a motivational speaker, sharing my story and journey at numerous speaking engagements throughout Connecticut. At the same time, I started promoting an invention motivated by a truly passionate drive to make a difference; it is geared toward saving infant lives by preventing them from tragically dying in hot cars. I call it, Hooked on Baby: A Lifeline to Your Baby. I shared it on social media and suddenly got the most amazing responses from caring families throughout the country who were interested in protecting their infants with this product. It was another true blessing! Once again proving that no dream is too big to dream!

So long as you can dream it, and believe in yourself, it can happen...it will happen!

CPSIA information can be obtained
at www.ICGtesting.com
Printed in the USA
JSHW042231310722
28728JS00002B/3